*Westerners in Gray*

# Westerners in Gray

## The Men and Missions of the Elite Fifth Missouri Infantry Regiment

*by* PHILLIP THOMAS TUCKER

*with a foreword by*
ROBERT L. HAWKINS III

McFarland & Company, Inc., Publishers
*Jefferson, North Carolina, and London*

British Library Cataloguing-in-Publication data are available


Library of Congress Cataloguing-in-Publication Data

Tucker, Phillip Thomas, 1953–
    Westerners in gray : the men and missions of the elite Fifth
Missouri Infantry Regiment / by Phillip Thomas Tucker.
      p.  cm.
    Includes bibliographical references (p.  ) and index. ∞
    ISBN 0-7864-0016-1 (lib. bdg. : 50# alk. paper)
    1. Confederate States of America. Army. Missouri Infantry
Regiment, 5th.   2. Missouri – History – Civil War, 1861–1865 –
Regimental histories.   3. United States – History – Civil War,
1861–1865 – Regimental histories.   I. Title.
E569.5 5th.T83   1995
973.7'478 – dc20                          94-27036
                                                   CIP

Manufactured in the United States of America

McFarland & Company, Inc., Publishers
  Box 611, Jefferson, North Carolina 28640

To my grandfather, Private Auzie Joseph Tucker,
a native of Hardin County, Tennessee,
and a veteran of the 64th Infantry Regiment,
American Expeditionary Forces,
Western Front, 1918

# CONTENTS

# PREFACE AND
# ACKNOWLEDGMENTS

It is especially ironic that the hard-fighting Fifth Missouri Confederate Infantry has remained one of the most obscure and little-known Confederate regiments in the annals of Civil War historiography. By any measure, this crack infantry unit from a Western frontier slave state was no ordinary command. Indeed, this elite command was the best infantry regiment of the finest combat brigade on either side during the Civil War, the First Missouri Confederate Brigade. For this and other valid reasons, the Fifth Missouri's role as a central player in some of the most decisive battles in the West deserves study, as do the lives of the common soldiers who served in this superb regiment.

Few, if any, Confederate infantry regiments compiled a more distinguished record during so many key battles in the West than did the Fifth Missouri. Compared to the well-known roles played by the Confederate soldiers from other states, the most obscure participants of the futile effort to win Southern independence were the Missouri Confederates.

This study is long overdue because the story of the Fifth Missouri is also the story of the other forgotten Rebels of the Civil War, the fiery Irish Confederates from the streets of St. Louis and the rural Missouri counties. The saga of the Irish Confederates from Missouri and their role in the war in the West has long been neglected. The fusing of an urban and rural citizen soldiery containing both Irishmen and pro–Southern Missourians of mostly Upper South ancestry created a unit possessing a unique blend of an unshakable esprit de corps, resiliency, high performance level, and iron discipline. These Missourians' role of serving repeatedly as shock troops on battlefields across the South forged them into a crack Western infantry unit of superior quality, durability, and resiliency.

The primary emphasis of this work has been to illuminate and understand the life and experience of the soldiers who became the elite Confederates of the Fifth Missouri. Consequently, as much human interest and personal information in the form of primary documentation as possible has been incorporated into the present work, which tells the intimate history of the Fifth Missouri by viewing it as a community of individuals. Rather than focusing primarily upon the standard interruptions of campaigns and battles, this study concentrates upon the humanity of the regiment by exploring the motivations, experiences, values, and beliefs of the average enlisted man in the Fifth Missouri's ranks. By this means, the lives of the forgotten common soldiers of the war, the Missouri and Irish Confederates of the West, have been illuminated as never before.

Many thanks are owed to the capable staffs of the State Historical Society of Missouri in Columbia and the Missouri Historical Society in St. Louis. Special thanks also go to St. Louis University professors Dr. Martin Towey and Father William B. Faherty and the interlibrary loan staff of Pius XII Memorial Library, St. Louis University. Mr. Edwin C. Bearss and his wife, Margia Riddle Bearss, made helpful suggestions and shared their expertise. In addition, I would like to thank Mr. George William Warren IV, the descendant of Lieutenant George William Warren, and his wife, Paula, and Mr. Warren's sister, Ellen Warren, for unfailing assistance, inspiration, and support over the years. From beginning to end, Dr. Leslie Anders provided invaluable support, encouragement, and guidance during the span of three decades with an amazing degree of patience and understanding.

PHILLIP THOMAS TUCKER
*Washington, D.C.*
*November 1994*

# FOREWORD

On a warm summer day in 1875, Jefferson Davis mounted a wooden platform at the Callaway County fairgrounds at Fulton, Missouri. Joining him were Governor Crittendon and United States Senator Francis Marion Cockrell, whose name adorned the brigade in which the Fifth Missouri Infantry served. Davis spoke not a word pertaining to the "late unpleasantness," but instead offered his prediction, rendered with great strength and eloquence, that the upper Mississippi Valley would lead America forward into great prominence and prosperity in the coming age.

This site, now known as Priest Field at Westminster College, is no stranger to momentous remarks or prominent speakers. Perhaps 100 yards away, Winston Churchill offered his famous "Iron Curtain" speech in 1946. Louis Mountbatten and Averill Harriman spoke here at the dedication of the Churchill Memorial in 1967, and Ronald Reagan delivered a moving address in 1990 upon the occasion of the dedication of the sculpture *Breakthrough* fashioned by Churchill's granddaughter from sections of the recently dismantled Berlin Wall. Most notably, some 10,000 people heard Mikhail Gorbachev declare the end of the Cold War here in the spring of 1992. It is interesting to note that none of these men of prominence drew crowds approaching the number of people who came to view the leader of the Lost Cause in 1875; estimates of the latter crowd have run as high as 25,000.

People sometimes have trouble remembering that the Confederate battle flag had 13 stars, not 11. Historians seem peculiarly subject to this affliction of diminished cultural memory capacity. It is as if a malevolent committee of the Chamber of Commerce decreed sometime after the Second World War that Missouri should be extracted from the column of Southern states, all for the best of business reasons to be sure. The great expansion of the St. Louis and Kansas City metropolitan areas in terms of geographical area, population, and influence have had effects not unlike

1

those Atlanta exerts upon the rest of Georgia or the impact that the growing suburbs of Washington, D.C., have had on the cultural identity of northeastern Virginia.

Yet the Southern heritage is there, rich and diverse, still waters running deep. Grandview, Missouri, near Kansas City, is known as "the Gateway to the South." Newspapers covering Churchill's visit to Westminster College in 1946 commented upon Callaway County's "particular disposition in favor of the cause of Jefferson Davis." Monroe County's centennial in 1931 produced a commemorative newspaper which included on the front page a statement declaring the Southern ideals of that region of northeastern Missouri. David McCullough's biography of Harry Truman describes Independence, Missouri, at the time of the future president's boyhood as being indistinguishable from Tuscaloosa. St. Louis has not entirely forgotten its French/Southern ancestry. Keytesville, Missouri, still enjoys Sterling Price Days every September. Nevada, Missouri, covers its town square in Confederate flags and celebrates J. O. Shelby Days each July. The Sons of Confederate Veterans and the United Daughters of the Confederacy thrive, Civil War Round Tables abound, and each May, Missouri's sons and daughters gather on the campus of St. Louis University to raise a glass in memory of the victims of the Camp Jackson Massacre, just as others gather on the last Saturday in October in Arrow Rock to commemorate Missouri Secession Day. An area of as many as 16 or 17 counties in central and northeastern Missouri is still known as "Little Dixie." Noted newspaper columnist and radio commentator James Wolfe offered an opinion on the traditionally Democratic politics of that region in the early 1980s when he stated that whether the inhabitants of that area were Democrats had a lot less to do with Walter Mondale or Jimmy Carter and a lot more to do with whether or not their great-granddaddy had fought for the Confederacy.

Missourians served in every theater of the War Between the States, sometimes by mistake. Only the most dedicated of historians are aware that when the Virginia Military Institute cadets made their famous charge at the Battle of New Market in Virginia, they were preceded by 66 Missourians under the command of Captain Charles Woodson. Relegated to this theater by mistake after being exchanged as prisoners of war, 59 of the 66 were casualties of this engagement; the survivors returned to create their own monument on the battlefield. Missourians served on board the C.S.S. *Virginia* in her famous engagement against the U.S.S. *Monitor* at Hampton Roads in 1862. The "Immortal 600" Confederate officers held as prisoners of war and used as a human shield by Federals on Morris Island, South Carolina, included a goodly number of residents of the Show-Me State.

This state alone suffered the depopulation of 3½ counties by order of the federal authorities. Here the war took on a particular viciousness never equaled elsewhere. Missouri was disproportionately represented in the group of revolutionaries who refused to surrender at the end of the war, traveling to Mexico with General J. O. Shelby and his Iron Brigade. Even Missouri Unionists, at least those who were not recent immigrants, predominantly thought of themselves as Southerners. A statue of Frank Blair in St. Louis commemorates his raising of the "first southern troops for the defense of the Union" (referring to St. Louis Germans) and also cites his efforts to return civil rights to ex–Confederates.

This is the state that produced the Fifth Missouri Infantry. These were the people who were never allowed — unlike the citizens of Tennessee, North Carolina, and Virginia — a second chance to consider secession after Lincoln's call for troops and the devastating impact of the Camp Jackson Massacre. This was the state which put its own army in the field to fight against federal troops without significant aid from the Confederate government, save that afforded during the Battle of Oak Hills (Wilson's Creek). This threadbare army led by officers identified by pieces of sumac on their shirt or hat, ill-equipped and sometimes unarmed, somehow developed into units such as the Fifth Missouri, which together with the other regiments of their brigade have been described by contemporary historians as the finest fighting unit in either army during that conflict. Speaking at a gathering in Columbia, Missouri, in May 1993, the chief historian of the National Park Service, Ed Bearss, declared in his own inimitable and direct manner, "Cockrell's Missouri Brigade makes the Stonewall Brigade look like the Little Sisters of the Poor."

They died valiantly, some would say futilely, and lie in graves in Missouri, Arkansas, Tennessee, Mississippi, Alabama, and Georgia. They are better remembered outside their state than within its boundaries, but that is not saying much. No school in Missouri regularly offers a class which will tell of the existence of these men, let alone of their accomplishments. Only in the organizations of their descendants and within the Round Tables are their suffering, sacrifice, and valor appreciated, though the numbers of persons in those groups are legion and growing.

In June 1993, I happened by pure chance to come upon a Confederate cemetery at Shelby Springs, Alabama, just south of Birmingham. Included in the hundreds of Confederate graves at that site were a number of Missourians, including several from the Fifth Missouri Infantry. Thinking of these soldiers who had died in a hospital and so far from home, I wondered if they ever imagined that they would be forgotten in the state for which they sacrificed so much. Did they ever suspect that the songs they loved, the cause they revered, and the symbols for which they struggled would some day be redefined to fit more neatly into the historical slot modern-day political orthodoxy demands of it?

Efforts such as this work will begin the process of showing to future generations what these men really were—a unique group of Americans fighting for home and hearth and political freedom. The author has done them justice. Let the reader carry the word to all who might wish to draw near and take inspiration from Southern valor in its purest form.

ROBERT L. HAWKINS III
*Commander-in-Chief*
*Sons of Confederate Veterans*
*Jefferson City, Missouri*

# I

## FORGING A LETHAL FIGHTING MACHINE

Along the creek bottoms of Lee County, the cottonwoods were already beginning to turn yellow-brown in the late summer haze around Saltillo, Mississippi, in the northeastern region of the state. Here, in the Rebel encampments of Major General Sterling Price's Army of the West, the First Missouri Confederate Brigade was reorganized on September 1, 1862, during a period of relative inactivity in this sector of the Western war. Since the fall of the all-important railroad town of Corinth, Mississippi, to an immense Federal army at the end of May 1862, no serious fighting had erupted in northeast Mississippi.

A distinguished past had already elevated the Missouri Brigade far beyond the level of the average Confederate brigade in either the West or the East. Indeed, since the battle of Pea Ridge, Arkansas, the Missouri Brigade acquired fame as the ever-reliable "Old Guard" Confederate troops of the West. Since December 1861, Colonel Henry Little had transformed his ex-members of General Price's Missouri State Guard into hardened Confederate soldiers. This elite command from a Western frontier slave state was, in the complimentary phase of President Jefferson Davis, now "the best drilled brigade in the Confederacy."

Not a better example of a famous Confederate brigade reflecting the character and ability of its commander could be found. Because Colonel Little had been elevated to a brigadier generalship in command of the Army of the West's First Division in June of 1862, Colonel Elijah P. Gates now led the First Missouri Brigade. This crack brigade consisted of the Second and Third Missouri Confederate Infantry, the Sixteenth Arkansas Confederate Infantry, the First Missouri Confederate Cavalry (dismounted) and Captain William Wade's Missouri Confederate Battery.[1]

Colonel Gates, age thirty-two, had earned a distinguished reputation as the most daring horse commander of Price's Missouri Army during 1861. He may well have been the best cavalry leader in the trans–Mississippi theater before the cavalry of the Army of the West was dismounted when it was transferred across the Mississippi River in April 1862. "Old Pap" Price declared that Colonel Gates "had no superior for bravery." The hard-fighting former hemp farmer from northwestern Missouri had successfully employed dismounted cavalry as infantry and had also used ambush and hit-and-run tactics in becoming a master of cavalry warfare on the Western frontier. At every opportunity, this elite Missouri Brigade of mostly middle-class farmers had served as the "Grenadier Guard" and shock troops of Price's army since the unit's creation during the winter of 1861-62. Under the command of capable Colonel Little, the Missouri Brigade had first won fame by playing these key roles during Price's risky withdrawal from Missouri to Arkansas and in the battle of Pea Ridge in the early months of 1862.[2]

September 1, 1862, was the same as any other late summer day in northeastern Mississippi, so breathless and humid that sweat poured off anyone leaving the shade of a pine. Consequently, there was not much activity on this day among the Confederate encampments nestled in the hot, windless pine and oak forests. Two disease-riddled Confederate infantry battalions of Missouri Confederate troops had earlier merged into the nucleus of a new regiment, the Fifth Missouri Confederate Infantry, after crossing to the east side of the Mississippi River. An ironic fate would follow the Fifth Missouri throughout its career. Unlike most of the other Missouri Brigade units, this regiment would never fight on home soil, struggling for years in the Deep South.

One of these Missouri Confederate battalions consisted primarily of four northeast Missouri companies led by Colonel Robert S. Bevier, a former lawyer from a small northeast Missouri town. Bevier's troops were joined by Colonel James C. McCown's five-company battalion, which was composed mostly of hardy yeomen from western Missouri. But the earlier combining of these nine companies had left the new unit one company shy of regimental status.[3]

The timely arrival of a company of southeast Missourians under Captain David Young Pankey from the Rebel camps around Tupelo, Mississippi, on the last day of August 1862 completed the necessary regimental quota of ten companies. These companies of the Fifth Missouri consisted of veterans who had served in the six pitched battles and twenty skirmishes of the Missouri State Guard under General Price throughout 1861. This newly arrived company of Missouri Bootheelers, named for the odd shape of their southeast Missouri region on the map, had earned a reputation for reliability in the Missouri State Guard.

With the formation of the Fifth Missouri had come elections for officers. Around campfires that illuminated the Confederate encampment in the darkness, flowery oratory, rhetoric, and semibribery highlighted the campaigning for high rank and prestige. The democratic principles of the frontier followed the Missouri Confederates into the military. Beardless youths and crusty Mexican War veterans, such as Noah Grant, made stump speeches far into the night. Enlisted men cast votes based upon promises of free liquor and good treatment from candidates if elected. As back in the Missourians' slave and border state of the West, the campaigning for rank exemplified frontier-style politics in the best democratic tradition. But such democratic excesses, ironically, would eventually undermine the caliber of the Confederate officer corps.[4]

No one saw a better chance to serve his regiment and country than James C. McCown. He sought appointment as colonel of the Fifth Missouri and succeeded. For years a shrewd politician from Johnson County, Missouri, McCown easily won the top leadership position of the newest Confederate regiment from Missouri. McCown had come a long way since serving as a private in his son's militia company of northwest Missouri Rebels. The second generation Irishman initially made a smooth transition from Warrensburg civic leader to military commander as colonel of a cavalry battalion, Eighth Division, Missouri State Guard. McCown served as a private in Captain Owen A. Waddell's company of the First Missouri Confederate Infantry Battalion after the expiration of his State Guard service. But less than three months later, he was elected the infantry battalion's lieutenant colonel.[5]

McCown was born and raised in the wilderness of Kanawha County, Virginia, now West Virginia. He often traveled west for work on the Ohio River boats. Between solitary sojourns, McCown established credibility in mountain society as a militia captain. But his wanderings were ended by a barefoot neighbor girl who was four years his junior, Mrs. Caroline McCown. In 1840 the newlyweds departed for Missouri, the bountiful land of opportunity in the West that most Virginians were raving about. The more than 700-mile journey ended on the fertile prairies of Henry County, Missouri. Here, in west-central Missouri, the task of breaking tough prairie sod with steel plows pulled by double teams, and sometimes four yoke of oxen, continued from sunup to sundown on the sprawling ocean of grass. With hard work and good fortune, McCown became one of the leading citizens of Henry County, winning election as constable of the local community.[6]

But the McCown family pulled up stakes around 1845 and moved to the county lying just north of Henry County. Settling near Warrensburg, Johnson County, the former boatman from Virginia envisioned the future with clarity. Investing in real estate with the belief that the quiet county seat would blossom with new growth one day, McCown snatched up 1,500 prime acres, including choice town lots. As back East, political power came with the extensive landholdings on the Western frontier. From the beginning, McCown dabbled in multiple community projects. He served as railroad promoter, church building committee member, masonry officer, and construction supervisor for the court house and also held other positions. The dream of a successful new life became a reality when McCown gained upper-class status on the frontier in a relatively short time. He also found his political niche in 1848 when he became circuit and county clerk of Johnson County at Warrensburg. McCown held the position for the next twelve years, until he was unseated by an outspoken Unionist as politics became sectionalized. It would have been unimaginable only a few years before how a Virginia heritage had suddenly turned into a liability.[7]

Ensuring a supply of sturdy farmhands, the county official brought six sons into the world. Three daughters also completed this frontier family. The Southern Methodist temporarily left behind the ever-growing McCown clan in 1857 when he won a position to the state legislature as enrolling clerk and traveled to the state capital, Jefferson City. As was the case for many Missourians of Southern ancestry, Virginia's secession in mid–April 1861 had a deep, emotional impact on the McCown family. Heated passion soon erupted into violence in Johnson County. Colonel McCown's well-educated son William shot and killed a leading Union spokesman in March of 1861 at the Warrensburg courthouse. Despite roots firmly implanted in the Warrensburg community life, the McCowns, father and sons, could not turn their backs on Virginia and the South when war came.[8]

McCown, consequently, early prepared for the struggle along with three sons who became State Guardsmen while most Missourians were naively dreaming of neutrality. For instance, he convinced Governor Jackson to pardon a convicted Johnson County horse thief to serve in his newly formed militia company. Even after donning a butternut uniform, Colonel McCown remained civic-minded. Under his directives, McCown's former deputy, now in Rebel ranks, smuggled the Johnson County records from the courthouse during the autumn 1861 invasion of Price's army north into Missouri. The county papers were hidden in a thicket from Union authorities until after the war.[9]

Chosen second in command of the Fifth Missouri was Lieutenant Colonel Bevier. Unfortunately for the regiment, he proved to be more of a political sort of officer than a fighter. Short on natural military ability but not on zeal, Bevier left Bolivar to fight in the Wakarusa War against the Kansas Jayhawkers during the winter of 1855. Three years later he opened a law practice in Macon City. Then Bevier became a Bloomington attorney for the Hannibal and St. Joseph Railroad. As an unsuccessful convention candidate, he accurately gauged the sentiment of Macon County and much of northeast Missouri in early 1861: "the graves of our fathers and our future destiny, our education, our interests and our inclinations all lead us to cast our fortunes with the South." He barely slipped through the net of General Nathaniel Lyon's Union forces and avoided capture with the pro–Southern Missouri militia force at Camp Jackson in May of 1861. Once with Price's army, Bevier served as division inspector, major of the First Infantry Battalion, and finally colonel of the Fourth Infantry, Third Division.[10]

Owen A. Waddell, a former Warrensburg attorney, was selected major. Handsome and intelligent, Waddell earned the reputation of being not only an excellent leader, but also of being the ladies' man of the Fifth Missouri. The North Carolina–born major, a devoted bachelor, took advantage of most opportunities in regard to the opposite sex. On the march or during furlough in the countryside, Waddell refined his well-honed skills of seduction. Such ardent pursuit won the polished Johnson County officer the title "the Chevalier Bayard of our regiment." The major became as famous for his conquests off the battlefield as on with his outgoing personality, good looks, and the clever stratagem of employing a chivalric facade in posing as "the politest of men." Waddell was the type of officer that the enlisted men idolized and the chaplains deplored. Many cold nights in camp were warmed by the tales of Waddell's nocturnal escapades, which became Fifth Missouri folklore. Like Colonel McCown, he was a Mason and a leading citizen of Warrensburg. Major Waddell demonstrated the same disregard for danger under the hottest Yankee fire as in the bedroom.[11]

Waddell, age twenty-four, helped organize the second Southern company from Johnson County, the Johnson Guards. He first won fame at the battle of Wilson's Creek during the summer of 1861, when he helped capture a Union artillery piece. Like so many other Fifth Missouri soldiers, Waddell would be killed in action.[12]

James T. Greenwood, a Warrensburg merchant, became the adjutant of the Fifth Missouri. Raised around Perryville, Kentucky, Greenwood became a Johnson Guard sergeant in part because of the influence of his native Bluegrass region and Virginia ancestry. The martial spirit had long been in young James's blood, stirred by listening to his grandfather's stories of battling redcoat invaders during the Revolution and the War of 1812. At the first chance, consequently, James Greenwood left the store counter to uphold "Southern rights" in Kansas. As was the case for so many people of Missouri, the sectional strife tore apart the Greenwood family. One brother enlisted in a Union regiment. But to give the family a decidedly Jeff Davis flavor, another sixteen-year-old sibling served in Company A, Fifth Missouri. The likable James Greenwood would be killed during the Missouri Brigade's first major battle of the Vicksburg campaign.[13]

Bright and competent, Benjamin Givins Dysart was appointed surgeon. He had recently been a leading Macon County physician at McGee College. Hailing from a distinguished lineage of doctors and ministers of the Western frontier, Dysart remained ever-mindful of his Southern heritage. His upper South ancestors of Scottish lineage were hardy fron- tiersmen "of wealth [who] brought slaves and came across the country with [their] possessions loaded on wagons drawn by ox teams." A robust figure who would stand up to the conflict's rigors until the war's end, Dysart served as the chief medical officer of Bevier's battalion. At age twenty-eight, he was a six-footer from one of the first families of Randolph County. Dysart's relatives grew rich by tobacco cultivation. On the large farm from where he hailed, his physician father owned twenty slaves and herds of cat- tle and thoroughbred horses in a rich agricultural area. But Dysart wanted much more out of life than to be a common tiller of the soil.

Benjamin Dysart, therefore, prepared for medical school at an early age. Even while helping to plant, harvest, and cure tobacco beside his father's slaves on their 400-acre family farm, Dysart dreamed of the future and the day when he would become a physician. So diligently had the mature youngster studied his father's textbooks and applied himself at local institutions that he taught school at age seventeen. After earning savings and much experience, Dysart entered McGee College and took general courses until he graduated in 1854. Then he returned to teaching once more. But after two years, Dysart decided to pursue his first love, medicine. After taking more medical courses from local physicians, he entered prestigious Jefferson Medical College at Philadelphia, Pennsylvania, in 1856.[14]

His dream finally came true, and Dysart graduated in 1859. The new physician then became an instructor-practitioner at his McGee College, which had been established by his forefathers. Despite his extensive educa- tion and upper-middle class roots, Dysart stands as a good representative of the typical Fifth Missouri soldier in terms of background. Instead of be- ing a fanatical revolutionary and slaveowner, he was a conservative tradi- tionalist of a yeoman society on the Western frontier. Dedicated to Jeffersonian democratic principles, this unmarried, middle-class Methodist pursued his father's vocation. Surgeon Dysart's accomplishments as a physician were widely known before the war's beginning. Dysart won fame throughout northeast Missouri for successfully removing a brain tumor from a female slave. This risky operation on a table on a College Mound street before students and other physicians became legendary in his frontier society.[15]

Complementing Dysart was Assistant Surgeon William Clarence Goodwin. He was brought up on the upper branches of Blackwater River near Columbus, Johnson County. Here his father owned slaves and a splen- did farm amid the prairie lands stretching to the horizon. Goodwin was dedicated and capable, with a State Guard regimental surgeon background. The twenty-six-year-old physician served as the First Battalion's assistant surgeon, after enlisting to defend the Confederacy. With Dysart destined to remain behind for extensive periods with the regiment's wounded after the first three engagements of the Fifth Missouri, Goodwin would be thrust into the regiment's top medical slot during the Vicksburg campaign.[16]

Martin Van Buren Mitchell was assistant quartermaster of the regiment, but he eventually would gain the top quartermaster position in the Fifth Missouri. Mitchell, age twenty-five, steadily rose through the ranks. He served as a private before becoming the quartermaster of the First Battalion. Like many other Missourians, Mitchell traveled to the Far West during the antebellum period. He served as an officer of a militia command known as the Polk County Rangers in prewar days, acquiring invaluable military experience. The eldest son of one of the first families of southwest Missouri, the quartermaster would serve with distinction from the beginning to the end.

Martin Mitchell enlisted with twelve Mitchells and other relatives, such as Private William A. Ruyle. The blue-eyed, fair-haired Mitchell clan members were together in family messes within Company C, Fifth Missouri. They left their homes among the hills and valley along the Little Sac River in southcentral Polk County, the "family base." This untamed region around the wide eastern plateau and above the valley of Little Sac River had been the Mitchells' haven since 1834. In pioneer days, the Mitchell settlers arrived by ox-drawn wagon from Tennessee to erect log cabins in the beautiful valley. Other clan members settled along the 2,000-foot-high ridges covered in giant hardwoods. Amid the sea of grass and dense forests, the native Volunteer Staters carved a home out of the wilderness. Here they prospered for generations in the new land of the Western frontier. The rolling terrain of the Ozark country suddenly dropped off into the gorgelike valley of the Little Sac in picturesque fashion. Wide fields along the bottoms produced generous yields of grain beside woodlands of untouched timber. Herds of deer and flocks of turkeys fed in the meadows in astounding numbers. At the war's beginning, this region remained an unspoiled paradise, but the sectional conflict would change the face of this beautiful land.[17]

From the highest point of the ridgetop, the Mitchell clan members could see the surrounding countryside for miles around. The Tennesseeans appropriately settled upon commanding ground reminiscent in some ways of the Smoky Mountains. After they cleared the bottom land along the Little Sac with the help of slaves, the black loam soil bestowed bountiful harvests of corn and wheat. For nearly three decades, only the Mexican War and the California gold fields lured a Mitchell boy away from his serene valley: a canyonlike rift nestled between Three Mound and Pleasant Prairies. With ancient ties stretching back to Tennessee and Virginia, every able-bodied Mitchell enlisted with the South except one. Following his own beliefs, the nonconformist donned a uniform of Yankee blue.[18]

Providence protected the thirteen Mitchell boys, all now of the Fifth Missouri, from danger for more than a year. Sergeant Benjamin Franklin Mitchell, known as "Franklin," was captured at Pea Ridge but later escaped to rejoin his command. For the clan's family members remaining in their secure valley in southwest Missouri, religion became the only means of assisting sons and fathers at the front. A number of Mitchells were ministers, including the clan's patriarch. During the battle of Wilson's Creek, the Mitchell families of the valley heard rumbling artillery southward and "spent the day [August 10, 1861] praying for their sons who they knew were fighting there." When Lieutenant Benjamin Looney Mitchell of Company C later heard of their prayers, he said, "I have felt that this resulted in our protection, for men were killed all around me by the score." Good fortune, however, ended for the Mitchell clan once on the east side of the Mississippi.[19]

Sergeant Benjamin Franklin Mitchell, a fiery Polk County preacher who may have been a Polk County Ranger as well, served as the clan's spiritual head in Company C. He gathered recruits and organized a local defense company at Bolivar in May 1861. Many of these volunteers later served in Company D, Fifth Missouri. Captain Mitchell and his unit departed to join Price before the Federal advance on Springfield in late 1861. The withdrawal before the German soldiers of St. Louis was swift, for "if we fell into his hands, his troops not understanding our language, [it then] would be the Alamo [massacre] on us." But Benjamin Franklin Mitchell would survive meeting the "foreign" Unionists until he took a mortal wound at Vicksburg.[20]

Since the start of the conflict, incredibly, only one Mitchell was cut down in action. That day which seemingly broke the good fortune of the Mitchell clan was May 8, 1862. At the skirmish of Farmington, Mississippi, Lieutenant James Redmond Mitchell, the quartermaster's brother, fell dying. With this death, the Mitchell settlement suffered its first loss far away in the hot lowlands of Mississippi. There would be more such sad tidings from the far-away South before the conflict's end.[21]

James Sprague Dysart became the ordnance sergeant of the Fifth Missouri. He could claim Tennessee ancestry and hailed from one of the first pioneer and leading families of Randolph County. In addition, he was the surgeon's relative and son of a Randolph County judge. James Dysart taught school for seven years after earning a McGee College education in the Dysart tradition. Then he set up shop as a College Mound merchant. Along with other residents, Dysart could only watch as his community was invaded by hundreds of Illinois troops in blue uniforms in June of 1861. This was enough to make him grab a gun and become a diehard Rebel. Young Dysart demonstrated talent as the ordnance sergeant of the First Battalion.[22]

To steer wayward Fifth Missouri soldiers toward God, Chaplain Charles H. Atwood provided spiritual guidance as regimental chaplain. A Renaissance man, Atwood was recently a merchant, dentist, and physician at Clinton, Henry County. Only after he had fought for some time as a Guard private were Atwood's talents discovered. He then served as a surgeon in a cavalry unit. But trying in vain to save lives without proper supplies, instruments, and medicine proved frustrating for the hard-working Atwood. He therefore dropped out of medicine and switched to a new position which might save more men than all the rusty saws, empty quinine bottles, and dirty bandages put together: the healing faith of religion. He spread the gospel while serving as chaplain of McCown's battalion. Atwood, a Presbyterian man of God known as "the parson" by the boys, found no contradiction in personally owning slaves and preaching about the brotherhood of man. During the dark and bloody days ahead, he would inspire hope and faith among the members of the Fifth Missouri when none existed.[23]

More adept in working with mathematics than with his Fifth Missouri comrades, William Henry Murrell was appointed commissary captain. He had been a competent and popular merchant in Leesville, Henry County. Murrell was elected state delegate by fellow citizens in February 1861. Staying true to his Southern beliefs, he cast a vote for Missouri to leave the Union. Murrell probably first served in the Henry County Rangers, like one of his relatives. He also demonstrated ability as a Guard commissary captain. The ex-representative of Southern interests on the frontier served in the same capacity with the First Battalion after entering Confederate service. But personal quirks that made Murrell a fine commissary officer aroused animosity among the always-hungry soldiers of the Fifth Missouri. Whenever rations were delayed for whatever reason, Murrell became the scapegoat. In the future, one highlight of Murrell's service would be the dishing out of mule meat during the siege of Vicksburg.[24]

Samuel Lyle Ramsey, lately farming the land near Columbus, Johnson County, was the ensign of the Fifth Missouri. A model soldier, Ramsey advanced to a sergeant's rank during the 1861 State Guard campaigns of six months. Samuel Ramsey, age twenty-four, was the eldest of five Company I Ramsey boys, including two brothers. All hailed from the area around Columbus, a half-prairie and half-timbered region along the north fork of the Blackwater River. Ancestors settled the area and defended their section of northwestern Johnson County during the 1830s. A Ramsey, for instance, led a mounted Ranger company against Sac and Fox raiders in pioneer days.[25]

Ireland-born John Learman was named drum major. After migrating West to begin life anew, Learman found ample opportunity for success in Warrensburg, a fast-growing community in a fertile agricultural region where manual labor was always in demand. Since there was not a large slave population in this frontier section of Johnson County as compared to the Missouri River counties to the north, young and ambitious immigrants from Europe could easily find work. The Irishman had learned to play the drum, perhaps while serving in the British army. Upon enlistment in Price's army, Learman became a musician. After his promotion to corporal, he was captured by Union forces at Springfield during the winter of 1861. Escaping from his captors, the drummer boy rejoined his unit within a month.

Perhaps Learman still had his favorite dog, a "saucy little fellow" found in Lexington, Missouri, when he was appointed the drum major of the Fifth Missouri. The musician and his pet were inseparable. During the withdrawal south from Lexington in the autumn of 1861, for example, Learman refused to abandon his pup. Marching across central Arkansas on the first part of the journey to reach the east side of the Mississippi River during the late winter of 1862, Learman carried his dog on his drum slung high over his shoulder while he crossed swollen bayous and streams in a cold rain. Perhaps the dog now served as the mascot of the Fifth Missouri.[26]

Royal G. Stokely, senior lieutenant, became captain of Company A with Waddell's election to major. Formerly a Kingsville, Johnson County, merchant, Stokely proved considerable leadership ability throughout his Missouri State Guard service. His hometown west of Warrensburg was such a hotbed of secession that Kingsville women roamed the streets to cut down Union flags during the secession spring of 1861. Stokely served with distinction as a major in Price's cavalry. He was shot off his horse at Pea Ridge, falling with an arm wound. In Confederate service, Stokely's rise in McCown's battalion was meteoric. In less than four months, he advanced from private to captain, a rank he attained by age twenty-seven.[27]

Company A members consisted of a hardy group of volunteers from Johnson County. Most of these men first organized at Warrensburg in the war's early days. They were part of the area's first Southern militia unit, the Johnson Guards. These soldiers later served under Captain Waddell. Some of these men, perhaps a majority, saw action against the Jayhawkers on the plains of Kansas before the war. Conditioned by years of battling Jayhawkers, the people of Johnson County were involved in civil war long before 1861.[28]

Mark Trumper was elected captain of Company B. He was an enterprising young man who would distinguish himself more for shrewdness than bravery. Despite being born in England, or perhaps because of it, Trumper received plenty of votes from the enlisted men of Company B. Immediately after the election, he readied the soldiers of his Macon County company for action. But the twenty-two-year-old Briton would lose interest in abstract principles and resign in less than three months, trading butternut for Yankee blue. Taking advantage of the solid currency of the United States, the Englishman would start a lucrative business venture as a Federal sutler. Unlike many of his comrades, Trumper probably walked away from the war with all limbs intact and many greenbacks, if he kept his Jeff Davis roots secret. Company B consisted primarily of Macon County troops from the state's richest tobacco lands and other northeast Missourians of the Audrain Prairie region.[29]

Asbury Coffee Bradford, a twenty-five-year-old from Bolivar, took command of Company C with wide approval. It proved no handicap that the popular captain had earlier lost his temper and "mashed his toe severely trying to give [Private] James [E.] Mitchell a fall from where he was lying." Coming from a long military tradition, Bradford adapted to the rigors of military life without difficulty. In the home where he had lived with his widowed mother and one female slave, he had long cherished a war relic, a powder horn worn by a Virginia ancestor during the American Revolution.

The son of one of the leading physicians of Bolivar, Bradford knew much about the business of war by an early age. In 1856, when he was a teenager, he joined the Polk County Rangers, which could trace its roots to the Bolivar Mounted Rifles. These mounted frontiersmen were the defenders of southwest Missouri. They had their own constitution, uniform, brass band, esprit de corps, and definite ideas about the best way to handle both Kansas Jayhawkers and, now, Uncle Sam. Despite his youth, Bradford played a large role in the company's formation and remained a "key [element] in the Polk County Rangers": a frontier cavalry unit of southwest Missouri which also faced regional threats since many of the area's slaves naturally felt that they had a right to determine their own destiny.[30]

A hard-riding Polk County Ranger was the "Minuteman" of the southwest Missouri frontier. He always had "his gun, blanket, horse, saddle and bridle at hand, to be used at a moment's notice." Far away from the nearest United States military post and with a national government providing little protection for his frontier community, the Ranger units for years protected their people in the Western frontier tradition against Indians, Kansans, rebellious slaves, or any other threat. This self-reliance was a key factor in loosening the loyalty of the people of western Missouri to the United States. On May 7, 1861, the Rangers accepted a new banner on Crisp Prairie with a good deal of ceremony. This emblem was not the "Stars and Stripes," but a Southern states rights flag.[31]

Bradford and other Polk County Rangers galloped northwest to the Kansas border "to repel invasion of our territory and protect our homes and firesides, and those near and dear to us," during December of 1860. By this period, wrote a journalist, the Rangers consisted of "the most erect, fine-figured, and comely set of men we ever saw." So famous was this frontier horse unit by the winter before the war that a St. Louis newspaper more than 300 miles away proclaimed in bold headlines to its readers: "The Polk County Rangers Ordered Out."

But trouble between the state militia's "St. Louis dandies" and the Ranger frontiersmen of southwest Missouri erupted almost immediately. In fact, the independent-minded Rangers actually came closer to an open clash with their St. Louis comrades-in-arms than with the Jayhawkers during the winter of 1860–61. When war broke upon the land, many of these southwest Missourians in navy blue traded uniforms for the butternut and gray uniforms of Companies C and D, Fifth Missouri. Much of the Rangers' veteran leadership also made the transition into the Fifth Missouri. Among those gaining invaluable prewar military experience were Captain Bradford and Lieutenants Robert S. Hearn and Martin Van Buren Mitchell and others. This cadre of experienced officers would greatly enhance the Fifth Missouri's overall quality.[32]

In 1861, Bradford's ex–Ranger influence and efforts first bore fruit during six weeks of recruiting in southwest Missouri. From the Polk County regions known as Buffalo, Flint, and Twenty-five Mile Prairies came thirty volunteers who banded together at Pleasant Prairie Chapel in January 1862. Bradford was unanimously elected captain of the horse company, which later became part of Company C.[33]

Captain Bradford and his troopers then joined Price's army at Springfield, Missouri. Here General Price designated Bradford's infant company as his personal escort. The Polk County soldiers faithfully guarded "Old Pap" throughout early 1862, but after the battle of Pea Ridge, the Missouri horsemen were dismounted. This unceremonious dehorsing was a cavalryman's worst fate in the view of these frontier cavaliers. Bradford's troopers nevertheless chose to stay with their captain as infantry instead of enlisting in another horse unit. Like Company C, some of the Fifth Missouri companies retained much of their fundamental Missouri State Guard composition upon entering Confederate service after the expiration of the six-month State Guard terms of service at the conclusion of 1861. Before the war's end, Bradford would die of disease far from his comrades and his Polk County home. The captain, ironically, would breathe his last at his grandfather's house in the picturesque mountains of East Tennessee. It would take a cruel civil war and a strange twist of fate to bring Captain Bradford back to his ancestral homeland to die.[34]

Twenty-year-old Alexander Campbell Lemmon had just opened his law practice in Bolivar when the struggle commenced. He hailed from a pioneer family which settled in southwest Missouri when buffalo and elk roamed the prairies and woodlands. These hardy settlers had wrested the land from Osage, Sac and Fox, and Delaware warriors. The Lemmon clan prospered, establishing the county's first grist mill on the Little Sac River around Hickory Grove. By 1860 these neighbors of the Mitchell clan were the masters of hundreds of acres, slaves, and political power.

After leaving his law books and office behind, the Tennessee-born Lemmon was elected captain of Company D. This was another unit of hard-fighting Polk County volunteers from the Ozark lands drained by Brush, Panther, and Bear Creeks. Among this group of frontier yeomen whom Lemmon recruited from Polk County were a father-son team of Company D, Privates James M. Williams, Jr. and Sr. As fate would have it, both father and son would be killed in battle less than a month apart. In gray pants lined with a red stripe and gray jackets, Captain Lemmon's soldiers became experts at a great deal of "red striped strutting," wrote one Rebel, before their first engagement. Confident and cocky, Lemmon's frontiersmen of southwest Missouri believed they "could whip any amount of men who would attempt to drive us from home and sweethearts."

Captain Lemmon first won distinction at Wilson's Creek while leading a Polk County company. But his struggle as a State Guard major came at a high price. Because of Lemmon's service on behalf of the South, the Unionsts threw his father into a Springfield prison, where he eventually died. It would be the second consecutive generation of Lemmon family heads to perish while serving their countries. Alexander's grandfather died on the long march home from Louisiana to Tennessee after helping whip the British at the battle of New Orleans during the War of 1812.[35]

Having recently recuperated from a summer bout with a life-threatening disease, James W. Fair was chosen captain of Company E. Like Captain Trumper, the twenty-seven-year-old Fair was raised in England. Near the Missouri River port of Miller's Landing, the Briton was a farmer in Franklin County at the beginning of the war. Fair was one of the first to answer the call, leaving a son barely a year old and a young wife. The Englishman was elected captain of a militia company by the farmers and hunters from the environs of the Gasconade and Bourbeuse Rivers.[36]

After escaping Federal pursuit and reaching Springfield, Fair and his volunteers united with Price's army to merge with the cavalry of the Sixth Division. The Confederate infantrymen of Company E still dreamed of glory in Mississippi during 1862 and were "determined the Feds will feel their power in the next engagement," as one Franklin County officer wrote in his diary. As subsequent events proved, these young Rebel volunteers were ill-prepared for the horrors that the first large-scale battle in Mississippi would bring.[37]

Captain Fair's most trusted lieutenant was George William Warren. Intelligent and honest, Warren early lost the fruits of his life's work because of his decision to fight for the South. Thanks to the vengeful Unionists, at least a $12,000 investment in his business and a labor of love had been lost forever. Warren was the postmaster and operated a general store forty miles southwest of St. Louis at Gray Summit, near the intersection of two of the state's main roads. With a railroad having only recently been built through the community, it seemed as if Warren was destined to succeed in life during the antebellum period. But the conflict changed everything and forever altered the destiny of young Warren. His store was ransacked by local Unionists and all of his personal property confiscated when Warren rode away with the Rebel troopers of Captain Fair's company.[38]

Company E's ranks were enlivened by Sergeant John Brennan. He was "a handsome young Irishman, gay and cheerful, ever ready with a kind word and a cheery song." Brennan was the second eldest son and was named for his father, a St. Louis laborer who brought his Irish family to America after 1840. John Jr. gained an early view of the ugly side of life in the world's greatest democracy not long after his arrival in America. In anti–Irish riots, the family saw discrimination not unlike that dealt out by the hated English in Ireland. In order to put barely enough food on the table, Brennan's father worked himself half to death just to make some arrogant native-born American richer. An older sister slaved for wealthy native-born Americans, and Brennan himself labored all day as a second-class citizen at a Second Street factory in the lifeless industrial zone of northern St. Louis.

Brennan was described by a Fifth Missouri officer as "a brave and faithful Soldier and always at his post." Probably because of the sting of racists' words and jokes, Brennan felt that he had something to prove. He seemingly fought longer and harder than most, as if to show he was as good as the next man. During the first attack of the Fifth Missouri, for instance, the sergeant would distinguish himself "for untiring persererance [sic] & bravery." Later, he would pay the ultimate price. Long one of the favorites of the Fifth Missouri, Sergeant Brennan would be fatally cut down by a Federal bullet.[39]

The most unique company of the Fifth Missouri was Company F. This unit was destined to earn distinction as the "Fighting Irish Company" of the Southern army's troops in the West. Company F was largely the product of Captain Joseph Kelly and, later, Patrick Canniff. Kelly was one of the best officers of the Missouri Volunteer Militia in antebellum St. Louis and then in Price's Missouri State Guard. Patrick Canniff also saw service in the prewar militia of St. Louis and with Price's army. Company F became "without doubt one of the best companies in the confederate army," wrote one soldier. This famous Irish company consisted primarily of first and second generation Irishmen from St. Louis and the rural Missouri counties.

Many Celts from these areas had served in the Missouri militia of St. Louis before the war. The Irish soldiers dominated in large part the companies of Captain Joseph Kelly's Washington Blues, Captain William

Wade's Emmet Guards, the Montgomery Guards, and other units. Proud of their heritage, these crack Irish companies long maintained their distinctive ethnic pride. Not only were the Irish troops the backbone of the best-drilled companies of St. Louis, they also were the most dedicated and high-spirited soldiers. During a militia encampment outside St. Louis, for example, the Emerald Islanders, wrote one journalist, "could be seen at intervals, engaging in the manly sports ... wrestling, fencing, pitching quoits, etc."

Company F was the most diverse unit of the Fifth Missouri from a socioeconomic, ethnic, and cultural perspective. A rural Missouri soldier complimented the Fifth Missouri's hard-fighting Irish as always being "in the foremost ranks of battle." In the heat of action, the Irish soldiers of this unit were motivated to vindicate "the honor and glory of that 'green isle of the sea.'" Each Rebel of Company F seemed especially eager in battle "to give his life and fortunes to a cause he loved."[40]

Many of Company F's Irish soldiers were upper- and middle-class products from St. Louis such as Captain Canniff and Lieutenants Walter Marnell and William Algernon Crow. These men immigrated from Ireland and pulled themselves up from their impoverished status by hard work and persistence in the New World. Company F had evolved primarily from the best military company of antebullem St. Louis, the legendary Washington Blues. This elite unit was the toast of St. Louis for years. A Kentuckian described Captain Kelly's unit in 1861 as consisting of "an exceptionally fine body of men, intelligent, educated, spirited young fellows, every one of whom held an excellent business position in the city. Yet without an exception or the least hesitation, they committed themselves to the cause."

Many members of Company F, including Captain Canniff, hailed from an Irish middle-class enclave around Market Street in the western suburbs of St. Louis. In this comfortable urban setting, they lived, worked, and loved. In relative terms, these socially elevated, middle-class Celts by 1861 were largely accepted by native-born Americans, unlike the masses of "shanty" Irish. By the war's beginning, most hostility was redirected toward a more dissimilar group of immigrants in St. Louis, the German people. Indeed, the Germans received the brunt of native-born Americans' animosity by 1860.[41]

But less fortunate Irishmen of Company F came from St. Louis's worst slum, Kerry Patch. This Irish ghetto was sandwiched between the middle-class neighborhoods and located near St. Louis University on the city's north side. Named for Kerry County in southwest Ireland, the unique, culturally distinct patch was a safe ethnic refuge from hostile Germans and native-born Americans. An entire community of Irish shanties filled a broad commons and became the immigrant's haven. Without streets or boundaries, Kerry Patch was a festering ghetto with open sewage, roaming swarms of loose goats, pigs, dogs, and children, plagues of disease and endless suffering, overcrowding and much dust or mud, depending on the season.

The Irish were the ethnic group most discriminated against in St. Louis besides African-Americans. Some of these St. Louis Irish of Company F were potato famine immigrants who came to America with little hope and even less money. These new Americans were shackled to the poverty and shame of Kerry Patch like prisoners. Large numbers of free blacks lived in this thriving city on the Mississippi, and slaves were only two percent of the population of St. Louis in 1860. This demographic reality guaranteed that the Kerry Patch Irish would primarily occupy the lower rung of the social ladder in the river city. As in Ireland, ironically, the majority of Emerald Islanders remained initially landless, illiterate, and destitute in St. Louis. For these Irish, the New World looked only too much like the Old World.[42]

Few Irishmen rose quickly above the squalor of Kerry Patch. By 1860 most St. Louis Irishmen worked in menial positions as laborers, boatsmen, and railroad workers. Many Emerald Islanders unloaded and loaded steamboats on the busy St. Louis levee. Wives and daughters toiled as domestics, and their labor served as another source of anger for Irish males. Because of the years of poverty and discrimination they had undergone, the Irish soldiers of Company F struggled harder, drilled longer, and maintained firmer discipline than any other Fifth Missouri soldiers. Officers who had been born in America were elated to have the St. Louis Irish unit in the Fifth Missouri, for it was the best "drilled company in the army, which had in former times constituted one of the regular city companies [mainly the Washington Blues] of St. Louis," in the words of one Confederate.[43]

Indeed, the Irish soldiers were destined to win widespread acclaim during the war. A Confederate officer from St. Louis serving in another regiment wrote upon first meeting Company F: "we were joined by Capt. Cunniff's [sic] company of the Fifth Missouri, without doubt one of the best companies in the Confederate army. It was drilled to perfection by that grand tactician, Col. Joe Kelly, and after his promotion transferred to Capt. Patrick Cunniff [sic], his protege and worthy successor. This company was like regulars in every movement it made. They were veterans, for they had been in all the engagements from Boonville, Mo., [and] it was the pride of the Missouri division." Indeed, this crack Irish unit "had no superior in either armies; they were simply perfection." As fate would ordain, few Company F Irishmen would survive the conflict and thus testified that their distinguished record on the battlefield was earned by blood. Less than a dozen Irish soldiers would be left alive after the war concluded. As one of Captain Canniff's soldiers lamented, "few of those in that noble band of patriots ever saw their homes or families after."[44]

Among the middle-class Irish of Company F, one of the most intellectual was a young man of much promise, Color Sergeant William W. Walsh. The twenty-eight-year-old Walsh was born in Ireland. When war came, he was a St. Louis merchant and a writer of poetry. Walsh's poems were published in the leading newspapers of St. Louis. For the Irishmen of the lowest social rank and those from Kerry Patch, enlistment into Confederate service was a quick ticket to instant equality and pay back for the past wrongs suffered at the hands of native-born Americans of European descent. The discrimination and prejudice against the Irish in St. Louis shifted mostly toward the Germans by 1860, who outnumbered the Irish three to one. With sectional antagonisms, native-born Americans were becoming increasingly hostile toward the more liberal, socially progressive, and culturally diverse Germans. By 1860 the Irish were less vulnerable to attack from the dominant Anglo establishment. Although much hostility remained in 1861, most of it was directed at the Germans, who now carried the banner of anti–Catholicism and abolitionism. The Germans' strong anti–Catholicism, anti–Irish sentiment, and Unionism caused many Irish to flock to the South's defense.[45]

The fondness of Company F members for liquor almost rivaled their reputation for perfect discipline and superior fighting abilities. These Rebels became known as the hardest drinkers of the Western army, while retaining the reputation as being among the most pious soldiers of the Fifth Missouri. These Irish Rebels were both Roman Catholics and Protestants, who closely embraced religion throughout the conflict. Captain Canniff, Sergeants Thomas Hogan and William Gillogly, Patrick Monahan, and other Company F members were former parishioners of St. John's Evangelist Church. At this beautiful church on the western edge of St. Louis, Father John B. Bannon, now the Missouri Brigade's chaplain, had held services each morning and afternoon during the antebellum period.

Many soldiers of Captain Kelly's militia company, including the captain, were also members of Father Bannon's temperance society. This unique paramilitary organization combined dual commitments to God and the military, neatly blending religion and the art of war. In looking at historical antecedents, this distinctive mixture could be traced back to Ireland, where a militant nationalism and religion had been fused into one, especially in County Kerry. In fact, during the antebellum period in St. Louis, these seemingly contradictory dual attitudes were meshed so thoroughly that Captain Kelly's Washington Blues and Father Bannon's Catholic Total Abstinence Society were considered one, "a military temperance company, composed of the flower of young Catholic manhood." Indeed, Father Bannon served as their prewar militia chaplain. And in terms of revolutionary sentiment, St. Louis was actually little different from the Emerald Isle because the yearnings of Irish nationalism continued to stir among the

Irish people, even though they were thousands of miles from their oppressed homeland. This spiritual longing for liberty by the St. Louis Irish was easily translated into Southern nationalism in 1861, for both of these revolutionary movements by two agrarian societies for self-determination were pitted against strong, centralized powers.[46]

Since January of 1862, Father Bannon had delivered spiritual guidance and words of faith primarily to the Irish Rebels, but also to the soldiers of other denominations in Price's army. Barely escaping Union authorities, Father Bannon left St. Louis on horseback at night and traveled south after learning from his former St. John's parishioners in Rebel uniforms that they lacked a Catholic chaplain in Price's army. He therefore departed his newly dedicated church, his life's work and dream, to join the St. Louis Rebels, and especially his former parishioners who now were in the Fifth Missouri. On almost any Sunday, Father Bannon could be found celebrating Mass at Captain Canniff's tent in the encampment of the Irish Confederates of Company F. He would serve with distinction as the "Confederacy's chaplain" of the Missouri Brigade during the first half of the war.[47]

The company commanders of the Fifth Missouri consisted of an exceptional body of experienced and highly motivated officers. The vast majority of regimental officers were "all young and full of life," wrote one soldier in his diary. Prominent among this elite cadre of company leaders was Captain Canniff, who commanded the Irish Rebels Company F. While in Missouri State Guard service, Canniff took over leadership of the company which consisted of the Washington Blues's nucleus after the promotion of Captain Kelly to colonel. He later led a company in Bevier's battalion after joining Confederate service.

Canniff probably came to America from Ireland with a brother, arriving by steamboat in St. Louis during the late 1850s to start a new life in America. For Canniff, the oppressed homeland was nothing more than an English colony under the exploitation of a harsh mercantile system. English authorities and the redcoats maintained supremacy throughout the Emerald Isle, where they were called "Hessians." Pro-Southerners in Missouri used the same term for St. Louis Germans. Experienced imperialists with a special talent for mercantilist exploitation, the British imposed anti–Catholic decrees and tried to mold the Irish peasants into good British subjects by stripping them of their dignity, heritage, and religion. Consequently, all hope of a bright future for young Irishmen like Canniff had long since died. Only the grim prospect of slaving as a lowly cotter remained for young Irishmen, whose homeland had become little more than a prison. But Canniff refused to waste his life digging potatoes, scything hay, and cutting turf from sunup to sundown on estates owned by English landlords. If endless toil, a hopeless future, and redcoat oppression did not break the spirit and body, then a potato famine and disease would complete the destructive process. No young Irishmen could ever forget the scenes on the miserable island that resulted from the greatest natural disaster in Ireland's tragic history and the British-imposed policy of unofficial genocide: starving women and children dying in the snow, multitudes homeless, plagues of disease, and no solutions in sight. Faced with a life of misery in the homeland, Canniff left for America to build a new life.[48]

Like many other immigrants coming to St. Louis, Canniff probably arrived on Missouri soil after a trip north up the Mississippi River via New Orleans, Louisiana. Canniff brought with him to the New World a distinct tradition of preserving one's native culture against a strong, centralized government. By 1861, Irish immigrants such as Canniff came to see that Ireland and the South shared an identical plight and historical burden: domination and exploitation by a strong centralized power. Consequently, a sense of Irish nationalism not only survived but also thrived more than 3,000 miles from their homeland on the banks of the Mississippi River in St. Louis before the war. At the shooting contests of the Washington Blues, for instance, prizes for the best marksmen consisted of medals "bearing on one side a head of Washington, and on the other Irish national emblems." This militia emblem tied together two comparable revolutionary and nationalist movements on opposite sides of the ocean. Hence, the identification with a third struggle, the Confederacy's fight, was easy for these Irishmen of St. Louis in 1861. Appropriately, during the antebellum period Canniff and other St. Louis Irish militiamen served in Captain Wade's Emmet Guards, named for martyred Irish nationalist Robert Emmet. The St. Louis militia company members wore shamrock-decorated breastplates, spoke with thick Irish brogues, danced "Irish jigs," and told tales and sang songs of Ireland.[49]

By 1861, secession was seen by many of St. Louis's Irish citizens as synonymous with Irish nationalism. A good example of the historical identification to worldwide nationalist and revolutionary struggles could be seen in the banner of the Emmet Guards. One side of the silk flag bore the portrait of George Washington, while the other side contained a hand-painted picture of Robert Emmet. Stitched above Emmet's portrait was his proclamation of the revolutionary sentiment which justified the struggle for nationalism and libery and historically linked the nationalist movements for American, Irish, and Southern independence: "I have wished to procure for my country the guarantee which Washington procured for America."[50]

In addition to the desire to obtain a better economic situation and personal freedoms, Canniff may have come to St. Louis to aid a female relative because there was one Canniff, a woman, living in St. Louis in 1858. By any measure, young Canniff migrated to the right town at the right time. With hard work and determination, Patrick Canniff was a self-made man, becoming an established saddle, harness, and collar-maker by 1859 and living at 81 South Fourteenth Street on the city's west side in St. John's parish. He had no time to find a wife, for the bachelor devoted his energies to taking advantage of the opportunities in thriving St. Louis which were not found in Ireland. Canniff's artisan skills in leather work were in demand in the West's busiest city, with throngs of immigrants preparing for the journey west across the Great Plains. The need for quality leather goods by those settlers bound for the West never ceased in St. Louis, Gateway to the West. Along with his own ambition and initiative, this boom period helped Canniff to escape the ghetto of Kerry Patch and rise to the middle-class status of an artisan. Additional prestige in St. Louis' antebellum society came with his enlistment as a private in Captain Wade's Emmet Guards.[51]

Canniff also volunteered to become a member of the Central Fire Company No. 1 of St. Louis. This community service gave him an opportunity to move up the social ladder, allowing even an illiterate Irish immigrant the chance to mix with his "superiors," gain status in the community, and engage in the city's most respected social events. Duty in the fire company might have helped Canniff gain entry into the prestigious militia of antebellum St. Louis. He also benefited financially as a volunteer fire fighter in August of 1859, when his blue-uniformed company disbanded. Like other fire company members, Canniff was paid $750 after the sale of fire company property. Canniff probably established his own private business with this financial gain.[52]

It is possible that Captain Canniff acquired British army experience before coming to America, which would explain his quick entry into the Missouri Volunteer Militia of St. Louis. By 1860, Canniff lived at a Twelfth Street boardinghouse which was distinguished by an international flavor. Although the residents included Scotsmen and Englishmen, this boardinghouse consisted mostly of Irish. It was located only four blocks east of Canniff's church, St. John the Apostle and Evangelist Church.

Canniff's first known military campaign came in December 1860, when the St. Louis militia marched to the western border to protect the state's citizens against Kansas raiders. During this expedition, the Irishmen in militia uniforms from the streets of St. Louis first received a close look at the terrified border and its refugees. Returning from the winter campaign before the new year with a firmer Southern stance, Canniff laid aside his militia uniform, a dark blue jacket, sky-blue trousers, and white crossbelts. Canniff became a peaceful civilian once more, but he would never be the same. Perhaps by now Canniff, age twenty-four, had already made his life's most fateful decisions: to support the doctrine of states' rights and "Home Rule" and to join the South's struggle for independence.[53]

Indeed, the Emerald Islanders of Company F had more than ample justification for linking their destinies with the South. After years of suffering from verbal abuse, discrimination, and even outright physical attack in St. Louis, Canniff and many other of his countrymen felt no great allegiance to a hypocritical democracy in which equality for them was a lie and a myth. During the anti–Irish riots in St. Louis in the mid–1850s, nativist assaults targeted Irish churches, "houses, shanties and groggeries," and even St. Louis University, the city's leading Catholic institution of higher learning. A new democratic and republican nation, the Confederacy, might offer less repression and greater chances for success and a better life, especially for those Irish who helped win that country's independence. Then equality would be a reality instead of a hollow dream mocked by the United States Constitution's false promises. If this infant Southern nation won its struggle for independence, then maybe Irishmen would not have to endure any more humiliation because of their nationality, heritage, and Roman Catholicism or feel the shame of mothers, sisters, and daughters toiling as domestics for well-to-do native-born Americans.[54]

In the New World, Celts of both sexes were treated as badly by native-born Americans as they had been by the British before they immigrated. Another key motivation for joining a revolutionary struggle was that these Kerry Patchers, "shanty" Irish, and self-made men of middle-class status from Ireland who enlisted in Company F, Fifth Missouri, did so because of ancient feuds against the Germans. Indeed, in St. Louis, the Irish had "in their blood an antipathy to 'the Dutch dating from William of Orange's days' and the 'infidel, Sabbath-breaking, beer-drinking Dutch who had invaded St. Louis' were of the same breed as those who harried Ireland and inflicted innumerable persecutions in 1689." In the Mississippi River port city of St. Louis as nowhere else in the nation by 1861, "the question of life and death for the Union is transformed into an ethnic feud" between Irish and German citizens.[55]

In the war's beginning, most St. Louis Irish sided with the South with the same enthusiasm that was described by a Southern journalist in another Mississippi River port town: "As for our Irish citizens — whew! They are 'spilin' for a fight with Old Abe." Some Irish militiamen of St. Louis early displayed the sentiment of those Celts destined for Fifth Missouri service when they raised a Southern banner over an inner city mansion, the Missouri Volunteer Militia headquarters, in early March 1861. Pro-Southern feeling among the Irish skyrocketed with the capture of Camp Jackson in May 1861, which drove the St. Louis "Irish to a state of frenzy," wrote one St. Louisan.[56]

Before the war's outbreak, life in the Emmet and Montgomery Guards and Washington Blues was most seductive. Admiring crowds socialized at the Capital Oyster Saloon, drinking "Green Tree" beer all night at the Green Tree Tavern near the Mississippi River front, participating in gala balls to celebrate the battle of New Orleans and the battles of the American Revolution, and marching in militia parades. On these festive occasions, militiamen such as Canniff, Marnell, and Crow "merrily passed the hours in social converse, mingled with the exhilarating mazes of the dances, and the no less exhilarating champagne, which flowed like the sparkling waters of the purling brook," according to one journalist. Best of all, militia brass bands delivered midnight serenades outside the houses of lovers, which probably ensured a successful conquest.[57] The romantic, antebellum world of the St. Louis militiamen was forever crushed, however, by the harsh realities of the Civil War.

As a young Rebel officer in 1861, Lieutenant Canniff first made a name for himself by becoming the top lieutenant under Captain Kelly, the "father" of drill, who was a key player in molding the Missouri State Guard into an army. Canniff became Kelly's "worthy successor" in discipline and drill proficiency after the colonel fell wounded at the battle of Wilson's Creek in August of 1861.

More responsibility came for Lieutenant Canniff when he took charge of Company A, Colonel Kelly's First Regiment, Sixth Division, after Captain Stephen O. Coleman's death at Wilson's Creek. In his first action leading a company, Lieutenant Canniff proved himself to be one of the army's finest skirmish officers. He aggressively drove the Federals from a strong point and secured an advantageous position at Lexington that contributed to a successful Rebel advance and siege. The fame won during Missouri State Guard service would follow Canniff into Confederate ranks and continue until his death in battle.[58]

With the expiration of State Guard service terms during the winter of 1861-62, Captain Canniff and his Irish Confederate company merged into Bevier's battalion. He led his unit with skill at the battle of Pea Ridge before crossing the Mississippi with Price's army. A Catholic of St. John's Church, the long-haired Captain Canniff worked closely with his former St. Louis priest, Father Bannon, who was now Missouri Brigade chaplain. Some of Canniff's duties consisted of touring various Confederate encampments and scheduling Mass for the Catholic chaplain. A Rebel of the Missouri Brigade long remembered meeting Captain Canniff's Company F for the first time and later wrote: "We connected ourselves with a company of Irishmen from St. Louis — all Irish from the captain down. They were recruited [from] the wharves of St. Louis. Brave men and good soldiers they proved themselves to be. Conniff [sic] . . . was the name of the captain." Even from the earliest State Guard days, some of the best soldiers of the Confederacy who saw these Irishmen of Company F often felt "how proud I would be to have been on the roll of this company." But, ironically, the reality was hardly glorious or glamorous, for enlisting in Company F was almost like signing a death warrant.[59]

The ever-aggressive Captain Canniff early demonstrated a natural instinct and ability which made him the premier skirmish captain of not only the Fifth Missouri, but also of the entire First Missouri Brigade. Summarizing Captain Canniff's influence, a Missouri Brigade officer was impressed "with the thorough confidence which the whole command reposed in Canniff. Many instances of great bravery are remembered of this gallant and unequaled Irishman, who was a favorite with all — never away from his post, always ready for duty — finished and complete in the study of the tactics, and considered by the Brigade as the best officer of his rank in the army." Whenever an obstacle needed to be overcome or whenever the most dependable soldiers were needed during the difficult campaigns ahead, Generals John Stevens Bowen and Francis Marion Cockrell and Colonel McCown and other leaders in the West would choose Company F and Captain Canniff to get the job done. Indeed, in the words of one Fifth Missouri officer, Captain Canniff's "fidelity to orders was almost proverbial."

With Celtic brogue and shoulder-length auburn hair, Captain Canniff cut a dashing figure on the battlefield. His value as the best skirmish commander of the elite Missouri Brigade would prevent Canniff from attaining a rank higher than captain, however. But after years of devastating losses in the Missouri Brigade, Captain Canniff would eventually command the Third and Fifth Missouri (consolidated) before his death in 1864. Canniff left behind an enduring legacy which carried on long after he was gone, however, for his skirmishers continued in their key role. Serving as the primary skirmishers for the Missouri Brigade and often for Rebel armies, this elite company of Irish soldiers became "the pride of the Missouri division," while earning the reputation of being the Missouri Brigade's best soldiers.[60]

The noncommissioned officers who made Company F the best skirmish company included such capable natural leaders as Sergeant Thomas Hogan. He was raised as the oldest son of a ten-member family headed by his former river boatman father. In one generation, the family rose from lower-class to middle-class status in St. Louis. Thomas Hogan was born on the Emerald Isle just before the disastrous potato famines of the 1840s, which caused the Hogan clan to depart. By 1860 both father and son worked as clerks at the same general store near the family church, Father Bannon's St. John's Catholic Church, to support their large family. The ex-clerk would survive dozens of hard skirmishes without a scratch while "many of my comrades were slain by my side." But Hogan's luck would run out when he was killed in 1864. In his last letter home, the sergeant told his St. Louis family how badly he wanted "soon to see them again, when the black clouds of war have blown over us, and the tranquility of peace returns again." No one would take the tragic news of Sergeant Hogan's death harder than his father, who would spend the remainder of his life grieving over the loss of his favorite son. The letters of the young sergeant from St. Louis "were printed and framed and hung in his home by his heartbroken father."[61]

Twenty-six-year-old Stephen Decatur Coale was elected captain of Company G. He was "a tall, lank Southwest Missourian, a perfect gentleman, brave as a lion," wrote one Fifth Missouri officer. The Henry County native left a teaching position at Clinton when he rode off to war. Coale's Company G consisted of soldiers from western and central Missouri, including three of the captain's relatives. But Henry County natives dominated the ranks. These Rebels first saw duty in such militia units as the Henry County Rifles and the Henry County Rangers. Living near the troubled Kansas border helped to instill within Company G's soldiers a desire to even up old scores with the hated Jayhawkers, who had long ravished the border. It is quite possible that Stephen led a forty-man Bates County company to the western border to join the St. Louis militia brigade, the Polk County Rangers, and other frontier militia units during the Southwest Expedition in the winter of 1860-61. Hardened by service on the western border, Coale served with distinction as a cavalry lieutenant in Price's army. Like his comrades, he was eager for the day they would ride west into Kansas to wage war and obtain revenge, but Coale left life as a cavalier behind forever to join the Fifth Missouri. Much suffering, a good many arduous campaigns, and a prison death awaited him.[62]

By far the least popular captain of the Fifth Missouri was crusty, autocratic, and hard-drinking Charles Thomas. He was elected commander of Company H before his many deficiencies were seen by his followers. A former United States lieutenant and perhaps the only Fifth Missouri officer with regular army experience, Captain Thomas would be driven half-crazy by the easygoing attitude of his undisciplined farm boys. No matter how much the grizzled captain raved, the enlisted men of Company H continued to slouch, spit tobacco juice, and ask stupid questions concerning the wisdom of even the simplest order. Captain Thomas, therefore, often turned into a raging madman when he attempted to discipline his individualistic soldiers. The large amount of rot-gut whiskey that Thomas, a serious-minded martinet, consumed soon brought these personal clashes to explosive levels. The Mexican War veteran, for instance, was enraged when Private Samuel Ellison, age eighteen, was unable to drill with his comrades because of sickness. Thinking that the young man was shamming, Thomas flew into one of his typical rages, screaming like a wildman, "God damn you, I will make you!" With Captain Thomas hurling obscenities and making threats, a sickly Ellison grabbed his musket, hobbled from his tent, and attempted to do his duty. Even though he escaped his captain's furies for the moment, Private Ellison was destined to be killed in the war.

The short-tempered Thomas often turned his wrath upon his whole company of northeast Missourians. The captain was especially fond of denouncing his Company H soldiers as a "God damn pack of hounds!" Repeatedly on the drill ground, Captain Thomas bellowed at his multitude of clumsy privates, "God damn you, can't you keep in line?" Private James McCann, an Ireland-born laborer from Warrensburg, became a special target for Captain Thomas's anger. After a minor infraction by McCann, Thomas went berserk as he so often did. In front of the entire company, he threatened to "break [McCann's] head." The much maligned enlisted men of Company H finally rebelled, filing charges of abuse and drunkenness against the hated Thomas. As a result, Captain Thomas soon stood before a court-martial. The captain would resign before 1862's end, despite winning acquittal during the trial.[63]

One butternut successfully enduring Captain Thomas's rages was Private John T. Tipton. He had his left arm amputated after a wound suffered during Missouri State Guard service. Despite this serious handicap, Tipton eagerly enlisted in Confederate service to join Company H, Fifth Missouri, and fought in the ranks like any other private. Refusing to be discharged for disability like others, he struggled beside his able-bodied Fifth Missouri comrades for years. At least two other Fifth Missouri Rebels who were missing arms as a result of amputations fought in the regiment. These other handicapped but stalwart fighters were St. Louis Celtic warriors of Company F, Privates Thomas Doyle, Ireland-born, and William Henry Hicks.[64]

Northeast Missourians of Company I elected young Benjamin Eli Guthrie as their captain. These volunteers, who came primarily from the fertile rolling grasslands of the Audrain Prairie region, made a fine choice in choosing Guthrie. Born near General Sterling Price's tobacco plantation near Keytesville, Missouri, Guthrie grew up hearing how his North Carolina ancestors had listened to the roar of the battle of Guilford Court House in 1781 from the security of their log cabin. Guthrie was a born leader and possessed an uncommon mixture of both intelligence and common sense at only age twenty-two.[65]

So eager was Guthrie to fight after seeing his community of College Mound, Macon County, invaded by Union troops, he departed immediately to raise a partisan force of Rebels from the countryside only two days before his long-anticipated graduation with honors from McGee College. Named after his preacher grandfather, who had drowned in the Missouri River attempting to save others, Benjamin Eli Guthrie seemed destined for great things. He matured early as the oldest of ten children on an Andrew County farmstead, especially with his traveling preacher father usually absent from home. His father's absence forced Guthrie to become the household head at an early age. His toil on the family farm seldom ended: there was always more land to clear, fences to mend, and fields to plow or harvest. Even in the midst of winter, Guthrie was out in the snowy woodlands before daylight, cutting down trees and hauling cord wood to town for sale to support the family. Despite the heavy workload, the young man not only managed to keep up with his studies at backwoods schools, but also excelled at academics. More demands were forced upon young Guthrie with his mother's early death. Saddled with more responsibilities, Guthrie now worked even harder, with more effort required to support his nine siblings. At an early age, the precocious young man learned more about the world around him and human nature as a livery stable driver. This position gave him an opportunity to visit surrounding Missouri counties, and thus he was able to talk to different people and to grasp the social and political ideas of the Western frontier.[66]

A fast learner, Guthrie gained more independence from familial responsibilities in 1855. He entered Chapel Hill College in Lafayette County, fulfilling a life-long dream. Higher education continued when Benjamin and his younger brother Robert, later a Company I sergeant, attended McGee College three years later. The sight of Illinois soldiers overrunning McGee College during the summer of 1861 convinced Guthrie that it was time to lay down his school books and fight, although he was within days of graduating with academic honors. Amid the dark hardwood forests along the Chariton River, "Eli" Guthrie was elected captain of a local militia unit of Rebels in August of 1861. The captain would lead a charmed life in the many bloody battles to come for the Fifth Missouri, always up front but never cut down by bullets. On the many battlefields across the South, the Guthrie brothers of Company I always would stay close together and survive the odds, even though "both had some narrow escapes." Reprieved by a six-month furlough during the summer of 1863, Benjamin Eli Guthrie would miss the Vicksburg campaign in which more than half the Fifth Missouri would be wiped out.

Guthrie was destined to be the only Fifth Missouri captain elected at Saltillo who would be left alive at the conflict's conclusion. This feat of survival was miraculous because the Fifth Missouri would engage in many of the war's most brutal campaigns in the West. The best-educated and youngest captain of the Fifth Missouri, Guthrie would travel full circle in his life, as if ordained by fate. He eventually would end up teaching in the academic world that he loved and at the same educational institution, McGee College, where his peaceful existence had been shattered by civil war in 1861. Guthrie had left not only his innocence and college degree behind at McGee College upon entering Rebel ranks, but also at least one broken heart.[67]

Of all the officers in the Fifth Missouri, Captain David Young Pankey best fit the stereotype of a slave-owning planter. Without hesitation, he was elected captain of Company K. While the vast majority of Fifth Missouri soldiers hailed from middle-class backgrounds, Pankey had only recently been a wealthy Virginian. Pankey, age twenty-nine, once owned gangs of slaves who worked hundreds of acres back in the Tidewater country. With a heritage of Revolutionary War and War of 1812 forefathers, a prestigious University of Virginia degree, and plenty of money, Pankey was a Southern aristocrat for most of his life. But the high life-style of a tobacco dealer, merchant, large slave-owner, and extensive landowner ended forever with sagging tobacco prices, worn-out land, and unsound investments wiped out during the 1857 depression.[68]

Forced to make a fresh start, Pankey journeyed west for a second chance. After selling most of his slaves in Virginia, the Presbyterian crossed the Mississippi River with a new wife and the determination to regain lost fortunes. Pankey planted roots in 1859 on the flat, wooded lands near Clarkton, Dunklin County. This section of southeast Missouri was so remote that the swampy area had been the last region settled in the state. In this rugged land near the Mississippi, the former blue blood of the Virginia aristocracy lived and worked on an average-sized farm and then opened a small store.

The Virginian of upper-class roots quickly merged into the democratic frontier of southeast Missouri. Despite almost forty years of statehood, the rugged countryside was untamed and wild, with only 5,000 people living in Dunklin County by 1860. In a fate that he could not have comprehended only a short time earlier, the refined Pankey became equal in social stature to the rough trappers, woodsmen, and hunters of the Bootheel region bordering the St. Francis and Little Rivers.[69]

Around Clarkton, the land was unbelievably fertile and unlike anything seen in soil-exhausted Virginia. The deep black soil of southeast Missouri produced high yields, more than seen elsewhere in Missouri. To the "Old Dominion" native, the unspoiled landscape of Dunklin County resembled the Deep South more than the Western frontier. For miles around lay a seemingly endless expanse of swamps, dark bayous, and cypress forests. But the wild region was a good place for a man of Pankey's abilities to start life anew. Despite their uncouth appearances and rough exteriors, the local people, who were mostly Tennesseeans who had migrated to southeast Missouri from across the Mississippi, were decent, God-fearing, and hard-working. Pankey successfully assimilated and was destined to outlive three wives, which was no small accomplishment in the 1800s. He became popular with the local population, some of whom served as Confederates in Company K, Fifth Missouri.[70]

The woodsmen, hunters, and farmers of Company K emerged from the wilderness of Dunklin County in 1861 after reading such southeast

Missouri appeals as: "So leave your plows in the furrow and your oxen in the yoke, and rush like a tornado upon our invaders and foes, to sweep them from the face of the earth." This emotional plea brought hundreds of Rebel volunteers from the dense forests of water tupelo, magnolia, gum, and cypress of the watery delta area known by those in revolt against the national government as "the glorious Little River District." This little-known region lay nestled between the Mississippi River to the east, the Ozark foothills westward, and Arkansas to the south. Appearing from the depths of the wetlands in pirogues with flintlocks, powder horns, and hunting knives, Bootheelers knew how to survive in their swampy domain. Their skills were honed to shoot a turkey off his cottonwood tree roost in the half-light of dawn, hit bounding white-tail deer on the run, and trap and net anything in or out of the water. Such experience in survival and self-reliance would soon prove invaluable to these soldiers on the forested battlegrounds of the Deep South.[71]

Despite the swamps, floods, and swarms of mosquitoes, this area of southeast Missouri was a trapper's paradise, a hunter's reserve, and a farmer's nightmare. Impassable and mysterious, Great Mingo, Little River, and Nigger Wool swamps were home to some Company K Rebels. Often flooded by the Castor, Little, and Mississippi rivers, the lush delta consisted of some of the world's richest and most productive alluvial soils and contained some of the hottest Southern sympathizers. It was an endless source of pride for the Confederates of Company K that not one Dunklin County resident voted for Abe Lincoln in 1860. In the Bootheel region as nowhere else in the state, cotton was king, but without the extensive plantation culture and large planter slaveocracy found in the Deep South. Middle-class farmers raised patches of cotton in the 10–20 foot black soil after clearing ground by hacking away the brushy tangles and thickets lining slight ridges. Only a small number of slaves, ironically, could be found in Dunklin County: barely 150 African Americans in 1860, and only 4 percent of the population. As indicated by the demographics evident in every Fifth Missouri company, the relatively few slaves from the home areas of Company K's soldiers reflected the primary socioeconomic makeup of these Fifth Missouri Rebels even amid a dominant cotton culture environment: they formed a middle-class yeoman society.[72]

Early in the war Dunklin County volunteers formed into a First Division infantry regiment of the Missouri State Guard, with Pankey serving as lieutenant colonel. He left behind a wife and a son less than six months old. As part of the Rebel forces under General "Swamp Fox" Jeff Thompson, Pankey's troops saw action for six months, fighting across southeast Missouri at Pattonville, Black River Bridge, Blackwater Station, Fredericktown, Bloomington, and New Madrid and engaging in numerous unnamed skirmishes. These frontiersmen in butternut struggled in guerrilla fashion from their swampy havens to the motto invoking the American Revolution: "Remember [Colonel Francis] Marion of the Santee and Pedee [River country of South Carolina], and dye every path, river and bayou with the blood of the ruthless invaders." Indeed, memories of the success of the colonial partisan bands in the South during the American Revolution rekindled a guerrilla tradition and the Swamp Foxes' nickname for these hard-fighting Missouri Rebels. Serving as a lieutenant colonel in the Swamp Fox Brigade, Pankey won "credit and distinction for himself in all [engagements]." The Bootheel Rebels' elusiveness and hit-and-run tactical skills earned them such titles as the Swamp Rats and Muskrats. After striking into the state's interior, the butternut partisans slipped back into their swampy strongholds during the autumn of 1861.[73]

With Brigadier General John Pope's Army of the Mississippi invading Thompson's swampy refuge during its drive on Island Number Ten, the Swamp Foxes abandoned their delta sanctuaries in early 1862. Then they escaped across the Mississippi and into Tennessee, becoming exiles like so many other Missouri Rebels who had to flee the Union-occupied home state. The Muskrat soldiers from southeast Missouri embarked upon Mississippi River duty in May 1862. These former guerrilla fighters became gunners and crewmen on the makeshift Confederate "cotton-boat fleet" to defend Memphis against the Union navy. Pankey's "sailors" contributed to the defense of the Mississippi, adjusting from a life as guerrillas to a life on the water.

After expiration of State Guard enlistments, Pankey organized a Confederate company consisting primarily of Dunklin County soldiers in June of 1862. Also included in this force were a sprinkling of Stoddard County Rebels, formerly from a unit called the Swamp Rangers. Pankey's contingent of veterans was the independent Confederate company which arrived at Saltillo from Tupelo, Mississippi, to complete the organization of the Fifth Missouri.[74]

Pankey's chief lieutenant was Ferrel Bennett Spicer, who would take command of Company K by November of 1862. In the pattern of other Upper South settlers, Spicer and family migrated by wagon west across the Mississippi via Cotton Point Ferry and through Nigger Wool Swamp to the West Prairie, Dunklin County, area. A Rebel company was formed from the Bootheel region swamps in the war's beginning, and it became known as the "Dunklin County Dead Shots." These "Dead Shots" were the nucleus of Company K, Fifth Missouri, and earlier saw action in General Thompson's command. The six-foot Spicer apparently served as a lieutenant of the "Dead Shots," an unorthodox body of frontier individualists from the swamps. The "Dunklin County Dead Shots" were initially so reluctant to join Confederate service because of states' rights enthusiasm that they ran off a Confederate recruiter with volleys. But this provincialism eventually vanished with the emergence of Southern nationalism and years of duty east of the Mississippi. These rawboned fishermen, trappers, woodsmen, and middle-class cotton growers were now veteran Confederates of Company K. Probably no one more than General Thompson would have been surprised to later learn of the accomplishments of his former Swamp Foxes, of Company K, Fifth Missouri, at the battles of Corinth, Port Gibson, Champion Hill, and Vicksburg. In these bloody engagements which were some of the most important of the Western war, the southeast Missouri troops of Company K "sustained the reputation of their state and added lustre to the Confederate glory."[75]

The Company K Bootheel soldiers added yet another diverse cultural group to the ranks of the Fifth Missouri. The Irish of Company F and the Company K Swamp Rats were the most dissimilar demographic contingents in the Fifth Missouri. They had little in common culturally with each other, but now stood side by side in northeast Mississippi for the cause of Southern independence. In contrast, some Fifth Missouri companies from different sections of Missouri were already well acquainted. For example, some of Canniff's Celts of Company F, including the captain, first met the Polk Country Rangers, now of Company C, on the Missouri-Kansas border during the Southwest Expedition of 1860. This meeting resulted in immediate friction based upon considerable urban versus rural differences, as well as cultural ones. Fate and the demands of war determined the destinies of both dissimilar groups of Rebels, throwing them together once again in northeast Mississippi on September 1, 1862. But now the Irish Confederates from the streets of St. Louis and the frontier Rangers of southwest Missouri were serving together in the Fifth Missouri and were united in violent revolution against the United States of America. It was a national tragedy which no rational American could have imagined during the age of innocence that preceded the most horrible war in the nation's history.[76]

A demographic analysis helps to reveal motivations. The Fifth Missouri Confederate Infantry consisted primarily of middle-class farmers, who comprised more than 70 percent of regimental members. The 822 soldiers listed by county from a total of almost 1,100 men represented 55 of the state's 115 counties. But three counties dominated, claiming 48 percent of the total number listed. Polk County tops the list, sending 161 Rebels into the Fifth Missouri's ranks, followed by Macon County with 135 men, and Johnson County with 105 soldiers.[77]

Most of Colonel McCown's Rebels had labored before the conflict on middle-class farmsteads of from two hundred to three hundred acres. On their small and average-sized farms on the Western frontier, these agriculturalists had primarily raised corn and hogs, the two fundamental staples of the West. These diversified farmers also produced smaller crops of wheat, oats and rye and sometimes grew patches of cotton or tobacco.

In western Missouri, gently rolling prairies of native grasses gave way to sprawling fields of corn. Hogs foraged on acorns along the heavily wooded creek and river bottoms.

Representative of the average agricultural unit was Ensign Ramsey's farm of 320 acres on the upper reaches of Blackwater River near Columbus, Johnson County. Along a Blackwater River branch, Ramsey's typical western Missouri farm included 50 hogs, 17 sheep, 12 horses, and 24 cattle. These agricultural farmsteads of Polk and Johnson Counties, ironically, were almost identical to those of Unionists from Illinois, Ohio, and Iowa. Colonel McCown's Missourians, strangely enough, had much more in common socioeconomically with their Northern counterparts than with the planter class of the Deep South.[78]

Macon County differed economically from Johnson and Polk counties. In the rolling countryside surrounding the Chariton and Salt Rivers, tobacco, not cotton, was king. More than one million pounds of tobacco had been produced in the county in 1860, ensuring strong economic ties with the South. But there were no sprawling plantations with numerous slaves as there were further South in the counties along the Missouri River.

The tobacco culture of Missouri's middle-class farmers at the war's onset had been brought by immigrants from Tennessee, Kentucky, Virginia, and North Carolina along with other cultural baggage of a distinctive Southern society and tradition. Branching out from self-sufficient farming to commercial farming for European markets, Missouri yeomen primarily raised crops on less than ten acres, producing the state's finest and longest-leafed tobacco in the shortest time. Because of the extensive work required to tend the large-leafed weed, known locally as "shoestring" and "yellow oker" tobacco, slaves worked more with this staple crop of the frontier economy in Macon County than they did in either Polk or Johnson counties. Less than 75 miles south of the Iowa border, Macon County had long held a tight grip on tobacco culture and a firm economic tie to the export city of New Orleans. So strong were the historic, economic, cultural, and social links with the South that Chariton, the oldest settled township in Macon County, had been nicknamed "South Carolina."[79]

Instead of being fire-eating revolutionaries who had everything to gain and nothing to lose, the men of the Fifth Missouri represented a solidly entrenched segment of frontier society. These citizens, levelheaded and conservative yeomen of a Jeffersonian democracy in the West, were the pillars of their frontier society, hard-working, traditional, and agrarian in perspective. Despite their relative isolation on the Western frontier, the soldiers of the Fifth Missouri were part of an educated group that adhered to Southern religious, cultural, and social values.[80]

Next to agriculturalists, students most dominated the Fifth Missouri's ranks. This high concentration indicated both the importance of education as a key foundation of the Jeffersonian democracy on the western frontier and the young ages of Fifth Missouri soldiers. Many of Company A's Johnson County men in the ranks had attended Chapel Hill College. This school was the key institution of higher education in western Missouri. Company H included a number of soldiers, both teachers and students, from Christian University in Canton on the Mississippi. McGee College alumni served faithfully in Company I's ranks. The importance of religion on the Western frontier likewise fused with respect for education to elevate Chapel Hill and McGee Colleges, both Presbyterian academic institutions, as bastions of learning in Missouri during the prewar years.[81]

After the high number of farmers and students in the Fifth Missouri could be found in descending order: laborers; merchants and carpenters; clerks, ministers, and printers; blacksmiths, physicians, lawyers, and teachers. Especially in a rural and Western society, these respected occupations clearly indicate that the Fifth Missouri consisted of the leading citizens and foundations of their frontier communities. As one soldier emphasized, the Fifth Missouri soldiery "counted the bravest hearts, the wisest heads, and the best blood of Missouri, who had voluntarily abandoned the peaceful delights of happy homes and the urgent ties of business and family duties."[82]

A distinctive Southern cultural heritage was one of the most important factor prompting these Missouri frontiersmen to unite their destinies with first the defense of the state against Union invasion and then the independence movement of the South. The symbolic and psychological importance of Southern ancestry had almost a magical quality in nineteenth-century American life. For instance, one Missouri Brigade member explained: "My Parents being of Southern blood it was only natural for me to espouse the cause of the South." Most Fifth Missouri Rebels had been born outside the state of Missouri. The vast majority of these men were natives of the Upper South: Kentucky, Tennessee, Virginia, and North Carolina. Interestingly, more regimental members were born in the lower Northwest territory region than in the Deep South.

Most of Colonel McCown's followers were young men in their 20s, still living and working on the family farm. In the prime of life and in good health from hunting and farming for years in the outdoors, the veterans of the Fifth Missouri had the physical conditioning and qualifications for a highly durable force. For example, one of McCown's officers described the physical appearance of the Fifth Missouri soldiers during a period of rigorous campaigning: "lithe, sinewy, ragged and bronzed, the very type of our Missouri rebels."[83]

From an early age, the men of the Fifth Missouri knew how to handle firearms. Hunting for dinner, target shooting for fun, and prior military and paramilitary experience ensured that training and experience in the use of firearms were early gained. Some of these frontiersmen had fought Indians, African Americans (Seminole War), Mexicans, and Kansans during the antebellum period. A Missouri Brigade member perhaps best analyzed the lengthy and extensive seasoning process during prewar days: "There were men who had driven 'Bull teams' across the plains, fought Indians, and endured the hardships [of] the plainsmen's life. There were men who had marched with Colonel Alexander Doniphan [sic] . . . and seen the American flag raised over the 'Halls of Montezuma'; men who had fillibustered [sic] with [William] Walker in Nicaragua, and [rode with the] 'Border Ruffians' [into Kansas] to capture 'Old John Brown.'" These antebellum experiences would help make the Rebels of the Fifth Missouri perhaps the Confederacy's finest troops in the West.[84]

The best example of this military conditioning before the Civil War could be found with the Polk County Rangers and the Missouri Volunteer Militia. Dan Frost's Southwest Expedition had provided excellent training during active campaigning in the winter before the Civil War. Dedicated and capable militia officers such as Colonel Bowen, "the best tactician in the city" of St. Louis, had applied West Point standards to the volunteers. Destined to lead the Missouri Brigade, Bowen had helped turn these rowdy citizens into disciplined soldiers. Most important, an espirit de corps had been born and a military tradition solidified when these militiamen defiantly resisted the Kansas threat during the winter campaign of 1860-61.[85]

These Fifth Missouri soldiers had gained invaluable experience during Missouri State Guard service. The six months of hard campaigning with General Price that consisted of six pitched battles and twenty skirmishes in 1861 provided early combat experience. The high quality of the Missouri Brigade owed much to its State Guard antecedents. Officers gained invaluable leadership experience and skills with General Price during 1861. For example, Lieutenant Colonel Bevier "did as hard studying as ever before in my life, even when in schooldays I had pored over algebra and vulgar fractions, and by Christmas had one of the best-drilled regiments in our brigade."

The motivation to redeem Union-occupied Missouri together with more combat experience than any other troops in the Confederacy made the Fifth Missouri soldiers highly disciplined and committed to fight to the end if necessary. The benefits of this invaluable militia and Missouri State Guard experience, superior discipline, and high morale would be reaped across the battlefields of the South, where the Missourians would consistently perform beyond the capabilities of most other Southern troops.[86]

Based upon the Jeffersonian agrarian model, the frontier society of Polk, Johnson, and Macon counties was the embodiment of a rural democracy in 1860. The primary blemish on this idyllic democracy on the Western frontier was the moral blight of slavery. Besides being a border state of the Upper South, Missouri was a new land of the West and part of "the Valley of Democracy," but it possessed deep Southern roots. Since before Missouri gained statehood in 1821, black servitude had existed, but it failed to thrive as it had in the plantation economies of the Deep South. By 1861, slavery was largely an obsolete appendage of the past in Missouri because of an emerging age of industrialism and the ever-changing economics and demographics of a modern era. Polk, Johnson, and Macon counties had few of the large slave gangs, white pillared mansions, or extensive plantations based upon a staple crop like in the Deep South. A Polk County resident in 1858 stated that in his yeoman society of southwest Missouri, "we have no distinction of classes or caste, no hide-bound sectarianism, no exclusive clans or intolerant cliques; and, what is best, we are entirely free from that vile abomination of small places — cod-fish aristocracy." By 1860 this dynamic but traditional society of mostly middle-class yeomen represented one of the earliest republican foundations of the American nation: an agrarian society of middle-class freemen on the Western frontier. For the soldiers of the Fifth Missouri, these economic, political, and social philosophies of a Jeffersonian democracy were identified with the Revolutionary generation of their forefathers and, by 1861, with the Confederacy's struggle for nationhood.[87] As in 1776, the fight was for self-determination.

But perhaps more significant, a distinctive Southern culture had not only survived in Missouri, but had also flourished during the decades of the frontier experience. Instead of fading away with the taming of the Missouri wilderness, a Southern cultural heritage had withstood the ravages of time and stayed alive throughout the state. Upper South settlers had poured up the fertile Mississippi and Missouri river valleys in the early nineteenth century. Like the European immigrants who flooded into Missouri during the decade before the war, these pioneers were hungry for a fresh beginning and the rich lands of Missouri.

Emotionally, symbolically, and spiritually bonded to the Southern ancestral homelands that they had departed with such high hopes for the future, these migrants had planted roots in those areas of Missouri which most reminded them of the distant Piedmont, the Bluegrass, and the forested hills and valleys left behind to the east. Erecting cabins along picturesque rivers and grassy meadows similar to those of North Carolina, Tennessee, Virginia, and Kentucky, "they loved the country here, because it looked just like" the far-away homeland. Across the fertile valleys of Missouri, frontier communities had popped up like magic along the streams, atop hills, and amid the grassy prairies. These isolated log villages bore the names of places out of the pages of Southern history, such as Williamsburg, Fayetteville, Richmond, and Louisiana.[88]

More important than middle-class ideology and an agrarian and yeoman value systems, a vibrant Southern culture had accompanied the flatboats and ox-drawn wagons into the promised land of Missouri. In the virgin country of the West, the ways of the Upper South were valued and preserved. They offered a means of survival in a harsh environment and thrived as constant reminders of the homes, relatives, and bluish mountain ranges left behind hundreds of miles away. Frontier communities across Missouri immediately took on the look of towns in Virginia, Kentucky, Tennessee, and North Carolina. In these frontier Missouri settlements, folklore, religion, traditions, language, architecture, mannerisms, speech, crops, farming methods, and the values of the Puritan ethic were those of the South. This transplanted Southern culture and heritage provided foundations for a latent Southern nationalism that ripened in the Civil War. As in the Upper South, there were full-moon hunts at night for fox, raccoon, and opossum; six-foot-high, "Virginia"-style split-rail fences; horse races that were community affairs; barbecues in meadows or woodlands; religious revivals in the open air; and patches of tobacco and cotton. Even the music of these early settlers had a distinct Southern flavor. During Macon County dances, recalled one Missourian, "the fiddler ... assumed an important bearing, and ordered in true professional style [because] that was the way in North Carolina."[89]

The evolution of Northern society into a more industrial, modernized, urbanized, and ethnic society that had allegedly become more "immoral" and less stable and less traditional further alienated Missourians of Southern background and pulled them toward the South. By 1861 the perception of a "radicalized" North pushed these Missourians away from the national government and toward the values of their Southern homeland and its more conservative and traditional society. A hostile North and intensifying sectional rivalries, especially those sparked by the Kansas struggle, had further widened the chasm between two diverse value systems, cultures, and societies that could not be bridged by compromise or reason in 1861.

To those of Southern heritage and sentiment, the capture of Camp Jackson in early May 1861 seemed to prove the Lincoln government's design to subjugate this distinctive Southern culture and society in Missouri. Abolitionist threats, the growing power of a strong central government with Lincoln's newly elected Republican administration, and a reactionary and hostile North were viewed as threats to the personal liberty of the pro–Southern yeomen in Missouri. To them, Southern civilization was the last defender and foundation of the true principles of the American Revolution. Missourians had long thrived under this traditional agrarian democracy in which the purest form of self-government was represented by the small landowner in the Jeffersonian tradition, who owned the land that he worked as he pleased with a minimum of governmental interference. A delicate balance of social equality, personal freedom, and economic security and opportunity were the republic's foundation. According to democratic theory, this equilibrium could only be maintained by a society of middle-class farmers who were guided by the principles of Jeffersonian philosophy. Because the Lincoln government had seemingly deviated from the traditional Constitutional, social, economic, and political values by upholding the interests of the business class, modernized industry, and a powerful centralized government, states rights and then secession became the natural defense for preserving the basic political philosophies of the republic and the Constitution.[90]

The secessionist delegates of Henry County — William Henry Murrell, the commissary officer of the Fifth Missouri, and Andrew Jackson Lee, a Company G, Fifth Missouri lieutenant — helped formulate provisions at the county courthouse in Clinton, Missouri, which emphasized the loss of personal rights and liberties to an overly powerful and radicalized national government. Murrell, Lee, and others concluded on January 9, 1861, "we regard the so-called Republican party of the North as a sectional and fanatical one, whose avowed principles are directly subversive of the Constitution, and whose ultimate triumph would be a national calamity."[91]

The Missourians' struggle was not simply a political contest for states rights; the Civil War in Missouri was also a societal conflict and cultural clash on a degree found nowhere else in the nation. For the Missouri Rebels, the war also came to be viewed as a struggle for their own personal individual and civil rights. Sterling Price, for instance, had warned fellow citizens how the unthinkable "fate of the Irish and Poles will be theirs," whenever Missouri's agricultural society fell under the grip of exploitation of Northern "greedy masters." According to many pro-Southern Missourians, the overall conflict was simplified as a contest between light and dark, good and evil. A "nation of shopkeepers" and Northern commercial interests were determined to economically, culturally, and socially enslave morally superior Missourians of "Southern birth and blood," reasoned those Missouri citizens of pro-Southern sentiment.[92]

No section of the state had been more concerned with the potential danger to its way of life than southwest Missouri, a land drained by the tributaries of the Osage River. A Bolivar newspaper, for instance, implored the people of Polk County in early May 1861 to rise up to defend their unique Southern heritage, for "the South is too refined, enlightened, brave and chivalrous to submit to the bands of Northern abolition fanatics and rebels, whose doctrines are obnoxious to every Southern interest."

Indicating the social rift and the encroachment of a variety of cultural threats upon Southern society, George Warren had joined the struggle against the "ignorant & bigoted supporters of Lincoln. When I left Franklin

[County], the Dutch & a class of Americans, the scum of society, were the only supporters of the Union cause." In December of 1860 a Polk County journalist analyzed two distinct cultures in the West and contrasted his people of Polk County with those of Illinois, where "Democracy is at a ruinous discount." Cultural differences of two dissimilar societies which caused the "irrepressible conflict" were easily discernible by perceptive individuals. As the southwest Missouri newspaperman noted with dismay, "the [Illinois] people are actuated by the inspiration of progression, and they seem to walk faster, talk and think faster, and certainly get rich faster than our people." But, qualified the Missouri editor, "morally and politically our people are a long ways ahead of the Egyptians here [but] the pulpit is made a political rostrum [and] true religion is as scarce here as money is in Polk county." Then, putting political differences in perspective, the journalist Polk County lamented: "true Democrats here are fully as hard to find as are true Christians — the great mass of the people being Douglasites or Republicans." This cultural, societal, and political rift between the communities of Polk County and Illinois only about 250 miles apart typified the differences between Unionists and Missourians of Southern heritage long before the first shot of the Civil War. As fate ordained, pro–Southern Missourians and Illinois Federal troops had met in some of the first clashes in the war for Missouri.[93]

To the soldiers of the Fifth Missouri, three social groups — the Germans, free blacks, and Northerners — posed the greatest possible threat to their Southern culture and society and the Jeffersonian democratic heritage. Songs which were sung for years during the campaigns of the Fifth Missouri throughout the South stressed the social nature of the conflict for these soldiers:

> The Dutch came to Mo as well you all do know
> To subjugate the rebel boys, but couldn't make it go
> They can't whip the Mo boys & will tell you the reason why
> The Mo boys made them git, root Abe or die.[94]

For the Fifth Missouri men, siding with the Confederacy was equated to the struggle of colonial ancestors against the British. So powerful were revolutionary stirrings in Missouri that a prewar Polk County editorial predicted: "the spirit of '76 still lives in the breast of the American people. They will not submit to oppression." Volunteers flocked to Price's Missouri army in 1861 with the vision that their uprising to defend their land against the national government was comparable to the minutemen's stand against the English invaders. Also, understanding this historical analogy, many Irish soldiers from Colonel Bowen's Second Regiment of the St. Louis militia, which was captured at Camp Jackson, were destined for the ranks of the Missouri Brigade.

The pro-Southern governor of Missouri, Claiborne Fox Jackson, also employed Revolutionary ideology and images. He had early implored: "Do not fail to remember those patriotic sires who wintered at Valley Forge — let their bright example encourage you: the cause is the same — 'tis liberty and equality for which we fight." More than any other historical event, the psychological, spiritual, and emotional impact of the American Revolution had a substantial influence prompting the Rebels of the Fifth Missouri to fight for what they believed to be right.[95]

The memory and spirit of the American Revolution had been nurtured for generations in Missouri, kept alive by oral tradition around the fire-places of settlers on cold winter nights and while fathers and sons labored beside one another in corn and wheat fields in the heat of summer. Stories of grandfather's military exploits during the War for Independence were told and retold over the years in the West, guaranteeing that the American Revolution lived in the hearts and minds of the Civil War generation as the most dominant historical experience in the nation's history. The heroic past was sacred to the people of the Western frontier, something never to be lost or forgotten. Cowpens and King's Mountain had special meaning to the farm boys of Polk, Macon, and Johnson counties. When they reached for muskets in 1861, they remembered the American colonists who took up arms at Lexington and Concord.

As the sectional conflict intensified after the election of 1860, the analogy between Lincoln and King George III was drawn by pro-Southerners of Missouri. As in the relationship between the colonies and the British Empire in 1775, a powerful centralized government now threatened to strangle Southern civilization in economic, cultural, and political terms, according to the beliefs of pro-Southern Missourians in 1861.

The profound psychological influence of the American Revolution was most readily seen in the names of Fifth Missourians. For example, there were at least 20 George Washingtons, 7 Benjamin Franklins, 7 Thomas Jeffersons, and 4 Francis Marions in the regiment. Not even Biblical names were more common among Fifth Missouri soldiers than were the names of the military and political leaders of the American Revolution.[96]

But the greatest impact of the American Revolution was in providing a historical identification and revolutionary idealism for the soldiers in the ranks. The men of the Fifth Missouri felt that they were not only engaged in a war of rebellion, but also were waging a holy crusade for "life, liberty and the pursuit of happiness," as explained one of McCown's officers. According to this theory, life under the Lincoln regime meant forfeiting individual rights and liberties to a despotic centralized government. One Fifth Missouri soldier rationalized the high cost of independence, writing: "should it be our unhappy lot to fall on some battle field or breathe our last in some distant hospital still it will be a great consolation to living friends to know that we died in the service of our country nobly battling for liberty and free institutions — May none of us ever shirk from this duty which we owe to our country and God."[97]

Ideology, however, failed as a primary motivator for the cynics and realists of the Fifth Missouri. But domestic problems, excessive debts, or unending farm drudgery provided enough impetus for these types to enlist. Among the officer corps, lawyers and physicians with little work were also quick to leave problems behind. For most of the volunteers of 1861, the excitement of adventure, the desire to whip Yankees, or the longing to see what lay beyond the next mountian range were strong motivations to become Rebels. Other men, such as Colonel McCown and his son, had to escape a hostile environment. In March 1861, the McCowns had both been targeted for lynching in Warrensburg by an enraged mob after the shooting of the pro–Union spokesman at the Johnson County, Missouri, courthouse.[98]

According to Cockrell, who had helped save the McCowns from the Warrensburg lynch mob, the most purely emotional motivation of the Fifth Missourians was to liberate "their loved and native Missouri — their home now groaning under an unparalleled [sic] despotism." Colonel McCown's Rebels fought and died because above all they believed that the occupying Union forces had to be driven from the home state at all costs. While fighting and dying hundreds of miles from homes and families for years, the Confederates of the Fifth Missouri prayed before each engagement "that the land of [their] forefathers would be freed from invasion and its independence won" after the one decisive victory which would unleash them to recross the Mississippi for the march on Missouri to liberate the Union-occupied homeland. Because they knew of the suffering at home from letters, the greatest urge of the Fifth Missouri soldiers, wrote Lieutenant Warren, was the simple "wish [only] to protect [their families] from the insults of their overbearing conquerors."

A Company E soldier gave voice to the worst mental anguish and torment for the men of the Fifth Missouri when he wrote, "[the] grand old State, the Home of those I hold most dear, [has been] trampled and crushed under the foot of the oppressor." The loss of Missouri resulted in considerable personal guilt and pain because the people of the state had been "left to the mercy of the thieving Jayhawker and murderous Hessian, their towns and their houses destroyed by fire, their property stolen, their country laid waste, and their wives and children driven from their homes to perish or to live as best they can."

While fighting for years in the Deep South, Lieutenant Warren, for instance, felt tortured by the haunting and bitter realization that his Franklin County people "do not know at what moment they may be burnt out &

turned upon the world penniless *[sic]*." Even long after hopes for success on the battlefield had disappeared, the soldiers of the Fifth Missouri would continue struggling east of the Mississippi, fighting and dying in the South for the vain wish of one day returning homeward with an invading Rebel army. The desire of Fifth Missouri Confederates to reclaim Missouri can be glimpsed in the words of a soldier who vowed: "as certain as God reigns in Heaven, we will return again and again, until the last man shall have perished, or we shall have reclaimed our homes."[99]

Clearly, Colonel McCown's men did not fight primarily to defend the institution of slavery. The vast majority owned no blacks, and not a single reference to slavery can be found in the scores of letters, memoirs, and diaries of Fifth Missouri soldiers. As declared one Missouri soldier, "among them all there was not a man who had come forth to fight for slavery." There were few Greek Revival–style mansions, and no sprawling cotton fields, or extensive hemp culture on the vast prairies of Polk, Macon, and Johnson counties. Middle-class farmsteads on the Western frontier, where diversified farming was the norm, could not support a thriving slave regime. Even though the highly labor-intensive tobacco culture was the staple of the economy in Macon County, African Americans amounted to only 5 percent of the county's populace in 1860. The same percentage of slaves existed in Polk County during the same year.

Because it was closer to the Missouri River and contained richer soil, Johnson County had in 1860 the highest percentage (15 percent) of slaves among the three counties most represented within the Fifth Missouri. But this percentage was relatively small in comparison to that of Lafayette County, lying just north of Johnson County and bordering the Missouri River, which had a slave population of nearly 50 percent. Clearly, the institution of slavery in the three principal counties from which the majority of Fifth Missouri Rebels hailed had not been a dominant factor in the economy in 1860, as it had been in the Missouri and Mississippi river counties of the state.[100]

Although slaves were sprinkled among the communities of Polk, Macon, and Johnson counties in small numbers, black labor had been instrumental in taming the wilderness before statehood and essential to the economic development of the frontier. Early settlers from the Upper South had brought African Americans with them, and both races struggled together to conquer the wilds of Missouri. Since pioneer days, black and white had toiled side by side clearing timber, splitting rails, erecting fences, grubbing out stumps, and planting and harvesting crops of middle-class farmers—corn, oats, and wheat. Laboring together, side-by-side, black and white had fought against nature to build a self-sufficient life out of the wilderness. Despite its obvious horrors, the institution of slavery in counties such as Johnson and Polk almost resembled indentured servitude in some ways when compared to the Deep South world of cash crops and plantation economies. Indeed, small middle-class farmers often hired bonded servants to work beside them, as well as young men who later served in the Fifth Missouri. Instead of being an institution based on the commercial and plantation model of the South, the slave system existed in the home counties of McCown's men primarily to support a diversified agricultural economy of the middle-class farmer. One visitor to antebellum Missouri, for example, had often seen "negroes and their masters ploughing side by side in the fields; or bared to the waist, and with old-fashioned scythe vying with one another who can cut down the broadest swath of yellow wheat or of the waving timothy; or bearing the tall stalks of maize and packing them into stout-built barns [and] when the long winter evenings have come, you will see black and whites sing and shout and husk in company [to] the music of Ole Virgininy [sic] reels."[101]

By any measure, a more integrated and racially mixed society existed on the Western frontier than in the Deep South. Despite the brutality of slavery, a greater closeness and interaction could be found between the races on the Western border of the Upper South than anywhere else in the nation.

Close personal interactions between black and white occurred on the Western frontier not only during work hours but also after the day's labors had ended. While the institution of slavery in Missouri was harsh and ruthless, it was not as horrible as slavery in the Deep South.

For instance, not only did whites and African Americans work side by side, but they also played, loved, prayed, and lived together to a greater degree in Missouri than in the Deep South. Both peoples fished and trapped together along the banks of the Little Sac and Chariton rivers and raced over forested hills on moonlit nights, following the distant baying of hounds in pursuit of game. During the horse races at the Prairie Course, outside Bolivar, the two peoples of Polk County had long freely intermingled. According to one Polk County newspaperman, the black and white sectors of society spent these horse racing days in "betting, swearing, drinking and anticipating the sport" together. African Americans and whites also joined together at Southern-style barbecues, religious revivals, and other frontier social events.

The close interaction between the two peoples in Polk County since the taming of the frontier caused one observer in 1860 to complain: "And right here we beg to volunteer the remark that we never have been able to understand what business slaves have at a horse race or an election." The close association and intermingling of these two peoples also accounts for Missouri containing one of the highest populations of "new people," or then called mulattoes, by 1860. Because of racism, this intermingling failed to raise the social status of mixed race peoples, however.[102]

By 1860 the economic importance of slavery had been on the decline throughout Missouri, "a slaveholding peninsula jutting up into a sea of free-soil." Only ten years previous, one slave could be counted for every four citizens. But the advent of modern economics and markets and heavy immigration from Europe, primarily Germany, during the 1850s had dwindled the institution's economic importance in Missouri by 1860. At the war's beginning, only one slave for every nine whites could be found in Missouri. A relatively small percentage of Fifth Missouri soldiers owned slaves. One typical slave-owning farmstead was that of Private Christopher Columbus Irwin, who was destined to die in prison. On the 900-acre Johnson County property near the sluggish Blackwater River, Irwin and a twin brother labored together in the broad corn and wheat fields with two male slaves. Another representative slave-owning family farm was that of Sergeant Zackariah M. and Corporal Robert L. Davis of Company A. Both of the Davis boys died in the war and far from home. The Davis farm bordered Post Oak Creek in Johnson County and included three male slaves. Such examples indicate that single black males best met the requirements of the small, middle-class slaveowner.[103]

Instead of employing black labor during the antebellum period, some Fifth Missouri men utilized the services of white bondsmen to help them improve the land. For example, Captain Fair had two bondsmen, one a fellow Englishman. Fair and his bondsmen plowed the green fields, planted crops, and girdled and cleared cottonwoods near the Missouri River in Franklin County. White bondsmen were also common in Polk County; "negroes were never good property in this section" of southwest Missouri, explained one resident of the county.[104]

Having grown up, lived, and worked together with African Americans for years, some of McCown's officers, such as Captain Pankey, brought slaves into service with them. Other Fifth Missouri officers, such as Lieutenant Colonel Bevier, found black servants while serving in the South. Duties for these blacks, who acted as body servants, consisted of cooking, caring for horses and equipment, foraging, and routine camp chores. African Americans, ironically, had similar menial roles in Union armies in this war. But the majority of Fifth Missouri officers had not owned slaves before the conflict and had none during active service.

To generally more enlightened officers who were natives of England, such as Captains Fair and Trumper, the concept of holding another human in bondage must have been especially repugnant. After all, many of these immigrants long had mothers, sisters, and perhaps daughters working like slave women in the households of wealthy whites. In addition, Irish officers like Captain Canniff might have viewed slavery with much distaste, for both the African American and Irish peoples shared the shackles of oppression and domination in America, and they had personally felt the sting of prejudice and discrimination. Even Colonel McCown rejected black servitude while leading the Fifth Missouri during its campaigns in the Deep South. In contrast to many regimental commanders, North and South, McCown had Private Philip Baxter, a thirty-year-old from Warrensburg, cook for his headquarters throughout the war years. In fact, some blacks gained a small measure of equality in the Confederate encampment, joining with the soldiers in favorite amusements during off-duty hours. Taking advantage of the typical white prejudices of the day, some poker-wise slaves often played the nonthinking role of "Sambos," before relieving Fifth Missouri farm boys of Confederate script on paydays by proving to be the sharper card players.[105]

The treatment of blacks varied with the owner's character and disposition. Before the conflict, Captain Pankey had owned many slaves in Virginia, whom he treated "in the most considerate manner and they were devoted to him." Emotional bonds between master and slave remained so strong that Pankey's blacks "never lost the feeling of affection and devotion towards him [and] would have cheerfully laid down their lives for him at any time." As learned by the author from a descendant of Captain Lemmon, this affectionate feeling between the Polk County Lemmon family and an African American family of Chicago, Illinois, endured for generations and remained strong well into the mid-twentieth century with periodic visitations between the two families that shared the tragic heritage of slavery.

Occasionally blacks who accompanied their masters to the Deep South made interment arrangements and brought home the personal possessions of Fifth Missouri soldiers who were killed on Southern battlefields. One example of the relative good treatment toward slaves in Polk County can be seen in the actions of a family member of Privates James C. and William H. Acock. The large land-owning relative of these Company C boys tenderly nursed his slaves during a fever epidemic in the winter of 1858. He wrote how "both duty and interest required me to stay at home and give them medicine and attend to them and it is probable was the means of saving some of them."[106]

Not so benevolent was Lieutenant Colonel Bevier. When angered over a minor infraction by the young African American who attended him, Bevier punished his personal body servant with a horsewhip as if he were an overseer on a cotton plantation in the Deep South. Such brutal treatment was ironic, for the lieutenant colonel's slave served faithfully and hated the Yankees. The African American had repeatedly begged to be allowed to join any attack of the Fifth Missouri. As explained Bevier, "We never went into battle that it did not require a peremptory command to keep him out." Had the ex-lawyer from Macon County been more enlightened, he might have allowed Shad to carry a weapon and fight by his side or freed him for his faithful service.[107]

Perhaps the only enlisted man of the Fifth Missouri who left for war with his own slave had been Private William Roe of Lexington, Missouri. As a Missouri State Guardsman who had served under General Price, Roe had distributed hidden powder from his house in town to Price's Rebels during the siege of Lexington in September 1861. This act would later cause considerable problems for Roe after he deserted Company F and returned to Lexington. His ex-slave obtained revenge by reporting Roe's Fifth Missouri past to Union authorities. A surprised Roe was thrown into prison, much to the delight of his former slave.[108]

While the vast majority of Fifth Missourians never owned a slave, most of them agreed that the peculiar institution fell under the personal property rights guaranteed by the Constitution, which seemed to be threatened by the Lincoln government. For the 1860s generation, indoctrinated by Jeffersonian ideology, the concept of private property was considered the most sacred guarantee and the foundation of their republican form of government. If the Republicans stripped away the institution of slavery, their opponents reasoned, then the abolition of other personal rights would surely follow. Personal freedoms, consequently, could only be preserved by a vigilant citizenry, which had to protect itself against a too powerful central government. By 1861 these Missourians sought to safeguard their liberties by rising up to protect their yeoman society against a hostile central government which represented the interests of a dissimilar society, culture, and political system. Colonel McCown's Confederates believed that the justification to go to war against the United States government stemmed in part from a defense of the principles of the Lockean natural right of revolution and self-determination in the tradition of their revolutionary forefathers.

# II

## IUKA BECOMES
## A DEADLY TRAP

Only a few more lazy days remained at Saltillo for the young soldiers of the Fifth Missouri. After the expirations of their furloughs, two Company E boys came into camp bringing several bottles of homemade brandy. The liquor was a good buy, only $5 per quart in Confederate script and enough to make a whole company of Franklin County Rebels drunk on September 4. As never before, these soldiers were determined to enjoy themselves before meeting the Yankees. Defeating the capable General Ulysses Grant would be tough: the Union's great hero was a Westerner like themselves, a hard-nosed fighter, and no soft, eastern "featherbed" general. So the Company E Confederates guzzled the distilled liquor as if there were no tomorrow. Captain Fair's brief absence allowed the frolicking to last longer than usual. John Barleycorn soon took command in Captain Fair's stead.[1]

The drinking spree shortly resulted in angry words and a personal squabble. Always a favorite diversion, a fist-fight drew hundreds of spectators from the Missouri Brigade's encampment. Even the sick hobbled from Surgeon Dysart's infirmary with renewed vigor to watch the action. More than slightly tipsy himself, although he now commanded the company, Lieutenant Matthew Townsend refereed the affair. While onlookers cheered, the combination boxing and wrestling match became "a pretty hard fight." Townsend did a commendable umpiring job until the antagonists tumbled too close. Flailing away in the dust, the combatants rolled over the former Stanton, Missouri, clerk. The impact sent Lieutenant Townsend sprawling over a mess table, shattering the company's dishes as he fell. But the fun ceased when a provost marshal's detail raced through camp to quell the disturbance. In record time "the crowd skedaddled." Captain Fair and Lieutenant Townsend were probably reprimanded by Colonel McCown, infamous for his hot Irish temper. That night Captain Fair "had to get tight" on the last bottle of brandy.[2]

But there was much more to this war than drinking and fist-fighting. To assist General Braxton Bragg's invasion of Kentucky, Price was directed to tie down Major General William Starke Rosecrans's forces in northeast Mississippi. If "Old Rosey" suddenly sprinted for Bragg's rear to thwart the Confederate dream of redeeming Tennessee and the border state of Kentucky, the Army of the West would follow the Yankees. To freeze Rosecrans in place, Price prepared to advance in early September. The autumn of 1862 would present the Confederacy with opportunities to win important victories, which would not come again. Indeed, General Robert E. Lee's Army of Northern Virginia was invading Maryland in the East, and Bragg was invading Union-held territory in the West that the Confederates had lost in 1861–62. Never again would the Confederacy launch simultaneous offensives in the East and the West which were more likely to succeed or win foreign recognition from Britain and France. In the Fifth Missouri's encampment, musicians Learman, Phillip William Molloy, a fifteen-year-old ex-printer from Bolivar, Polk County, and other drummers sounded the long roll around two o'clock, splitting the stillness in the early morning of September 6. Before a rising sun had burned away the fog lining the creek bottoms, the soldiers of Colonel McCown's long column were already trudging north up the railroad. General Price's northward thrust had begun. The Army of the West of two divisions pushed forward, eager for the battlefield successes vital to the life of the Confederacy.

Not having taken the offensive since crossing the Mississippi River in April of 1862, the soldiers of the Army of the West were hardly in campaign-ready condition after a relatively quiet summer. Blistering heat made the trek miserable, and thick clouds of Mississippi dust hovered over the Rebel ranks. A yellowish tint of dust covered cotton uniforms in a sweltering humidity only found in Mississippi. The difficult march continued for seventeen miles through the broiling countryside. Accouterment straps cut into shoulders, and feet were blistered raw under a scorching sun. But worst of all, wooden canteens could not be refilled in the dry creeks along the route, for northeast Mississippi was caught in one of the worst dry spells of recent memory.[3]

The soldiers of the Fifth Missouri found no respite as they moved swiftly through tiny Boonville. They continued to plod northward, skirting the parched cotton fields and shortleaf pine forests of Prentiss County. Despite their aching feet and the weight of full gear, wrote one Rebel in his diary, the Missourians remained "in fine spirits, although it is oppressively warm and dusty marching." Few men straggled that day despite the scorching heat. Eagerness to meet the Yankees kept everyone pushing onward. Soldiers like Adjutant Greenwood felt a sense of anxiety. The former clerk knew that a march north into his native Kentucky might mean facing his Yankee brother in the Army of the Cumberland on the battlefield.[4]

As the day neared its end, Fifth Missouri gear lay strewn along the route after weary Confederates had lightened their heavy loads. McCown's soldiers finally stumbled into a shady grove as the sun dropped in the west. Here they made bivouac, six miles north of Boonville. Cutoff from supply lines and mired in a parched countryside, McCown's Rebels dug wells to find water and relieve their suffering. Shouts of success erupted when foul-smelling water oozed into holes. That night, a handful of the regiment's stragglers gradually stumbled into the encampment, often going instantly to sleep where they fell.[5]

Cautious about advancing toward Grant's domain, General Price attempted to ascertain Rosecrans's location and strength with probes for the next several days. If Rosecrans were withdrawing toward Tennessee, then Price would hit the Unionists on the open road. Meanwhile, there was now little for the average soldier to do but stay in the shade, while the army's mounted soldiers skirmished to the north with the blue cavalry. One Rebel who probably enlivened the regimental encampment in the pine forests that night was sixteen-year-old Private David H. Music. According to a Fifth Missouri soldier, he was "a little mite of a fellow, a mere boy, with no beard upon his face, but in his heart all the mischief of a big man." The Company G enlisted man, wrote one officer, was one of the Fifth Missouri's comics and "at the bottom of more fun and practical jokes than any other member of our command, and his activity in that direction fully compensated for his deficiency in size."[6]

General Price pinpointed Rosecrans's lead elements at Iuka, Mississippi, on September 11. Thinking that Corinth had been evacuated and fearing the Federals were headed for Tennessee, Price decided to immediately strike Iuka, twenty miles southeast of Corinth. The advance of the Army of the West, therefore, continued with renewed vigor. After pushing forward another fourteen miles by hard marching, the Missouri Confederates settled into camp along the Tombigbee River just to Marietta's east. But the rest was brief. The Rebels, including the Fifth Missouri, dashed north toward Iuka during the predawn hours of the following day. The morning sun unmasked the heart of Unionist county in Mississippi: an ironic setting for a battle in the Deep South.

Lieutenant Fountain F. Smith, who was filling in for Captain Bradford due to sickness, led Company C onward through the choking dust with added responsibility. One of Bradford's most trusted lieutenants since State Guard days when Smith was twenty-two, the Polk County farmer had only a few weeks to live. Much complaining rose from the ranks during the march; the boys "don't like to carry knapsacks," wrote Lieutenant Warren in his diary.[7]

While the lengthy Rebel columns advanced toward the small town of Iuka, some Fifth Missouri Rebels died in filthy hospitals around Saltillo from diseases contracted during the past summer, in part from spoiled rations, swamp water, warm weather, and no sanitation. One of the regiment's most popular members to perish was musician James R. Hale, a teenager and brother of Captain Hale. The drummer and former McGee College student died on September 12, while far from the command and his Macon County home.[8]

Colonel McCown's foot soldiers halted within striking distance of Iuka as the sun set on September 13. Muskets were stacked, and the aroma of supper shortly spread through the hot Mississippi air. Amid patches of timber bright with autumn colors, the Fifth Missouri soldiers stretched out on the grass, lit pipes, and talked loudly of the victories and glories that lay ahead, including perhaps even marching all the way to the Ohio River. With their ranks thinned from the disease-ridden summer, fewer than three hundred Fifth Missouri Confederates now remained. The bivouac stirred with excitement when Colonel McCown ordered his soldiers to be ready to march by midnight.

With the Unionists near, General Price wanted to strike Iuka quickly before the element of surprise vanished. No time could be wasted if "Old Rosey" Rosecrans were hurrying to reinforce the forces opposing General Bragg. Under a moonlit sky in the cool darkness, the Missouri Rebels of General Little's First Division, Army of the West, filtered silently along the narrow road hewn through the pine forests. General Little summed up the representative attitude of his Fifth Missouri soldiers with the prayer, "God give us victory." The ruins of once-beautiful northeast Mississippi homes, recently burned down by Yankee raiders, deepened the resolve of McCown's troops to punish the Federals.[9]

Rebel scouts suddenly burst out of the blackness, saying that the Unionists were thick in the inky woodlands ahead. Colonel McCown halted and deployed his regiment. In the darkness, the Missourians rammed down buck and ball loads into muskets. The Fifth Missouri prepared for a night battle less than two weeks after the completion of its organization. With fixed bayonets, grayclads passed briskly up the tree-lined, dusty road leading to Iuka. Immediately south of town, Colonel McCown aligned the Fifth Missouri in the moonlight. Tension mounted each hour. But now only the Union rear guard remained in Iuka. Some of Rosecrans's forces had withdrawn toward fortress Corinth, while other units were dispatched to Kentucky.[10]

"Sore & stiff" Fifth Missouri Rebels got to their feet for the push to take Iuka, while Price's silent column inched north up the road toward one of Grant's richest supply depots. As the eastern sky lightened, McCown's Rebels emerged from the patchy mist to come suddenly "in sight of town [when] their rear guard was leaving." Price's butternut cavalry routed the Unionists before they could destroy the warehouses. Like a chicken hawk after its prey, the Army of the West descended upon its prize. Brimming with tons of supplies, Iuka was soon all Confederate. Savoring the victory with other Company C comrades, Lieutenant Avington Wayne Simpson, a twenty-two-year-old yeoman from Polk County's Sentinel Prairie, wrote, "the Yankees got up and dusted [and we] got all their commissary stores and many other things." McCown's troops poured through the deserted town, hunting for snipers and something to eat. Ragged Confederates dashed from house to house, rounding up a handful of Union stragglers. Flames about to engulf some of the storehouses were extinguished.[11]

As in Missouri State Guard days, the enlisted men of the Fifth Missouri immediately broke into warehouses. The always underfed Southerners especially relished the notion of "Old Abe" donating breakfast in the small northeast Mississippi community. After the boys consumed their fill of captured supplies, Colonel McCown ordered the party stopped. Details were sent to guard each storehouse. As soon as the colonel departed, however, the soldiers gathered the spoils for their mess mates. The lieutenant colonel, in charge of the guards, faced a dilemma among the riches because of his rank, but his black servant came to the rescue, doing the pilfering for Bevier.[12]

From prisoners or captured dispatches, Price now learned that Rosecrans and around 10,000 troops had retreated toward Corinth. Price decided to remain in Iuka, eyeing Rosecrans for his next move. No one yet knew if the Federals were going to remain in Corinth or head for Tennessee. To guarantee Rosecrans would not swing north, Price had appealed to Van Dorn for a combined strike against Corinth. But confusion in the Confederate command organizational structure and Bragg's pleas for reinforcements complicated the situation and resulted in Price's subsequent indecisiveness. An adversary like General Grant, who had overall command of Union forces in West Tennessee and took advantage of most opportunities presented to him, could turn such Rebel uncertainty into disaster. To relieve pressure in Tennessee and perhaps deliver a knockout punch, General Grant jumped at the chance to strike the stationary Price at Iuka.[13]

While General Price's Army of the West languished at Iuka, Grant agreed to a bold scheme proposed by Rosecrans for destroying Price with a swift blow before he could unite with Earl Van Dorn. An 8,000-man Union force under General Edward Otho Caesap Ord therefore marched southeastward from Corinth toward Iuka. Grant gambled that the Missouri general would pounce on Ord. To further set up the elaborate plan, Grant held Van Dorn in place around Holly Springs, Mississippi, with a feint. As a result, Price was alone and out on a limb, isolated at Iuka. While the Army of the West dallied in Iuka and focused its attention on Ord, Rosecrans's 9,000 Unionists would slip around from the southwest to slam into Price from rear and flank. The classic entrapment of the Rebels between the

forces of Ord and Rosecrans seemed guaranteed to snare the old militia colonel, who had never before faced Grant.[14]

Indeed, Price's Army of the West stayed too long at Iuka, remaining
five days and risking encirclement. While Ord probed southeastward
through the forests to hold the Rebels' attention, "Old Pap" hurried troops
back and forth to various sectors of his defensive line to parry threats that
would not come. With "some sign of fight" northwest of Iuka, the double-
quicking Fifth Missouri soldiers zigzagged over the dry countryside,
deploying whenever skirmishing intensified. On the rainy evening of
September 17, a battle seemed so imminent that General Price, in a colorful
battle shirt and farmer's hat, readied the Fifth Missouri and other units for
action against Ord's forces. He endeared himself to the young men of Company C by passing down their ranks and imploring them to "shoot 'em low,
boys, whack 'em about the knees."

That night the Fifth Missouri Confederates remained on the field in the
cold rain. Slipping back into old militia ways, General Price was mesmer-
ized into inactivity by the reconnoitering advance elements of Ord's
Unionists. The Army of the West now lay vulnerable as never before.
Rosecrans's troops maneuvered at will as the Rebels remained stationary in
Iuka's environs. An unknown country, effective Union ruses, contradictory
orders from superiors, and faulty intelligence froze Price firmly in place at
Iuka as Grant had planned.[15]

For McCown's troops, meanwhile, a series of alarms and counter-
marching resulted in little sleep, no tents for shelter, and few rations. Like
the other Confederates at Iuka, Lieutenant Smith, now commanding Company C, was unable to decipher the grand strategy. As a steady rain pelted
through the trees at a bivouac site northwest of Iuka, Smith silently celebrated his third wedding anniversary to a pretty Polk County girl he would
never see again. Nobody liked the looks of the confusing situation in the
water-soaked forests around Iuka. Indeed, Ord was poised only six miles
to the northwest near Burnsville on September 18, playing the part of an
aggressive commander. While Ord kept Price guessing and immobile,
Grant plotted the Army of the West's annihilation for September 18. He
gambled that Price's entire army could "be driven against the Tennessee
River" and destroyed.[16]

As towering pines began to cast longer shadows on the evening of
September 18, McCown's soldiers settled into camp. Active campaigning
for the first time in months and recent rains had reactivated many of the
lingering diarrheal illnesses and other ailments of the past summer, sending
some Fifth Missouri soldiers to the infirmary. Exhausted men ate dinner,
tried to stay dry, and were getting "nicely fixed to sleep when the Drums
beat the long roll to fall in. We were up dress[ed] and in line in 15 minutes,"
wrote one soldier in his diary. Skirmishing erupted northwestward in

Price's front, shattering the solitude of the woodlands. It seemed that Ord now had to be heading their way.

Consequently, the Missouri Confederates grabbed muskets and raced through the dimming light to meet the challenge. Not long thereafter, McCown's companies deployed in the deepening darkness. Here, northwest of Iuka, the Missourians spent a long night in formation amid the damp pine thickets. While Price's troops faced northwestward before Ord, Rosecrans's strong columns swung east from Jacinto, Mississippi, to hit the distracted Southerners from rear and flank. The audacious Union trap was about to be sprung.[17]

"Old Pap," having long lost the initiative, was fooled badly about the tactical situation. But fortunately General Rosecrans ran into serious problems which ruined the delicate timetable upon which the strategy hinged: roads resembling trails, oceans of mud, tangled woodlands, and confused guides. Clearly, Price had an invaluable ally this September in good fortune. Rosecrans could not get into position for the attack from the flank and rear on September 18. General Grant, consequently, had to delay the scheduled attack until September 19.[18]

The first light of dawn that day revealed Price's forces and the Fifth Missouri still stationary at Iuka, and the Union battle plan intact. But fate would further undermine the complicated strategy of the Unionists. Ord's troops patiently waited in formation for the opening of Rosecrans's guns to signal them forward. A stiff northwest breeze, however, howled toward Confederate fortunes and away from Ord. Thousands of bluecoats under Ord to Iuka's northwest, therefore, would hear no firing from Rosecrans to the southwest. The Union pincer movement would fail to close. Price's army would be miraculously spared from a knockout blow from which it probably could not have escaped.[19]

After finally getting his Union troops into position, General Rosecrans launched his assault from the southwest of Iuka in the afternoon heat of September 19. Federals rolled en masse up Jacinto Road like an avalanche. Wisely "Old Pap" had earlier thrown out pickets along the Jacinto Road, and these now opened fire and skirmished with the foremost Yankees. After being apprised of the crisis, Price responded with alacrity. He turned his troops about-face from Ord toward the threat to his army's rear southwest of Iuka. To rescue the Army of the West, Price directed General Little to lead Rebel units south to counter the threat from rear and flank. Luckily, Ord's Yankees meanwhile stood in neatly dressed lines as they leaned on their rifles and listened to the wind whistling through the pines. Unable to hear Rosecrans's firing to the south, Ord's troops failed to launch their attack. But Colonel McCown's soldiers heard the crashing musketry, which sounded as if hundreds of Federals were attacking behind them.

After perceiving no serious Union demonstration before them, the

Fifth Missouri Confederates swung around and raced for the brewing battle around five o'clock. Colonel McCown's fast-moving Confederates dashed across the tracks of the Memphis and Charleston Railroad and splashed across Indian Creek to Iuka's southwest. The Rebel infantrymen crossed swampy woodlands along the Jacinto Road before pushing up higher ground sloping south toward the escalating action.[20]

Although he was still half-sick with fever and hardly able to ride his horse, General Little hurled the available troops of his First Division down the dusty Jacinto Road. With the aggressiveness of Price's top lieutenant, he slammed into Rosecrans before the Union soldiers could fully deploy and thus stole Rosecrans's initiative and saved Price's army. The fury of Little's attack disrupted Rosecrans's plan to gain the westernmost of the two parallel roads leading south from Iuka. Indeed, the Fulton Road, the only escape route south for Price, was wide open to the Jacinto Road's east.

General Little, Price's "most trusted lieutenant," blunted Rosecrans's drive with this furious counterattack. And he bought time for more units of the Army of the West to arrive in the autumn-hued woods that covered the rolling hills southwest of Iuka, which were turned into a bloody battleground. Little's cheering men charged headlong into Rosecrans's Union soldiers, overrunning an Ohio battery. Superior numbers of Unionists soon told, however, and darkness cheated Little's attack out of greater gains. While he was saving the day at Iuka, General Little was shot off his horse, dying at the zenith of his distinguished career. Father Bannon brought back the body of the man most responsible for molding the Missouri Brigade into an elite force. By the time Colonel Gates's Missourians reached the field with another brigade after a six-mile sprint, hundreds of demoralized Southerners were fleeing to the rear, but Little had stabilized the situation.[21]

Victory remained within Rosecrans's grasp if the Fulton Road could be reached to cut off Price's line of retreat. After receiving orders to help solidify the position around the battered Fortieth Mississippi, Colonel McCown led his troops onward to enter the battle of Iuka. Amid the chaos, yelping Fifth Missouri Rebels headed straight toward the bloody knoll. The regiment's drive steamrolled over body-littered fields, while surrounding forests grew dark with a six o'clock dusk. Some Confederates would later claim that it was too late an hour for General Little's counterattack to destroy Rosecrans.

The near darkness and the smoke-laced fields proved a godsend for the attacking Fifth Missouri, for no concentrated Union volleys riddled McCown's advancing lines. According to young Lieutenant Warren, the Fifth Missouri arrived on the field in time to "receive one round when the enemy withdrew because of darkness." Seldom to be repeated hereafter, this initial good fortune saved untold Fifth Missouri lives. When the Fifth Missouri finally "got near enough for the bullets to whistle through our ranks it was dark as pitch."[22]

As minié balls zipped by, the regiment fired its first volley, unleashing a spontaneous, ragged musketry in the smoky twilight. The unordered firing nearly cost the lieutenant colonel his life. Half-blind in the gathering darkness amid drifting smoke, Bevier was caught ahead of the lines as his anxious soldiers rushed ahead with yells and took aim in the foggy half-light. He later recounted how they had "in their eagerness, shot under my horse and over him, and made a rest of both ends of him." Yellow and red spurts of fire exploded in the blackness, dropping four Fifth Missouri soldiers in the noisy confusion. As fate would have it, the Fifth Missouri suffered almost half of the Missouri Brigade's total losses at Iuka with the initial volley.[23]

Company C, on the far right, received the brunt of the regiment's baptismal fire. Lieutenant Simpson, who described the engagement at Iuka as "one of the hardest little fights imaginable," fell seriously wounded. Simpson, ironically, had joined the fight despite being on the sick list. The injured officer from southwest Missouri was helped off the field with an ugly arm wound. But the most serious loss of Company C was fifteen-year-old Private William Henry Acock, who went down with a bloody leg wound. Private James Acock, an older brother, probably carried his sibling back to Surgeon Dysart's field hospital behind the lines. The Acock boys brought with them onto Iuka's field a fine military tradition, deeply ingrained in Polk County folklore. They seemed bent on outdoing the Mexican War exploits of their ancestors. The Acocks were blue bloods from a leading family of southwest Missouri that was prominent in politics and owned thousands of acres and slaves. These young men were some of the first to enlist. But far from home and family, all their money and influence could not help them now in northeast Mississippi. Competent Surgeon Dysart would rule out amputation and patch together Billy's leg. Soon the teenager would be back in the ranks, fighting until he was killed in action.[24]

Also downed in the volley was one of the most spirited natural fighters of the Fifth Missouri, the gregarious Private Daniel Monahan of Company F. And true to the Irishman's fortune, the wound came right after he joined the command from Virginia service. But Company F would miss Monahan's jokes and songs for only a short time. He would soon be back on his feet with the regiment. The volley's final victim was James A. Huffman, "a stalwart Democrat" of Company B. In the near-dark, the Macon County corporal went down with a bullet in his right leg. The teenager of German ancestry would be forced to retire from active service because of the wound's severity.[25] Fortunately, most of the Federal bullets had whistled over Fifth Missouri heads on this bloody last Friday before the autumn of 1862.

After the Federal volley whizzed past, the Missourians swept onward across the field of bodies with determination and cheers. Darkness and smoke palls obscured the vision of McCown's attackers. Colonel McCown relieved those troops who were battered by the Federals earlier and helped solidify the Missouri Brigade's front for the night. Colonel McCown at last halted and aligned the Fifth Missouri in an advanced position. But Captain Canniff's Company F kept moving forward in the blackness. The Irishmen splashed over swampy ground and patches of woods, which were now covered with fog, low-lying layers of battle smoke, and injured soldiers. These veteran skirmishers of Company F dashed toward the Union-held knoll, slipping on patches of bloody grass and stumbling over the human wreckage. One of McCown's Confederates felt sickened because "the dead & wounded are lying around so thick that you can scarely [sic] help steping [sic] on them."[26]

With his usual skill, Captain Canniff hurriedly fanned his men out in a thin gray line to cover the front. After scrambling for shelter, the Celts hugged the cold ground, being now the closest Rebels to the Yankees. Out in the darkness in the black forests beyond a glade lay the Federal lines only a short distance away. Throughout the dismal night, a "heavy dew fell cold and cheerless — not a soul was allowed to stir, as the breaking of a twig might cause a fire." Once again Company F was placed in a precarious position.

The position of the Fifth Missouri likewise remained tenuous. Although they were a good distance behind Company F, some of McCown's men were unnerved by the hellish night on the field. Imagining blue demons in the darkness and feeling sick of the horror and fighting, Company K Privates James Ward Bodine, an eighteen-year-old, and Samuel Donscomb slipped out of line and left for their Bootheel region homes. Hungry Fifth Missourians, shivering from the cold, lay flat among the damp weeds. There was nothing left to do but hope for the sunrise and pray that the Yankees would not attack.[27]

The dying horses of the Eleventh Ohio Battery screamed throughout the night, making a surrealistic nightmare come alive amid the sulfurous blackness and the horrors of the battlefield. Union wounded kept calling for water and family members far away. The pathetic cries of the injured soldiers nauseated McCown's men, sending chills down their spines. Although they had orders not to move from their positions, some of McCown's Rebels scoured the battleground on errands of mercy, giving water to the wounded bluecoats. Thinking the Army of the West was stirring, the Yankees opened fire on the samaritans in butternut and gray.[28]

But McCown's angels of mercy only compounded the water shortage. Most Rebel canteens had long since been emptied. Now the only nearby water trickled in a shallow, muddy creek between the lines. With the promise of another blistering day and a renewal of battle, Colonel McCown understood the urgent need for water before more serious fighting on September 20. The colonel therefore called for a volunteer to undertake a risky mission. Lieutenant Joshua Lippincot, a New York–born ex-clerk, stepped forward without hestitation. Because of his haughty demeanor and perhaps his Northern background, Lippincot never gained much respect from the enlisted men of the Fifth Missouri. The former adjutant of McCown's battalion crept into the inky darkness on his own, with twenty canteens and newfound popularity.[29]

Lieutenant Lippincot's sortie between the lines went well until he approached the creek. At that point the St. Louisan stumbled noisily into a mudhole, and the Federals opened with a brisk fire. With minié balls whistling past him and splashing in the muck, the twenty-four-year-old officer panicked. He backtracked on the run with canteens banging loudly and dashed for the Fifth Missouri's position. It seemed as if hundreds of Yankees, who "supposed our whole army was charging up them," now unleashed a heavy fire at the racket between the lines. The former St. Louis clerk, muddy and frightened, miraculously escaped without a scratch. But, wrote one officer, he "tumbled over three or four of his superior officers and landed full length on me, nearly knocking the breath out of me." Evidently Lieutenant Lippincot's deeds at Iuka failed to win him accolades. The young officer would be cashiered for cowardice within the next few months.[30]

As Unionists blasted away at the Fifth Missouri's position, Captain Canniff ordered his Celts to return fire. A hot skirmish flared up and down the lines throughout most of the night as a heavy dew covered the fields. Lieutenant Warren complained how "the enemy would give us a volley, whenever we made the least noise." Shrouded in mist and darkness, the Fifth Missouri defenders aimed and shot at the muzzle flashes of the Unionists. The danger and horror grew as the night lengthened. According to one of McCown's followers, piles of injured and dead Confederates lay in every direction.

Sobered by the death of his top lieutenant, General Little, and his subordinates' wise arguments for not continuing the battle on September 20, Price began to grasp the overall tactical situation and the danger of remaining at Iuka. It was clear that lingering any longer at Iuka might spell certain disaster. Now Price acted like the "Old Woodpecker," which was Rosecrans's complimentary nickname for Price because of his craftiness. On the brink of disaster, General Price at last regained his most valuable military asset, the "home-bred common sense" which had made him successful in Missouri during 1861. The Army of the West prepared to withdraw down the Fulton Road at midnight on September 19. This was the only escape route south out of Iuka. On his finest day in Mississippi, General Little paid with his life to keep this road open for the safe withdrawal and escape of the Army of the West. The evacuation of Tishomingo County's seat would proceed "with great promptness."[31]

Trains of wagons full of captured Union supplies rumbled out of Iuka.

A lengthy Southern column ambled south in the darkness. Before leaving, Father Bannon conducted the midnight funeral for General Little by candlelight. The sad funeral service was held in the backyard of a citizen's house in town, while the ranks of the Army of the West trudged by.

Not until around three o'clock that morning did the Fifth Missouri get word to retire by the left flank. As at the end of the battle of Pea Ridge on the west side of the Mississippi, General Price selected the Missouri Brigade to cover the army's rear. But more important, Colonel Gates gave the Fifth Missouri the task of guarding the Missouri Brigade's withdrawal. After the Confederate Army pulled away, McCown's soldiers, sore and stiff, arose from dew-covered grass and formed in a column in the blackness "with as little noise as possible," as Lieutenant Warren noted in his diary. In a swift and stealthy movement, the Missouri Rebels were gone with the thinning dawn.

By any measure, the battle of Iuka was a hard fight. The vicious two and a half hour contest cost Price around 700 casualties. The Unionists suffered about 100 more casualties than they inflicted.[32] But, thanks largely to General Little's efforts, Confederate success could be measured by Price's escape from Grant's trap at Iuka.

As the last Rebels to depart from the Federals' presence and to leave the front, the Fifth Missouri Confederates performed risky duty in bringing up the rear of the Army of the West. Soon Captain Canniff and Company F were the only grayclads left before Rosecrans's forces, as they covered not only the Fifth Missouri's, but also the Army of the West's retrograde movement. Then the Irish captain eased his soldiers through the damp fields and forests skirting the road, following Price's withdrawing army. The chore of guarding an army's rear was nothing new for Captain Canniff and his crack Irish soldiers. Since the war's beginning, he had served as leading officer of the crack St. Louis company. This unit had led Missouri State Guard advances and covered withdrawals throughout the early history of Price's army. After the battle of Iuka, Captain Canniff and his company had the experience necessary for such an important role within the Army of the West.[33]

Expecting to find Price transfixed around Iuka, the Yankees only found empty fields, evacuated positions, and rising dust clouds with the sunrise of September 20. Union cannon bombarded Iuka while the Fifth Missouri Rebels pushed through the agricultural community on the run, racing through the shell-fire. A few of McCown's seriously ill soldiers were carried into Iuka's Methodist Church, private homes, and other buildings, which were now makeshift hospitals. One Fifth Missouri Confederate abandoned to the Federals was Private John T. Banning, a former McGee College student. Banning felt some solace that Surgeon Dysart, his friend and former college instructor, would be administering to the regimental sick and wounded at Iuka.

Another enlisted man too weak to go on was Private David Green Nickols, a Bootheeler of Company K. Nickols would eventually gain enough strength to escape his captors. Making a choice that would again be repeated, Dysart volunteered to remain behind and be captured in order to assist the wounded of the entire Missouri Brigade. Surgeon Dysart would later be released to rejoin the command, after helping to stabilize the chaotic medical situation at Iuka.[34]

After leaving behind the almost fatal trap of Iuka, the Fifth Missouri turned south down the dusty Fulton Road leading to Baldwyn. For the entire night and most of the next day, McCown's unit followed behind both the Missouri Brigade and the Army of the West. Company F's skirmishers protected the command's rear in the cool half-light of dawn. While ever-alert and constantly on the move, Captain Canniff and his Emerald Islanders scanned the dark woodlines and distant cotton fields for advancing Yankees, while the sun inched higher in the hot sky of September. As the hours of daylight increased, the Rebels leap-frogged methodically rearward in protective fashion.

Lieutenant Robert Salmon, a thirty-one-year-old St. Louisan detected unnatural color in a thicket. Sneaking over with cocked revolver, the second generation Irishman yelled, "Come here, ye divil!" An Illinois major in command of scouts popped up from the underbrush with hands extended. The former tobacconist from St. Louis motioned with his pistol and said, "come along and be quick about it," while the boys of Company F darted past with smiles.[35]

The sprint for Baldwyn was as tough as the rear-guard duty was hazardous. After a sleepless night with no water, dozens of McCown's Rebels fell out of the ranks suffering from heat exhaustion and sunstroke. Along the dusty route, weakened Confederates lay under trees and next to split-rail fences. Hour after hour, the Fifth Missouri soldiers dropped beside the road in the dust and heat. Lieutenant Warren staggered to the ground from heat exhaustion. While the young officer from Franklin County waited for the dizziness to pass, "a light-haired, blue-eyed, handsome fellow" and one of "the lightest-hearted and gayest among the gay" came along. Like Lieutenant Warren, this soldier tumbled in a heap "to rest near me, and in less than five minutes he was dead." The sun's heat, ironically, took more Fifth Missouri lives than Union bullets at Iuka.[36]

The young man's death was the first in the Fifth Missouri after the completion of the regiment's organization, and the sight of him lying "pale and rigid, but beautiful in death" caused many regimental members to long remember the loss of this young soldier. The hasty burial by the roadside made the Missouri Rebels reflect more seriously on a lonely death far from home. As recalled one officer: "Many a sincere tear was dropped on his obscure grave. As we laid him tenderly to rest, I thought of the distant mother." Chaplain Charles H. Atwood performed the hasty burial service beside the road. Despite suffering "very much from fatigue," the Fifth Missouri soldiers resumed their journey south toward Baldwyn under the hot Mississippi sun within minutes of the sad ritual on the dusty road.[37]

General Rosecrans's cavalry meanwhile harassed Price's rear. But the Army of the West made good its escape. Footsore Missourians reached Baldwyn as the sun of September 23 dipped below the western landscape. In a patch of woods along the Mobile and Ohio Railroad, the Fifth Missouri encamped with Price's other units. The Army of the West had been fortunate to survive Price's first meeting with Grant. Rest at Baldwyn was well-deserved, for the withdrawal's fast pace took a toll. The difficult trek caused Lieutenant Warren to declare in his diary: "I feel perfectly exhausted. I have never suffered so much on the march before."[38] But before the war's conclusion, the Iuka withdrawal would seem like a Sunday stroll in St. Louis.

# III

## STORMING THE
## FORTIFICATIONS
## OF CORINTH

Active campaigning this fall for the Fifth Missouri would not end with the battle of Iuka. Indeed, the third and last phase of the three-part Confederate offensive during the late summer and autumn of 1862 was about to begin. Orders came on September 25 for the Fifth Missouri to prepare to move out in preparation for again meeting the Yankees. In high spirits, McCown's infantrymen swung northwestward at daylight on September 26, with the long butternut-colored columns pushing over the brown rolling hills. The destination of the Army of the West was Ripley, a small town east of Iuka where Van Dorn's troops were assembled. The uniting of Price's Army of the West with Van Dorn's forces to form the newly styled Army of West Tennessee would muster around 20,000 Southerners. As if in repayment for "Old Rosey's" plan which had almost entrapped Price's army at Iuka, Van Dorn now meant to capture Corinth and destroy Rosecrans's army. Linking four corners of the Confederacy, Corinth was the most crucial railroad intersection in the West.[1]

At Corinth, the Memphis and Charleston Railroad served as the South's most vital lifeline, connecting west with east: an invaluable asset for this war which revolutionized the use of railroads. Iron rails meeting at Corinth connected "the three great arteries of the South." Since the war's beginning, Trans-Mississippi supplies and troops poured east from Louisiana, Arkansas, and Texas. Likewise, munitions and volunteers came up from the Gulf region along the Mobile and Ohio Railroad. Corinth was "the key to the Tennessee and Mississippi Valleys." Without Corinth and the most direct railroad routes for Confederate reinforcements and materiel, the South's heartland would have eventually strangled and died.

The Union-held stronghold at Corinth seemed especially vulnerable to Confederate leadership by the autumn of 1862. General Grant's defensive line stretched eastward across 80 miles of rough country from Memphis to Corinth. Federal troops were scattered throughout the southern Tennessee

countryside and garrisoned key strong-points along the Memphis and
Charleston Railroad. Isolated on Grant's far left, Corinth stood as a great
prize to be picked off by aggressive Southern action during the fall of 1862.
In addition, a Rebel conquest of Corinth would assist Bragg's invasion and
disrupt any ideas that the pesky General Grant might have of embarking
upon a campaign to reduce Vicksburg.[2]

General Van Dorn had a bold plan to exploit Grant's weakness. First,
the Army of West Tennessee would march north and bluff toward Bolivar,
Tennessee, to freeze the nearby Unionists in place and decoy the Federals
at Corinth. Then thousands of Rebels would turn and push rapidly southeast to snatch Corinth from the rear. These quick maneuvers by Van Dorn
were calculated to leave the Union garrisons at Jacinto, Iuka, and Rienzi
stationary and unable to assist Corinth when the Confederates struck a
mighty blow. Then after capturing Corinth, the Southerners would link
with Bragg in Kentucky, push farther north, and perhaps march all the way
to the Ohio River.[3]

With high hopes, Colonel McCown's Confederates poured briskly
northwest for the rendezvous with destiny. Long Southern columns skirted
the fields and forests parched from the long summer, which had been exceptionally hot and dry. Captain Guthrie and his Company I men would have
been incensed had they known of recent atrocities committed by Union occupation troops back in their Macon County, such as the execution on
September 25. Ten pro–Southerners, who were captured after taking oaths
of allegiance, were executed by a Union firing squad just south of the town
of Macon. The Fifth Missouri soldiers of Macon County in Companies B
and I now had even more reason to take the war "beyond the Ohio" and
obtain revenge during the Confederacy's autumn of hope.[4] Indeed, this was
a holy war for McCown's soldiers.

The Missouri Confederates and the Army of the West pushed onward
for Ripley and Van Dorn. A line of thunderstorms approached near sunset
on September 27. Colonel McCown's infantrymen double-quicked through
the darkening forests and sudden gusts of winds, as if in a futile attempt
to escape the storm as treetops swayed against a churning sky. Lieutenant
Warren wrote: "[It] commenced raining. We had five miles to make to get
water, when it commenced it became so slippery that I could hardly stand
up. I fell down at least 5 times. We were scattered for miles. I could not keep
in sight of the Regment [sic]. I put up under a tree for the night, I was wet
from head to foot."[5]

The gently rolling countryside of northeast Mississippi turned into a
morass. On the open road, the soldiers of the Fifth Missouri were caught
amid a dripping darkness and a sea of mud and water. With rain coming
down in sheets, those Rebels yet in column struggled toward Baldwyn. One
of McCown's men described the deluge in his diary: "One of the heaviest

rains I ever saw fell. It was so dark we could hardly see our hands before us. The country was very hilly and the roads very muddy. I have never seen such muddy men before or since." Wet Confederates of the Fifth Missouri straggled into their Baldwyn encampment throughout the night.[6]

General Price's Army of the West finally linked with Van Dorn on September 28. The veteran troops of Van Dorn's only Missouri regiment, the First Missouri Confederate Infantry, eagerly awaited the arrival of Colonel McCown's soldiers, whom they had heard so much about. The St. Louis Irish of the First Missouri Infantry were eager to see Captain Canniff's Irish company once more. Lieutenant Joseph Boyce, First Missouri, described the meeting: "[The men] quietly awaited the arrival of [McCown's] heros of Wilson's Creek, Lexington, etc. 'Here they come, boys!' and we rushed to the road to welcome them. Many old friends met who had parted at Camp Jackson, and our pleasure was great, indeed, to meet so many friends and former comrades. They presented a very soldierly appearance, marching and moving like veterans. They were well armed but indifferently uniformed." The long awaited third Rebel offensive of late summer–fall 1862 would begin now with the uniting of the two Confederate forces, which resulted in the formation of the Army of West Tennessee. Almost immediately, Van Dorn's Southerners turned and headed northeastward, beginning the daring maneuver to snatch Corinth from under the nose of General Grant.[7]

Not long thereafter, McCown's troops rejoiced when they left the Magnolia State and entered Tennessee on October 1. Setting foot on the ancestral ground of their forefathers caused many Fifth Missourians to celebrate their arrival in Tennessee. For Colonel McCown's Rebels, the state of Mississippi had brought nothing but misery and bad luck since the Missouri Confederates first arrived in the state during April 1862. Sergeant Ruyle rejoiced when the Fifth Missouri "crossed the line into Tennessee. I hope we have bid farewell to Miss[issippi] for a long time." It was a vain wish because hard duty, bloody battles, and death in the Magnolia State had only begun for the Missouri Confederates.[8]

As shadows deepened in the dense forests bordering the Hatchie River immediately east of Pocahontas, the Missouri Rebels unrolled their blankets and made preparations to spend the night in Alcorn County. Weary Confederates stretched out near Davis's Bridge under blackening skies. Uncertain of their fates, McCown's butternuts sat around campfires thinking of the homes hundreds of miles away that they might never see again. With a big battle imminent, little poker playing, drinking, or cursing of generals occurred in the encampment that night. Indeed, on this night, reading the Bible suddenly became more popular.

A foreboding hung in the air on the night of September 1. Sleep did not come easy for many of Colonel McCown's boys that night, with a major engagement on the horizon. With the cynicism of a veteran, Sergeant Ruyle expected the worst. He had already scribbled on the front leaf of his diary: "If I should fall on the battlefield or die in any other way while the war lasts, I hope some friend will finish my letter [diary] by giving a detail of my last days, the manner of death, burial, etc. This I desire some friend to do for the satisfaction of my father and family."[9]

In a quirk of fate, Private Patrick McGrath, age twenty-six, had enlisted in Company F at Corinth the preceding summer. As a member of the Irish peasantry, he was raised in Ballymartle, Ireland, on a small farm. Like his company commander, Captain Canniff, McGrath left the misery of the Emerald Isle to "escape the oppressions of his own country." The former St. Louis clerk would be one of the first fatalities of the Fifth Missouri at Corinth, where his Confederate career had begun so recently.[10] Foremost among the thoughts of McCown's soldiers on this peaceful evening was that only a short distance to the southeast and down the Memphis and Charleston Railroad tracks stood the massive fortifications of Corinth and about 23,000 Unionists. And if Rosecrans grew wise to the Tennessee feint, Corinth would be more formidable after being reinforced.[11]

But for now Van Dorn held the initiative. General Grant remained uncertain if the Confederates meant to have Bolivar, north of Pocahontas in Tennessee, or Corinth. Rosecrans also had not yet ascertained the Rebels' objective. After a wrecked bridge across the river was repaired, lengthy Southern columns pushed across Davis's bridge early on October 2, passing over the turbid Hatchie and unraveling the mystery of Van Dorn's objective to the Yankees. The march of the Rebels east along the tracks toward Corinth continued across the Tuscumbia River.

That night the Fifth Missouri soldiers bedded down in lines of battle beside the railroad south of Chewalla. McCown's troops were now less than ten miles from their objective, Corinth. October 3 dawned warm and clear, bringing forth another hot Indian summer day. The Confederate army drove southeastward toward the most important railroad center in the West to reverse Rebel fortunes. In a repeat of the Pea Ridge campaign, General Van Dorn, obsessed with grandiose visions of Napoleonic victories, felt confident of success, thinking that General Rosecrans was confused and badly outnumbered for the climactic showdown at Corinth.[12]

But "Old Rosey" was not fooled by his former West Point classmate (1842), who had underestimated the ability of this fine Union commander. At West Point, Rosecrans had graduated four places from the top, while Van Dorn finished a like number from the bottom. Gaining insights just in time, General Rosecrans reasoned that Van Dorn was targeting Corinth for capture. He therefore marshaled thousands of troops from surrounding garrisons. To slow Van Dorn's advance, Union forces filled the town's outer defensive ring about three miles northwest of Corinth. As at Pea Ridge, Van Dorn's West Point strategies had gone awry once again. The anticipated element of surprise that Van Dorn so desperately needed for a successful attack upon Corinth from the rear was already lost. The sound of cavalry skirmishing meanwhile swelled higher in the early autumn air. Excited butternut scouts reported that the woodlands and outer works before Corinth were teeming with bluecoats: the possibility of overrunning Corinth by a "coup de main" had vanished.[13]

Even worse, Van Dorn had little knowledge of Corinth's new inner network of fortifications. This was the best evidence of a critical failure of intelligence because of the lack of a proper reconnaissance, and this failure would result in a greater loss of Southern lives. To McCown's veterans, the increasing volume of musketry seemed to indicate that the entire Corinth garrison, almost twice as large as the army Van Dorn expected to meet, had marched out to do battle. Around 9:30 A.M., escalating gunfire snapped many Confederates into thinking about life after death, as Chaplains Atwood and Bannon had often urged them to do.

With a fight brewing, Colonel McCown's more superstitious followers threw playing cards from knapsacks. Few soldiers wanted to face bullets without God on their side as rifle-fire crashed louder through the forests up ahead. With no more atheists in the ranks, the Missourians hurried down Chewalla Road. Ten minutes later, Colonel McCown's soldiers loaded muskets with a clatter of ramrods. As they had practiced on many drill fields, the Confederates from Missouri then fixed bayonets on the run, while a wind scattered playing cards through the thickets.[14]

The impending conflict seemed all the more ominous because a morning earthquake had shaken northeastern Mississippi. The seemingly ill portent was most appropriate, for now Van Dorn's Rebels continued "hastening to the feast of death prepared by the weird sisters of Destiny." More feelings of foreboding came with the sight of the powerful outer works, the Beauregard Line, which stood northwest of Corinth. Van Dorn deployed his three divisions in a long arc. Price's troops shifted left, crossing the Memphis and Charleston Railroad forming for action north of the fortifications. Still assuming that Rosecrans had been tricked by the Tennessee swing, Van Dorn prepared to launch a massive attack. Colonel McCown's companies filed into assault formations along a wooded hilltop as temperatures and skirmishing continued to rise on an autumn day as hot as summer. Despite the blistering heat, Price's corps of two divisions aligned on the left in a short time.[15]

About to lead the Fifth Missouri in its first charge after the completion of its organization, Colonel McCown awaited orders to assault the fortifications. Rebels sweated under a hot sun, leaning on muskets atop their forested perch. Word finally came to advance. Drawing his saber while on horseback, Colonel McCown screamed, "Charge!" With battle flags flying, the five infantry regiments of the elite Missouri Brigade swung downhill and over a slight rise. Artillery boomed within the Union entrenchments, sending flashes of fire and smoke from the earthworks. Cheering Confederates poured through a belt of woods and into a hollow filled with the tangles of a dense abatis. Colonel McCown's assault slowed upon encountering the obstacles. As the Confederates picked through the entanglements, Federal volleys whizzed high over their heads, whistling above the hollow. To slow the Rebel advance and buy time for the Corinth garrison, Rosecrans was fighting only a delaying action at the outer defenses. Had the Unionists made a stand here, the Fifth Missouri would probably have been decimated. After much effort, the Confederates finally broke free of the cheval-de-frise. Rebel soldiers now raced up the opposite high ground to be the first inside the Unionists' earthworks. The Federals, meanwhile, retired toward Corinth, heading south for either a second defensive line or the main, or inner, line before Corinth a mile distant.[16]

Eager for revenge, the tide of Fifth Missouri attackers scaled the parapet while howling to celebrate the victory. One soldier leading the regiment over the top was Sergeant William W. Walsh, the St. Louis poet and former Washington Blues member. With waving swords and revolvers, the mounted officers of the Fifth Missouri spurred their horses to ride over the high parapet. But in the face of the obstacle, the animals slid down the steep earthworks. Missouri leaders dismounted to lead their horses across on foot, joining the cheering foot-soldiers pouring over the defenses. Once across, Colonel Gates's Missouri troops captured supplies, several cannon, and groups of stragglers. Sitting astride a brass cannon, a dust-covered private greeted McCown, "Well, Colonel, you mounted fellows are tolerably useful in camp, and serve a good purpose on the drill ground but we don't need you much in a fight." Amused by the spunk of the enlisted man, Colonel McCown replied, "No, I'll swear you don't and you boys can out-run the devil when you are after a Fed." The wild charge of the Fifth Missouri had swept everything before it. In one soldier's words, "we did not get a man hurt" during the attack.[17]

Barking orders, officers quickly reformed the Fifth Missouri for more fighting. To the right, meanwhile, Brigadier General Martin E. Green's brigade ran into stiff resistance. Providing timely support, Colonel McCown hurried his troops toward the rattling gunfire. The Missouri Brigade took position on Green's left rear, reinforcing these hard-fighting Rebels at a critical moment. Behind Green's Missourians and Arkansans, McCown's soldiers found refuge in a brushy hollow to escape the volleys. Seeking shelter from the leaden storm, Fifth Missouri boys hugged the ground while bullets clipped the tall weeds overhead and made the air sing.[18]

Finally the last and most obstinate bluecoat resistance collapsed. The Missouri Brigade quickly aligned on Green's left for the advance upon the inner works of Corinth. On the double, McCown's Rebels splashed across a creek with clanging gear. Upon the colonel's signal, the Fifth Missouri formations went crashing through a cornfield and then into the parched forests from which the Federals had been chased. As the sun hovered on the horizon, cheering Missourians surged forward in the last push of the day. The Fifth Missouri soldiers halted upon reaching the high embankment of the Mobile and Ohio Railroad, after the long advance south toward Corinth. Securing good cover, Colonel McCown's infantrymen filed behind the natural breastwork only about a mile north of Corinth and caught their breath in the suffocating heat.[19]

With daylight fading fast, Colonel McCown worried about the dark woodlands before him and immediately summoned Captain Canniff to ascertain what lay in the Fifth Missouri's front. No sooner had Company F pushed southeastward through some oak thickets than heavy skirmishing erupted. Despite the stiff resistance, the ever-aggressive Captain Canniff ordered his crack skirmishers to continue forward. On the run, the Rebel soldiers drove the Union soldiers rearward during stubborn fighting at the end of the day. The Unionists made repeated stands during the running fight through the belt of woods, firing from the timber.[20]

Driving the Unionists back a good distance exacted a toll, however. Indeed, some of the best skirmishers of Company F were cut down. Twenty-two-year-old Private John M. Miller, a Randolph County farmer, fell mortally wounded. Corporal Thomas Hogan, age twenty-two, had numerous brushes with death. Lately a tobacco store clerk, he escaped harm during the struggle amid the darkening woodlands, "although the men next to me, on both my right and left were shot."[21]

Against the odds, both Company F and Company G, Second Missouri, finally secured the wooded area in the Missouri Brigade's front, but the skirmishing continued with intensity. Company F's Confederates held their own and then hurled the Federals back in one last drive before dark. In stubborn fashion, the blueclads continued to fight back while heading slowly toward Corinth's main line. One of Company F's finest noncommissioned officers, Sergeant Joseph D. Rumpf, age thirty, fell wounded when a bullet cut across his scalp. The former St. Louis printer would survive the bloody gash and soon be back in the ranks. But the sergeant, destined to be killed at Champion Hill, would never see his Russia-born wife again. In one of the hardest skirmishes to date for Captain Canniff's warriors, two more Company F members were hit before the blazing sun of October 3 dropped.

"Western Sharpshooters," consisting of Missourians in blue uniforms, punished Canniff's soldiers with a severe fire. These expert Union marksmen, ironically, were led by Colonel Patrick E. Burke, a prewar St. Louis militia officer who had once commanded some of the Rebels of Company F. The two former St. Louis militia members—Captain Canniff and Colonel Burke, who had served together during the Southwest Expedition— now led opposing skirmishing parties in advance of two American armies which were trying hard to destroy each other that day. Both Canniff and Burke, two Irish officers from St. Louis, exemplified not only how Missourian fought against Missourian, but also how Irishman fought against Irishman, one of the best examples of the brothers' war on the Western frontier. Ironically, Colonel Burke would be killed in the same year as Captain Canniff, bloody 1864.[22]

The Fifth Missouri soldiers, meanwhile, clung low behind the railroad embankment. Orders were given to stay down as bullets zipped overhead. But many of these rambunctious Confederates could not stay inactive while Canniff's boys fought and died before them. Some of McCown's butternuts scampered atop the embankment and popped away over the friendly heads of Company F. But the firing only drew the Unionists' wrath and musketry, and a few Confederates tumbled down the incline with bullet holes in them. Sharp-eyed Federal snipers "would shoot our men whenever they would poke their heads above the railroad [and] killed and wounded some of our best officers and soldiers who were anxious to get a shot at them," Sergeant Ruyle wrote bitterly in his diary.

One soldier eager to shoot a Yankee this evening was Sergeant Samuel Lane, who was destined to die in the fighting during the next summer. A natural leader of Company C, Lane was hit in the forehead by a minié ball. As the sunlight and the skirmish finally faded away, an early autumn coolness embraced the land. Worn and dirty, Colonel McCown's soldiers behind the railroad shivered from the cool snap "without blankets or coats and almost without rations, occasionally shooting at the Feds and getting water out of the mud holes" on the dangerous side of the railroad embankment.[23]

By this time, Captain Canniff's unit had advanced a quarter mile through the tangled woodlands to a creek near the cleared ground before the main fortifications of Corinth. With a yellow moon rising and the Union artillery pounding the area, the skirmishes of Company F retired a couple hundred yards toward the railroad for the night and maintained an advanced position in protective fashion before the Missouri Brigade. Regimental members at the railroad watched silently as the dying and wounded skirmishers, splashed in blood, were carried rearward over the railroad embankment. These were the first battle fatalities after the organization of the Fifth Missouri was completed.[24]

The Missouri Confederates slept that night with arms at the ready. Many of McCown's men felt confident that "the foe had fled," and they believed that they would take Corinth "with hardly a struggle." But in the darkness, Johnny Rebs listened to the movements of a busy Federal army around Corinth and contemplated the implications of this activity. It seemed Rosecrans had to be evacuating after the day's beating. Braying mules and creaking wagons and caissons seemed to indicate that Rosecrans was moving out of Corinth. Fifth Missouri Rebels lying with their arms near them in the dew beside the railroad grew more apprehensive by the early morning hours. Many of McCown's young exiles still dreamed of invading Tennessee and Kentucky before turning west to reclaim Missouri. No one had forgotten how "Old Pap" Price promised to lead them "back to the fertile prairies, the rich woodlands and majestic streams of our beloved Missouri — that I may the more certainly restore you to your once happy homes and to the loved ones there."[25]

Fearing that many of his Catholic followers would be wiped out with the sunrise, Father Bannon spent the entire night administering his services. Bannon took the confessions of the Irishmen of Company F in the black woodlands after waking up many of the Catholic warriors. Amid the moonlight and the dark forests about a hundred yards east of the railroad, a number of young Emerald Islanders gave their last confessions on the night of October 3.[26]

As daylight approached, the worst possible scenario developed because the Unionists were ready for action. Instead of evacuation, the night sounds were Rosecrans's bolstering his front with artillery and reinforcements and concentrating his forces within a two-mile-long inner defensive line. Strongly fortified redoubts bolstered the Federal line. Now the opinions of Generals Price and Bowen seemed verified: the Rebel assaults the previous evening should have continued toward Corinth.

Dozens of Confederate guns to Corinth's northwest and north opened around dawn. The last hope of the Southerners entering the city unopposed was shattered when Union batteries responded at 4:30 A.M. McCown's soldiers understood the truth when shells suddenly exploded around them in the tree-tops. Clearly, Rosecrans had decided to stand and fight to the finish at Corinth.[27]

Explosions around the Fifth Missouri Rebels alerted them more quickly than bugles or drums. As could be expected, some confusion ensued during the heavy bombardment. With the agility of veterans, Colonel McCown's Confederates dodged the shells and dropping limbs while the unit hustled into formation behind the embankment. As Yankee cannon growled to announce the contest's opening and the first rays of light filtered through the trees, the sun rose brightly into a clear sky to illuminate the showdown for the possession of Corinth.[28]

General Van Dorn must have been enraged by the brutal reality of October 4. The Mississippian had been supremely confident only hours before. In fact, he had already bragged about the October 3 success in a telegram to Richmond. Van Dorn seriously miscalculated the tactical situation at Corinth, thinking the Union garrisons had been tricked by his Tennessee detour and believing that the strongest earthworks had been already overrun. But the defenders of Corinth had not been surprised nor had they fled. Van Dorn badly underestimated his old West Point classmate and the quality of his veteran blueclads from the West. The destiny of strategic Corinth was yet to be determined on October 4.[29]

As during the severe contest of the evening before, Captain Canniff's skirmishers and the Missouri Brigade's other premier skirmish company — Company G, Second Missouri — hurled Colonel Burke's tenacious Missouri bluecoats from their front. The Irish Rebels trotted through the last belt of forest in the half-light of dawn, surging toward the open ground before the fortifications. Elated over having the Yankees again on the run, the Missouri skirmishers pushed across a dry creek-bed with Rebel yells and renewed confidence. Colonel McCown, meanwhile, ordered the Fifth Missouri over the embankment around nine o'clock to follow Company F's advance. The Irish Confederates halted on the wood's edge and fanned out before opening fire. After another job well done, Captain Canniff now waited for the arrival of the Fifth Missouri and the Missouri Brigade. By this time, Colonel Gates had sent forward two additional companies of skirmishers to assist Canniff. One of these units was Company E, Fifth Missouri, under the capable Captain Fair. After advancing around two hundred yards to the rear of the Missouri Brigade's skirmishers, the Fifth Missouri deployed near the creek and east of the railroad. Soon the two divisions of Price's corps were aligned for the great assault on Corinth.[30]

A killing field, the cleared ground spread before the Fifth Missouri for several hundred yards. The slopes led upward to a commanding ridge-top where a Union artillery bastion — Battery Powell — dominated the horizon. This imposing earthwork to the Fifth Missouri's left stood as the primary fort protecting the northern approach to Corinth. To Powell's right, or southwest, along the same ridge could be seen Fort Richardson, a strong fortification erected during the night: a reminder of the cost of not attacking late on October 3. Along the summit, lengthy blue formations lined the commanding ground as far as the eye could see. Colorful Federal banners, clumped together in bunches, dotted the ridge-top. Rows of brass cannon were poised along the opposite heights, crammed practically wheel to wheel. The thick abatis which promised to destroy Confederate attack formations sliced across the intervening ground. Except for the felled timber, the whole slope was wide open.[31]

Van Dorn hurriedly made dispositions from the attack. According to plans, General Louis Hebert's division of Price's corps would begin the assault on the left by swinging around the Unionists' right to strike their flank at daybreak. Major General Mansfield Lovell's division would simultaneously do the same on Rosecrans's left. To further complicate the scheme, Brigadier General Dabney H. Maury's troops of Price's other division were directed to smash into the Unionists' center while the Army of West Tennessee's remainder — the divisions commanded by Generals Hebert and Lovell — ripped into the Unionists' flanks. Van Dorn would have been taxed to develop a more delicately timed and difficult assault. If everything went according to plan, then "Old Rosey" would be destroyed and vital Corinth won for the Confederacy. But the best chance for victory had already vanished during the evening of October 3.[32]

Nothing would go right for Rebel fortunes on the morning of October 4. Van Dorn's three divisions stood motionless as if paralyzed at the scheduled time of attack. A scorching sun inched higher in the sky. No cheering or heavy musketry could be heard on any sector at the front. Only the busy skirmishers of both sides banged away in their own vicious, private war. Clearly, Van Dorn's carefully laid plans were upset. A courier bearing instructions for Hebert to open the engagement had fallen asleep at a farmhouse. Then to add to the confusion, General Hebert stumbled into Van Dorn's headquarters around seven o'clock and requested to be relieved of command due to illness. Although his battle plan was self-destructing around him, Van Dorn refused to revise it. The general meant to strike a blow before any more reinforcements bolstered Corinth's defenses. But little did Van Dorn know that Union troops from the surrounding area were already positioned within some of the strongest fortifications in all the West.[33]

At least the long delay assisted Chaplain Bannon. As was his usual practice before a battle, Father Bannon now sought out soldiers in need of spiritual uplifting. He went along the attack formations to listen to the hardened Rebels from the Western frontier during the final moments before the suicidal charge. Soldiers in the ranks made last-minute preparations for the attack. Perhaps final good-byes were said by the more pessimistic, or realistic in this case, men and boys from Missouri.[34]

Skirmishing, meanwhile, continued to escalate along the front. On the edge of the woodlands, Captain Canniff's skirmishers from St. Louis's streets and rural Irish communities steadily peppered the Union skirmishers before the earthworks. Perhaps a few Company F sharpshooters climbed trees along the creek to pick off Federals on the crest. Canniff's skirmishers dropped a number of Yankees with their marksmanship and drove back their Missouri counterparts in blue. Chasing the Yankees uphill, they swept over them "in a jiffy." Colonel McCown aligned his 225 Fifth Missouri Confederates along the woodline beside the dry creek about 325 yards before the defenses. Before the first charge of the Fifth Missouri began, the uniforms of McCown's troops were covered in dirt and dust.[35]

Upon the colonel's order, McCown's Rebels attached bayonets to muskets, while eyeing the hilly ground they would soon have to cross. The ridge before them seemingly rose like a mountain out of the open fields. Seconds lingered like hours, and it seemed that time stood still for the Confederates standing in ranks. No doubt some Fifth Missouri soldiers with premonitions of death now passed letters, diaries, or last words to comrades to be relayed home. Some of McCown's soldiers placed Bibles in breast pockets to ward off minié balls.[36]

Probably no one seemed more out of place in the Fifth Missouri's line than Color Sergeant Walsh, age twenty-eight. Standing at the formation's head in the sticky morning haze of Indian summer, Walsh proudly held the regimental colors, a bright red banner with thirteen white stars sprinkled over it and a white quarter-moon crescent in the upper corner. The former St. Louis merchant was the poet of the Fifth Missouri. A young man of much promise and great expectations, Walsh had been considered one of the budding talents of St. Louis. The works of the Ireland-born sergeant were published in more than one St. Louis newspaper.[37]

Motivation was high among McCown's soldiers that day. The Fifth Missouri Rebels felt determined "to regain their prestige of victory seemingly lost at Iuka." The motto of the Missouri Confederates during this autumn of hope was to "conquer or die." Within only a few hours of this hot October morning, some of the best and brightest of the Fifth Missouri would be slaughtered.[38]

Just when it seemed as if the attack had been canceled, General Green ordered his four brigades forward in echelon. Casting aside any pessimistic feelings that he might have had, Colonel McCown yelled, "Steady, there; come up a little on the left. All right. Forward, double-quick — march!" Rebel waves rolled up the slope with bayonets sparkling in the sunlight just before ten o'clock. Shells began exploding overhead with great crashes. Explosions knocked down attackers as soon as Gates's Missouri Brigade poured out of the woodline like a flood. The Fifth Missouri skirmishers of Companies E and F charged before the advance with wild yells, firing and chasing Colonel Burke's Missouri skirmishers toward the main line.[39]

Price's corps swarmed forward on its own to hit Corinth from the north. General Lovell, on the right, advanced his division, but failed to launch a determined assault. He evidently reasoned that Van Dorn's assault orders seemed suicidal and "not in accordance with West Point tactics." Consequently, Maury's and Green's [formerly Hebert's] divisions swarmed on the defensive network ringing the city without support. Butternut formations of Price's two divisions headed forward toward a cruel fate with battle flags flying and drums beating in the smoke of battle. At long last, and only after invaluable hours passed, the Southern attack to reverse the Confederacy's fortunes in the West began.[40]

Leading the Fifth Missouri southeastward toward Battery Powell, drummers Molloy, Learman, and others pounded away on their instruments. The drum beating of the regimental musicians mingled with that of dozens of other drummer boys. Both Battery Powell and Fort Richardson were formidable. The strongest artillery bastion and most formidable earthwork anchoring Rosecrans's right-center, Battery Powell dominated the ridge on the southern horizon. Bristling with six 20-pounder Parrott rifled cannon of the First United States Artillery, the fortified redoubt jutted north to form a salient on Rosecrans's northern defenses to the road's left, or west. In addition, six pieces of the Sixth Wisconsin Light Artillery stood near the four-sided redoubt. The earthen defensive structure was crammed full of guns, limbers, caissons, horses, and expert artillerymen. But the Battery Powell sector had a chink in its armor. The weak link was from the railroad eastward across Purdy Road and on to Battery Powell. Along this sector, not an earthwork had been erected except for Fort Richardson. The Federals had not had time to dig rifle pits.[41]

At last, the moment came for the final rush. McCown's officers roared, "Forward!" when the Fifth Missouri was within 300 yards of the fortifications. Ignoring the casualties and carnage, Fifth Missouri leaders led their troops up the ridge and "steadily to death." The Confederates unleashed a spontaneous Rebel yell, which mingled with the boom of artillery. War cries from the Western frontier combined with the shouts of "On to the battery! Capture the battery!" White puffs of smoke from Union artillery bellowed forth on the horizon. More shells burst overhead, exploding in swirls of red and yellow light. Great upliftings of earth sent dirt and shrapnel pelting over the charging waves of howling Rebels. Dead and wounded Southerners tumbled to the ground in bunches and lay tangled together in grotesque piles. Despite the holes blown out of Fifth Missouri formations, the brownish-colored ranks mechanically closed up. Farther up the slope, meanwhile, the retreating blue skirmishers fled toward the main line with thousands of attacking Rebels behind them.[42]

The momentum of the charge broke when the attackers encountered the abatis, however. While cannonballs and shells whizzed by, the Missouri Rebels frantically pushed sharpened branches aside. Other veterans zigzagged down narrow picket lanes that were cut through the entanglements. As bullets zipped around them, McCown's men tore through the felled timber in what seemed like an eternity. Once clear of the abatis, Gates's First Missouri Brigade, with Green's Third Brigade to its right, converged en masse toward the fiery defensive bastions, Fort Richardson and Battery Powell.[43]

The charging Missourians continued up the ridge, yelling their quavering Rebel scream, which was a blend of the frontierman's and the Indian's war cry from the Western frontier. Sergeant Walsh led the fierce attack uphill with the Fifth Missouri's colors flapping through smoke and dust. The distance gained across the open ground was expensive, for the slope was now covered with many bodies scythed down by the artillery. Determined to plant the flag of the Fifth Missouri on the earthworks, Walsh surged ahead on his own. He suddenly fell backward after a minié ball tore through his head. Captain Fair rushed over and picked up the colors to carry on so that Sergeant Walsh would not have died in vain. Waving both sword and tattered flag amid the tumult, the British Rebel continued forward into the murderous fire.[44]

The whole ridge-line belched fire and flame. Batteries Robinette and Williams, across the railroad to McCown's right, or southwest, poured an enfilading fire on the Fifth Missouri's formations, which suffered severely under this pounding. Now the regiment paid the price for the inactivity of Lovell's division. The lack of cooperation in other sectors and the enfilade fire resulted in "the unneccessary slaughter of the [exposed] Missourians." Perhaps it was at this time that in Company K's front Captain Pankey took an ugly wound across his chin which later could only be hid with a thick beard.

In the words of one soldier, the "shot and shell from more than a hundred guns crashed and whistled around us incessantly and deafening. No orders could be heard, but as wide gaps were made in our ranks, the men closed up and pushed steadily forward." The onrushing Missourians, "yelling and hollering," stumbled over seemingly countless bodies. Two brothers, privates Alonzo Hollowell, a medical student of twenty-seven, and Miles Hollowell, a twenty-one-year-old aspiring lawyer, dropped wounded. Despite the slaughter, discipline was maintained, and no one halted to return fire.[45]

Green's Second and Fourth brigades on the division's left wavered and recoiled under the severe punishment. Few of these regiments would gain the defenses, but both brigades maintained pressure on the Federals. To the west, meanwhile, the First and Third brigades of Green's division kept charging up the ridge, oblivious to the left's repulse and the right's inactivity. Now even more Union guns turned toward the Fifth Missouri's lines to unleash what Bevier called "the most terrific hail of lead and iron I ever saw." Thousands of yelping Rebels swarmed toward the Battery Powell salient.

General Thomas A. Davies's Second Division, to Powell's left, and General Charles Hamilton's Third Division, on the stronghold's right, were braced along the crest for the onslaught. These veteran Yankee troops continued delivering volleys off the dominant terrain. One Unionist wrote, "As the shower of bullets struck the Rebel front, hundreds of men went down."

While he was encouraging his Fifth Missouri onward, Colonel McCown and his horse tumbled into a heap. Getting to his feet and leaping upon an aide's mount, the colonel continued galloping toward the summit covered in flame. Private James W. McAffee, age twenty-two, threw down his musket and raced rearward, permitting him to live to a ripe age.[46]

With less distance to cover than other commands, Colonel Gates's attackers neared one of Rosecrans's weakest sectors. The First Missouri Brigade swarmed toward the Unionists' right-center, where not a breastwork linked Fort Richardson with Battery Powell. Here, along the crest of the ridge, stood the troops of Davies's division, mostly from the "Union Brigade," which had been mauled the previous day.

Dropping like autumn leaves back in Missouri, Colonel McCown's infantrymen continued falling across the cleared slopes. The Fifth Missouri, wrote Sergeant Hogan in a letter to his St. Louis father, charged "through open hilly ground on which there was not even a single bush to screen a person from the terrible storm of shot and shell from their heavy siege [sic] guns [in Battery Powell], which were in full view for over a mile, and looked like if hell had been let loose. Shells bursting all around you; round shot ploughing the ground everywhere; grape and cannister sweeping down the hill almost by the bushel, it is a miracle how any one escaped." More than half of McCown's regiment would not escape the bullets and artillery projectiles on October 4.[47]

Rows of Union cannon sprayed fire from three sides, roaring unceasingly until the "very earth shook," wrote one Missouri Rebel. As Confederate swarms closed in on the run, Colonel Burke's blueclad skirmishers piled up at the abatis nearest the crest and crowded toward Battery Powell. While Rebel hordes poured closer by the minute, Ohio and Iowa soldiers on Powell's flanks could not fire for fear of killing their own troops. Spared from the worst frontal volleys, meanwhile, the Missourians' attack toward the northern apex of the Federal line gained impetus.[48]

With their skirmish comrades finally within the lines, the Ohioans, Iowans, and hundreds of other Union defenders unleashed a blistering volley that exploded in the faces of McCown's attackers. Battery Powell's gunners of the Sixth Wisconsin on the ridge's crest switched to double-shot canister, the foot-soldier's nightmare. Pulling lanyards almost before sponge-staffs were removed, the Union artillerymen sent hundreds of iron canister whizzing point-black into the butternut throng.

Ignoring fallen comrades Missourians steadily charged onward and into the hurricane of fire. Captain Fair held the regimental banner while it flapped through smoke layers and exploding shells.[49] Pounding away at shotgun range, the Wisconsin light pieces and 20-pounder Parrotts within Battery Powell jolted from recoil after spraying death in wide sweeping arcs. Clusters of canister hit before the brownish masses and then bounced up to break and mangle the legs and hips of the attackers.

In addition, the Twelfth Wisconsin Battery, 400 yards in Powell's rear, lobbed shells over the bastion to smash into the surging Rebel tide. Three Wheatley relatives of Company A went down in the murderous fire. But help suddenly came from the left, or east. Green's Second and Fourth Brigades poured an enfilade fire on the right flank of Davies's unsheltered troops along the crest around Battery Powell and on the Unionists farther eastward. The exposed salient was swept with musketry from the troops of Texas, Alabama, Louisiana, and Mississippi. The combined effect of Green's enfilade fire on their right, the Third Brigade's attack on their left flank, and the Missourians' charge in their front caused some of Davies's formations to crumple and break. Likewise, portions of General Charles S. Hamilton's line were hard-hit and wavered.[50]

The panic among the Unionists grew contagious. More soldiers in blue caught the scare. Additional Federals melted away, fleeing toward Corinth. Emitting screams that practically drowned out the artillery's roar, the onrushing Missouri Rebels continued sprinting toward the ridge-top. With Davies's support on the right around Battery Powell dissolving, the crest position was untenable. The Iowans on the bastion's right wavered under the Rebel onslaught and then were crushed by the butternut avalanche. Battery Powell, the foundation of Rosecrans's defense on the right-center, was now vulnerable as never before with infantry support melting away.

As some of Davies's and Hamilton's units buckled under the shock, Confederate cheers rang over the summit. Despite the odds, Colonel Gates's elated troops were on the verge of driving a wedge between Davies's and Hamilton's divisions just to Battery Powell's left.[51]

Union cannoneers refused to abandon their guns, however, even though some of their infantry support was slipping away. Battery Powell's field pieces continued roaring and ripping mammoth holes into the Rebel mob converging on them. With the bobbing red battle flags of Gates's Missouri Brigade almost on the summit, the commander of the Sixth Wisconsin Battery shouted to his men to hitch their guns to caissons and get out. But in the crowded redoubt, it was too late to flee from the onrushing tide of Missouri Rebels. Terrified artillery horses plunged and reared, tangling reins and making removal of the pieces impossible in the cramped earthwork.

To stop the firepower bellowing from the Wisconsin and United States cannon, McCown's attackers finally sighted muskets on their tormentors. The Missouri Rebels opened a close fire that swept Battery Powell end-to-end. As they tried to manhandle pieces rearward, Federal artillerymen fell in the close volleys that they could not escape. Nothing could now blunt the Missourians' fierce "charge [which] in the history of the war [there was none] more daring or bloody," in the words of one Southerner.[52]

A tidal wave of screaming attackers neared the key to Rosecrans's defenses on the north, Battery Powell. The Missourians blasted away at artillery horses with deadly accuracy, slaughtering animals in bunches. Bullets splintered wood from caissons and limbers, cut reins, and ricocheted off barrels. In the hail of lead, artillery horses fell riddled in their traces by the dozen, sealing the fate of the Wisconsin cannon. Yankee gunners struggled to control horses, while they attempted to hitch field pieces to limbers. The high-pitched yip-yip of onrushing Confederates meanwhile indicated the victors of Battery Powell. Veteran Rebels shot down more artillerymen and horses in the smoky haze. Union cannoneers undoubtedly cut traces from dead animals so makeshift teams could take guns off the field, but it was too late for the Sixth Wisconsin Light and the First United States Artillery trapped in Battery Powell.[53]

Leading his attackers, Captain Fair reached the top with the Fifth Missouri's colors, but he was mortally wounded and dropped the flag. Canister shattered the Englishman's left knee and leg. A soldier grabbed the banner and sped onward. The regimental color guard had long been wiped out. Colonel McCown took a wound in his right wrist, but he continued onward toward the blazing earthwork overflowing with Yankee cannon and defenders.[54]

With almost half of the company leaders of the Fifth Missouri cut down, corporals and sergeants now took over the role of officers. One soldier rising to the challenge after the death of Captain Fair was Sergeant Brennan. The Irish sergeant led Company E through the drifting smoke, racing straight into the cannon's mouths. Artillery blasts dropped handfuls of Rebels, blowing great holes in the onrushing, jumbled horde. Corporal James A. Mitchell went down with a leg smashed by canister shot.[55]

Howling Missouri Confederates at last gained the crest and poured over the high ground en masse. Colonel McCown's Rebels piled into the deep ditch and continued over the parapet with victory cheers. In Company D's van, Captain Lemmon fell with a badly broken right arm. Leading the former Polk County Rangers, Lieutenant Smith was one of the first to scale the earthworks, but he instantly tumbled backward into the ditch when riddled with bullets. As Lieutenant Smith lay dying beside the redoubt's walls, the swarming butternuts smothered Battery Powell and its remaining defenders.

The Fifth Missouri's fifth color bearer of the day planted the blood-red flag atop the fortifications. Yankee artillerymen picked off the first Rebels to appear atop the parapet, but then the Southern masses flooded into the bastion as if a dam had burst. Streaked with dirt and powder, screaming Missourians leaped inside the bastion with gleaming bayonets and prepared to meet the Federals face-to-face in a hell on earth. Some Yankee gunners, meanwhile, prepared for one last shot.[56]

Colonel McCown's attackers dashed up to cannon muzzles, which spat canister for the final time. The foremost Missourians took the full impact of the artillery explosions and were blown to bits. But the Fifth Missouri men kept moving forward and then plunged their bayonets into the remaining defenders. Other Confederates swung musket butts, beating to death those who had wrecked so many comrades' lives. Vicious fighting swirled around the field pieces for hectic minutes during a bloody nightmare that no one would ever forget.

Every Union artilleryman who refused to abandon his gun was killed, wounded, or taken prisoner. The vicious struggle finally ended when the last Wisconsin and United States cannoneers fell. Defiant to the last, the Federal gunners finally went down, resisting to the end with sponge-staffs, fists, and revolvers. But the colors of the Fifth Missouri waving from the breastworks indicated that Battery Powell had fallen. After taking Battery Powell and its plentiful artillery reserves, the frontier Confederates smashed into the remaining infantry support with an abandon and tenacity not often seen. The "Union Brigade," consisting mostly of Iowa farm boys with some Illinois troops, and the Fifty-Second Illinois Volunteer infantry were hurled off the ridge by Colonel Gates's savage onslaught.[57]

As never before, the Missouri Rebels cheered their amazing success. Downhill to the south before them were the all-important intersecting rail lines and the most strategic railroad center in the West, Corinth. At all costs, therefore, the attack had to be resumed. But the price of capturing the strategic redoubt had been fearful. Almost 50 percent of the Fifth Missouri's manpower was now sprawled dead or wounded before the earthworks. Commanders of Companies A, C, D, E, I, and K — Captain Stokely, Lieutenant Smith, Captains Lemmon, Fair, Guthrie, and Pankey, respectively — had been cut down. More than half of the top company leadership of the regiment had been knocked out of action. But a giant hole had been ripped open in Rosecrans's center and right-center by Green's Third Brigade and Gates's First Missouri Brigade, respectively.[58]

Surveying the carnage strewn throughout Battery Powell, Sergeant Ruyle wrote in disbelief: "We had possession of a large number of cannons [totaling nearly seven full batteries] which they had deserted [and] this was one of the bloodiest places I ever saw. On all sides of me I could see both the enemy and our men lying killed and wounded, shot in every way you could think of, groaning and dying in the bleaching sun in the dust which was about six inches deep." No one yet realized the full extent of the Missourians' success on the right-center. But rising smoke gradually lifted to reveal the unbelievable sight. A seemingly endless number of abandoned Federal cannon lined the ridge-top and no Unionists in sight.

Seldom if ever in the war did so few troops — Northern or Southern — capture so many pieces of artillery on a battlefield. The Missouri Brigade, incredibly, claimed an impressive list of prizes: the Battery Powell redoubt and its six 20-pounder Parrotts and six guns of the Sixth Wisconsin Light Artillery, field pieces of some First Missouri Light Artillery companies, and Rosecrans's reserve cannon, consisting of several First United States Artillery companies of large guns. Incredibly, the soldiers of the First Missouri Confederate Brigade captured a total of at least 40 cannon and perhaps more.

Never before had Colonel McCown's veterans seen so many artillery pieces. One Missouri officer wrote in his diary: "Never will I forget the sight that now presented itself to my eyes as I stood upon the breast-works. That our small force had obtained the position they now occupied, could hardly be believed; around us stood about forty pieces of artillery, deserted by the enemy." First Missouri Brigade members held in their possession at Corinth on the morning of October 4 the greatest prize that the Army of West Tennessee would ever win.[59]

But the victory celebrated in and around Battery Powell by the Fifth Missouri conquerors was brief. Batteries Williams, Robinette, and Fort Richardson delivered an enfilading barrage that forced many Fifth Missouri Confederates and other Missouri Brigade veterans to take cover along the crest and within Battery Powell. Here the Rebels caught their breath, bit off cartridges, and reloaded as rapidly as possible in case the Federals launched a counterattack. But large numbers of other Missouri Brigade Rebels raised cheers and continued onward with battle flags flying. The elated horde of Confederates swept past cannons, heaps of dead, and the wreckage of the Union batteries, which had been wiped out. Colonel Gates's troops on the right, with bands of Fifth Missouri soldiers, mingled with Green's brigade to surge forward and widen the gap in Rosecrans's center. After uniting, the brownish-hued masses "swarmed like tigers," wrote one Yankee, off the high ground and down into the valley of Corinth. This renewed Confederate onslaught rolled along the ridge to hit Fort Richardson from the northeast, out-flanking other Federal units. With General Lovell's division for all practical purposes out of action, Price's corps continued attacking alone and without support.[60]

Everywhere could be seen routed Union commands fleeing the field. In addition, Davies's division of three brigades was shattered, along with the left of Hamilton's division to the east of Battery Powell. Roaring like a freight train out of control, Colonel Gates's juggernaut rolled over the ridge and gobbled up more guns in Fort Richardson to Battery Powell's southwest. Packs of Rebels swarmed over the handful of Federal cannoneers like hungry wolves after injured prey. In the final seconds before their five cannon were captured, Missouri artillerymen in blue swung "their rammers high over their heads as the enemy, yelling like demons, surround and literally smother the little squad of men fighting for their guns." After the savage flurry of killing, Fifth Missouri soldiers spun artillery pieces around and sent shells whizzing toward Corinth. With Confederate flags now waving from its earthen walls, Fort Richardson fell to the howling Rebel tide, as had everything else in the path of Gates's hard-fighting Missouri Brigade.[61]

No one was more aware of the center's weakness than "Old Rosey." Massed reserves of Unionists, consequently, stood poised 400 yards to Battery Powell's rear. In addition, Rosecrans had ample troops available for redeployment after the failed Rebel assaults elsewhere. But even some of the rear echelon Union reserves were shaken when hundreds of victorious Confederates charged toward them. Runaway caissons, frightened teams, and streams of panic-stricken bluecoats poured through the reserve formations after they were routed by the Missourians. The Southern attack that pierced the Union right-center now threatened to cut Rosecrans's army in half.[62]

Before the attacking Missouri Brigade, the Fifty-Sixth Illinois, the Tenth Missouri Volunteer Infantry, and the Twelfth Wisconsin Battery stood squarely in the storm's path. In a hollow behind Rosecrans's last reserve line in this sector before Corinth, Union ammunition teamsters panicked. A good many wagons joined the Federal stampede churning rearward toward Corinth. Braced for the onslaught, Yankee formations unleashed a volley "from our whole line on the exultant enemy, who were rushing forward in large masses, flushed and yelling at their success," penned one Unionist.

But the cheering Rebels kept coming, charging into the streets and plaza of Corinth, capturing Rosecrans's headquarters and nearly taking the Union army's supply trains. Now hundreds of grayclads from primarily the Third Brigade and portions of Colonel Gates's First Missouri Brigade as well surged through the town "with a yell of triumph[,] hopefully trusting to greet there Lovell's command equally successful on [Corinth's west] side." With Lovell's failure to strike a meaningful blow on the right, however, "the [only] greeting they received was the red hand of carnage & of death."

At this crucial juncture, with victory in sight on the right-center, the six Wisconsin cannon roared furiously. Double-shot loads of canister left the ground littered with horses, piles of bodies, and flags in one tangled mass, the remains of some of Colonels Gates's and McCown's finest troops. Indeed, wrote one Yankee, "never could any battery do more effective service at a more critical period."[63]

Also blowing McCown's men to bits were the rows of cannon belonging to the Eleventh Ohio Light Artillery and another company of the First Missouri Light Artillery. Simultaneously Union divisions on both sides of the break blasted into the flanks of the butternut horde. The gap bored into Rosecrans's line grew smaller with each passing minute. Now, with clumps of downed attackers seemingly scattered everywhere, the momentum of what appeared to be one of the most successful charges of the war was broken.[64]

With their dead and wounded littering the ground in bunches, Missouri Brigade survivors fell back to the ridge, losing more soldiers and at least one captured United States flag. As wrote one Federal, the punishment was "too much for even rebel courage." Those Fifth Missouri soldiers who had charged upon the town now rejoined their comrades holding Battery Powell and the commanding ground. But some Rebel bands continued to pour over the crest, attacking downhill to meet with certain destruction. But the suicidal charges off the ridges only resulted in more heaps of Confederate bodies, providing a bloody testament of "their fidelity to the cause."[65]

Here, along the bloody ridgetop, Colonel Gates's Missourians, including the survivors of the Fifth Missouri, made their stand to fight against fate and the inevitable counterattack. The Missourians were not yet ready to abandon at least 40 pieces of artillery won by so much blood and effort. If Van Dorn hurled still more Southerners into the breach, perhaps success could yet be gained. But poor Confederate timing and the lack of support throughout October 4 would continue to snatch defeat from the jaws of victory. As minutes passed, more Federal regiments, both fresh and rallied units, converged on the ever-narrowing gap. Hanging precariously to the toehold inside and around the redoubt of Battery Powell, Fifth Missouri soldiers and other Missouri Brigade members now took even more punishment: "a fatal cross-fire was enfilading us, and more than half our men were killed and wounded," explained Lieutenant Colonel Bevier in his description of the horror.[66]

Fighting against impossible odds as thousands of Yankees swarmed forward to retake Battery Powell and seal the gaping hole in Rosecrans's line, Sergeant Hogan was "shot in the head, just above the forehead, at one of the forts which our brigade had taken; not, however, without having some narrow escapes." Hit by raking musketry from three sides, McCown's survivors rapidly loaded and fired while they were pinned down. More Confederates dropped after they were struck with minié balls from different directions. One Fifth Missouri Rebel described the nightmare on the bloody ridge-top of Corinth: "Every second it seemed I could see some comrade fall dead or wounded." Battery Powell, Fort Richardson, and the open ridgetop were now death traps for the Missouri defenders.[67]

Outnumbered Rebels furiously bit off cartridges as they loaded, and blood flowed from their parched, cracked lips. Dust and sulfurous smoke choked throats under a hot sun. But worst of all, the cartridge boxes of the Missourians were almost empty. Fighting against fate, Private Absalom

Dyson blasted away with his musket until he "received a wound in my right arm between the wrist and elbow which was quite an ugly affair [and] also received a wound from a ball just behind my ear." No doubt his younger brother, Private Elam Dyson, the youngest of five Company E brothers, who had been shot in the stomach at Pea Ridge, assisted Absalom as best he could.[68]

The Missouri Confederates hung to their gains tenaciously, praying for succor before they were wiped out. There was nothing left to do, according to Sergeant Ruyle, but continue standing "up side by side, [while Colonel McCown's troops] fought and died like men and true patriots." Many soldiers had already expended their forty rounds. Consequently, some diehard Rebels prepared to defend Battery Powell with bayonets and musket butts. Other Missouri boys grabbed rounds from the cartridge boxes of dead comrades and fought on with renewed desperation. Armed with .69 caliber smoothbores, the Fifth Missouri defenders could not use the smaller sized Federal ammunition from the cartridge boxes of Yankee dead and wounded. Rebel gunfire, consequently, diminished from the ridge overlooking Corinth at the most critical time.[69]

The dilemma of the Fifth Missouri soldiers around Battery Powell grew more desperate according to Lieutenant Colonel Bevier, for his men held the "inside [of] the breastworks of the foe, and hold a portion of their guns; and if Cabell [General William L. Cabell, commanding an Arkansas brigade of Maury's division] only would come! Why don't they help us on the right? A division hurled in that direction would attract that terrible cross-fire which is turned upon us because it has nothing to do in front [Lovell's sector] of it. But we expect in vain. Imploring eyes are cast around to see if no help is at hand." As Colonel McCown's band was further decimated, not only Lovell's troops remained largely inactive, but also Cabell's regiments were idle only 700 yards away awaiting orders to charge. The Fifth Missouri and her sister regiments of the Missouri Brigade were left to fight and die alone around Battery Powell and Fort Richardson. No officer, unfortunately, had bothered to direct Cabell's Arkansans to follow closely upon the Missourians' heels to exploit the break.[70]

To the Missouri Confederates, it appeared that Rosecrans's whole army, meanwhile, now surged upon Battery Powell and Fort Richardson. Through drifting smoke, surviving Fifth Missouri Rebels spied lengthy formations of unidentified troops sweeping toward them from the left. It looked as if Green's Second and Third Brigades had finally broken through and rolled up the Unionists' flank. It seemed possible that victory was yet at hand for the Missourians, but it would never be. Only after anxious seconds did the truth unfold to the outnumbered defenders on the ridgetop. In Bevier's words, the onrushing columns were "not for us. Long, dark lines of Federal infantry we perceive, beneath the dim cloud of powder smoke that lowers over the field, moving swiftly against us." The only relief for the stranded Missouri Confederates along the ridge-top would come with bullet holes.[71]

Without help, luck, or cartridges, the Fifth Missouri, and the Missouri Brigade as well, did not have a chance. The steamrolling blue avalanche could not be slowed with either meaningless heroics or cold steel. Some of Colonel McCown's survivors, probably cursing incompetent Southern leadership and capable Union leadership, felt like dying in the captured forts beside the rows of artillery rather than running for their lives. Everything had happened so quickly in the first big battle east of the Mississippi. Indeed, one minute they were on the verge of success, the next they faced a stunning defeat. Now for the doomed Missouri Confederates, "to stand their ground was but ingloriously to die." Nevertheless, the Westerners in gray and butternut continued to hold their ground stubbornly and face a cruel fate.[72]

With the end near, Colonel McCown's men were unable to disable the vast array of captured Union artillery. The attackers failed to bring any spiking equipment with them when they broke through Rosecrans's line. As Cabell's Arkansas brigade belatedly hastened forward to solidify the Missourians' gains, Union masses prepared to close in for the kill. The aggressive colonel of the Tenth Missouri reasoned that a bayonet charge would sweep his fellow staters of Colonel McCown's regiment off the bloody ridge. With blue battle flags leading the way, the Missouri and Illinois regiments were the foremost units in the counterattack to recapture more than three dozen cannon with fixed bayonets. Rallied "Union Brigade" units, including some regiments of General Jeremiah C. Sullivan's brigade and other commands followed as well, adding impetus to the charge that could not be stopped.

Surging toward the crest in the Missouri Union regiment came Macon County soldiers and former McGee College classmates of some of the members of Captain Guthrie's Company I, another example of the brothers' war. While Union hurrahs echoed closer and louder, the surviving handful of McCown's infantrymen aimed their last rounds into the wall of steel bayonets glistening in the early autumn sunlight. A close volley of buckshot and ball from the Rebels swept the head of the hollow, dropping the foremost counterattackers, including fellow Missouri Yankees. But the point-blank fire could not slow the momentum of the blue tide pouring out of the hollow. As the charging Tenth Missouri converged on Battery Powell with cheers, the bullet-tattered banner of the Fifth Missouri still waved from the earthwork's parapet, which was strewn with bodies of both blue and gray.[73]

But to remain beside the regimental flag in the face of the fierce Union counterattack now meant suicide. Unwilling to give up at least 40 cannon even at the last moment, Colonel McCown finally choked out the most painful order that he was ever forced to give: the order to abandon Battery Powell and Rosecrans's reserve artillery. After receiving the order to withdraw, the Missourians could only curse at the directive that meant defeat. For McCown's veterans, the hardest part was to abandon their many wounded comrades to the victorious Federals. As Union cheers that proclaimed victory grew nearer, some butternuts said good-byes to injured friends and relatives for what they knew would probably be the last time. The bloody ridge of Battery Powell had now become a graveyard for the Fifth Missouri and Colonel Gates's "Old Guard" Missouri Brigade as well.[74]

Amid the carnage and piles of bodies, Lieutenant Colonel Bevier kneeled beside Lieutenant Stephen M. Hendricks, a former McGee College instructor and "a dear friend." Like so many other Fifth Missouri Rebels, the scholarly Hendricks, shot in the head, lay splattered in blood within Battery Powell. A semiconscious Hendricks, age twenty-seven, still gasped for breath in the noon heat and suffocating battle smoke. Knowing that the popular young officer would never survive, the lieutenant colonel mumbled a brief, emotional farewell before joining the Rebel throng streaming off the ridge. The redoubt of Battery Powell and the ridge-top attested to the Missouri Brigade's desperate but futile efforts to win the day, for the "ground was literally covered with the dead and wounded of both friend and foe, the killed and wounded of the enemy being nearly if nt fully two to our one." Perhaps some of his former students-turned-captors in blue of the Tenth Missouri would help make Lieutenant Hendricks's last moments less painful.[75]

Life and death were at stake during the frantic race off the ridge to the woodline more than 300 yards distant. Some Confederates huddled in the deep ditch and abatis to be captured. After retiring through the fallen timber and reflecting upon the horror of October 4, the Fifth Missouri's survivors slowly began to realize the terrible cost of the attack. Indeed, dozens of regimental comrades "were [last] seen in heaps, having fallen across one another." Within and around the deserted bastion of Battery Powell, six 20-pound Parrotts and six field pieces stood unspiked because the Confederates had brought no hammers or rat-tail files with them. Consequently, all of those large caliber pieces, the Wisconsin guns, and the clusters of reserve artillery remained untouched. Now the rows of cannon which had killed so many Missouri Confederates stood alone as silent sentinels watching over the heaps of the dead of both armies. At least two score artillery pieces of Rosecrans's army were arrayed exactly where they had been captured, waiting in place to be retaken after the surviving Missourians departed.[76]

Hundreds of blueclads meanwhile raced to gain the crest, shouting and cheering their success. Fifth Missouri soldiers sprinted down the slope as they had never run before. A mob of hundreds of disorganized Rebels covered the ground before the earthworks drenched in smoke. Blue waves of Tenth Missouri attackers shortly overran Battery Powell, while the Fifty-Sixth Illinois poured through Fort Richardson like an avalanche. Here a handful of desperate Missouri officers still struggled to rally their survivors for a fight to the death. In yet another bloody encounter exemplifying the horror of the brothers' war, the Yankees of the Tenth Missouri drove Fifth Missouri Confederates out of Battery Powell in a bitter flurry of savage fighting with bayonets, fists, and musket butts. At last, after some of the most vicious fighting seen at Corinth, the Union right-center was secured.

In addition, Green's Third Brigade to the west had been hurled from the avenues of Corinth along with elements of the First Missouri Brigade. As expected, losses among the attackers had been frightfully high. The gap that had been torn open so wide by the two Confederate brigades of Price's First Division was now slammed shut forever. Every Southerner left within the forts was either killed, wounded, or captured by the onrushing blue tide. General Rosecrans had thwarted the most serious challenge of the day, repulsing the Rebel assault on his center and right-center.[77]

One of the last Fifth Missouri boys to depart the nightmarish ridge-top that day was Lieutenant William B. McCarty, a Warrensburg carpenter. Dashing only a few yards down the slope, McCarty was thunderstruck to turn and see the tattered Fifth Missouri's colors, half-obscured in the smoke shrouding Battery Powell, still atop the parapet. With the color guard of the Fifth Missouri annihilated, the flag had been forgotten during the hasty withdrawal. Running back uphill, McCarty made an audacious attempt to retrieve the bullet-shredded banner. The Kentucky-born lieutenant snatched the colors off the parapet with a mob of Tenth Missouri Unionists only ten feet away. Disbelieving their eyes, the bluecoats were initially too startled to take aim and fire on the ghostlike apparition of an apparently half-crazed Confederate soldier suddenly popping out of the dense smoke in their midst. Against the odds, Lieutenant McCarty, age twenty-three, carried the prize safely off the ridge, saving the precious regimental colors of the Fifth Missouri from the ultimate humiliation: capture by "renegade Missourians," which was the derogatory name given to Missouri Yankees by Missouri Brigade members.[78]

The contest soon turned into a fox-hunt style chase for the victorious Federals, who enjoyed inflicting damage and exacting revenge on their fellow Missourians in gray. A Tenth Missouri soldier recalled how "every man [was] trying his best to reach the top of the hill first, to get the best shot at them." Hundreds of Yankees aligned along the high ground and opened a murderous fire after gaining the crest. Fleeing for their lives, the fast-moving Rebels now blanketed the slopes as far as the eye could see. Hit in midflight, additional Southerners dropped dead or wounded when the murderous volleys swept down the hillside. Private John B. Trammel, a twenty-year-old Macon County farmer, took a minié ball in the back. Other Fifth Missouri men went down, including Tennessee-born Private William E. Fullerton, age twenty-two, who tumbled down the slope when a bullet tore into his heel.[79]

Having only recently escaped disaster themselves from the most devastating Rebel attack that they had ever seen, the Federals delivered punishment upon the exposed Southerners without mercy. Many Missouri men received their death strokes before they reached the woodlands bordering the creek. Colonel Gates's survivors ran a deadly gauntlet, taking the wrath of Union infantry and artillery from rear and flank. The slaughter among the Missouri Confederates caused one Fifty-Sixth Illinois soldier to write, "our voleys [sic] mows them down as grain before the sickle."[80]

The cannon of Battery Powell and those artillery pieces in its vicinity were also turned upon the fleeing Confederates. The Twelfth Wisconsin Battery, the Missourians' nemesis that day, rumbled up to unlimber along the ridge-top and then hammered McCown's survivors in wild flight. Sickened by the killing, General Price could not believe the sight of his best troops being so severely punished and now running for the first time. "Old Pap" openly wept, exclaiming: "My God! my boys are running! How could they do otherwise — they had no support — they are nearly all killed." By any measure, the butchery of Corinth was unprecedented, as had been the Missouri Confederates' fierce "assault on so formidable a fortification [which] has never been excelled on any field."[81]

Once clear of the killing zone, Colonel McCown's officers attempted to rally the decimated regiment. But many Fifth Missouri soldiers continued heading rearward "in spite of all officers" and their efforts to rally the command. Moving across the same hard-fought ground where his Company F had lately distinguished itself in the skirmish contest, Captain Canniff might have reflected with bitterness upon how 20 out of his 35 prized Irish skirmishers had been killed or wounded. One casualty of Company F included dying Private Patrick McGrath, age twenty-six. He had journeyed from St. Louis the preceding summer with the express purpose of joining the famous Emerald Isle company, but he found death, not glory, at Corinth.[82]

Not until they reached the timber would Fifth Missouri survivors rally largely on their own, especially after so many officers had been killed. Fortunately for the Rebels, Rosecrans decided against an immediate pursuit, which would have dealt perhaps a fatal blow to Van Dorn's army. While basking in the glow of decisively repulsing Southern attacks all along the line, "Old Rosey" perhaps let a complete victory slip away.[83]

Victories in the West for the Confederacy continued to be ever-elusive. Superior Union generalship, firepower, logistics, and materiel had once more saved the day, the usual equation for Federal victory in the Western war. The desperate Confederate gamble to snatch Corinth under Grant's nose had resulted in disaster and devastating losses. Southern blunders and miscalculations had allowed the worst scenario to become a brutal reality for Confederate fortunes once more. Van Dorn's careless strategy, approach, and attack upon Corinth failed to assist Bragg's invasion of Kentucky as planned. The only bright spot for the South was the resolve of the common soldier in the ranks, which failed to dim with the disaster.

But the dream of a decisive Confederate victory that would help guarantee independence would never become a reality. Now there would be no triumphant march into Kentucky and Tennessee to assist Bragg's northern invasion.

The addition of the Army of West Tennessee might have been decisive in providing the conquests in the Kentucky Bluegrass necessary for foreign recognition and independence. After hurling back Van Dorn's offensive, General Grant now would hasten reinforcements north to help thwart the last legitimate Northern offensive carried out by the Confederacy west of the Appalachian Mountains. The South's high-water mark in the West would consequently ebb before mid–October 1862. In addition, the Missouri Rebels' all-consuming ambition of invading their home state likewise receded with Confederate fortunes. From now on, Western Rebels would fight little more than losing battles without regaining a comparable offensive thrust in the West.[84]

Corinth's nightmare had only begun for the thousands of Rebel wounded. As at Iuka, Surgeon Dysart stayed behind to care for the multitude of injured Rebels. The Fifth Missouri had suffered severely at Corinth, establishing a pattern of high losses which would not cease until the end of the war. Official reports indicate that the Fifth Missouri lost 6 killed, 62 wounded, and 19 missing, a total of 87 casualties. But these figures underestimate the full cost. For instance, a Fifth Missourian immediately after the battle wrote in his journal that 100 of Colonel McCown's Rebels were cut down out of the 225 Fifth Missouri soldiers who charged the fortifications of Corinth. Lieutenant Colonel Bevier wrote that the Fifth Missouri lost more than half of its strength, at least 113 soldiers, but probably more of Colonel McCown's men were lost at Corinth. Clearly, the Fifth Missouri at the battle of Corinth lost many more dead than the 6 killed that the official records figure indicates. Counting those soldiers who later died in hospitals from Corinth injuries, the actual loss of Fifth Missouri dead would eventually swell to 25 soldiers.[85]

Among those regimental members killed or soon perishing were: Privates McGrath, Miles Hollowell, John Martin Wheatley, W. Miller,

John Henry Miller, James Lawrence Henry, Daniel D. Shawver, George M. Huntsman, William Maley, W. They, John Gregory, George Washington Sears, William L. King, Joseph W. Chapman, and William Mallony. Fatalities among noncommissioned officers included Corporal James D. Richardson, Sergeants Walsh and Epaminondas A. Smith, a Kentucky-born teacher from Warrensburg. Earlier in the war, a Confederate recalled the Company A sergeant with the Biblical first name who had led General Price's personal escort, "a very fine company numbering 114 men ... whose captain rejoiced in the euphonious name of Epaminondas A. Smith."[86]

The officer corps of the Fifth Missouri had been badly chewed up at Corinth. Captain Fair, Lieutenants John Fletcher Boone, Hendricks, Patrick H. Gallaher, an Irishman, Hugh M. C. Gray, Joseph G. Parsons, and Fountain F. Smith were killed or were shortly to die. Many of the Fifth Missouri's best and brightest were sacrificed in the bloodbath at Corinth, one of the most sanguinary contests of the war. Van Dorn lost nearly 5,000 troops on one short October morning. In contrast, Rosecrans suffered about half as many casualties in a key victory in the West at a critical time, a victory which helped the Confederacy along the road to extinction.[87]

At least 19 of McCown's soldiers could not be accounted for after Corinth's storm passed. A number of Fifth Missouri Rebels charged into Corinth's valley of death never to be seen again. No one knew if comrades were killed in action or lay rotting in hospitals or prison camps. As late as 1865, for example, Fifth Missouri Confederates would still be attempting to ascertain the fate of Lieutenant Boone, a nineteen-year-old farmer. The Company I officer had been last "seen in the works during the charge of 4 Oct and when we were repulsed was seen no more." Unknown to his family in Columbus, Johnson County, Boone had been killed in the attack on Corinth.[88]

Seldom would information of the fates of soldier-relatives filter through the Union lines and back to Federal-occupied Missouri. But whenever such tragic news came to families, it usually appeared months after the battle. Not until December of 1862, would a Company E, Fifth Missouri, Confederate report to the home folk that Private Benjamin Franklin McCulloch, a twenty-two-year-old farmer of Franklin County who was listed as killed at Corinth, "is yet living & doing well & wishes you to convey word to his parents at St. Clair [Missouri]." One rare instance of the public notification of the death of a Fifth Missouri soldier to reach a St. Louis family would appear on February 1, 1863. The Walsh family of St. Louis printed the following in the obituary section of a major city newspaper: "Walsh, Sgt. William of Co. F, 5th Reg Mo Vols C.S.A., killed at Corinth, MS; he had written poetry published in local papers signed Wilhelm."[89]

This would be the only listing of a Confederate killed at Corinth in St. Louis's newspapers. The obituary was a tribute to one of the Fifth Missouri's first heroes killed in action. Many of McCown's soldiers would gain recognition for Corinth valor.

Perhaps because they captured Union flags or artillery, or inspired their comrades forward, 12 soldiers of Company E earned "mention for bravery at Corinth." This group honored by comrades consisted of 3 sergeants, 1 corporal, and 8 privates. The most distinguished of these soldiers was handsome Sergeant John Brennan. He "behaved admirably" on October 4 and was one of the main driving force behind Company E. Lately a St. Louis machinist, the Ireland-born Brennan could make his men want to follow him to hell and back if necessary. Sergeant Brennan would be killed before the war's conclusion. Of the 12 Company E soldiers cited for gallantry at Corinth, 7 would be dead in less than two years. The heroic feats of the men of Company E were not exclusive to that one unit. One of McCown's officers wrote that "on the glacis north of Corinth every man was a hero." Raw courage demonstrated by the ragged Confederates had not been enough to win Corinth or bring victory in the West, however.[90]

# IV

## LULL BEFORE THE STORM

After barely escaping two Union forces, General Edward Otho Cresap Ord from the west and Rosecrans from the east, and avoiding entrapment and perhaps destruction between the Hatchie and Tuscumbia rivers on October 5, the badly bruised Army of West Tennessee retired deeper into the safety of Mississippi. Once more the Fifth Missouri played a key role in protecting the rear of a withdrawing and roughly handled Rebel army. Captain Canniff and his Company F were conspicuous in this rear-guard duty as in the past. Less than 130 men made up what remained of the Fifth Missouri when it encamped just below Holly Springs on October 10.

With the Fifth Missouri's ranks decimated by more than 50 percent casualties at Corinth, company leadership was restructured. Since Captain Stokely lay near death in an Iuka hospital, Lieutenant Barnett J. Atkinson took over Company A. Company B also lost its leader when Captain Trumper deserted and became a Federal sutler. Now commanding the company was Captain Samuel G. Hale.

The rainy and dreary winter of 1862-63 would see the arrival of Captain Bradford, who had recovered from disease to once more command Company C. Seventeen soldiers of Company D were cut down at Corinth; this was a higher number than those men remaining now for duty. After Captain Lemmon's death at Corinth, Lieutenant William Hughes Lemmon, a younger brother, assumed the leadership of Company D.

Captain Fair of Company E had been captured and carried to what soon became a vast sea of human suffering engulfing tiny Iuka, where he died in a hospital. Filling Captain Fair's place to take charge of Company E was Lieutenant Matthew Townsend. Matt's twin brother, Edmund, had been wounded and captured at Corinth. As usual, Captain Canniff had escaped Corinth's wrath and retained command of Company F. Change came to Company G when Captain Thomas finally resigned that winter to the great relief of everyone among the enlisted ranks. A most dependable replacement, Captain Noah Grant took charge of the unit.

Company I had been fortunate at Corinth, not taking high losses among its leadership as had most Fifth Missouri companies. The ever-reliable Captain Guthrie remained in command despite a hand wound suffered at Corinth. Undergoing considerable change was Company K. Captain Pankey made his way back to Missouri to heal from a Corinth wound. Soon Lieutenant Ferrel Bennett Spicer, age twenty-three, took over Company K. But he had to wait for a Corinth thigh wound to mend before he could lead the former Swamp Foxes of the Missouri Bootheel region.

Despite the devastating losses of Corinth, the winter of 1862-63 found the Fifth Missouri more consolidated and even stronger in some ways. Indeed, the overall quality of leadership had not dropped dramatically. Enough soldiers of ability remained in McCown's ranks to fill the voids. In fact, the fall campaign weeded out those commanders such as Captain Trumper who had lacked both resolve and ability. Incompetent leaders like Captain Thomas also left after Corinth. The solidification of the officer corps of the Fifth Missouri left a body of "good and kind officers," noted Warren in his diary. Those men who were less dedicated simply quit the struggle and went home after the nightmare of Corinth. By this period, wrote one of McCown's soldiers, "Our numbers have been terribly reduced. Regments [sic] that numbered last spring when we entered Miss[issippi] 7 or 800 men, can scarcely muster 2 & 300 men [but] what are left are Veterans." Indeed, the Fifth Missouri was now superior in terms of leadership and experience than it had been at Saltillo. Political-type officers, who talked much and fought little, had been exposed by this time. From now on, company commanders would remain with their units until they met with death, crippling wounds, or the struggle's conclusion.[1]

Other changes came for the veteran soldiers of the Fifth Missouri by the autumn of 1862. A subtle maturation and great commitment evolved with the long months of hardship and realization of the war's realities. Away from the farm for the first time, beardless boys became men and hardened veterans. New attitudes, for instance, developed from association with Confederates from the Gulf Coast, middle Tennessee, the Kentucky Bluegrass, the cotton plantations of Mississippi, and the French-speaking Creole regions of Louisiana. Marching, fighting, and dying together forged divergent elements of the Western army into one soldiery. Provincialism was replaced with a stronger and deeper Southern nationalism. Fewer petty jealousies and rivalries now existed among the men than existed in the summer of 1861. Indeed, the ever-observant Private Dyson detected the transformation, noting in a letter how "all of us boys are stronger for the South than we were before we left home."

By this time, the Missouri Rebels had become much more open-minded and less provincial. Just a year ago, for instance, as much animosity had existed among the Missourians for General Ben McCulloch's Trans-Mississippi Rebels as for General Nathaniel Lyon's United States regulars. And only two years before, the Polk County Rangers, now of Company C, were indignant when St. Louis militiamen of the Southwest Expedition had marched to the Missouri-Kansas border to assist them in deterring the raids of Jayhawkers. These proud Missouri Rangers of the frontier declared that they needed no "St. Louis dandies" to come to their aid. But burying a good many comrades in the red clay soil of Mississippi, becoming adopted members of Southern families, and defending a strange land that they had never seen before caused Colonel McCown's soldiers to gain new perspectives and lose old prejudices. Time, experience, and sacrifice bound the Missourians' hopes and aspirations to Rebels from Texas, Alabama, Mississippi, Louisiana, and Tennessee. As the narrow provincialism of states' rights mentalities diminished, the common goal of winning independence for the Confederate nation became paramount for McCown's warriors in gray.[2]

Clothing shortages grew acute as December winds howled and the weather became colder. As throughout the conflict, shoes were in short supply for the exiles stranded on the east side of the Mississippi. Many Missouri boys stood barefoot during roll call on frosty mornings. Lieutenant Warren, therefore, boarded a train at Grenada for the 300-mile journey southeastward to the Gulf port of Mobile. The young officer with a sound business background was a good choice for the assignment of shoe procurement. Mature and responsible, he was not the type to indulge in booze, fine food, and prostitutes in the South's wildest city.[3]

As the days shortened toward the year's end, cold rains and cold winds lashed the Fifth Missouri's encampment along the dark Yalobusha. When they were not holed up in tents during the deluge, Colonel McCown's soldiers drilled four hours a day. Occasionally these exercises were conducted by General Bowen, who was now division commander and a martinet. Granted a winter reprieve from battle, the Fifth Missouri Rebels perfected already legendary discipline and drill skills for the upcoming spring campaign. During a late October review, for example, Colonel McCown's men and other Missourians were singled out by a Confederate general, who reported to President Davis of the exiles' drill proficiency: "I have attended reviews of the armies of General Pierre G. T. Beauregard, Bragg, Albert Sidney, and Joseph E. Johnston, and also in the old United States service, and I have never seen a finer looking body of men nor of more soldierly appearance and efficiency, nor have I ever witnessed better drill or discipline in any army since I have belonged to the military service." Such praise for the elite soldiers of the Fifth Missouri would be common during this fall and winter.[4]

Indeed, the First Missouri Brigade's reputation had first been established at Pea Ridge, where the Missourians fought as the army's shock troops. Their performance prompted General Van Dorn to state: "I have never seen better fighters than these Missouri troops." This tradition and legacy of reliability on the battlefield only grew on the east side of the Mississippi. So impressed was General William J. Hardee, the author of *Hardee's Tactics,* that he wrote that the Missourians were "the finest, most efficient, best drilled and most thoroughly disciplined body of troops in the [principal] Army" of the Western theater. And this elite reputation, which had spread across the Confederacy, increased with each passing month. Another Southern general, Dabney E. Maury, admitted, "the Missouri troops of the Army of the West were not surpassed by any troops in the world." During this fine-tuning period of winter, consequently, one of the Fifth Missourians' favorite anecdotes described a popular Confederate general inquiring during a review of an Arkansan, "Where is your cap box, sir?" The private then loudly asked Joseph E. Johnston, "What do I want with a cap box with this damned old Flint Lock musket?" As never before, intensive and hard drilling now became a way of life for McCown's troops.[5]

When the Fifth Missouri joined this crack Missouri Brigade, standards were raised in the regiment to new heights. And no one did more to improve Colonel McCown's regiment than Captain Canniff. To meet the challenge, the Fifth Missouri had the good fortune of containing the nucleus of the best-drilled unit of the Missouri State Guard in 1861, the Irish soldiers formerly of the prewar militia and now Company F. Canniff and his top lieutenants, such as dependable Marnell and Crow, went to work with a zeal. They had already helped transform Price's mob into an effective Rebel army of the Wesern frontier in the war's beginning, so the job of now making good troops even better was a task well suited for such experienced officers. The skills to make elite soldiers had been honed in prewar militia days in St. Louis's parks and streets by these officers, who would now make the Fifth Missouri the most superbly drilled unit, most dependable, and best infantry regiment of the famous Missouri Brigade.[6]

Drilling along the muddy Yalobusha intensified to levels never seen before. McCown and Canniff were determined to make the Fifth Missouri the finest regiment of the Missouri Brigade, and they would succeed in their mission. Even during the seemingly never-ending light rains of winter, Colonel McCown's already highly disciplined butternuts splashed through the river bottoms in neat formations for long hours amid the mud and water to perfect their craft. One Missourian complained that his officers would "turn loose and drill us till the tongues hung outen our mouths." The nearly barefoot Confederates of the Fifth Missouri stomped around the bottoms seemingly from sunup to sundown in uniforms which resembled dirty rags. But all the while they were becoming as proficient in drill as the finest regulars in Europe. Indeed, Colonel McCown's men were destined to earn the coveted reputation as being the Confederacy's most expertly and thoroughly trained troops. All the hard work by the soldiers of the Fifth Missouri would pay high dividends during the upcoming Vicksburg campaign. Then the Missourians would earn renown as the Confederacy's "unsurpassed Brigade," "the noble Brigade," and "the gallant ... Missouri brigade" from none other than President Davis.[7]

One Company A, Fifth Missouri, soldier who grew especially weary of the drizzle, mud, and drilling at the winter encampment was Private Benjamin Wheatley, the last surviving Rebel of the six Wheatley clan idealists from western Missouri. By any measure, the year of 1862 had been one of tough luck for the family from southeast Johnson County. A cruel fate began to alter the destiny of the Wheatley family in 1859, when the Wheatleys left the Blue Ridge Mountains of Wilkes County, located in northwest North Carolina near the Virginia border, and headed west for Missouri. Once the war began in Missouri, some of the Wheatley Tar Heels fired the first Rebel shots in Johnson County. Union Home Guards from the German settlement of Knob Knoster only a mile to the east had struck the Wheatley settlement in retaliation. Initially, under the leadership of their elder statesman, fifty-two-year-old William W. Wheatley, Sr., and Benjamin's father, who was later killed at Wilson's Creek, the clan had resisted the "Hessian" invasion. In defending their homeland as hard-riding partisans, the outnumbered Wheatleys were hunted as "bushwhackers" and were persecuted accordingly.[8]

Well-organized bands of Unionists had chased eight Wheatley men, ranging from ages sixteen to fifty-two, out of Johnson County, and General Price soon had these North Carolinians in his ranks. Ill fortune continued to haunt the Wheatley Rebels. The youngest Wheatley soon died of disease, while another departed the army because of sickness. William L. Wheatley was also in bad health and had been left behind in an Arkansas hospital. The remaining five Wheatleys now in Confederate service had marched to the east side of the Mississippi with McCown's battalion.[9]

The Blue Ridge Mountaineers expected William, age thirty-eight, to rejoin them in northeast Mississippi upon his recovery. But William would never rejoin his relatives of Company A, Fifth Missouri, across the Mississippi. Instead of heading for Mississippi, he traveled north after he recovered from his bout with disease and left Arkansas. He finally reached his 87-acre farm in Johnson County late one night, after more than a six-month absence. But instead of a joyful reunion with his wife, William found her in bed with another man, possibly a Unionist to add insult to injury. During the ensuing altercation, the interloper shot and killed the returning butternut, who had survived some of the bloodiest battles in the West, only to die in his own home. Word of William's tragic fate never filtered back to Mississippi. Consequently, the Fifth Missouri soldiers assumed that he had died of disease in Arkansas.[10]

But William's murder would be only the beginning of the tragedies befalling the Wheatleys of Company A. On October 4, three of them were cut down and captured at Corinth. Private George Wheatley, whose son had already perished of illness in a dirty Confederate infirmary, was paroled but was disabled for life. Two brothers, Privates John Martin and James Wheatley, died at a hospital and in an Alton, Illinois, prison, respectively, in early 1863. On November 28, the clan's solitary survivor, Benjamin, also in Company A, was beside Private Calvin Wheatley, when he died of disease in a Mississippi infirmary. After seeing seven relatives wiped out in less than eight months and learning the horrifying news of his civilian in-laws being killed by Union militia back home, Private Benjamin Wheatley remained the clan's lone representative in the ranks of the Fifth Missouri.[11]

The high casualties of the Fifth Missouri at Corinth and deaths in hospitals across Mississippi only emphasized the urgency of liberating the home state before the Missouri Confederates were all killed off east of the Mississippi. It made little sense for Missourians to be slaughtered in the Deep South while the homeland suffered under the reign of Union occupation troops. Sitting out the long and lonely winter in mid–Mississippi with a Confederate army while their homes were only a few hundred miles to the northwest caused much discontent among McCown's exiles. General Price warned President Davis of the rising discord, declaring how "the troops here . . . are clamoring to be led back to Missouri."[12]

President Davis reviewed the Western troops on December 24. Luckily, Missouri Confederates at Grenada did not know the full truth of their fates nor the strategic realities of the West, or President Davis might have seen a mutiny. As deemed by the government at Richmond, Missouri had been forsaken by Confederate strategists since the battle of Pea Ridge.

Vicksburg now remained the top priority in the West for both sides. With Missouri abandoned forever by Rebel strategists and the contest for Vicksburg imminent, General John C. Pemberton was determined to keep the Missouri Confederates with the Vicksburg army east of the Mississippi. This was one of his few wise decisions of the Vicksburg campaign. General Pemberton refused to risk losing his finest troops in the army destined to protect fortress Vicksburg.[13]

President Davis, consequently, played a politician's role at Grenada, covering up geopolitical realities and military necessities to the elite soldiers who would be sacrificed to a futile attempt to save Vicksburg. With a good grasp of the importance of an elite cadre of veteran troops in the defense of the most strategic citadel in the West, President Davis knew that the First Missouri Brigade would become Pemberton's "Old Guard" and would never be sent west. Ignorant as to their fates, Colonel McCown's soldiers would never learn of the fateful decisions of politicians who had already determined their destiny. Nevertheless, five Fifth Missouri boys slipped out of camp in December, heading for home and leaving the Western Rebel army which never won battles.[14]

Colonel McCown's veterans aligned in neat rows at the December 24 review. On the day before Christmas, few soldiers of the Fifth Missouri realized that the President's attitude and the military requirements east of the Mississippi guaranteed they would never be ordered back to Missouri. Therefore, the Fifth Missouri Rebels cheered their President with enthusiasm. Knowing that the Western Confederates already had been sentenced to be sacrificed in his own home state of Mississippi and not their own, Davis "stated that he perceived the necessity of sending the Mo's [Missourians] on the other side [west] of the Miss River, and that it was his intention that we should be sent over in time to commence the Spring Campaign." But before the campaign's end, a large percentage of the Missourians would be lying in shallow graves across the Confederacy thanks to the betrayal of a host of Southern politicians, bureaucrats, and military leaders. Missouri's new Confederate governor, Thomas C. Reynolds, would shortly convince Price to join in a compromise by returning to the Trans-Mississippi without the Missouri Brigade in order to ease political tensions between the state and national government.

An optimistic Private Dyson, destined to die east of the Mississippi like so many others, wrote to his wife that they soon would meet again, for "we will in all probably [sic] cross over into Ark. with our whole division in a few months." Buoyed by President Davis's half-truths, another Fifth Missourian could hardly wait for the long-awaited return to the Trans-Mississippi. He predicted that when the Fifth Missouri crossed to the west side of the "Father of Waters" to "recruit out decimated ranks, depend upon it, we shall make a mark in old Mo yet." Dreams of an imminent invasion of Union-held territory which would never come true fueled the desire to meet the Yankees as soon as possible in a decisive clash.[15]

Exchanged and returning wounded soldiers bolstered the Fifth Missouri's strength throughout the winter. The vast complex of field hospitals in northeastern Mississippi had finally almost emptied. Only the slight mounds of red dirt dotting the landscape around Iuka bore mute testimony to the many Fifth Missouri men who would never rejoin the regiment. One of the last injured Rebels remaining at Iuka was Private Dyson, who related in a letter: "there are not very many in the Hospital now, some gone to the country and others to the command while some have gone to their long home."[16]

The Yuletide season caused much celebration among the Missouri exiles. Dreams of independence still burned brightly in December of 1862. For
Christmas festivities, McCown's men scoured the brown forests bordering
the Yalobusha, hunting for suitable logs with which they could celebrate
soldier-style. Utilizing pioneer skills and ingenuity, these Rebels from the
Western frontier then would "bore a hole in a log and fill it with powder
and drive a pin in it and touch it off, it would roar like a cannon, but this
was against orders." Spare time was spent gathering enough food from the
surrounding countryside for feasting on a scale not yet seen by the exiles
in Mississippi. Christmas Eve led to wild celebration. As one Fifth Missouri
officer wrote in his diary: "Many of the soldiers drunk on whisky . . . at
night much confusion in camp, firing of guns & pistols. Some making
speeches some swearing & fighting & some gambling." While enlisted men
played pranks, shot off their homemade wooden cannon, and drank rotgut
whiskey, Fifth Missouri officers dined at the stately mansion of a leading
cotton planter. Western frontiersmen of middle-class origins were mixing
with the South's upper class for the first time in their lives. Although socioeconomically they were closer to the native "crackers," who would not get
through an aristocrat's front door, than to Southern aristocrats, McCown's
largely slaveless yeomen were now suddenly social equals with the planter
class elite of the Deep South. Gold braid on uniform sleeves and an invading Union army on Mississippi soil broke down class distinctions and
fostered a social acceptance in war not seen in peacetime. Fifth Missouri
officers drank toasts throughout much the night, hoping that the ill-fortune
and the bitter defeats of 1862 would not be repeated in 1863.[17]

Confidence and optimism were high among McCown's Confederates.
The defeat of Grant and a successful spring campaign in Mississippi might
bring foreign recognition and independence to the fledgling Southern nation. Lieutenant Colonel Bevier felt optimistic and recorded: "The northwest is becoming dissatisfied; the [Horace] Greeley faction are talking of
peace; France is muttering threats of intervention." But the common
soldiers in the Fifth Missouri's ranks failed to gauge accurately the Northern
people's determination to save the Union. Indeed, the fiber of union would
prove stronger than Southern nationalism. Waiting for such impossibilities
as foreign recognition and a negotiated peace to become reality cost time,
which the Confederacy could not afford to waste in a war of attrition. All
the while, the industrial-technological giant that was the modernized North
churned out a seemingly endless stream of military hardware, materiel, and
supplies, easily mustering the necessary strength to extinguish the flickering
flame of independence of a backward, agrarian nation. Unable to fully
understand how this total war would be determined by the most centralized
war effort of the more modernized society and how God stood on the side
of the heaviest legions, a romantic and naive Lieutenant Colonel Bevier

boldly predicted that the Confederacy would win its bid for independence "ere the end of 1863."[18]

But not all of McCown's soldiers felt optimistic about the future. Seeing only too clearly how the plentiful reserves of Union manpower and firepower had been swiftly mobilized at Corinth to destroy everything that Van Dorn threw at them, a realistic Private Dyson knew the worst loomed ahead for the outnumbered ghosts in gray who were trapped in a brutal war of attrition which was almost impossible for them to win. As if reading into the future, the former schoolteacher wrote in a letter of the many fallen Southern soldiers who were no more, understanding how there eventually would be thousands more to follow for little or no gain. In a sad letter, Dyson solemnly reflected, "It grieves me to know that so many of our friends and relatives [including two Company E relatives] are gone, gone, gone, forever." In the upcoming campaign for Vicksburg, the Missourians would suffer higher casualties than any other Rebel troops in the Vicksburg army.[19]

The new year of 1863, nevertheless, began in grand style, beguiling a cruel reality. On January 1, Lieutenant Warren instantly raised morale when he arrived from his Mobile mission. With much fanfare, he distributed 120 pairs of shoes and 100 pairs of wool socks to soldiers in great need, including those who were barefoot. Indeed, it had been a thankful Thursday and seemingly a good start to the new year for the men of the Fifth Missouri. The year's first day could have been much better for McCown's soldiers, however, because on his return trip, Lieutenant Warren accidentally broke a precious five-gallon jug of apple brandy that cost $120 in script. This inflated price indicates the Confederacy's inability to finance its war effort except by printing money; the resulting inflation helped undermine an already fragile economy and diminish the Southern people's will to resist.

The never-ending regime of drills and rains continued with hardly a break. During one downpour which trapped everyone in the encampment, an officer of the Fifth Missouri lamented in his diary: "It has been raining all day and everything is flooded with water. We have been amusing ourselves in the Tent, playing 'seven-up.'" These card-playing gamblers naturally stayed out of sight of Chaplains Atwood and Bannon. Soldiers also found merriment in dancing to music and fiddling well into the night, enlivening the dark winter nights in the Missouri frontier tradition.[20]

January 8 proved to be a memorable day. Most Fifth Missouri men, believing President Davis's inspiring words about their imminent return to the Mississippi's west side, signed up for the war's duration. An ever-optimistic Lieutenant Warren, blind to the truth, bragged in his diary: "All of the twelve months men have been continued in the service for the War. All over the ages of 45 will get their discharge in three months after their term of enlistment expires. I am sorry to say that there has been some cases of desertion among the 12 months men. ... Our company [E] have reenlisted for the War." Now Fifth Missouri soldiers had linked their destinies closer with an indifferent centralized government in Richmond, which maneuvered them like pawns and manipulated them beyond their comprehension. These Missourians were now destined to fight and die for years east of the Mississippi. As the dream of liberating the home state faded farther away and became a myth, McCown's soliers had in reality signed up to serve as little more than "cannon fodder" for interests other than their own and in defense of states and peoples east of the Mississippi and hundreds of miles from their homes.[21]

The greatest problem confronting Colonel McCown during this quiet period before the storm was the large numbers of "hospital rats" of the Fifth Missouri. Admitted weeks or even months before by Surgeon Dysart for valid reasons, the "rats" found hospital life soft and comfortable. They consequently decided to stay in the infirmary because it was an ideal place to escape the endless drilling. Indeed, life in the infirmary was something like a vacation, with no early morning roll call, picket duty in the rain, nor gathering wood for fires or cooking. These Rebel shammers were healthy enough to leave the hospital and successfully raid the regimental commissary department, where they stole two barrels of whiskey. Putting them back into the Fifth Missouri's ranks became one of the colonel's top priorities. But the problem of the "hospital rats" would be temporarily forgotten during the New Year's Eve celebration.

For young Fifth Missouri officers attending balls in Grenada, all that mattered was to get drunk, find a lover for the night or a mate for life, and dance as long as possible into the morning hours. There would be no limits on New Year's Eve just as there seemed to be no limit to the conflict's increasing destruction and cruelty. Indeed, the grim prospect of incredibly brutal and bloody fighting, as at Corinth, would become commonplace from now on.[22]

The year 1862 had been disastrous for the young Confederacy. The year had started badly with the forsaking of Missouri, the summer was disease-ridden and without glory, and the fall brought the slaughter at Corinth. The Fifth Missouri suffered more than 50 percent casualties on that one October morning in a man-made hell in northeast Mississippi. But, ironically, the greatest loss for these Missouri Confederates did not come from Union bullets and shells. The ravages of diarrhea, pneumonia, and typhoid fever had taken more lives during the four months since the completion of the Fifth Missouri's organization than the military might of the Yankee army. Without adequate medicine, sanitation, and diet, disease proved to be the foe that could never be defeated. A Fifth Missouri officer reflected on the past twelve months of struggle in Missouri, Arkansas, and

Mississippi: "It has been a year of stirring events and stern realities. Its beginning found me quietly domiciled in Springfield, Missouri; its ending reaches me a thousand miles away. Looming up, as landmarks in its troubled records, are Sugar Creek, Elkhorn, Farmington, Iuka, Corinth, and the Hatchie, while the chinks are principally filled in with long, weary, disheartening retreats — an almost continuous countermarch. The never-lagging wheels of Time will soon roll another year on the stage of life. Can it be possible that this, too, will be a luckless one?"

The answer to this question for the Missouri exiles would be in the affirmative not only for 1863, but also for 1864 and 1865. To the out-numbered Southerners battling against the military muscle of a Northern industrial complex, fate had cruelly stacked up the odds against the "band of brothers native to the soil" and especially the Missouri Confederates.[23]

Since it appeared that General Grant would remain inactive during this winter of 1862, the Fifth Missouri soldiers prepared to erect sturdy shelters to replace their flimsy tents. The area around Camp Rogers had long been stripped of timber and other resources, however. Colonel McCown therefore shifted the encampment a short distance to a pine thicket on January 11. Trees shortly dropped by the hundreds, falling to the efforts of the Rebels turned lumberjacks. One soldier described in his diary how without iron nails but knowing pioneer ways of the frontier to create homes from the conifer woodlands, the Missourians started "building Cabins, which looks like they [are] going to stay sometime." Some of McCown's butternuts, having seen fathers and grandfathers adapting in this way to the Missouri wilderness, erected elaborate log structures from the pine forest. But other soldiers' cabins resembled shacks or trapper's lean-tos.[24]

Commenting on the winter quarter's variety, Lieutenant Warren recorded that "the architecture and design of some of them, is quite Com-ical, some above ground, & some below." While the busy noise of hammer-ing and chopping echoed over the wooded hills, soldiers turned architects worked for weeks on their new Mississippi homes so far from their Missouri homes. A log community took shape across the brown hillsides of Grenada County.[25]

It was not all hard work for McCown's carpenters and homespun engineers. Indeed, social life at the Fifth Missouri's log town had boomed. In the words of one soldier, the "cabins, huts, shanties, and banked-up tents assumed the appearance of a village with regular streets and the busy scenes of peaceful life, occasionally beamed upon by the fair ladies of Grenada and the vicinity." The only news to dampen spirits came with more deaths. Even as late as mid-January, word filtered into camp of the death of Lieu-tenant Patrick H. Gallaher in a Vicksburg hospital. Exchanged after his capture at Corinth, the Ireland-born brick mason of Warrensburg lingered near death when complications developed after the amputation of his left leg. The Irish Rebel, age forty-three, finally died of infection on January 13.[26]

One group of Missouri Confederates not basking in Camp Roger's comfort were the men of Company I. The Macon County soldiers had had enough of defeat and death in the Magnolia State. Because they had not been sent to Missouri as they had been promised and because they resented Bowen's harsh West Point standards, Captain Guthrie's men mutinied. Many of Company I's soldiers, members of the Fifth Missouri's most free-thinking and independent-minded unit, had been part of McGee College's faculty and student body. They consequently more freely spoke their views on what they perceived to be a political conspiracy and the cynical politicians and military leaders who had betrayed them. The entire company defiantly "refused to appear on Dress Parade." An angry Colonel McCown dispatched armed guards to quell the miniature rebellion, which had the potential of sweeping the largely Missouri division because of already existing bitterness over its exile east of the Mississippi. But the mutineers refused to be intimidated by the show of force. As if they were facing Yankees in 1861, these butternuts stood up for their rights and stood their ground, loading muskets and fixing bayonets. Faced with the crisis which was about to result in bloodshed, McCown's enforcers backed down. The colonel then ordered Lieutenant Townsend and his Company E to the rescue. Rushing to the scene, these Franklin County soldiers faced Macon County men, hailing from the opposite side of the Missouri River, for long minutes with rifles and bayonets ready. It seemed as if the Fifth Missouri was on the verge of self-destructing. The trigger-happy guards of Company E surrounding them only strengthened the resolve of Company I members to hold firm and not be intimidated. Consequently, these revolutionaries from the Chariton and Salt River country swore "never to be taken alive."

Just as bloodshed was about to erupt, other Fifth Missouri companies sided with Company I. Much of the whole Fifth Missouri revolted against Confederate authority. Shortly, Colonel Gates's regiment joined the mutiny as well. Indeed, these ex-cavalrymen were still angry because they had been dismounted after they crossed the Mississippi in April 1862. A tense situation and stand-off developed largely from discontent arising from the Missourians' most sensitive issue: returning to the west side of the Mississippi to liberate home and families from Union occupiers. Despite their efforts, Lieutenant Townsend and his Company E soldiers could not subdue hundreds of armed and veteran Rebels, who were as mad as hornets. "We could do nothing with them without causing bloodshed," and this would include much Company E blood. An uneasy stalemate developed for the remainder of this tense day in January.[27]

Neither side offered concessions or talked of compromise. General

Green, who had been the Missouri Brigade commander before he took Colonel Gates's place in late October, galloped into camp the next morning. Perhaps the absence of General Green's leadership had additionally sapped morale, for he was one of their own, a hard-fighting Missourian who had struggled across the state in 1861. Discontent at the replacement of the popular Colonel Gates, the most popular officer in the Missouri Brigade, seems partially verified by the fact that the First Missouri cavalrymen sided with the mutineers.[28]

Tempers cooled during the night. A stern lecture from General Green and "the persuasion of" McCown convinced the men of Company I to throw down their muskets. Guthrie's Confederates marched themselves voluntarily to the guardhouse. The crisis passed for the moment, but widespread discontent among the elite troops of Pemberton's army simmered just below the surface. General Price continued to demand the transfer of his division when he was in Richmond near the end of January, but President Davis, General Pemberton, and the Confederacy had different ideas about the destiny of the crack Missouri troops. Indeed, Price would be going back to the Trans-Mississippi to raise an army for an effort to reclaim Missouri, but the Missouri Brigade would remain on the east side of the Mississippi. Confederate military leaders, strategists, and politicians were determined "to retain troops so valuable" to Vicksburg's survival. The luckless Missouri Rebels would continue dying for years hundreds of miles from home, while their families suffered under Federal occupation. As fate would have it, the majority of Fifth Missouri soldiers would never return to their home state again.[29]

Calm finally returned to the rustic community of the Fifth Missouri on the Yalobusha. Light snows and rains came with increased intensity, sweeping McCown's encampment more frequently. Still half-injured from his Corinth wound, Lieutenant William Henry Johnston reached camp in early February. Wanting only to serve the regiment, Johnston had declined a disability discharge taking charge of the Fifth Missouri's baggage train. But his devotion to duty would soon cost him his life, for the young lieutenant would meet death in Vicksburg's trenches during late May.

For the common soldiers of the Fifth Missouri, Sunday was the best of all days, with no drills or work details. Lieutenant Simpson caught the spirit of the Sabbath day and noted in his diary: "It being Sunday many of the boys singing, some reading [the Bible] and some talking of home &c." This quiet period would be the last in the lives of many of McCown's men, however. Although they were confident and optimistic that winter, the majority of these Fifth Missouri soldiers would soon be killed, wounded, or captured during the fast-approaching Vicksburg campaign.[30]

After the threat of mutiny faded away, the rapid pace of cabin-building continued and even progressed to new heights. Menacing black skies and occasional snow flurries increased the speed of the carpenters in gray. Missouri Rebels split, shaped, notched, and chinked pine logs for days. One Company E group of officers, according to the diary of one soldier, after much toil, "completed our Cabin to day. It is ten by fourteen, built of Pine logs, has a large fire place and two bunks. It will be fine for cooking in, as the continued rains make it impossible to cook out of doors." It appeared as if the remainder of the winter would be pleasantly spent by the Fifth Missouri Confederates at their new quarters.[31]

But life in the comfortable winter quarters would be brief. After his communication lines were snapped and the major supply depot at Holly Springs destroyed, Grant was forced to abandon his advance upon Vicksburg through northern Mississippi. As part of a two-pronged drive to capture Vicksburg, Major General William T. Sherman advanced and threatened the city on the north. General Pemberton, therefore, began to redeploy his forces to counter the Unionists' threat from the Mississippi north of Vicksburg. When he gave orders to move out on January 23, prospects and hopes for a soft winter were dashed. A disgusted Lieutenant Warren lamented in his diary: "We did not sleep in our Cabin a single night." To add to the misery, the Missouri column snaked eastward for Grenada under a cold drizzle and a chilly wind. But morale remained high because the Missourians, as one soldier wrote in a letter, were "anxious to have a tussle" with the Missouri Yankees in Grant's army, who had helped win the state for Lincoln.[32]

Colonel McCown's mud-splattered Rebels crowded into a Grenada warehouse on the rainy evening of January 23. Soldiers immediately slipped out of the barnlike structure and headed for the nearest store to buy liquor. Bottles of rum were freely passed around. Sergeant Ruyle described the cramped quarters with "five hundred soldiers, a good portion of them drunk, hollering, laughing, sweating [and] it rainy and the mud a foot deep anywhere outside." A model officer, Lieutenant Warren did not engage in the fun. The sober young man recorded: "The boys have plenty of Whiskey and there [are] a great many of them tight." Indeed, complained the lieutenant, "More than half the Regment [sic] were drunk [and] carousing all night. They drink Louisiana Rum at $10.00 gal."[33]

Groggy Fifth Missouri boys piled aboard cattle cars of the Mississippi Central Railroad around ten o'clock on the following morning. As a rising sun eased the morning's chill, the train rumbled southward for Jackson, the state capital and concentration site of Rebel reserves. The twisting route over central Mississippi's forested and rolling hills added to the nausea caused by the previous night's drinking. With little sleep but with much rum left in wooden canteens, trouble was bound to break out at the first opportunity. The home-brew liquor finally asserted itself as during the night before. When the train stopped to refuel at Canton, just north of

Jackson, thirty-seven-year-old Corporal Peter Moran, a hard-drinking soldier born on the Emerald Isle, got into a fray with one of the Confederate provost guards at the railroad. He was shot and mortally wounded during the altercation. Moran would die on January 27. The rowdy Irishmen of Company F once again maintained their wild reputation as they would do throughout the South for years.[34]

In spite of Company F's fine officers, the Irish unit had been an endless source of difficulty from the beginning, although the Celts in gray also had the reputation of being the best-drilled and hardest fighting troops among the elite Missourians. This reputation was hard-earned from service in the prewar militia, Missouri State Guard service, and Confederate duty east of the Mississippi. Even Captain Canniff could no more control the Irishmen's turbulent spirits than he could influence the weather, however. But Canniff could do a better job handling these Irish Rebels than anyone else in the Fifth Missouri. Because of the Irishmen's pugnacity, anti-authoritarianism, and free-spirited nature, regimental officers could not tame such rowdy spirits. No one was more frustrated at trying to restore order among Company F's soldiers than the lieutenant colonel. By 1863, Bevier had long since given up the task, concluding that these Irish Confederates would simply remain "the best soldiers on duty and the worst off, the best fighters and the most troublesome men in the army." The only one brave enough to quell such violent outbursts and assert his authority was Father Bannon, and he had God on his side. Himself of imposing physique and unafraid of either high-strung Rebels or Yankees, the Irish priest occasionally stepped in to break up the fist-fights among the Irishmen of Company F.[35]

As it was for the men in other companies, liquor was the source of much of the trouble in Company F. Captain Canniff's Rebels remained sober only "when it was impossible to get enough whiskey to get drunk on," swore one officer. Indeed, fist-fights often erupted to break up the peace of Company F's bivouac. Bloody noses, deep cuts, and broken bones among the sons of Erin kept Surgeon Dysart more busy with these types of Confederate-inflicted injuries than with wounds received from the Yankees. Fights among the Irish Confederates often resulted from the slightest provocation. One contest between two Celtic Rebels of Company F raged among the tents over something as insignificant as the ownership of a stick of firewood. Missouri Brigade members marching past the encampment could often see the soldiers of Company F rolling, biting, and jabbing in the mud, rain, or snow, as if they were fighting back home on St. Louis's infamous "Battle Row," a seedy den of boarding houses, taverns, and bawdy houses along the Mississippi.[36]

Another disaster struck Company F before it reached the capital of Mississippi. A railroad car jumped the tracks, injuring Private John

Chambers, age thirty. Formerly a St. Louis stone cutter and meat market worker, the Ireland-born soldier died two days later. Meanwhile, Colonel McCown's column swung through the bustling town of Jackson after disembarking from the train on January 28. Here, a mile west of the Magnolia State's capital, McCown's troops encamped near the Pearl River.

To the complete surprise of the Fifth Missouri, new Confederate uniforms arrived on the last day of the month. It was about time that an indifferent government, which appreciated the worth of the elite Missourians and played with their destiny as if a reckless gambler, finally provided Confederate uniforms to its exiled troops. Although they had fought for the South since 1861, these were the first Confederate uniforms given to Colonel McCown's veterans. Indeed, the soldiers of the Fifth Missouri had charged Corinth's fortifications while wearing parts of Union uniforms and gear, carpet-clothes, civilian clothes, cotton garments dyed with walnut hulls (for the butternut color), and even slave apparel. Even while fighting as elite Confederate troops, these Fifth Missouri soldiers maintained their distinctive Missouri State Guard look of hardened Rebels from the Western frontier. Most of the other soldiers of the Missouri Brigade, in contrast, had worn Confederate gear, such as "C.S." belt buckles and other accouterments, which had been issued during January 1862.[37]

Colonel McCown's Confederates shed tattered clothes for gray uniforms trimmed in blue, which probably had come from North Carolina storehouses. Cartridge boxes, cap pouches, and "C.S." buckles soon adorned the Fifth Missouri Rebels in their new gray uniforms. Soldiers tossed slouch and old militia hats aside for regulation gray kepis trimmed in blue. Fifth Missourians were transformed by the uniforms. Instead of looking like a bunch of farmers and militiamen, they now looked more like the crack Confederate troops that they were. McCown's newly attired Confederates "feel very proud of them, being the first uniforms that they have received." A proud Lieutenant Warren wrote in his diary that each Fifth Missouri infantryman could now boast of owning "Grey Pants, grey Jackets & grey Caps. The collars & cuffs of the Jackets are trimmed with light blue."[38]

As the Federals pushed south from Memphis to cut the Confederacy in two, Pemberton continued rushing units southwestward to concentrate on the defense of the Mississippi River citadel. After spending a week and a half at Jackson, Colonel McCown's regiment received word on February 8 to head toward Vicksburg.

Fortress Vicksburg had to be successfully defended to give the South a chance at life in this war of attrition. The eastern half of the Confederacy needed to keep the Mississippi River open for the invaluable resources, material, foodstuffs, and supplies from the Trans-Mississippi. The rich frontier lands of Texas, Arkansas, and Louisiana were a most critical economic base for the young Confederacy. After the Davis government had made the eastern theater its top priority, only the manpower from this region could provide the reinforcements necessary for Vicksburg's survival in the summer of 1863.

With the first opportunity to show off their new uniforms, Colonel McCown's boys marched to Jackson's depot with "music & flying colors." From the capital, the Fifth Missouri was whisked by rail westward toward the bone of contention. An excited population along the route "cheered from all sides as we passed by the ladies," long remembered one soldier.[39]

The Fifth Missouri encamped sixty miles east of Vicksburg near Big Black River. A seemingly endless deluge of cold rains soon turned the bivouac area of the Missourians into a quagmire. No dry wood could be found for campfires in the swampy bottoms, and as a result, rations could not be cooked. Wet, cold, and huddled in tents, Fifth Missouri Rebels went hungry as winds lashed and sheets of rain pelted the canvas. One officer wrote gloomily: "[It] has been raining very steadily for two or three days, we are surrounded on all sides by swamps. The ground is very muddy [sic], and it is impossible to go out of our Tents." The late winter storms along the turbid Big Black at last subsided, but it became necessary to erect bunks to escape the constant threat of flash floods. According to Warren, the completed dry quarters were "quite a treat after sleeping on the wet ground. [Lieutenant Hamilton E.] Kelley [destined to be brutally murdered by Home Guards in Missouri after Vicksburg] & I played Gus [Augustus St. Mary, a Company E lieutenant] and Eli [Guthrie] a game of seven up to see who should have the lower 'Bunk.' We beat, and now luxuriate on the lower Bunk." By this period, gambling had become a central feature of camp life, despite the preaching of the Rebel chaplains.[40]

As winter faded into spring and the Confederacy's decisive spring campaign for the possession of the Mississippi River was about to begin, less rain fell and the nights became warmer. Fairer skies and dry fields along the river meant longer hours of drill in preparation for some of the most vicious fighting of the war. Some free time of the Fifth Missouri soldiers was probably spent hunting and trapping small game in nearby bayous and cypress swamps. These activities that supplemented dull army rations of cornbread and bacon particularly suited the Company K soldiers from the swampy Bootheel region. In addition, the sluggish Big Black River probably supplied plenty of catfish and turtles just like the Chariton or Blackwater rivers back home.

The refreshing warmth of spring weather came early to central Mississippi and Hinds County this year. Schools of fish from the river had already spawned in the shallows of the half-flooded bottoms. Descending from gray skies in swarms, large flocks of ducks and geese filled the watery woodlands to feed as they stopped briefly on their northward journey up the Mississippi flyway.

Like the hectic activity in the world of nature around them, the advent of warmer temperatures caused McCown's Rebels to become more frisky and ardent in the pursuit of neighborhood women, well-educated and aristocratic Southern belles in fine petticoats as well as slave women in common work clothes. Sports became a physical outlet which kept McCown's men out of trouble. A handful of soldiers, probably from the urban environment of St. Louis, fashioned a ball and bat. The Big Black River games began when the fallow fields bordering the watercourse dried. Entire Fifth Missouri companies played baseball for hours on the level floodplain. Enjoying himself, Lieutenant Warren watched the fun, feeling content that "the boys amuse themselves at games of ball."[41]

General Price finally received orders to travel west at the end of February to join the struggle in the Trans-Mississippi theater. His division, including the Missouri Brigade, assembled to hear "Old Pap's" tearful farewell. Based upon what he had been told and promised by Confederate authorities, Price swore to his troops that they would soon be going home to rejoin him in the attempt to win Missouri. But many of McCown's more realistic veterans had grown cynical and wise, no longer believing the false promises of a brighter future. When the lieutenant colonel surveyed the Fifth Missouri's formations, he saw that "the hearts of the men were sad, for they truthfully apprehended, notwithstanding his cheering words, that it might be a long time ere they would again follow the banner under which they had endured so much and had achieved so many successes."[42]

It was an emotional good-bye between the Missourians in gray and General Price, the "George Washington" of Missouri's struggle. Losing their former commander whom they had fought for since the war's beginning was as painful as parting with a family member. For the young men who had left kinfolk and their rural communities almost two and a half years before for the first time, the benevolent Price had been a father figure since the spring of 1861. Sergeant Ruyle recalled how on March 1, "I never saw so many & sad faces as I did when all the boys found Old Pap was surely going to leave us in Mississippi."

Indeed, a sense of abandonment weighed heavily on the Fifth Missouri Confederates on the first day of March. General Price had long been identified with the effort to free Missouri from Union occupation. A deep trust and a mutual admiration between the general and the men in the ranks had also been established since the beginning. Indeed, Price constantly worried and fussed like an old woman about his soldiers' welfare, making sure there was enough food, rest, dry quarters, etc., for his men. The rough-hewn Missouri enlisted men could never forget the many acts of kindness demonstrated by General Price. Sergeant Ruyle, for instance, would always remember how General Price had lifted exhausted Rebels who could march no farther to ride behind him on his horse and helped some soldiers across icy streams during the Arkansas withdrawal.[43]

Manpower shortages became acute before the opening of the Vicksburg campaign, especially among the frontier exiles. The largest manpower reserve of the regiment became even less accessible when Price crossed the Mississippi, for Missouri Rebels west of the Mississippi would rally to his standard. As if to compensate, five Fifth Missouri officers took recruiting assignments in Missouri during the first week of March. Confederate recruiters from other Missouri Brigade regiments also were selected. This risky duty in Union-occupied Missouri could get these isolated Confederate recruiters executed by Yankee firing squads if they were caught on their secret missions. The five recruiters from the Fifth Missouri were lieutenants George T. Duvall (Company A), Simpson (Company C), Warren (Company E), and Andrew Jackson Lee (Company E) — who was sure to have influence on western Missouri soil in part because he had been elected one of Henry County's convention delegates — and Captain Guthrie (Company I). In a strange twist of fate, this hazardous duty in Federal-held Missouri would be safer than staying with the regiment during the upcoming Vicksburg campaign. Indeed, the Fifth Missouri would suffer more than 60 percent casualties during the upcoming spring and summer months of 1863.[44]

Yet another new challenge came to the Missouri Brigade when Colonel McCown ordered tents struck on March 9. The Missouri Brigade pushed sixty miles southwest to Grand Gulf on the Mississippi. But the soldiers of the Fifth Missouri would not be forsaking the environs of Big Black, for the river emptied into the "Father of Waters" just north of Grand Gulf. The memorable three-day march through the Magnolia State's western half was almost like triumphantly entering Missouri for these elite Confederates. Crowds welcomed them along the route, cascading cheers upon the frontier exiles so far from home.

Colonel McCown's Missourians, resplendent in new uniforms, basked in the attention while women tossed flower bouquets, shouted, and tried to look their best for the young soldiers in gray. As in the past, the Fifth Missouri's reputation had preceded it, for these troops were already known as the hardest fighters of the Confederacy. Citizens were determined to catch sight of the Westerners. "Such imperishable renown have the Missouri troops gained in the late battle of Corinth, that all are anxious to witness and cheer the brave fellows who have suffered so much the Southern people will never forget," wrote one Southern lady who was duly impressed.[45]

With the savvy of veterans, some Missouri boys took immediate advantage of opportunities. At one plantation along the road to Grand Gulf, for instance, some Company G soldiers slipped away from Captain Coale and the company. One angry planter, whose patriotism had suddenly disappeared, complained that these ever-opportunistic grayclads "broke into my house, killed some of my chickens, mussed up the sugar and lard and such things, and cooked a meal big enough for forty men." In part, such indiscretions were possible because Lieutenant Colonel Bevier and Major Waddell had been ordered by Colonel McCown to keep "a sharp look-out for stragglers, with the pleasure of straggling ourselves." While two of the Fifth Missouri's highest ranking officers prowled for attractive women and free dinners along the way, numbers of enlisted men dropped out of column to forage and frolic on their own.[46]

After arriving in the Grand Gulf vicinity, the Missouri Brigade encamped on the only level ground southeast of town, the Hamilton Plantation located a mile and a half from the river. If these Missourians envisioned a blossoming of social life at Grand Gulf along the Mississippi, they would shortly learn differently, much to their dismay. Only recently a booming cotton export community, Grand Gulf now lay in ruins, the victim of a Yankee naval and army raid during June of 1862. But the bluffs which rose from the river's floodplain and overlooked the blackened debris of a city that had once rivaled Vicksburg and Natchez were now important to Confederate strategists. Anticipating that General Grant's scheme to slice a canal through DeSoto Peninsula to bypass Vicksburg might fail, Southern leaders correctly ascertained the urgent need to fortify the high ground above Grand Gulf to protect the southern flank of Vicksburg.[47]

Still retaining much of their distinctive frontier individualism, the soldiers of the Fifth Missouri had reservations about their new commander, General Bowen, during this period. He had first won acclaim on the battlefield at Shiloh, taking serious wounds and having two horses shot from under him. Would Bowen now be the same unbending officer who had imposed harsh discipline on deserters in Kentucky during the winter of 1861-62? Some of Colonel McCown's soldiers had expected the worse with Bowen's appointment to command Price's division.

No doubt Canniff, Marnell, Crow, and other officers who had served under the rigid Bowen on the Southwest Expedition, when he was a Missouri militia colonel and General Frost's adjutant, had spoken freely about what to expect from the serious-minded West Pointer. As a result, threatening talk of shooting the brigadier general if he intended to treat the men high-handedly had spread throughout the command. But the Chatham County, Georgia, native had softened by this time, perhaps in part because his wife had only recently joined him. Or possibly General Bowen feared a musket ball through his back in the first battle after he learned of the threats. The brilliant West Pointer, however, made the right impression on McCown's soldiers from the beginning, for "on going into their first

Camp they found their comfort so well provided for. Bowen's tent in their midst [made] the Cheers [break] from them; he was ever after their idol." In addition, wrote Sergeant Ruyle, General Bowen now "gave us more liberty than we ever had before and all the boys loved him, almost equal to Old Pap himself." This, of course, was the ultimate compliment from the enlisted men of the Fifth Missouri.[48]

General Bowen, in fact, had become too liberal. A Claiborne County plantation owner came raging to the general's headquarters, located between the batteries and the infantry camps, to complain that the Missouri soldiers had abused their privileges and were raising hell in her slave quarters. Officers and enlisted men of the Fifth Missouri and other Missouri Brigade units were slipping out of the Confederate encampment at night and trekking north through the forests for Pattieson's Plantation along Big Black River. Here, at the plantation's slave cabins in the bottoms, McCown's restless men found kindred spirits among the blacks, who had a vibrant social and community life of their own from sundown to sunup when away from the dreary fields and overseers and masters. In contrast to practices in the Deep South, the closer intermingling of the two peoples in antebellum Missouri in part resulted in the Fifth Missouri Rebels — like Missouri Yankees — interacting with African Americans in Mississippi.[49]

Around roaring fires and rustic cabins, the slaves played fiddles, banjos, and perhaps native African instruments throughout the night. Black and white freely mixed, laughing, drinking, and dancing together. Sexual encounters occurred, and the Missouri soldiers probably forced their attentions upon unwilling black women. At any rate, these sexual contacts were destructive to African American family bonds. Domestic turmoil, especially of the nocturnal variety, equated to poor production in the fields in the eyes of the planter. An enraged Mrs. Pattieson, consequently, demanded to talk to the leader of the home-wrecking Rebels, who were "raising Caine" among her slave quarters each night. Such practices were known among Union soldiers in the South as well.[50]

General Bowen ordered Bevier to solve the problem immediately. The strict Presbyterian general from Carondelet, Missouri, refused to have his men scandalizing the countryside and acting as if they were in a Mobile or Vicksburg whorehouse on furlough. Not at all shocked by the recreational behavior of his troops, the cynical lieutenant colonel merely philosophized: "When far away from all the wholesome restraints of social life soldiers, although they may wear swords and carry commissions, are sad dogs." Perhaps Bevier himself had been among the participants, for he soon would have charges placed against him that resulted in a court of inquiry. Indeed, he later harbored some ill-feeling toward Bowen. To round up the offenders as directed, the lieutenant colonel called upon Captain Grant. If Grant could help win Lewis County, Missouri, for the South, then he could surely handle "so delicate an enterprise" in Mississippi. Clearly, the Mexican War veteran was a fine choice for such a sin-cleansing mission because he was "one of our oldest company commanders, a most excellent leader, as brave a man as ever headed a charge, at home a prominent member of his church, and to the regiment a model of all things." But Company H's commander could not be found.[51]

Captain Canniff, therefore, received the assignment. With rifled-muskets on their shoulders, the Irishmen of Company F soon swung through the Missouri encampment, heading northwestward for the river landing at Grand Gulf. To mask their mission, Canniff's troops loudly complained about having to unload a steamboat, a dirty job that many of these Irish Rebels had performed on the St. Louis levee before the war. But once outside of camp, the Emerald Isle captain signaled his troops off the road and into a thicket shadowed by a dropping sun. Here, the Celts of Company F would remain until eleven o'clock. Then, with a moon casting a soft yellow light over the Mississippi River delta, the Irish soldiers pushed north toward Pattieson's cabins of iniquity. After hearing the shouts and music rising from the river bottoms nestled between the forested hills, Canniff halted his files along a ridge-top. The captain, a devout Catholic in gray, could hardly believe his eyes at the scene which was presented to him: "each shanty was brilliantly lighted, the music of fiddle, guitar and banjo kept time to the thumping of many feet, comely saddle-colored girls were engaged therein and in passing around refreshments; the loud laugh and sharp halloo mingled with an occasional shrill 'yip' that would have done credit to an Osage Indian war dance, gave zest to the festive gathering."

With the Celtic indignation he had exhibited during a dozen skirmishes, Captain Canniff deployed Company F to sweep the entire slave community clean. Charging through the cabin village and past campfires, the warriors barged into the log houses of the African Americans. No doubt, some offenders in gray were caught in embarrassing positions of intimacy. Company F rounded up sixty intoxicated Fifth Missouri Rebels within minutes. Captain Canniff had effectively stamped out sinful recreation at Pattieson's Plantation. Not until two o'clock in the morning did the Paddies return to camp with their prisoners. One captive was Captain Grant, who swore that he had only gone to the Big Black River "whorehouses" in order "to keep the boys straight." For all his poor excuses and bad acting, Grant was "heartily laughed at." Shortly the captain would be sitting before a court-martial. Mrs. Pattieson's dilemma had been solved at last, but for McCown's revelers, many more cotton plantations and slave quarters around Grand Gulf existed for nocturnal activities. No one was probably more proud of the success of Company F's police-action than Father Bannon.[52]

In order to bolster Grand Gulf's bluffs, Bowen's soldiers and Claiborne

County slaves had been erecting fortifications since the second week of March. Black and white worked side by side digging an extensive network of earthworks both at the bluff's base and 100 feet atop the high ground. Union leaders would compliment the Missourians' labor and Bowen's excellent engineering skills by christening the powerful defensive position "Little Gibraltar." The Missouri Brigade's artillerymen of Captains Wade's and Henry Guibor's batteries were positioned at Grand Gulf, adding strength. Captain Landis's guns, meanwhile, commanded the mouth of navigable Big Black River, just north of the town's ruins. Grand Gulf had suddenly become second in strength on the Mississippi only to fortress Vicksburg. By March 27, Bowen confidently reported, "I am satisfied that if they attempt a Bombardment they will be sorry for it."[53]

The defenses of Grand Gulf were completed just in time. Two Federals warships tested the new fortifications on March 19. Bowen's orders were not to open with artillery unless Federal troops landed, but an eager Missouri cannoneer lamented to his comrades, "It['s] a damn shame to let 'em pass without givin' 'em a round!" Captain Guibor responded with the order to open fire. During the artillery exchanges, Missouri cannoneers raked the Union ships with shot and shell, convincing the Yankees of the earthwork's strength and their own determination. Effectively chastised, the Union navy's "scouts" steamed down the Mississippi. But additional Federal warships would be coming soon to reconnoiter.[54]

Amid the grassy fields of the Hamilton Plantation, McCown's encampment stood close enough to Vicksburg for General Bowen to rush troops north to aid the city if necessary. Spring rains had already produced a landscape along the Mississippi that was budding with new life and bright green. A wet freshness filled the air, promising the fulfillment of nature's beauty. Blooming dogwoods, azaleas, and magnolias added fragrance and colorful luster to the countryside that teemed with new life and vitality. Honking and flapping upriver in the coolness of early morning, the flowing, V-shaped waves of geese heralded the end of winter. Like so many other Fifth Missouri soldiers, Sergeant Ruyle, rejuvenated by the beauty of the budding woodlands and fair weather of springtime in Mississippi, felt at home in the bivouac area in a belt of "trees [that] are putting forth their leaves and everything becoming very green, which brings new thoughts of home to mind" at "the most pleasant place we had ever camped."[55]

Homesickness diminished with intensified "sparking." A liberal granting of furloughs by General Bowen coincided with the fairness of the spring weather. A good deal of time was devoted to finding temporary mates, whose husbands or lovers were off in Confederate service, or prospective wives. Indeed, the "ladies around Grand Gulf were pretty, far above average, and we enjoyed ourselves among them as if no war was brooding over the land." With no romantic illusions remaining, one shanty St. Louis Irishman, sensing a rare chance to gain upward social mobility via the belles of the Southern aristocracy, courted with "the deliberate determination of falling in love with some plantation with a pretty girl attached if such a thing be possible," as he revealed his personal strategic plan in a letter.[56]

The nearest town to the Fifth Missouri's encampment was Port Gibson, only eight miles to the southeast, which became the center of social activity. Lifelong friendships and relationships developed among McCown's men and the local citizens at one of Mississippi's most beautiful communities. Company F's Private Dan Monahan, for example, spent almost every evening with his newfound family. The people of the quiet town along Little Bayou Pierre embraced its Missouri defenders, while McCown's soldiers adopted new homes and families. Indeed, "every private had his 'home' and his circle of acquaintances, where he was always welcome." Thanks to the tireless efforts of the resourceful General Grant, the tranquility and social bliss would be fleeting, however.[57]

Even now the war loomed much closer to the Fifth Missouri boys than they wished to believe. Just across the river, Major General John A. McClernand's corps pushed southward through eastern Louisiana and ever closer to Grand Gulf. With the failure of Grant's canal plan, the Unionists now sought a base on the Mississippi's west bank from which to cross the river and invade the Magnolia State. Amid the swirl of romantic evenings and talks of marriage, McCown's veterans were unaware of the larger strategies now taking place around them, which even now controlled their destinies.[58]

On the last day of March, Rear Admiral David D. Porter's transports and gunboats sped past Vicksburg's batteries in preparation for the great crossing of the Mississippi. Bowen's men were ready when the considerable might of the Union navy suddenly appeared. With the accuracy of experienced veterans, Rebel gunners hammered the warships with everything they had in their arsenal, including homemade canister. The Fifth Missouri's soldiers, meanwhile, lay in reserve hidden among the wooded hills above the river. If the Yankees attempted to land on the east bank, then Southern infantrymen would pour off the bluffs and drive the invaders into the Mississippi.[59]

Sergeant Presley S. Stark of Company I did not like sitting idly by while Guibor's and Wade's cannoneers and the artillerymen of a Louisiana battery worked their siege guns with precision. The righteous teachings of the Cumberland Presbyterians at McGee College, where he had been "an eminent educator and literateur," had stirred a deep hatred in Stark for the invaders. Consequently, an angry "Pres" grabbed his Enfield rifle and dashed down the bluff above Grand Gulf in a "War-like mania." Explosions from Union artillery fire rocking the hillside failed to deter the Tennessee-born sergeant. Eager for action, Sergeant Stark jumped into the trenches with the Missouri Brigade's defenders. Shooting at navy "Jack Tars" and peppering warships with bullets somewhat satisfied the pious Stark. Despite the spirited defense, no serious damage was inflicted on the Union gunboats, however.[60]

Bowen's well-founded concerns about an attack on Grand Gulf can be partly glimpsed as early as March 17, when he pleaded to General Pemberton to release some experienced Missouri officers, including some of McCown's men, from court duty. Not long thereafter, General Bowen begged of headquarters "that every man and gun that can be spared from other points be sent here." But Pemberton did not share Bowen's conviction that Grant intended to cross the Mississippi from Louisiana. Even by mid-April, Pemberton mistakenly thought Grant would reinforce Rosecrans in north Mississippi. He consequently prepared to hurry troops north and away from Vicksburg. Not even the valuable intelligence gathered by Colonel Cockrell's Louisiana reconnaissance had convinced Pemberton otherwise. Now there would be no sizable numbers of Southern reinforcements for Bowen at Grand Gulf until it was too late.[61]

For the men of the Fifth Missouri, the balmy days of early spring quickly passed in western Mississippi. Although they had received some Confederate supplies and Warren's Mobile purchases, some of McCown's boys remained ill-shod and even barefoot before the hard fighting of the Vicksburg campaign. Mischievous Private Music, for instance, became disabled when he accidentally dropped his Enfield rifle on his naked foot during a difficult drill maneuver.

With steady rains and cool nights and mornings, cases of fever and pneumonia increased among McCown's graycoats. Surgeon Dysart soon had a full field hospital containing not only plenty of sick men but also many shammers. In Lieutenant Colonel Bevier's estimation, "the generous and open-handed hospitality of the people of Port Gibson, Grand Gulf and vicinity had utterly demoralized our soldiers." As a result, the numbers on the regimental sick list skyrocketed. Now a good many Fifth Missouri Rebels came up with "every excuse for sickness that could be devised." Tired of the boredom of army life and badly missing their families after such a long absence from Missouri, these soldiers, often "desert[ing] for days at a time," usually spent both recreation and recuperation periods in private homes at Port Gibson or in the surrounding countryside. Payday became regular for once, prompting soldiers like Private Dyson to have their "likeness" taken at Port Gibson's tintype studios.[62]

Whenever the Mississippi rains subsided, long hours of drilling continued for McCown's Rebels during most of the morning and afternoon. Serious-minded and a perfectionist, General Bowen had high expectations.

One of McCown's officers complained that the general's "discipline was strict and inexorable. It made us soldiers but sometimes made soldiering irksome." For one drill match competition with other veteran units, Bowen unhesitatingly chose the Fifth Missouri to represent the First Missouri Brigade. Once again, the prewar militia experience of Kelly's well-trained officers from St. Louis came to the fore. By the spring of 1863, Colonel McCown's troops were thoroughly conditioned to follow only "those orders that were correctly given according to the Manuel [sic]."

Company G's Captain Coale was more eager than usual for the beginning of the competition because many of the army's highest ranking officers and numerous spectators were present. Coale's lack of confidence and inability to fully decipher the complex maneuvers found in Hardee's Tactics caused the young officer considerable anxiety. In a jittery attempt to begin, the ex–Clinton teacher ordered Company G to "open ranks three paces to the rear, backward, march!" When the improperly given directive jumbled the gray ranks, Captain Coale, "more nervous than he ever had been in the hottest fight," frantically yelled orders to countermarch on a fixed pivot in close formation. This directive restored order and straightened out the lines. Under immense pressure, the captain forgot the proper command to halt, however, and the crack soldiers of Company G were too thoroughly "drilled to stop without it." The Henry County company kept moving forward and plowed through the crowd of spectators, scattering them without losing a step.

Captain Coale, still unable to recall the correct order to halt, continued shouting hysterically for his soldiers to stop. In frantic haste, he raced in pursuit "to head them off, his long legs making remarkable time and his heavy sabre swinging and clattering around them, threatening every moment to trip him." At last gaining the company's front, the former educator implored, "Stop! Stop! Darn it all, can't you stop!" But the captain's hysterics were ignored. The men of Company G continued marching briskly in mechanical fashion as the shocked onlookers watched in amazement. Coale finally recalled the magic word and yelled, "Halt!" But the captain's most embarrassing moment provided the best proof of Company G's superior discipline, and the Fifth Missouri won the first prize.[63]

This inactive period for the Fifth Missouri did not preclude losses. Private James W. Stewart, an eighteen-year-old farmer of Polk County, paid for his youthful rambunctiousness. The Tennessee-born Stewart suffered an injury when he had his "left leg broke by falling out of a tree," as one soldier recorded in his diary. Private Stewart, however, soon recovered from his nasty fall and earned promotion to sergeant in just over a month after his leg healed. But the worst damage inflicted came when a thunderstorm lashed the encampment of the Fifth Missouri. During the stormy night, high winds blew down a large tree, which landed squarely across a tent filled with sleeping soldiers. The tree trunk crushed two of McCown's men to death, and Chaplains Atwood and Bannon faced the sad chore of a burial service on the following morning.[64] But for the young soldiers of the Fifth Missouri, a far more destructive storm was about to descend upon Grand Gulf with a fury seldom seen.

# V

## DRUMBEATS
## IN THE CANEBRAKES
## OF PORT GIBSON

With Grant about to hit attack Grand Gulf, General Bowen would soon be vindicated. Indeed, he had been the first high-ranking Confederate commander to decipher Grant's plans. The invaluable 13-day Louisiana reconnaissance from early to mid–April conducted by a portion of the Missouri Brigade, including the Fifth Missouri, provided the critical intelligence upon which Bowen based his prophetic views. Pemberton and other Confederate leaders, however, remained unconvinced, believing that the Unionists would strike from Vicksburg's north.[1]

By any measure, the Confederacy was ill-prepared to meet the greatest challenge in the West because of decisions made months before by Southern leadership. President Davis had failed to draw troops from the Trans-Mississippi theater and enough units from the Army of Tennessee for an adequate defense of Vicksburg.[2] In addition, Davis's poor choices of commanders in the West—Johnston, Bragg, and Pemberton—practically guaranteed an uncoordinated effort to save Vicksburg. The president's departmentalization of the West led to a dangerous dispersal of forces which could not be galvinized to meet Grant's threat.[3]

Perhaps President Davis's most ill-fated decision was to have given an inexperienced commander, Pemberton, what was probably the most difficult assignment of the war: beating Grant and saving Vicksburg.[4] To compound the problem, General Pemberton was handicapped by having too few troops and too large of an area to defend in confronting both Grant's immense army and the Union navy.[5]

President Davis and his government had again focused too much attention on the Eastern theater.[6] As a result, Pemberton and his Rebels had little hope for success even before the beginning of the campaign.[7] Few examples can be found in this war of the Confederacy being more unprepared for a decisive campaign.[8] But General Bowen and his Missourians were determined to do their best against heavy odds, Grant, and a cruel fate.[9]

As General Bowen had so accurately predicted quite often, Grant was ready to strike Grand Gulf a powerful blow. On the morning of April 29, the Union navy prepared to knock out Grand Gulf's artillery to pave the way for the landing of thousands of Union troops on Mississippi soil. Grant reasoned that Grand Gulf had to be taken before he launched his Mississippi invasion to capture Vicksburg, split the Confederacy in half, and win control of the vital Mississippi. To make one of the largest amphibious assaults of the war, the Union fleet steamed close to the east bank as if nothing could stop them, firing all the way. Not far behind the Union warships, 10,000 bluecoats waiting aboard transports were prepared to storm ashore. General Grant felt more confident than perhaps at any other time in this conflict. Only five days before, he had bragged with confidence that Grand Gulf "will easily fall."[10]

During the emergency at Grand Gulf, the soldiers of the Fifth Missouri assembled and advanced to resist the landing after the first cannon shot disturbed the stillness of morning. With a ferocity not yet seen on the Mississippi, the swarm of Federal ships relentlessly pounded the bluffs at close range. The explosions forced the Rebels of the Fifth Missouri into a ravine near the bluff's crest. Here Colonel McCown's command remained in readiness if the Union divisions should force a beachhead and charge up the slope. Hour after hour, the steadfast Confederates remained in position and held firm under the most intense shelling that they had ever faced. By early afternoon, powder-stained Confederate gunners continued to return fire with spirit.

Defying the odds, they kept a tight grip on the high ground "that had the apperance [sic] of a mountain almost," in the words of one Yankee. About 3,000 shells from seven of the Union navy's warships hammered the defenses, including Forts Cobun and Wade, named for Bowen's chief of artillery. In a lopsided contest, in which the Confederate guns were outnumbered more than ten to one, the Missouri and Louisiana cannoneers won the duel despite the heaviest naval bombardment of the war. General Grant finally gave up the idea of quickly eliminating the Missouri and Louisiana artillery after more than five hours, and he canceled the invasion of the Magnolia State for the moment. The Union general had especially feared the mobile firepower of Captains Guibor's and Wade's field pieces lining the bluffs of Grand Gulf. Indeed, these guns could quickly be shifted downhill by these veteran artillerymen to oppose the landing. Taking the Federal high command by surprise, Bowen's tenacious defense upset Grant's well-laid scheme for a mighty invasion of Mississippi.[11]

The defenders of the Fifth Missouri soon learned of Colonel Wade's tragic death. The colonel's head was torn off by a shell which whistled through Fort Wade along the bluff's base. Colonel Wade, ironically, received his death stroke ten years to the very day that he had advanced his economic standing in life by forming a lumber company with partners in St. Louis. The forty-two-year-old Wade had commanded the Emmet Guards of the St. Louis militia with distinction. This fine antebellum unit, which had included Captain Canniff, had consisted of what Wade termed an exceptional "Body of fine Young Irishmen to a Man Good National Democrats [militant Southerner sympathizers]."

Despite Colonel Wade's death and the terrific pounding from the Union navy, Grand Gulf had stood firm at the crucial hour. But General Grant had an alternate plan to subdue Vicksburg which called for the transports to pass Grand Gulf, load troops below Grand Gulf, and then continue farther downstream in order to cross the Mississippi at another point and place his army in a position to eventually gain Vicksburg's rear. Bowen, however, expected that Grant's warships would return to try again to land troops at Grand Gulf. Consequently he ordered several Missouri regiments into the trenches, including the Fifth Missouri.[12]

Indeed, firm Confederate resistance at Grand Gulf had only made the tactically flexible Grant more determined to succeed. He therefore continued southward down the Mississippi, hunting for a river crossing in Claiborne County which was unknown to Southern leaders. General Grant found one at an obscure landing near the mouth of Bayou Pierre. From the east bank landing, a dry road, the Rodney Road, sliced eastward toward Port Gibson through the sprawling grain fields along the river bottoms, a former cotton region that now fed the always-hungry Rebel armies. The ribbon of dirt had long been an avenue for hauling cotton to the Mississippi River steamboats for the trip south to New Orleans. But more important, the road led east to the strategic high ground where the land suddenly rose and stood on edge. Grant had to have this high ground to solidify his landing on Mississippi soil. Only a mile to the east stood the line of wooded ridges where the country abruptly dropped off to the floodplain of the Mississippi. Besides his own tactical skill, the rugged terrain and semitropical wilderness would aid General Bowen on May 1. Through this almost impenetrable jungle, General Grant had to move an immense army and secure the high ground for his Mississippi invasion to have a chance to succeed.

The worst nightmare of Colonel McCown's soldiers became a reality on April 30, when the first of 23,000 Unionists crossed the river on transports and waded ashore 10 miles south of Grand Gulf. While the blue hordes poured into Mississippi, four Confederate divisions stood motionless around Vicksburg, thanks to the confusion of Southern leadership. Warnings that Bowen had sent as early as April 27 to General Pemberton about Grant's impending invasion of Mississippi below Vicksburg went largely unheeded. Consequently, the war's most critical landing on Southern soil was made without a Rebel in sight.[13]

Confederate leadership had failed to react properly because of poor communication and misunderstanding between commanders, and the lack of Southern cavalry to gather intelligence. Sherman's feints north of Vicksburg had badly fooled Southern leadership and had tied up two-thirds of Pemberton's army at Snyder's Bluff, north of Vicksburg, for attacks which would not come. Not until the evening of April 29, when Grand Gulf was attacked, had Pemberton ordered Major General Carter L. Stevenson's 5,000-man division south to reinforce Bowen. But this reinforcement was far from being enough for General Bowen. With no working rail lines leading to Grand Gulf, any additional Confederate reinforcements from Vicksburg would have to march 45 miles along dusty roads in hot weather and in full gear.[14]

Masses of Federals raced eastward through Mississippi to gain the high ground to guarantee a permanent landing. Eight miles to the northeast beyond the elevated and heavily forested terrain, Port Gibson now became the principal objective for Grant. Nestled on the south fork of Bayou Pierre, Little Bayou Pierre, Port Gibson was suddenly strategic and became the bone of contention on May 1. Because of Port Gibson's dirt roads snaking through the fertile countryside and leading to Grand Gulf, Jackson, and Vicksburg, Grant had early realized the community's strategic importance.[15]

To cut off Vicksburg's garrison from Bowen's force, General John A. McClernand's troops swarmed toward the suspension bridges spanning both Bayou Pierre's north and south forks. McClernand's legions had poured over the highlands, gaining their objective before sunset on April 30, and they now continued toward the bridges. Only Bowen's small division at Grand Gulf stood close enough to meet the Confederacy's greatest threat in the West during the late spring of 1863. If the Unionists gained Port Gibson, then in one stroke the "Little Gibraltar" would be flanked, and Vicksburg would lose its protection on the southern flank.

Handicapped by little assistance from superiors or the Vicksburg garrison, Bowen formulated strategy at Port Gibson largely on his own without his "eyes and ears." Gray horsemen now chased Colonel Benjamin Grierson's Illinois raiders throughout much of Mississippi. To add to Bowen's problems, Pemberton had warned him that the raiders might try to capture Grand Gulf from the rear or the east. But worst of all, Pemberton had ordered most of Bowen's cavalry out in a futile effort to stop the bluecoats. Hence General Bowen had no choice but to reluctantly send out his Port Gibson–based cavalry from the area where they soon would be needed the most. As a result, Grant's landing and movements toward Port Gibson could not be exactly or early pinpointed. Now half-sick from illness, Bowen understood better than anyone that at least 15,000 to 20,000 Confederate troops were necessary to beat Grant at Port Gibson on May 1. But, in reality, the ill-starred General Bowen would have to confront the mighty Union invasion with only a fraction of the troops needed to defeat Grant's juggernaut.[16]

To ascertain the Federals' movements on Mississippi soil, Bowen had already dispatched 500 Arkansas veterans of Green's Second brigade for the risky assignment. These Rebels hurried southeastward from Grand Gulf on the evening of April 29, heading rapidly toward Port Gibson. This reconnaissance force shortly swelled to 1,000 troops, who awaited the arrival of thousands of veteran Yankees. On the evening of April 30, Green's men were bolstered by the arrival of a 1,500-man Alabama brigade and a Virginia battery sent by Bowen. To slow the Unionists until hopefully more of Vicksburg's garrison arrived, Bowen formed his Arkansas and Alabama troops astride the Rodney Road, which led east to Port Gibson.[17] Here, near a wood-frame house of worship known as Magnolia Church about four miles to Port Gibson's west, General Green and his soldiers prepared to meet the onslaught of 23,000 Federals.[18]

Upon arrival at his Grand Gulf headquarters, General Bowen found more of the dismal news which seemingly would never end. He was thunderstruck to learn that "Pook Turtle" ironclads had entered and eased up Bayou Pierre. If these probing Union gunboats destroyed the bridges over the sluggish bayou, then Bowen's forces would be cut in half, and his units would be isolated from Pemberton and Vicksburg. But even more disturbing for Confederate fortunes at Port Gibson, an adequate number of Southern reinforcements for the almost impossible task at hand would not be forthcoming from Vicksburg. To impede the warship's passage up Bayou Pierre, Bowen hastened one of Cockrell's regiments with its artillery to defend the bayou.

General Bowen's fortunes, however, continued to be ill-fated as throughout his military career. Many of the Confederate infantry and artillery units that Bowen would muster to defend Port Gibson on May 1 were destined to run out of ammunition during the battle. Besides tearing up the vital logistical support system in Vicksburg's rear, Colonel Grierson's blueclad raiders had intercepted and destroyed precious supplies of munitions that were bound for Grand Gulf and Port Gibson.[19]

Unable to respond in force to Grant's landing, most of Bowen's division was pinned down guarding four defensive points: Grand Gulf, the mouth of Big Black River, Thompson's Hills, and Bayou Pierre farther upriver. The Federal naval probes succeeded in causing the dispersal of Bowen's division and giving the young brigadier general additional headaches. Much of Bowen's artillery, consequently, remained north of Bayou Pierre to face the probing Union gunboats, while the contest at Port Gibson brewed to the south.[20]

Even with two additional Confederate brigades sent from Vicksburg, General Bowen still had less than 7,000 graycoats to defeat 23,000 veterans

of the Army of the Tennessee. Bowen had to place all his faith in Pemberton's promise to send sizable assistance his way before it was too late. Most
Southern reinforcements would fail to arrive in time from Vicksburg,
however. Soon General Bowen and his outnumbered forces would fight a
bloody delaying action at Port Gibson, vainly awaiting the arrival of large
numbers of Confederate reinforcements.[21]

West of Port Gibson, a loud crackle of gunfire broke loose around 1
A.M. on April 30, when blue formations smashed into Green's units. Hundreds of Federals scattered the Arkansas pickets, who fought gamely
against impossible odds in the dark forests. Skirmishes echoed throughout
the night, warning of the hard fighting which lay ahead. General Bowen
was now alerted to the harsh reality that Grant had definitely landed in
force to the south. Fortunately, for Bowen, the Unionists called a halt amid
the tangled and darkened woodlands. The Federal attack was to resume at
daybreak on fateful May 1. Bowen, therefore, had been granted some
precious hours to manufacture a defense with what little he had at hand.[22]

As the black forests were lightened by the sunrise or May 1, a full
Army of the Tennessee corps stormed eastward up the Rodney Road.
Thousands of blueclads swarmed forward along the open ridges toward
Port Gibson as if nothing could stop them. A diversionary Northern force,
meanwhile, poured up the Bruinsburg Road north of, and parallel to, the
Rodney Road. The two roads intersected two miles west of Port Gibson,
and Grant knew that he needed to obtain possession of the key junction as
badly as Bowen needed to hold it. With increasing momentum, the main
Union thrust pushed toward the Magnolia Ridge line. Tracy's Alabama
Brigade, most of whose men had arrived during the night, and Green's
regiments gamely held their positions. As in so many past battles, General
Green's forces refused to give ground, although his hard-pressed units were
nearly overwhelmed. Meanwhile, two-thirds of Pemberton's army remained
inactive around the citadel, which made Bowen's job of stopping Grant
almost impossible. Only General William E. Baldwin's Mississippi and
Louisiana Brigade raced toward the field of strife with the sunrise. And, as
fate would have it, no additional Southern troops followed these reinforcements south to Port Gibson.[23]

On the bluffs overlooking the ruins of Grand Gulf, meanwhile, the
whippoorwills and owls had ceased their nocturnal serenades which had
echoed eerily during the night and through the sombre forests of Mississippi.
Draped in an early morning coolness across a sprawling field of a Claiborne
County plantation, the Fifth Missouri's encampment was quiet in the early
morning hours of May 1. Doing the domestic chores of their messes, only
a few soldiers stirred in the half-light while most of McCown's men continued to sleep.

The skirmishing of General Green's troops to the south had started early in the morning but caused no undue alarm in the encampment of the Fifth Missouri. Glowing in the east, a fiery sun "rose bright and clear" over the fields and forests of Claiborne County, guaranteeing hot summer-like temperatures and another beautiful day. Flowering dogwoods and redbuds illuminated the hillsides surrounding Colonel McCown's camp. The brightly colored blossoms spread the fragrance of spring over the rows of tents of the Missouri Confederates, beguiling the cruel reality that this would be the last sunrise for many Missouri Brigade members.[24]

As General Bowen had planned, his crack Missouri troops were in solid defensive positions at the "Little Gibraltar" for good reason. If the Bruinsburg threat proved to be yet another feint and if Grant's forces attacked Grand Gulf again, then Bowen's finest troops would be ready to meet the crisis. During the morning hours, these veterans of Colonel McCown's regiment contemplated the meaning of the peals of rifle fire escalating to the south. All signs indicated a big fight brewing to initiate the spring campaign to determine the fate of Vicksburg, a contest for which both armies had prepared all winter.[25]

West of Port Gibson, meanwhile, the situation for Bowen's defenders rapidly deteriorated. Federals poured through the forests by the thousands, charging forward with the confidence that they could eaily brush aside the Rebels. After galloping back to the battlefield a few miles east of Port Gibson after sunrise, General Bowen realized that the whole Yankee army was swarming into Mississippi. Indeed, Grant's troops pushed eastward to try to snatch Port Gibson from under Bowen's nose before the arrival of substantial reinforcements from Vicksburg. General Bowen consequently dispatched couriers northwestward with orders for Colonel Cockrell and all available Missouri units to hurry south to Port Gibson. Bowen now understood that "no hope [remained] unless the promised reinforcements [from Pemberton] should reach me in time."[26]

Around ten o'clock, a messenger in gray rode into the Missouri Brigade's camp. The courier yelled that General Bowen needed help and fast: the invasion of Mississippi had begun to the south, and a mighty Union army was pouring inland like a great flood. Clearly, it was now obvious that Grand Gulf had ceased to be Grant's main target. With Colonel McCown sick or on furlough, Lieutenant Colonel Bevier now commanded the Fifth Missiouri for one of its greatest challenges to date. Shortly, graycoat drummer boys beat the long roll. Musicians Learman; Peter McHugh, a Cass County farmer; teenage Molloy, the former Polk County Ranger; Junius Hart, an eighteen-year-old printer of the pro–Southern Cass County Gazette [which had been censored by Union authorities]; and Hugh Hayes pounded their drums in the morning sunshine. Jolted by the cadence of the drumbeats ringing over the hills, the soldiers of the Fifth Missouri quickly strapped on gear, grabbed muskets, and rushed into formation.[27]

Adjutant Greenwood cantered down the ranks, tightening alignment of the regiment. But with the many lengthy furloughs and the soft winter, Fifth Missouri leaders expected not a hundred soldiers to respond to the beating drums today. The problem of the numerous "hospital rats," or malingers, had not been solved. But to the surprise of all, Surgeon Dysart's infirmary emptied in a hurry. Answering the hoarse booming of the cannon below Bayou Pierre and west of Port Gibson, dozens of "hospital rats" scurried into line with rifles, in addition to many Fifth Missouri soldiers who were actually sick.[28]

Tennessee-born Color Sergeant Stark, the ex–McGee College student from Macon County, stood in front of the Fifth Missouri. Young Stark held the regimental flag which was soon to be stained with his blood. Never before had so many Fifth Missouri soldiers formed into ranks at the onset of a major battle. More than 350 soldiers of the Fifth Missouri assembled, more than twice as many men as had stormed Battery Powell and Fort Richardson last October. While the dueling artillery of both armies roared angrily to the south, few of Colonel McCown's graycoat warriors wanted to be left behind at the Grand Gulf encampment on May 1.[29]

But one Fifth Missouri soldier staying behind that day in camp was Private Dyson. The former schoolmaster's right arm was still unhealed and half-crippled from a bad Corinth wound. Missing his first action since the war's beginning proved a traumatic experience for the dedicated and duty-minded Dyson. Firmly believing he had let Company E down by not marching south to Port Gibson with his comrades, Private Dyson felt overwhelmed with guilt. Later, he expressed his feelings in a letter: "Dear as life is to me I would sooner risk my chances on the field action with the rest of the boys than [be] left in that situation."[30]

A dejected Dyson watched as the gray ranks of the Fifth Missouri marched by, including a younger brother Elam who was fated to die in this war like himself. Also in Colonel Cockrell's reinforcement column heading for Port Gibson were the Third and Sixth Missouri Infantry Regiments, Captain Guibor's Missouri Battery, and a section of Captain Landis's Missouri Battery. The fast-moving files of the Fifth Missouri quickly vanished like a long, gray serpent into the woodlands bright with spring colors. Private Dyson could not have realized that nearly one third of his Fifth Missouri comrades would not survive the upcoming engagement in the forests near Port Gibson.[31]

The Missourians double-quicked along the road twisting southeastward toward Port Gibson at midday, while scorching temperatures of the year's hottest day broiled the land of the Deep South. After crossing the two Bayou Pierre bridges on the run, McCown's panting troops continued onward toward Port Gibson without a break. Cheering citizens lining the town's streets greeted the Rebels, who had raced eight miles through

Claiborne County. In response, the Fifth Missouri boys probably raised a cheer before turning west for the final sprint to the battlefield.[32]

In defying the Yankees, General Bowen, meanwhile, had barely held his own against impossible odds. With too few men and no luck that day, Bowen was attempting to simultaneously block both roads leading east to Port Gibson. Around noon, the breathless Missouri Confederates at last reached the intersection of the Rodney and Bruinsburg roads two miles west of town. Luckily, General Baldwin's brigade had arrived on the field just before Colonel Cockrell's units to help bolster the sagging Rebel lines. Bowen now made quick calculations about how to deploy most effectively his three Missouri infantry regiments, Guibor's battery, and part of Captain Landis's battery, which were the last reserves that would reach the battlefield on May 1. Earlier, a desperate General Bowen had recalled those First Missouri Brigade soldiers who were assigned to guarding Big Black and Bayou Pierre. But this veteran contingent of Colonel Cockrell's force, as well as other Southern troops sent from Vicksburg, would not arrive in time.[33]

General Bowen, nevertheless, could not have hoped for better reserves during such a serious crisis than he now had at Port Gibson. The veterans of the Fifth Missouri and their comrades had just covered the 8 miles from Grand Gulf from ten o'clock to half past noon. Commanding the Sixth Missouri was Henry Clay's grandson, Colonel Eugene Erwin, who had compiled a fine record on both sides of the Mississippi. The handsome Erwin, a twenty-six-year-old born in Kentucky, had only recently recovered from a Corinth wound. Leading the Third Missouri was Colonel William R. Gause, age twenty-four. He had taken command of the regiment since Corinth, where he had been shot down. This ex-lawyer born in Ohio likewise compiled a distinguished service record.[34]

Captain John Christopher Landis was a Kansas City blue blood from a wealthy family, and he had a West Point background. His father had been thrown into prison because of his son's service, and this injustice spurred the resolve of Captain Landis, whose high-spirited nature made him an excellent artillery commander. The exploits of Captain Guibor's battery had already reached legendary proportions. Guibor's "long arm" unit had been the Missouri State Guard's first and best battery. Captain Guibor, of French-Canadian ancestry, and his St. Louis cannoneers of this crack artillery unit were destined to have their careers intertwined with the Missouri Brigade throughout most of the war. The battery's demographics were cosmopolitan. Its members consisted of Irishmen, Germans, Frenchmen, Italians, Scotsmen, Creoles, Englishmen, and other colorful mixtures. This reinforcing contingent of 1,259 battle-hardened Missouri Confederates from Grand Gulf would perform far beyond their numbers on May 1.[35]

Only General Bowen's masterful defense, tactical brilliance, and the forbidding terrain of Mississippi had saved the Southern forces west of Port Gibson to this point. But the thin gray lines of resistance could not long hold back the might of the powerful Army of the Tennessee. Brigadier Peter J. Osterhaus's division slashed toward the Bayou Pierre bridges via the Bruinsburg Road. McClernand, meanwhile, tore savagely into Bowen's over-extended center astride the Rodney Road. Green's troops finally could take no more punishment. The Magnolia Ridge line dissolved under the pounding of McClernand's blows. Howling Yankees overran the high ground, capturing a couple hundred prisoners, two Virginia guns, and an Arkansas battle flag. With the Rodney Road defense shattered, it appeared the day had almost been lost. Not even a counterattack led by Bowen which overran a Union battery and briefly drove the Federals back could stem the blue tide.[36]

To the north, Tracy's Alabamians wavered under Osterhaus's attacks. After a forty-four-mile march, Baldwin's brigade had just been directed by Bowen to align across the Rodney Road, a mile and a half east of the shattered Magnolia Church position and closer to Port Gibson. General Bowen deployed the Louisiana and Mississippi troops on good terrain west of Irwin Branch to hold the Unionists at bay long enough to use his last ace, the Missouri troops, who had already acquired fame as some of the best fighters in the Confederacy. To stabilize the Southern line to the north, Bowen rallied Green's units and hurried them to Tracy's aid. Colonel Erwin's Sixth Missouri likewise rushed north to reinforce the battered gray lines below Bayou Pierre.[37]

It was not long before Baldwin encountered trouble. Hundreds of Federals converged on the isolated Confederate brigade that was fighting for its life. Tracy's Alabamians had expended much of their ammunition after blasting away for hours at the swarms of attackers. Utilizing the crossroads as an interior line to reinforce his widely separated wings, Bowen dispatched the Fifth and Third Missouri south to stabilize Baldwin's hard-pressed lines. Colonel McCown's soldiers, worn from their eight-mile sprint in the heat, raced west down the Rodney Road under a singeing sun, before turning south and leaving the road. Correctly ascertaining that Bowen's strategy was "to hold me in check until reenforcements [sic]" arrived, General Grant hurled brigade after brigade into the fray, hoping to overpower Bowen's thin lines by weight of numbers. General Bowen, meanwhile, patched together a defense along the best, and last, high ground west of Irwin Branch.[38]

After another long run south of around 1,000 yards to Irwin Branch's east, Colonel McCown's troops and the Third Missouri gained the new battle line along the ridges above the watercourse. Here the perceptive Bowen expected the Unionists to exert the most pressure and attempt to turn his left. Colonel Bevier halted his infantrymen in a stubbled cornfield and wooded ravine to the Fourth Mississippi's left-rear and took cover. If McClernand hit Bowen's left flank, then the Missouri exiles would be waiting and ready for the challenge.[39]

Soaked in sweat, the Fifth Missouri Rebels now caught their breath in the suffocating heat and rested in the Mississippi humidity. On a ridge above and behind them, Captain Guibor's artillery bellowed in defiance, providing support to the Missouri infantrymen as so often in the past. Lieutenant Colonel Bevier ordered Captain Canniff and his skirmishers into the valley of White's Branch. Hot skirmishing immediately erupted from the woodlands filling the valley, serving notice that a big battle in this sector was on the verge of erupting.[40]

Fighting increased as McClernand threw more blue skirmishers forward over the open ridge between White and Irwin branches. The big Yankee push to smash the Rebel center along the Rodney Road had resumed once again. Despite the odds, Captain Canniff's skirmishers held their ground as long as possible. Captains Guibor, the Mexican War veteran, and Landis, the frontier aristocrat, had their cannoneers working hard and sweeping the ridge with canister and shells. These Missouri guns slowed the blue avalanche with an enfilading fire, punishing the attackers. But McClernand had now amassed a heavy force of five-brigade strength to steamroll over Baldwin's infantrymen and Captain Landis's and Guibor's artillery.[41]

As never before, the situation was critical for the heavily-outnumbered defenders. Confronted by his greatest challenge, Bowen knew that he now faced a no-win situation and assessed by early afternoon: "We have been engaged in a furious battle ever since daylight; losses very heavy [as] they outnumber us trebly. There are three divisions against us [and] the men act nobly, but the odds are overpowering." Clearly, General Bowen now had to gamble that Baldwin's 1,600 butternuts could hold out against McClernand's hordes and buy time for him to receive additional reinforcements or to launch a counterstroke. Meanwhile, Captains Guibor's and Landis's batteries along the ridge skirting Irwin Branch would have to put up a bolder front.[42]

With the crisis brewing along the Rodney Road, Bowen ascertained even greater danger to the south. What he now detected transpiring in that direction was most alarming and posed the greatest threat of the day. For hundreds of yards atop the open ridge between the two branches sprawled an array of blue formations: McClernand was rapidly deploying units southward to turn Baldwin's, or the army's, left flank. In extending beyond the southern, or left, flank of Baldwin's Fourth Mississippi, the Unionists hovered closer to the battlefield's key at this critical time — the Natchez Road — than did the Rebel forces. If the Federals gained the dirt road, then Yankee columns could swing eastward, bypass Bowen's force, and march

into Port Gibson unopposed. Gaining the Confederate rear would probably mean the destruction of Bowen's force.[43]

Now, with the day's most severe crisis at hand, this was the battle's
turning point. A guaranteed victory for Grant lay only around 1,000 yards
farther south down the ridge beyond his right flank: an open avenue
leading to glory. At this critical juncture, General Bowen formulated his
most audacious strategy of the war, as he later recalled: "[Viewing] the
enemy's right rapidly deploying and occupying a ridge that gave them ac-
cess to the Natchez Road, I determined to check their movement.[44]

While McClernand's 13,000-man tidal wave of victorious bluecoats
crested to break upon Baldwin's 1,600 defenders, the Missouri Confederates waited in reserve for more than an hour. The long wait and inactivity—the lull before the storm—had caused McCown's veterans to
"almost [conclude that] we were forgotten." But General Bowen galloped
over to the Fifth Missouri's position around one o'clock. Here, to Baldwin's
left-rear, Bowen pulled up hard, and the Missourians could hardly believe
the sight. The general was splattered with blood from the swishing tail of
one of his horses that had been shot earlier in the day. Scrambling to their
feet with a clanging of accouterments, Colonel McCown's enlisted men
quickly fell into formation. Above the noise of Guibor's cannon roaring to
the rear, Bowen announced a bold plan, revealing the details of an audacious charge for all to hear. He explained the dire situation and probably
mentioned that a good many Sixth Missouri soldiers were dying to the
north. Indeed, Colonel Erwin's troops had charged, fought tenaciously,
and recaptured two Virginia cannon of the Botetourt artillery. Without
orders, the "Bloody Sixth" Missouri had attacked Grant's entire left wing
and advanced a quarter mile. But, with only his regiment taking the offensive, Colonel Erwin's amazing success in the dark forests to the north could
not be exploited.[45]

Eventually, overwhelming numbers of Unionists would force Colonel
Erwin's troops off the field and batter Tracy's brigade in the Bruinsburg
Road sector. Attacking Federal units under Bowen's old West Point
classmate (Class of 1853), Major General James B. McPherson, rushed for
the Bayou Pierre bridge. If the bridges across both of the bayou's forks fell,
then Bowen's forces would be cut off from Pemberton, stranded south of
the bayou, and doomed. In addition, both Rebel gunners and infantrymen
in this sector were short on ammunition and had no hope of being resup-
plied in the dense woodlands west of Port Gibson. But the worst threat
from the attackers was to the south. Here McClernand's line was steadily
gaining strength, and as the Union advance gained momentum from a
steady stream of fresh units arriving from the river landing, it eased closer
to the strategic Natchez Road. After Bowen's speech, the Fifth Missouri
soldiers understood the hard day's work before them and knew that many

of them probably would not live to see the sunrise of May 2. In a desperate bid to save Bowen's forces and buy time for the arrival of Pemberton's reinforcements, the frontier exiles were chosen to be sacrificed to preserve the Rebel forces which could not be lost if Vicksburg were to be saved.[46]

General Bowen spoke emotionally to the gray band as he gave the men a virtual death sentence. Correctly making the proper decision at the moment of crisis, he reasoned the best defense against vastly superior numbers was a bold offense. There was no longer time to wait for Pemberton's reinforcements that had supposedly been dispatched from Vicksburg. Baldwin's troops had been taking a beating at the edge of the woods for too long and might break. Ammunition would run so low in this sector that Mississippi officers yelled to fix bayonets and "if they come bleed 'em!" Indeed, the Rodney Road sector might collapse at any moment.[47]

An audacious gambler much like his former neighbor, General Grant, General Bowen would be forced to leave Baldwin's outnumbered Mississippians and Louisianans largely on their own while he struck with his elite Missourians. With much of Grant's Army of the Tennessee surging up the Rodney Road, Bowen prepared to strike with his only available reserves.[48] Fortunately for Bowen and the South, some of the Confederacy's finest troops, the veteran soldiers of the Fifth and Third Missouri, stood ready with high spirits and cartridge boxes filled with forty rounds. Supremely motivated today, these Johnny Rebs from the Western frontier were eager to avenge the Corinth defeat and to win the kind of victory which might unleash them in an effort to reclaim Missouri. As fate would have it, it was now the task of slightly more than 700 Missourians to reverse the day's fortunes by charging headlong into the right flank of the Army of the Tennessee. To save Bowen's force from destruction in order to win perhaps a better opportunity to whip Grant at a future date, a good many Missouri lives had to be sacrificed on one throw of the dice. Without exaggeration, President Davis called the Fifth and Third Missouri's effort to save the day at Port Gibson a "forlorn hope."[49]

General Bowen had wisely placed his final reserves to meet the crisis which was developing to the south. He now had his crack Missouri troops in a perfect position to play his last hand in order to save the day. With his defensive lines at most every point of the field near the breaking point, Bowen led his two Missouri regiments on the double toward Irwin Branch. After surveying the terrain with the care and skill of a great tactician, General Bowen formulated an audacious strategy.[50]

Bowen's desperate scheme to reverse the tide was as simple as it was bold. These Missourians in gray would trek southward up Irwin Branch's hollow. After moving several hundred yards from the Rebel army's left, Bowen would then turn and lead the two regiments westward. The Con-

federate band would then cross the wooded watershed between Irwin and
White branches to hit McClernand's right flank. If these Confederates could
slam into Grant's flank before the main line of grayclad resistance melted
away, then Bowen's command might survive the nightmarish clash in the
forests of Claiborne County to fight another day.[51]

With high hopes for the success of the plan, the Missouri Rebels
pushed into the forested ravine of Irwin Branch in the early afternoon heat.
As Bowen and Cockrell led the way, the column turned left and struggled
up the brush-choked hollow. Included in the task force was at least one section of Guibor's battery. With the Third Missouri following, McCown's infantrymen slapped away vines and thorny limbs clogging the dark hollow.
Summerlike foliage and the depths of the hollow screened their southward
march from Yankee eyes. Also masking the risky maneuver through the
wilderness was another section of Guibor's battery. These Missouri cannon
blasted away and convinced McClernand that the woodlands to Baldwin's
left were swarming with butternuts.[52]

Sixteen-year-old Sergeant Richard M. Lee made sure no Company H
member straggled during the most important mission in the Fifth Missouri's
history. Lee was the kind of noncommissioned officer who could keep the
formation of his primarily northeast Missouri company tight during a
march that must be disciplined. In an ironic twist, the last time that
Sergeant Lee had seen his Audrain County homeland was when an Illinois
colonel named Ulysses S. Grant and his bluecoats had occupied the community in the picturesque Missouri Bluegrass region.[53]

General Bowen and his Confederates in the forested hollow of Irwin
Branch could see little in the junglelike growth, but a Union lieutenant on
the ridge above and west of White Branch could see a good deal from his
elevated perch. The Federal spied sunlight flashing off the muskets of
McCown's men or off Captain Guibor's guns, which evidently were having
difficulty in keeping up with the infantry in the rough terrain. Brigadier
General Alvin P. Hovey, an Indiana lawyer commanding a division, also
saw Rebel bayonets glittering in the sunlight along Irwin hollow. Consequently, much of Bowen's element of surprise suddenly disappeared.[54]

General Hovey flew into action, erecting a strong defense in record
time. He gathered as many infantry reinforcements as he could to meet
Bowen's attack. Eventually thirty Union artillery pieces would be unlimbered atop the ridge. Thanks to Hovey's efforts, Bowen's chances of rolling up the Unionists' flank as he had recently envisioned had now dimmed
considerably. Ascertaining the tactical situation as best he could in the
heavy foliage and timber after marching his troops several hundred yards
up the hollow, Bowen ordered the Missouri column from the sheltering
ravine. With a clattering of gear and on the double, the Missourians crossed
and swung out of Irwin Branch near its headwaters. These stealthy

Confederates moved up, or westward, over the watershed between the two branches and pressed on. Bowen apparently deployed Guibor's section of artillery in a position not far from Irwin Branch. Opening a heavy fire, these cannon now raked McClernand's right.[55] The angry reply was not long in coming.

Twelve Sixteenth and Second Ohio Light Artillery pieces soon bounced along the road topping the ridge above White Branch. This timely reinforcement of Union firepower bolstered the twelve cannon already roaring from the open ridge-top. Along the ridge that Bowen's graycoats were approaching, General McClernand would eventually have the largest artillery concentration of the campaign, thirty guns. Unaware that his audacious movement had been betrayed, General Bowen led his troops straight toward a trap. In a belated effort, Union cannon bellowed from the heights, and shells exploded in the bottom of Irwin Branch. The Rebels were long gone, however.[56]

Moving as fast and quietly as possible, the Fifth Missouri soldiers were first across the timbered watershed as the Federal shells streamed overhead. Colonel Gause and his Third Missouri followed closely behind Colonel McCown's regiment. With Guibor's guns barking behind them and providing inspiration, the Missourians spilled into a deep hollow like a gray flood. Perspiring butternuts struggled through the underbrush and down the slope. The Missouri Confederates pushed onward through the omnipresent wilderness drained by White Branch. For the Rebels in the ranks, the heat and humidity were overwhelming. McCown's soldiers plunged onward without making any unnecessary noise, marching under the heavy timber that masked their trek. Trying hard to ascertain the Unionists' dispositions, General Bowen could only hope that immediately ahead lay the Union army's right.[57]

But much had changed since Bowen had first formulated his strategy. The Union right now extended much farther southward down the ridge and closer to the Natchez Road, and more Union troops and artillery than ever before bolstered the dominating position that Bowen would have to attack. As precious minutes ticked by, the slim possibility of the attack's success grew even less likely on this May afternoon in Mississippi that no Fifth Missouri soldier would ever forget. A formidable array of massed Federal cannon and blue formations now spread along the ridge to greet slightly more than 700 Missourians.[58]

Beneath the heavy timber that almost shut out the sunlight, the Southern files inched onward toward a rendezvous with destiny. But the pace of the Confederate march slowed in the tangled forests as Rebel soldiers groped forward through the woodlands blanketed in the lush growth of late spring. Pushing onward, or what they thought to be a westerly direction, in a lengthy Missouri column organized by battalions, the Confederates continued to push forward with high hopes. The young farm boys in their new gray uniforms prayed that no sudden gust of wind stirred nearby trees and that no musket's accidental discharge betrayed their movement. Bowen's flank march slowed as the Rebels picked through the underbrush which choked the hillside of the second to last ridge before White Branch. In the column's van, dismounted Confederate officers encountered difficulty in leading their horses through the trackless wilderness. Not even the shadows of the woodlands eased the early afternoon humidity and heat for McCown's soldiers, who pressed onward with a determination to make Bowen's plan a success.[59]

But the summery foliage and wooded ridge just east of, and roughly parallel to, White Branch provided concealment as Bowen had hoped. The thick foliage provided a natural screen, ensuring that this audacious maneuver to strike Grant's right flank would be stealthy. Hovey knew that the Confederates were headed his way but could not ascertain their strength or at what point they would strike. General Bowen was equally blind. Hemmed in by forest, he could not exactly pinpoint the position of the Union flank up on the ridge-top. And there was no time to reconnoiter, for the Southern lines elsewhere might be smashed before the ever-changing tactical situation was sorted out. Bowen could only roughly guess at the location of McClernand's right flank.[60]

Figuring that he had trekked close enough to his objective, General Bowen shifted his two regiments a short distance through a canebrake and up a ridge which was parallel to the Union-held ridge to the west. Atop the high ground, Bowen must have been astounded by the scene before him. On the opposite ridge directly west and across White Branch spanned the lengthy lines of Federals and rows of cannon. Bowen now must have realized what had happened: he had marched too far in a northwesterly direction instead of West, bypassing the Unionists' right flank. As a result, thousands of Yankees stood braced along the commanding terrain the Missouri Rebels.[61]

Hardly had Colonel McCown's men gained the ridge-top when at least four Union batteries belched fire across the valley. Close enough to the Confederates to do damage, the well-served Illinois, Missouri, and Ohio cannon barked like thunder, echoing across the valley below. Salvos from Union artillery bombarded the Rebel line, informing the Missourians of the hard day's work ahead. McCown's regiment, in the foremost position, took the brunt of the artillery punishment.[62] As shells whizzed by, Bowen carefully scrutinized the topography before him and hunted for a weakness in the Federal position from his hilltop perch. The stream's wide valley lying before the Union-occupied ridge was clogged with brush, a forest of saplings, and a 100-yard-wide canebrake. In addition, another slight ridge stood before the Confederates as well. On the cleared ridge opposite the

Missourians stood a most formidable array of much of the Army of the Tennessee's might.[63]

Ever the tactical opportunist, General Bowen finally spied a vulnerable point. Unaware of the Rebel movement toward him, Colonel James R. Slack had swung his Second Brigade, Twelfth Division, over an isolated finger of high ground which jutted out eastward from the ridge on the other side of White Branch. This hill stood east of the main ridge and held no Union artillery. The exposed salient was just far enough before the main ridge, crowned with artillery and blue formations, to be gobbled up. Hitting the right flank of Slack's brigade was a good opportunity — much less ambitious than smashing into the extreme right flank of Grant's army — to yet strike a serious blow and perhaps reverse the day's fortunes.[64]

With the Southern lines about to snap in other sectors, General Bowen understood that no more precious time could be wasted. Spurred by a new sense of urgency, Bowen hurled his troops northwestward off the ridge. The onrushing Rebels surged over a hollow and the last high ground, around 300 yards southeast of Slack's right, before the valley of White Branch. One Rebel wrote that as the two Missouri regiments swept onward, "The enemy began to come out of the woods and the slope on their side was soon covered, it seemed about as thick as they could stand."

Vanishing into the valley, Colonel McCown's and Gause's troops continued forward across sloping ground until they reached the dense canebrake. Here the Southerners caught their wind and made last-minute dispositions for the attack to redeem the day. While the shouting of orders and clanging of gear rang across the bottoms, more than 350 Fifth Missourians prepared to reverse the hands of fate with one blow. Simultaneously Colonel Gause hurriedly shifted about 300 Third Missouri Rebels to the left of the Fifth Missouri. The drummer boys of McCown's regiment, some of whom had not yet shaved, scampered ahead of the gray lines stretching through the canebrake, which filled the level floodplain of White Branch. Before the tall cane shoots, Confederate officers prepared their troops for "one of the most desperate charges of the war."[65]

The situation looked most grim in the Third Missouri's front facing to the west. Too many Yankees and cannon, more concentrated here than in McCown's sector, stood before Colonel Gause's regiment. The foremost Union defenders safeguarding the artillery were from Brigadier General George F. McGinnis's First Brigade of Hovey's division. McGinnis's troops had swarmed forward to protect Slack's regiments, which had begun descending into the stream's valley. The formidable might of McGinnis's bulging 2,800-man brigade pouring down the slopes to Slack's southwest was a sobering sight to the handful of Missouri Rebels.

Maneuvering rapidly to meet the crisis, General Bowen positioned the Third Missouri to deal with McGinnis's largely Indiana brigade to the west.

Blue reserves closely behind McGinnis and the spectacle of Slack's movements caused Bowen to conclude that at this point there were "three
brigades in front of a battery to receive our charge."[66]

The Yankees now lavished insult upon the grayclads standing at attention. Spunky Westerners in blue, who had whipped General Green's troops
earlier in the day, waved forage and slouch caps overhead and cheered,
issuing a direct challenge to the Missouri Rebels. The Unionists' heavy
formations all across the slope were "drawn up to receive us, with flags flut-
tering defiance," wrote one Confederate who would never forget the
scene.[67]

But the prospects for success appeared higher where the Fifth Missouri
faced northwest toward Slack's knoll. Preoccupied with the noisy and
pesky Rebel skirmishers before them, many of the Iowa, Indiana, and Ohio
troops were distracted from Bowen's threat encroaching from the bottoms
to the southeast. Slack's right flank, on open ground atop the knoll, and
his rear were unprotected and exposed. Apparently few, if any, blue skirmishers watched the southern end of the line. Now these Federal forces in
the wake of the Missourians' advance were vulnerable.[68]

Before Colonel McCown's soldiers, the northern tier of the main ridge
held by the Unionists consisted of three separate spurs. To Slack's rear and
right, these hilltops bristled with six Second Ohio guns divided into three
sections: a much less formidable array than the eighteen cannon of the First
Missouri (Company A), Second Illinois (Company A), and Sixteenth Ohio
batteries massed before Colonel Gause's troops. Another six cannon eventually bolstered this Second Ohio artillery concentration for a total of
thirty guns that the Missouri Rebels would face this afternoon. The Fifth
Missouri would be directly attacking a narrow front defended primarily by
only one Federal battery. But if the advance of the Third Missouri faltered,
then most of the Union cannon would turn to enfilade McCown's unit with
the most concentrated firepower they had ever seen.[69]

Although his original plan had been thwarted, General Bowen was
determined to attack immediately. He had no choice but to launch an offensive strike at any cost. The Fifth Missouri, perpendicular to Slack's unwary
right flank, was in an excellent position to do considerable damage. Clearly,
every Confederate would be needed in the ranks that day. Even Lieutenant
Colonel Bevier's teenage black slave, who fairly "panted for the blood of
the foe," was in the Fifth Missouri's formation and ready to charge. While
sunlight flashed off bayonets at the edge of the canebrake, McCown's
soldiers stood in formation near the tall cane and again prepared for a
bloody meeting with the men in blue. Knowing that hard fighting was imminent, company leaders of the Fifth Missouri drew revolvers and swords
from scabbards. The killing was about to begin in earnest.[70]

In one of the most desperate attacks of the war, General Bowen prepared to hurl two "very small" regiments — the Missouri Brigade's most diminutive units — of slightly more than 700 troops into the midst of two almost full Union brigades. Meeting one of its greatest challenges, the Fifth Missouri contained the smallest number of soldiers. Facing a gauntlet of cannon and thousands of Federals, the Missourians' situation became even more precarious with a concentration of Union reserves just behind the foremost lines. In addition, two parallel and deeply eroded forks, or gullies, of White Branch stood as obstacles before the Fifth Missouri. These natural barriers promised to break the regiment's alignment at the most crucial moment. The 100-yard-wide canebrake in the valley's lowest point posed a natural obstacle to impede the attack as well. This canebrake "was about thirty feet high and so thick one could not see into it more than a few feet." In addition, Guibor's cannon would not be available to knock out Federal artillery because these guns, now out of ammunition, had withdrawn to the Rodney Road sector.[71]

Determined officers such as Adjutant Greenwood, Colonel Bevier, and Major Waddell rode down the lines to make final adjustments in formations and to speak their last words of encouragement to those young men of the Fifth Missouri who were about to meet their Makers. No doubt the former Warrensburg clerk, Adjutant Greenwood, wondered if he would encounter his brother in blue during the next few minutes.

Calm and poised as usual, General Bowen rode to the front, pointed his saber, and screamed, "Charge!" Cutting loose with their high-pitched "regular Missouri yell," the Missouri soldiers surged toward Slack's exposed flank like an avalanche. The Rebel yells of the attackers shook the bottoms. In their most desperate attack to date, the Missourians charged over the northern edge of the knoll about 300 yards to Slack's southeast "with the ferocity of demons," as one Rebel recalled.[72]

Moving swiftly through the cane, Colonel McCown's formations charged straight toward the vulnerable right flank and rear of Slack's Second Brigade. Cheering Southerners rushed forward with colorful battle flags waving, maintaining alignment "as if only on parade." Slack's right, the Twenty-Eighth and Twenty-Fourth Iowa Volunteer Infantry, was advancing in the branch's floodplain and was shattered by the gray onslaught which engulfed it. In tangling with the Confederacy's best troops, the Iowans never knew what hit them amid the woodlands. The most advanced blue units took the brunt of the assault and were hurled out of the valley. Panic-stricken Federals fled back up the knoll from which they had come. Colonel Slack was now alerted to the full extent of the danger. Responding quickly, he threw his two remaining regiments, the Fifth-Sixth Ohio and Forty-Seventh Indiana Volunteer Infantry, into the gap left by the beaten Iowa men.[73]

Around 1,000 Ohio and Indiana soldiers hurriedly deployed on the eastern slope of the knoll and stood ready for action. At about the same time, the 500-man Twenty-Fourth Indiana Volunteer Infantry, one of McGinnis's regiments to Slack's left, also swung downhill to greet the onrushing Southerners. Gaining momentum, Colonel McCown's attackers continued rolling headlong into White Branch, which ran parallel to the advancing gray ranks. The eroded branch bed, twelve foot deep and twenty foot wide, presented a serious obstacle. McCown's once neat formations disintegrated upon hitting the moat-like ditch. Groups of Fifth Missouri soldiers angled off in various directions as exploding shells blew holes in their lines. Scrubby growth clogging the wash further fragmented the attacking waves of howling Confederates. After splashing through water and mud, Colonel McCown's enlisted men scurried across the ditch and scaled the gully's opposite side. Once on the other side, the frontier exiles realigned instinctively as they had practiced on dozens of drill fields.[74]

Despite being hard-hit by the murderous fires, the veteran soldiers of the Third Missouri rushed quickly to form to McCown's left. The battered but intact gray formations soon stood poised amid the underbrush and the blistering shell-fire. With the two heavily outnumbered Missouri regiments stretching across the bottoms, General Bowen and Colonels Cockrell, Bevier, and Gause once again led their men forward with a ringing shout and grim determination to carry the field at any cost. The rugged terrain and the bombardment of the Union batteries above them slowed, but failed to break, the most desperate Confederate attack launched at Port Gibson. Seldom had any charge in the Civil War faced greater odds or seemed more suicidal than Bowen's audacious bid to reverse the day's fortune with the Fifth and Third Missouri.[75]

In a half-circle hugging the knoll's base, a new Union wall of resistance quickly took shape to confront Bowen's challenge. The Fifty-Sixth Ohio and Forty-Seventh Indiana stood astride White Branch and faced southeastward. Meanwhile, the Twenty-Fourth Indiana deployed along a dry stream and these soldiers faced east. Parallel to the valley and perpendicular to the Fifty-Sixth Ohio, on Slack's right, the Indiana soldiers held a key position at the angled defensive line. Veteran Federal troops hustled into formation with alacrity, as a solid Union defense formed in the valley's heavy woodlands at the base of the high ground. On the Forty-Seventh Indiana's left, the bluecoats of the Twenty-Ninth Wisconsin Volunteer Infantry likewise shifted down into the bottoms to meet the ragged Rebels.[76]

But the worst development for Fifth Missouri fortunes occurred when the booming Union cannon atop the ridge turned to the left to rake Colonel McCown's onrushing ranks. Canister from the Yankee artillery blew great swarths in the Fifth Missouri's formations, leaving a good many grayclad bodies strewn throughout the bottoms. The Federal infantrymen, meanwhile, could see nothing before them in the dense canebrake. With fixed bayonets and cocked muskets, the Unionists could only listen as the screams of hundreds of McCown's attackers grew louder. The Fifth Missouri, with the Third Missouri to the left, continued rolling onward through the canebrake like an avalanche pouring down a hill with ever-increasing momentum. Rows of Union artillery pieces hammered away from the heights above them, inflicting terrible damage.[77]

Facing a fierce Confederate attack, the Federal troops became uneasy. From the canebrake roared the din of pounding drums, Rebel yells, and hundreds of thudding feet, which blared ever higher in the lush growth. Nothing could be seen before the defenders but the cane stalk forest. At the Missourians' head, General Bowen led the Fifth Missouri "sabre in hand into the thickest of the fight [while] officers and men followed with the confidingness of children."[78]

Then all of a sudden hundreds of Fifth Missouri Confederates swarmed out of the cane less than 90 feet distant from the masses of Yankees. Behind Confederate officers came a throng of wild-looking enlisted men in dirty gray with faces contorted from shouting at the top of their lungs. Yelling Rebels trampled over the cane en masse, shooting on the run and shaking bayonets. Flowing above the sea of green stalks, the Missourians' blue regimental colors with their white Latin, or Christian, crosses flapped in the sunlight. Only now did Colonel Slack realize the full extent of the serious challenge, for his troops were about to meet the famous "flower of the Southern Army."[79] Braced for the worst, the Unionists sighted muskets on the howling Confederates ripping through the canebrake with the force of a tornado.

Ohioans, Indianans, and Wisconsiners opened with a murderous volley at a range from which they could not miss. Scores of Rebels crumpled to the ground after the whole Yankee line exploded in flame. The Fifth Missouri charged headlong into the face of two fires erupting from the north and west. According to one Missourian, the "minié balls [flew] into our ranks as thick and as fast as hailstones from a thunder cloud or rain drops in an April shower."[80]

General Bowen and his horse tumbled hard when swept by bullets. Somehow surviving, the general crawled from under the dead animal and sprang up. Swinging atop an aide's horse, Bowen continued leading his troops onward into the fiery cauldron. The galling fire decimated the Fifth Missouri as never before, with soldiers "falling by the dozen."[81] So concentrated was the Unionists' firepower, wrote one survivor, that "the very trees and underbrush were cut away by the incessant fire." But through the raging holocaust, the Confederates of the Fifth Missouri continued onward with flags flying and wild screams. Captain Coale fell while exhorting Company G into the hurricane of fire. A perfect target on horseback, Adjutant

Greenwood galloped across the lines until he was riddled with bullets. Spinning off his mount, the native Kentuckian tumbled to earth to rise no more. One of the first to die, Greenwood breathed his last among the cane stalks, while his cheering soldiers rushed by and then fell themselves. Veteran Yankees before the Fifth Missouri maintained their poise under the onslaught and blasted away. Sheets of fire rippled across Slack's and McGinnis's densely packed ranks, exploding in the faces of the Missourians.[82]

Commanding the unit in his first action, Lieutenant Townsend saw Company E cut to pieces. One soldier killed by the scorching fire was Private Thomas G. Childers, age twenty-one, and a good many other Franklin County boys were cut down. In the Fifth Missouri's van was Color Sergeant Stark, waving the bullet-tattered banner for all to see. Suddenly he crumpled in a pile when a minié ball shattered his right arm. While bullets toppled cane stems beside the fallen colors, Sergeant James M. Walton, a Polk County farmer, snatched the shredded flag from the body-littered ground and charged onward into the smoke. Dropping to the ground as if cut down by a giant scythe, the stalks of cane snapped as a storm of projectiles ripped them in half. Never having faced such a murderous fire before, one Missourian believed that "there was enough ammunition shot at us to have killed or wounded the entire army, and then had enough left for another battle."[83]

Striking an exceptionally strong point, Colonel McCown's left took severe punishment, raked by the defenders' volleys at the fiery defensive angle of the Yankees. The Fifth Missouri's right, meanwhile, met less resistance but also suffered damage and high casualties. The right-most companies of the charging Fifth Missouri swarmed toward an isolated northern spur of the main ridge. Here two Ohio guns were exposed after the artillery's infantry support melted away before the Missourians' fierce onslaught. If the Fifth Missouri's left could continue to advance and gain ground, then Colonel McCown's right would have a good chance to capture the blazing cannon, which dominated the spur just southwest of Slack's knoll.[84]

Colonel McCown's attackers made headway at every point and struck hard with the slashing impact of "the South's Finest." Swinging eastward, the Fifth Missouri zeroed in and tried to encircle the Twenty-Ninth Wisconsin, which was aligned perpendicular to the Forty-Seventh Indiana. Delivering a powerful blow, these easternmost Fifth Missouri attackers slammed savagely into the right flank of the Wisconsin regiment. Some 500 blueclads from Wisconsin, who had not seen action before, were left for the most part to fend for themselves on McGinnis's extreme right when other Union troops bolted. If the wavering Wisconsin regiment broke, then the Missouri Rebels might well be on their way to turning Grant's right flank. All the while, the distinctive "Missouri yell — a cross between an Indian war-whoop and a Yankee huzzah" split the air, the Federals further unnerving. But the advantages in momentum and hard-hitting shock power of the attackers would not last long. The Fifth Missouri Confederates only had a few minutes to roll up McGinnis's right flank before powerful Union reinforcements would arrive to make that objective an impossibility.[85]

The slaughter among the Fifth Missouri soldiers continued unabated before the ridge. Lieutenant Stokely, twice wounded in previous battles, was hit for the last time. The young officer was leading and "gallantly cheering" his Company A onward when he was killed in the merciless fire.[86]

Just when it appeared that the Fifth Missouri attackers would smash the Federal lines and turn the right of both the Forty-Seventh Indiana and Twenty-Ninth Wisconsin, a wave of blue reinforcements arrived in the nick of time. More than 1,000 Yankees of several Union regiments swung over the ridge and poured down the slopes to engage the onrushing Missourians. At almost the last moment, the arriving Union reserves bolstered the Forty-Seventh Indiana and Twenty-Ninth Wisconsin, hit hard primarily by McCown's right, and the Fifty-Sixth Ohio, under the assault of the Fifth Missouri's left. These timely Union reinforcements opened a withering fire upon the howling Southerners in the valley below.[87]

The Missourians' attack slowed when they encountered a White Branch fork. With the punishment from an ever-increasing amount of Union firepower and with Rebels dropping all around, the charge lost momentum and faltered. The situation was especially grim on the left of the Fifth Missouri. Here the Twenty-Fourth Indiana, at right angles to the Fifty-Sixth Ohio, enfiladed Colonel McCown's left flank with volleys at close range. As never before, thousands of bluecoats now swept the bottoms with a musketry which seemed never to cease.[88]

Now the turning point of Bowen's desperate bid to reverse the tide at Port Gibson occurred. The deep gully had to be crossed by the Missouri Confederates for the attack to succeed. But despite a valiant effort, it could not be done in the face of such a withering fire. Musketry exploding in the Confederates' faces and dozens of Union cannon pounding lines to bits were too much for even these elite veterans. Bloodied and bruised, the Rebels headed back several yards to the shelter of White Branch. Seemingly possessed with a death wish on May 1, General Bowen once more went down while leading the charge. His horse was one of four unlucky mounts killed from under the general that day.[89]

Faced with a solid wall of fire, Colonel McCown's soldiers jumped into the twelve-foot-deep natural trench for shelter from the storm. Now probably less than 600 Confederates fanned out and took firing positions against the bank of the gully. Expecting such badly cut-up adversaries to flee, Colonel Slack expressed surprise when McCown's veterans stood their ground in the canebrake of White Branch and "soon recovered" from the terrible punishment.[90]

The Third Missouri, on Colonel McCown's left, suffered the Fifth Missouri's identical fate; after initially achieving gains, it was hurled back with heavy losses. The timely arrival of a Sixteenth Ohio section of guns and another Indiana regiment on the buckling Union right had solidified resistance. These Union reinforcements then added their wrath to the enfilade fire punishing McCown's left. Indeed, to the Fifth Missouri's left, or west, there arrived two Indiana regiments of around 1,000 soldiers. These units had beaten Colonel Gause's Missouri troops at Pea Ridge barely a year before and played a key role in denying Colonel McCown's soldiers victory at Port Gibson. Blunted from achieving additional gains, both the Fifth and Third Missouri Rebels, therefore, took cover in the brushy environs of White Branch to gamely continue the fight despite heavy losses and little hopes for success.[91]

With more reinforcements adding might to the Federal resistance, even more Northern firepower poured into the branch and punished the survivors of the Fifth Missouri. The Yankees seemed to swarm everywhere: blue legions stood atop the ridge, were strewn across the slopes, and were aligned at the base of the high ground. So many Unionists had converged to repel the Missourians' assault that only one explanation was possible: the Confederates had struck closer to Grant's right-center than Grant's extreme right flank. Indeed, the Union right had extended farther south down the ridge toward the Natchez Road as Bowen had feared. By the time of the assault, Bowen's Rebels had slammed into an ever-widening front which was more powerful, in terms of numbers of troops and artillery, than anyone dared believe.[92]

The ravine of White Branch, nevertheless, had to be held at all costs to buy more time. A last stand would have to be made along the brackish watercourse choked with thorny bushes and cane if Bowen's command were to survive bloody May 1. The Fifth Missouri Confederates, according to one surprised Federal officer, were solidly dug-in and returned fire "with great spirit and pertinacity." Concealed amid the saplings and thick underbrush, Colonel McCown's soldiers blasted away from "under the protection of the creek banks not ten feet distant from them, while they [the Yankees] were on the open ground and suffered immensely from our fires." The men of the Fifth Missouri had the Fifty-Sixth Ohio in an especially bad fix. Exposed on the treeless slope only a few yards distant, the Ohio soldiers made fine targets for the sharp-eyed and veteran Missouri marksmen. Unable to aim at targets hidden along the smoke-covered low ground, the Unionists sent volleys that were mostly high and crashed into trees well above the ravine.[93]

The Ohioans, first bloodied at Shiloh, had been practically invincible so far today. They had captured an Alabama battle flag, overrun Southern artillery, and aligned in a fine defensive position just before they were hit by McCown's charge. But the tables were now turned. Along the length of the bank, fast-working Confederates fired point-blank at the "U.S." buckles and breastplates on blue uniforms, which made excellent targets on the higher ground as they glistened in the sun. "Stars and Stripes" and regimental colors of the Yankees flowed in the smoky haze and fluttered in Rebel faces so near they could almost be grabbed. With such advantages, Colonel McCown's soldiers decimated the blue ranks. Loads of .69 caliber ball and buckshot from Fifth Missouri muskets brought down finely uniformed officers and color bearers. Serving as a well-dug trench, the length of the ravine spat fire, flaming along the rim for hundreds of yards. Ohioans steadily dropped to the well-aimed fire of the Missouri Confederates like leaves on a windy autumn morning.[94]

To the Fifty-Sixth Ohio's right, the Twenty-Fourth Indiana likewise took a severe beating. The Indiana Yankees blazed away so fiercely that their rifles overheated and could not be fired. The close-range duel raged along the brush-choked environs of White Branch and continued with an intensity seldom seen in this war. However both sides refused to budge and relinquish ground.[95]

More than 500 hardy loggers, woodsmen, and fishermen of the Twenty-Ninth Wisconsin faced the firepower delivered from the Fifth Missouri's right. This inexperienced Federal unit was hit on the right flank and took severe punishment. Swept by McCown's enfilade musketry, the unseasoned Wisconsin boys were in serious trouble. Dead and wounded Wisconsin Yankees piled up at a rate equaled by only one other Union regiment at Port Gibson. Despite suffering under a murderous baptismal fire, the Wisconsin soldiers initially held firm and withstood the wrath of the more experienced Missourians.[96]

Behind the front lines of blueclads were reserve formations, stretching across the slopes and along the ridge-top. These Union troops also swept the ravine's length with gunfire which found Fifth Missouri victims and made the lower position a living hell for the defenders. But the Federal artillery inflicted the most damage. Because White Branch curved slightly northeastward at this point, the ten First Missouri and Second Illinois field pieces enfiladed McCown's position from the southwest, sweeping the Confederate line with a vicious fire.[97]

It appeared to Colonel McCown's soldiers as if Grant's whole army was pouring down the hillsides to confront the Missouri regiments and unleash an unceasing fire into the gully. A veteran officer, Colonel Cockrell estimated that his two smallest Missouri regiments had charged into the midst of impossible odds. Indeed, fewer than 700 Rebels had initially smashed into at least several thousand Unionists, and even more Northern reserves had since flooded over the ridge-top to join the fight. General Bowen later concluded that his band had plowed into twelve regiments, but actually the strength of the Federals eventually increased to almost two divisions.[98]

Never before had the Missourians been subjected to such a withering fire. From the ridge-top, the slopes, and the base of the high ground poured an immense concentration of Union musketry and cannon-fire at an unprecedented rate. More Fifth Missouri boys fell in the cyclone, dropping into the bottom of the bloody ravine to rise no more. Teenage Sergeant Lee went down without a sound when a minié ball struck him in the head and passed through his brain. Trapped in a muddy ravine which might soon become a final resting place of the Fifth Missouri, McCown's soldiers fought back "with the desperation of brave men anticipating death or capture."[99]

Only a few yards distant, the Fifty-Sixth Ohio began to waver under the pounding. Ohio boys in blue fell in clumps, while Union officers tried to keep their hard-hit and skittish troops in line in the face of McCown's blistering fire. But, unable to take any more punishment from the rapidly firing Missourians, some Yankees fled across the ridge and seemed to be headed back to Ohio. Fifth Missouri soldiers raised a cheer when most of the Ohio regiment bolted rearward, leaving their dead and wounded littered across the slope like cordwood. But the Ohioans retired only a short distance until they were bolstered by one of McGinnis's regiments, and resistance solidified once again. Then the Ohio boys once more resumed fighting as gamely as before. As so often during the brutal fighting in this bloody sector, Union reinforcements had once again plugged a gap.[100]

The Twenty-Ninth Wisconsin had also suffered enough of the devastating fire of the Fifth Missouri. With his command being cut to pieces, the desperate Wisconsin colonel warned Colonel McGinnis that his regiment was being destroyed. Stung by McCown's enfilade volleys sweeping over his regiment's length from right to left, the Wisconsin colonel faced a grave crisis. To save the Wisconsin regiment, McGinnis hurried an Indiana regiment downhill.[101] In timely fashion, the Eighth Indiana charged down the slope to rescue the nearly surrounded Twenty-Ninth Wisconsin, "which was being hotly pressed with great slaughter." Indeed, in one final offensive effort of the day, the Fifth Missouri Rebels were still trying to turn the right flank of the Wisconsin regiment. But hundreds of fresh Indiana soldiers entering the contest ended such ambitions of the never-say-die Fifth Missouri attackers. Cheering Federal reinforcements soon added their raking volleys to the inferno enveloping the ever-dwindling defenders along White Branch.[102]

Lieutenant William C. Fincher, age twenty-six, staggered mortally wounded along the muddy branch. A minié ball had crashed through his body with devastating effect when the soft lead bounced off bones and tore holes in flesh. Bleeding Rebels of the Fifth Missouri lay sprawled in grotesque positions throughout the gully. Drummer boys quit attending the wounded to grab muskets, and they shot at Yankees in fits of rage after seeing so many friends and relatives cut down.[103]

Besides Lieutenant Fincher, the Leesville community lost another of her sons when Corporal George Washington Parks fell. One of the Parks boys of Company G, the seventeen-year-old, died in the ravine. The situation of the Fifth Missouri became more critical as blue formations converged on the isolated Missourians from three directions. Enfilading fires came from different directions and elevations, sweeping the gully with a vengeance. More of Colonel McCown's graycoats dropped when they were hit simultaneously from multiple angles in the ravine, which was becoming a death trap.

General McClernand's right, meanwhile, continued to extend southward down the ridge, lengthened by arriving Federal reinforcements. Before the flaming ravine, the Union lines spanned everywhere for hundreds of yards. The blue formations continued growing in size and inching ever-closer, causing one of McCown's officers to conclude that the Union hordes were "rapidly closing [in] around us" on this day of death.[104]

Far from rolling up Grant's right flank, McCown's band was pinned down, and it was being slaughtered to purchase time and help save the day. Decimating one Federal line after another only to have new blue lines suddenly appear like magic merely demonstrated the futility of battling against such superior odds.[105] Union batteries to the far left atop the ridge caused the most havoc among the ranks of the Fifth Missouri. Sighting field pieces northeastward to fire down and sweep White Branch, cannoneers of the Sixteenth Ohio section, First Missouri, and Second Illinois Light Artillery enfiladed McCown's position from left to right. Thirty massed cannon played the decisive role in breaking the Missourians' desperate bid for victory on May 1.[106]

These Union batteries roared as one for nearly two hours, as double loads of canister cut down brush and defenders. Sergeant Robert Guthrie, the former McGee College student, was sent sprawling end over end when he was hit "in the breast by a cannon ball."[107] But the young sergeant, the brother of Company I's captain, would survive. Thirty cannon bellowed above the smoke-filled valley and steadily delivered death. So fast did one Ohio artillery piece fire that it overheated and was permanently impaired.[108]

But each Fifth Missouri left unhurt in the ravine helped to steal a complete victory from Grant. A decisive victory slipped through Grant's hands as the ravine resistance ate up the clock and sapped the strength of Union attacks elsewhere. Every hour won by blood and audacity in holding the gully added up to a victory of sorts. Those Yankee troops who would have shattered the thin Rebel defensive lines along Bayou Pierre and Centers Creek at the Rodney Road sector had rushed to the right to counter the Missourians' unexpected attack. Although it had not rolled up the Union flank, Bowen's strategy was successful because the effectiveness of the attack by the Fifth and Third Missouri had stolen Grant's momentum. The thin and battered lines of Bowen's army would not snap that day.[109]

But the price was high, and now the survivors of the Fifth Missouri were in grave danger and in the worst fix of their lives. Cartridge boxes ran low of rounds after the Missouri Rebels banged away at opponents for nearly two hours. Confederate fire gradually slowed, sputtering to only the level of a hot skirmish. With fixed bayonets, Colonel McCown's survivors prepared for a fight to the finish if necessary.[110]

Company E, on the Fifth Missouri's left, was devastated. Hit by the flank fire, Lieutenant Townsend's dead and injured soldiers were piled-up throughout the gully. Casualties were especially heavy in one small Franklin County mess of Company E. Twenty-two-year-old Private John Jacob Momon, who was killed, was referred to in a comrade's letter as "a fine looking Soldier and as brave as they make them." Momon had been cited for gallantry at Corinth. Also going down in this one Company E mess was Private Heszekiah Joyce, who dropped with a mangled right shoulder. Both Momon and Joyce had been students of Private Absalom Roby Dyson, also a mess member, at a Japan, Franklin County, log schoolhouse, before the war changed their lives forever. Another messmate, Sergeant James McMeeken, crumpled to the ground with a shattered left leg. He had also been commended for bravery in storming Battery Powell and Fort Richardson.[111]

The return fire from the Fifth Missouri dwindled with no resupply. McCown's Confederates scoured the cartridge boxes of dead and wounded comrades, who now lay in heaps at the gully's bottom, but only a few rounds were secured. Commanding Company D for the first time, Lieutenant Hearn was knocked out of action with multiple wounds when a shell exploded practically atop him.[112] Powder-stained soldiers of the Fifth Missouri often glanced rearward, hoping to see the reinforcements that General Pemberton had sworn would be sent to their aid. During what seemed like an eternity, no reinforcements were forthcoming, and the canebrake to the rear stayed empty except for the battered stalks drooping over bodies. As at Corinth, the Missouri Rebels had been abandoned to fight and die alone against odds that could not be beat. Even Private John N. Cates, whom Captain Bradford could never get to shoot a musket at the bluecoats, was now blazing away in the depleted ranks of Company C with newfound determination.[113]

First Missouri cannoneers in blue had the best angle to blast down the gully and enfilade the position of the Fifth Missouri. One casualty of the artillery hell was Private Thomas B. Halstead, age twenty-two. Halstead was killed instantly when a cannon ball passed completely through his body.[114] Pinned-down Fifth Missouri defenders now returned little fire, making the best of a bad situation. Most Confederates hugged the banks of the gully, finding some shelter. After almost two hours of vicious fighting along bloody White Branch, still no succor had arrived to the relief of the Missouri Rebels. With his Missourians more than holding their own, Bowen had by this time departed the ravine area to stabilize other sectors. He now dispatched messengers to tell the two cutoff Missouri regiments to withdraw before they were destroyed: The attack and the defense of the ravine had already exceeded the general's expectations, buying time and succeeding tactically. But these orders failed to arrive because the couriers were unable to locate the advanced and isolated position of the Missourians.[115]

At last a Rebel courier reached the surviving Fifth Missouri Confederates. The graycoat messenger dashed through the bloody canebrake and the storm of projectiles to deliver the instructions that would save the Fifth Missouri from annihilation. By any measure, Colonel McCown's boys and the other Missouri Rebels had accomplished a great deal during the bitter struggle along White Branch in a "forlorn hope" to reverse the day's fortunes.

Placing the slashing assault of the Missourians in a proper perspective, General Bowen later wrote: "I am of the opinion that this attack saved the right from being overwhelmed and kept the enemy back until nearly sunset." And, most important, the attack had ensured a successful retrograde movement to safety.[116]

Anger spread through the Fifth Missouri's ranks with the orders to retire. On this afternoon in hell, Bowen had expected his exiled Westerners to perform at a high level, and he had not been disappointed by the stirring accomplishments of the hardest fighting troops of Vicksburg's army. The young general from Carondelet worte that the Fifth and Third Missouri's "desperate move carried out with a determination characteristic of the regiments making it, saved us from being flanked and captured, and gave us until sunset to prepare for our retreat." Seldom in the Civil War had so few soldiers done so much against so many and at a more critical moment in a decisive campaign.[117]

Grimy with powder stains, company commanders of the Fifth Missouri zigzagged down the ranks and indicated withdrawal procedures by gestures because the roar of battle made speaking useless. Now more powerful than ever before, the Federal lines stretched as far as the eye could see "away for nearly a mile on our left [and right as well], and [were] rapidly closing around us" in a final bid to destroy the two small and decimated Missouri regiments, which were isolated, badly exposed, and without support, ammunition, or hope.[118]

A desperate rearguard action and a solid defense by a few Missouri boys were now needed to ensure a safe withdrawal of the Fifth Missouri. Either Lieutenant Colonel Bevier ordered a company to provide a delaying party or the handful of volunteers in dirty gray simply responded to the challenge. At any rate, these veterans of Company I stepped forward for one of the most dangerous and unforgettable missions of the Civil War. It would be the task of seven of Colonel McCown's Rebels to attempt to freeze the foremost Unionists in place while the Fifth Missouri escaped eastward.[119]

Clearly, a strong sense of duty and a deep motivation caused this handful of northeast Missouri soldiers to volunteer for a suicidal mission. For these ragged Confederates of Company I, this war was a very personal fight. The Barton brothers, for instance, had a good many personal scores to settle and were eager for revenge. Covered with powder, dirt, and sweat, and looking like anything but some of the Fifth Missouri's elite soldiers, the two young ex-farmers from near Woodville, Macon County, had good reason to volunteer for this desperate undertaking. Carrying on a military tradition of Kentucky antecedents, Corporal Stephen Allen Barton, age twenty-three and destined to die in this war, and Private Elias Taylor Barton, five years Stephen's senior, were the last of six brothers in Rebel ranks.

The Barton clan from the Chariton and Salt River country had already sacrificed much in this war. A younger sibling had been taken from his Missouri home before his horrified family and was killed by Federal militiamen. Private George Washington Barton now lay near death in a Deep South infirmary. The Company I enlisted man, age twenty-five, would perish before autumn, dying of disease like so many other Fifth Missouri soldiers. Another Barton brother had been thrown into the hell-hole of a prison in Alton, Illinois, where he died on the frozen bluffs above the Mississippi. In addition, one other brother would succumb to Yankee minié balls. Clearly, the Barton family paid more than their fair share in the cause of their nation's independence.[120]

Reasoning that they might as well end it here and together, the Barton brothers of Company I gathered the last few remaining cartridges and prepared to hold out to the last man if necessary. It must have seemed to Stephen and Elias that many years had passed since the idealistic brothers had in 1861 eagerly joined Captain Guthrie's band of partisans at Penny's Bridge along the Chariton to defend their homeland against the invaders in blue uniforms. One of Colonel McCown's finest noncommissioned officers, Sergeant Thomas D. Moore, a former McGee College student, led this elite group of Fifth Missouri stalwarts. Like other Company I members from the college, Sergeant Moore could never forget how hundreds of Illinois troops had overrun his hometown and school on that fateful April day in 1861.[121]

Also preparing to buy time by holding the Federal legions at bay was a reliable father-son team of Company I: Virginia-born Private Allen Marion Edgar, a fifty-two-year-old Macon County farmer, and his son Private John Henry Edgar, a twenty-two-year-old farmer who would perish at Vicksburg. One volunteer of this cadre of some of the Fifth Missouri's finest soldiers was Sergeant Charles B. Leathers, another hardy middle-class farmer from Macon County. The sergeant had ancestors from the North Carolina Piedmont, and his Southern heritage was also indicated by an older sister's name, Louisiana. Few Fifth Missouri Rebels would ever forget the tall and slim yeoman of the Western frontier, who remained compassionate and uncorrupted by the horror and brutality of this war. Sergeant Leathers's mild manner and quiet ways beguiled his tenacity on the battlefield, where he was as tough as nails. In addition, this grizzled soldier was an excellent leader of men, especially during an emergency such as this rearguard action. A good judge of character, Surgeon Dysart considered Leathers "one of the best soldiers I ever saw," and the hard-fighting sergeant from Macon County would once again prove his worth on this hot afternoon in Mississippi.[122]

Perhaps the most irrepressible volunteer of this elite group of Company I soldiers was Private John D. Dale. Long a natural leader in the ranks, Dale would nevertheless remain a private for four years. He had been a common tiller of the Randolph County soil, living peacefully on the land that he loved until Union soldiers from another state crossed the Mississippi and invaded the agricultural paradise that he called home. As no other enlisted man in the regiment, Private Dale epitomized the heart and soul of the Fifth Missouri.[123]

While the seven Company I Rebels made their last stand in the gully, more than three hundred Fifth Missouri soldiers retired eastward on the double. Union volleys continued to sweep the ravine end to end, but Colonel McCown's Confederates were able to escape. In fact, the volume of fire from the Unionists had escalated to a steady din and a constant roar, and the noise and palls of smoke meant that the bluecoats failed to decipher the Fifth Missouri's diminished rate of fire and the pell-mell flight to the rear. Colonel McCown's Rebels, meanwhile, raced back through the canebrake, heading rearward to regain Bowen. Sulfurous clouds of smoke hanging low over White Branch helped screen their wild dash to safety and saved the lives of countless Fifth Missouri soldiers. Abandoning the body-littered ravine must have been especially hard for the Mitchell clan. Two severely wounded cousins, Privates Thomas Wesley Mitchell, a yeoman of twenty-two, and Arthur Ewing Mitchell, age twenty-three, had to be left behind by their seven relatives of Company C. The surviving Mitchell boys trusted that God and the mercy of the victorious Yankees would spare the lives of their two injured Mitchell men who were now farther away from their Polk County home and families than ever before.[124]

Taking the shortest route back to the Rodney Road sector, McCown's Rebels dashed northeastward over a cane-covered hill as they ran for their lives. Whenever they were able to see through the smoke of battle, some Unionists now turned their fire on the jumbled gray mass vomiting out of White Branch. Federals dropped more soldiers of McCown's regiment in the cane patch, which had become a killing field. Some Fifth Missouri wounded, such as Private George Washington Parks who had gone down with a smashed leg, were half-carried and half-dragged over the top of the hill. Private Parks, a teenager, escaped through the canebrake, but he would later perish of infection.[125]

As demonstrated by the hard-hitting attack of the Third and Fifth Missouri, General Bowen's unpredictability and boldness on May 1 not only slowed but also caused the blueclads to be more cautious by the afternoon of that bloody day. Additionally, the Barton brothers, the Edgar father and son team, Sergeants Moore and Leathers, and Private Dale continued holding the masses of Federals at bay with little more than audacity. It seemed to the Unionists that the Missourians continued to hold the wooded ravine, while other Missouri Rebels might be maneuvering to strike another blow on the right flank. Frozen in place and made cautious by Bowen's hard-hitting tactics and audacity, thousands of Unionists held their ground and failed to advance. The survivors of Colonels McCown's and Gause's regiments meanwhile escaped to the main line to fight another day.[126]

The tenacious last stand by the seven Company I boys worked better than anyone expected. Under a lowering four o'clock sun and a slight diminishing of the day's heat, the Rebel band continued firing, purchasing time with audacity and its last few remaining bullets. Fearing that the Yankees had gained the Natchez Road and swung behind him to reach Port Gibson, General Bowen worried about the meaning of the sudden silence before the Rodney Road defensive line. General Baldwin's troops, therefore, were ordered forward to ascertain the Unionists' locations and intentions. A good many seasoned Yankees remained before Baldwin, but these Unionists would not move forward until the Northern army's right advanced over the ravine obstacle.[127]

Thanks to the aggressive efforts of the Missourians that day, so tentative had General Hovey become that not for some time would the Twelfth Division commander take action. Finally, however, Hovey ordered two Indiana regiments to sweep the length of the gully. Meanwhile, Dale, Moore, the Barton brothers, Leathers, and the Edgars blazed away with their last remaining rounds, while hundreds of Indiana soldiers pushed up White Branch from the north.[128] Just before the Indianans converged upon them, the handful of grayclads of Company I expended their final rounds. In one of the war's most daring exploits, the seven Rebels from the Fifth Missouri had incredibly, in the words of Captain Guthrie at the time, "held in check the advance of a whole Fed[eral] Div[ision] after their Regt had fallen back expending all their ammunition." After squeezing off their parting shots, the last defenders of Company I scrambled out of the ravine and headed for safety. The men of Sergeant Moore's detachment passed by the bodies of comrades as they ran through the cane after successfully fulfilling their mission. With this final act of a stirring drama, the bloody struggle for the gully of White Branch had at last ended.[129]

After some of the most severe fighting of the war, the blue conquerors took possession of the ravine. A great length of the gully was bloody and strewn with debris. Clumps of grayclad bodies, fouled muskets, accouterments, bloodstained bandages, and torn vegetation were scattered everywhere. Barely able to step over the piles of fallen Confederates, the Indiana troops eventually gathered 30 badly wounded Fifth Missouri soldiers as prisoners.[130]

Captain Coale was the highest ranking Fifth Missouri officer taken captive. While lying among the torn bodies of his Clinton, Henry County neighbors, Coale probably handed over his saber to the nearest Federal. The gully was officially surrendered after nearly two hours of bitter resistance. As fate would have it, Captain Coale would spend the next twenty-two months, in his words, in the hell of the "damned old Isle [the Johnson's Island Prison]." After his exchange in early 1865, Captain Coale would make a valiant attempt to rejoin the Fifth Missouri. But a fatal disease, lingering from the wintry nightmare on the bleak island in Lake Erie, would place him in an early grave far from home.[131]

Relishing his victory, Colonel Slack arrived at the ravine to inspect the scene of his success. He wrote with much pride how in "this engagement the Fifth Missouri Regiment was almost annihilated, there being but 19 of them left, who were taken prisoners." Eleven other regimental members would later be taken prisoner when they were found among McCown's fallen soldiers, who were scattered throughout the smoke-laced woodlands and canebrake. Other injured Fifth Missouri Rebels would not be discovered until the following morning. From the appearance of the gully, it seemed as if a whole Confederate regiment had been destroyed as Colonel Slack had speculated. Demonstrating compassion for their fellow Americans in gray, the Federals attended to the needs of the wounded Confederates of Colonel McCown's regiment.[132]

Even Colonel Slack paid homage to the fighting prowess of McCown's soldiers, praising the Fifth Missouri as dutifully meeting its fate in the bloody gully of Port Gibson. This veteran and well-respected officer further complimented Colonel McCown's hard-fighting Rebels as having fulfilled their reputation of being the "flower of the Southern Army." Another Union leader felt relief in the fact that his seasoned regiments had survived a savage contest with "the veteran troops of the Confederacy, who gloried in the laurels won upon the earlier fields of the war."[133]

Indeed, the Fifth Missouri had been crippled and badly cut-up. More than 100 of the regiment's best men had become casualties in the fierce counterattack. Captain Hale's Company B had taken the worst beating, suffering a loss of 4 killed, 1 mortally wounded, and 10 wounded. Company E suffered the second highest loss of any Fifth Missouri company at Port Gibson. Lieutenant Townsend now commanded 13 fewer soldiers from the Meramec and Gasconade river country than before the suicidal attack.[134]

Around 250 Fifth Missouri soldiers survived one of the bloodiest battles of the Vicksburg campaign and assembled once again near Baldwin's left. In the stubbled cornfield beside the Irwin Branch hollow, the exhausted graycoats fell to the ground for some much-needed rest. Color Sergeant James M. Walton, an Illinois-born bachelor who had led a charmed life and dodged much danger on this hot afternoon in Mississippi, planted the regimental flag for the Fifth Missouri to rally around. With Color Bearer Stark splashed with blood and lying near death in the canebrake, Walton now had responsibility for the Fifth Missouri's emblem.[135]

Hobbling on muskets and assisted by comrades, a steady trickle of McCown's wounded soldiers limped through a scattered fire and over the hill to rejoin the regiment. Against the odds, Company I's Sergeant Robert J. Guthrie had miraculously survived the contest. The McGee College scholar would live to tell his grandchildren about being struck by a cannonball. After stabilizing his defensive sector around Centers Creek, Bowen rode over to the two decimated Missouri regiments. General Bowen, who had lost friends whom he had served with in the prewar militia of St. Louis, attempted to pay a glowing tribute to Colonel McCown's survivors. During an emotional speech, General Bowen tearfully spoke his thanks to the exiled soldiers who had paid such a high price that day, saying, "I did not expect that any of you would get away, but the charge had to be made, or my little army was lost." General Bowen then galloped north to patch up other defensive sectors for the inevitable Union onslaught.[136]

By any measure, General Bowen had seen perhaps his greatest day on May 1. He had held nearly 24,000 Federals at arm's length for eighteen hours with fewer than 7,000 troops. He performed with a tactical brilliance seldom seen in the West, especially among the mediocre corps of Confederate generals. One of the most gifted West Pointers in the West, General Bowen would win a major generalship for the leadership qualities and skills that he demonstrated during the decisive campaign for Vicksburg.

In one of the most audacious gambles of the war, Bowen's attack with the Fifth and Third Missouri had sapped the momentum of Grant's juggernaut with one hard hitting blow and won the Yankee general's rare respect. Not only had he blunted Grant's advance into Mississippi, Bowen had also flirted briefly with victory after unleashing his Missouri troops. Barely had McClernand's right flank avoided being rolled up by Bowen's hard-hitting strike. Had Bowen received only one division of the promised reinforcements and employed them with his crack Missourians, he might have hurled Grant's forces into the Mississippi by turning his right flank.[137]

Sergeants Moore and Leathers, the Edgar father and son duo, Private Dale, and the Barton siblings rejoined the Fifth Missouri after performing their mission and miraculously surviving. Yankee skirmishers meanwhile popped away from the high ground to the west, alerting McCown's soldiers of more action to come. After bolstering his lines with fresh reserves, McClernand had once again resumed the offensive. To meet a new challenge, Colonel McCown's veterans instantly assembled for more fighting.[138] Lieutenant Colonel Bevier bellowed for his skirmishers of Company F to push the probing Unionists rearward. Springing into action with the blast of a bugle, the Irish Rebels sprinted across the open field with clanging gear to perform another mission. As so often in the past, Captain Canniff and his elite Emerald Isle skirmishers drove the aggressive Federals rearward. Meanwhile, the pressure was maintained by the advancing Unionists and continued to mount on Bowen's thin lines. Around six o'clock, General Bowen ordered his battered units north across the bridges of Bayou Pierre to avoid getting cut off and trapped on the south side. The Fifth and Third Missouri had bought the critical time necessary to allow the escape of Bowen's forces.[139]

After chasing the sharpshooters off the ridge, Captain Canniff's successful skirmishers returned to the cornfield. Anxious not to be left behind, the Fifth Missouri soldiers soon joined the sullen Rebel withdrawal, swinging north and crossing Baldwin's rear. For the beaten Confederates, it was now a race north to reach the chocolate-colored bayou. Colonel McCown's troops reached the crossroads safely, barely avoiding being cut off by aggressive Union pursuit.[140]

Heading up the narrow roads hewn northward through the forests, which were now growing ever darker, the Confederates marched along the open ridges slanting toward Bayou Pierre in the twilight. It proved difficult and painful for the Missouri soldiers to abandon Port Gibson to the invader. During March and April, many of Colonel McCown's men had established close familial bonds with the local residents of Claiborne County and especially the people of Port Gibson. But the Fifth Missouri Confederates could now no more protect Port Gibson's citizens than they could help their own families back in their Union-occupied home state.[141]

Finally, with a red sunset shimmering off the bayou's black waters, McCown's regiment reached the watercourse minus more than 100 soldiers. The Fifth Missouri Rebels quickly hustled across the bayou and then set the bridges on fire to prevent Yankee pursuit. One embittered Fifth Missouri officer could only lament upon crossing the swaying suspension bridge that "to retain possession of [the structure] we had sacrificed all those valuable lives."[142] No cheering erupted when the soldiers reached the north side of the bayou, where Pemberton and Vicksburg lay farther to the north. McCown's soldiers could feel the pain in their bruised shoulders from firing far more than their issued forty rounds, but more painful was the bleak realization that one of the best chances of this campaign to beat Grant had been missed at Port Gibson. A huge Union army was now firmly planted on Mississippi soil and was a greater threat to Vicksburg than ever before. At this point, Grant had a firm grip that he would never lose and an opportunity to gain Vicksburg's rear.

But General Bowen had not stopped fighting on May 1. Yet planning to contest Grant's bridgehead, Bowen deployed his units along the north bank of the bayou. Expecting General William W. Loring and his Confederate troops to arrive to reinforce his Bayou Pierre defensive sector, General Bowen "felt confident of whipping them in front." Although they had not eaten since they had left Grand Gulf that morning, the Fifth Missouri soldiers went to work with newfound energy and erected earthworks while a sinking sun seemed to forebode the beginning of the end of Confederate hopes in the West. McCown's Rebels dug feverishly as the surrounding cypress forests grew darker and Grant's forces approached in ever-greater numbers.[143]

Daylight on May 2 ended far from glory with the Missouri Rebels squatting silently in black mud, feeling thankful that they had survived the fight.[144] To these savvy veterans, it now appeared that more Fifth Missouri lives would be lost in making this stand along an obscure bayou in Mississippi. The thinned ranks of the Fifth Missouri indicated that some of McCown's most dedicated soldiers had been lost and could never be replaced, and before long, more would die. Once again the same old Pea Ridge and Corinth pattern had been repeated: no ammunition or reinforcements, incompetent Southern leadership, overemphasis of the Confederate government on the Eastern theater, shortage of materiel, poor Southern strategic planning, logistical breakdowns, another near-battlefield success slipping away, and more good men sacrificed for little or no gain. All these factors had again further diminished the band of Missouri exiles.

As if to compensate for the absence of victory in the Western war and the realizaiton that they would never return to the west side of the Mississippi, the will of the Fifth Missouri soldiers to continue struggling against the odds grew stronger. The Missourians' efforts would be dedicated in the days ahead to those comrades who had been killed in Mississippi. Hence, the conflict was turned into an effort to keep the Fifth Missouri's fallen from having died in vain.

Best exemplifying this common attitude was the Missouri Brigade commander, Colonel Cockrell. Combining nationalism and a religious-like zeal, Cockrell now swore to God that he and his Missouri Confederates would dedicate their future efforts on the battlefield to the Port Gibson dead. More committed than ever before, Colonel Cockrell solemnly promised that "by our acts we will avenge their deaths."[145] This commitment grew stronger as the war progressed and became as important as the goal of an independent nation to the exiles.

Port Gibson's populace would never forget the Missourians' high sacrifice in defending their town in vain against the Yankees on May 1. The citizens of Claiborne County grieved for the many dead Missouri exiles who had been like adopted sons. One Port Gibson woman was grateful for what "the brave and noble and the true Missourians have done. Long will there [sic] name be remembered by us."[146] But today, ironically, the Missourians' sacrifices have been largely forgotten across the South and in the annals of Confederate historiography.

Back in Union-occupied Port Gibson, meanwhile, Colonel McCown's prisoners went hungry and endured the humiliation of being captives. Rounded up like cattle by Yankee guards, even the walking wounded of the Fifth Missouri were herded toward the Mississippi during the night. Since General Grant had no supply base at this stage of the campaign, the Union navy provided rations for the captives. Three of McCown's men would endure an interesting fate after their capture at Port Gibson. Privates James T. Nelson, a former minister, Charles P. Duncan, age twenty, and Corporal John T. Browning, a twenty-four-year-old farmer, would find themselves in Virginia after an early exchange. The trio became members of Company A, First Missouri Confederate Cavalry. Company A would be unhorsed and attached to a Virginia infantry regiment by the spring of 1864. At a critical moment during the battle of New Market, Virginia, in May 1864, the 62-man Missouri orphan company charged a Union battery. The exiled cavalry unit lost 40 members as it almost silenced the Federal guns and helped stabilize the wavering Rebel battle lines by taking the tactical offensive.[147]

With his capable Union medical counterparts, Surgeon Dysart worked day and night on the multitudes of wounded men in Port Gibson. According to one Port Gibson nurse, "the poor dear brave Mo soldiers were put in a hospital together." Now perhaps the Missouri Brigade's best physician, Dysart would struggle for two months to save a good many lives in the filthy and nightmarish hospitals. The community of Port Gibson rallied and pulled together to alleviate the suffering of these young men, and especially the

Missouri Rebels, who were so far from homes and families. As one Port Gibson angel of mercy in petticoat wrote, "the ladies here all took a very active part in nursing the wounded [Missouri] soldiers and so we all have made the hospital our home for nearly 6 weeks." Also "good nursing [came] all the time from the Missouri soldiers who were paroled prisoners."[148]

Performing medical miracles under miserable and unsanitary conditions, Surgeon Dysart's operations often resembled innovative experiments in medical science. For instance, he always tried to preserve the limbs of badly wounded soldiers rather than utilizing the standard procedure of amputation. A tireless worker, Dysart saved a good many lives at Port Gibson throughout the late spring and early summer of 1863. One such special case treated by Surgeon Dysart was Sergeant Stark, who lingered near death with a bad compound fracture from either a bullet or shell fragment. Less capable surgeons of both armies usually handled this type of injury by an immediate amputation. Proudly explaining to a cousin about the risky operation and its success, the Macon County surgeon wrote in a letter with understandable pride: "Pres Stark is fast recovering from his wound received at Port Gibson. I took one bone out of his arm from the wrist back about 8 inches."[149]

Sergeant Stark's mangled right arm was spared, but his flag-bearing days were over. From now on, the former McGee College scholar with a fiery nature could only relive in his mind his role in leading the charge through the canebrake of Port Gibson. But dreaming of past deeds was not in the sergeant's nature. Refusing a disability discharge, the soldier from College Mound left the Fifth Missouri to become a courier and continued to serve for the remainder of the war.[150]

As if in reward for defending this Deep South land far from their Western frontier homes, Fifth Missouri dead received better treatment from the local people than could be obtained from Union burial details. Besides assisting Surgeon Dysart, the citizens of Claiborne County combed the canebrake, hills, and ravines of the battlefield to gather McCown's fallen soldiers. The people of Port Gibson then had the exiled Missouri soldiers buried and headstones erected in Wintergreen Cemetery for the young men, so hopeful and idealistic, who had come hundreds of miles away to give their lives to defend a people and country that they had never seen before. This last tribute would be one of the few given to the Fifth Missouri's dead in the South.[151]

The high sacrifice paid by the Missouri Confederates at Port Gibson deeply affected Colonel Cockrell, who had seen more of his men killed for no gain and too little glory. The newly appointed Missouri Brigade commander wrote: "Among the dead we mourn the irreparable loss of [Captain] R. G. Stokely, Company A, Fifth Missouri Infantry [an] efficient, reliable, and chivalrous [officer] who fell at the post of danger, in the full discharge of duty, regardless of personal safety, gallantly leading his men. For the dead we shed tears — the true test of friendship; in our hearts we cherish their memories." Young Stokely, the ex-merchant from Johnson County, posthumously won promotion to a captain's rank for bravery at Port Gibson. The Fifth Missouri Confederates especially mourned the loss of teenage Sergeant Lee, whose "noble spirit had gone to the shades of the unknown land, where there is a home for the good and rest for the brave."[152]

More Fifth Missouri wounded than usual would survive because of the good care of Port Gibson's nurses and Surgeon Dysart's medical skill. Typical of those wounded men destined to recover and rejoin the regiment before the year's end were two soldiers from St. Clair, Missouri, Sergeant Edwin H. Jefferies and Private Wilson B. Hurt. Both of these excellent soldiers had been cited for heroics at the battle of Corinth. Jefferies, age twenty, had taken a head wound, and Hurt had suffered a mangled thigh at Port Gibson. The young sergeant from the Bourbeuse River region hailed from a distinguished pioneer family. His Virginia ancestors had come by ox-drawn wagon to settle the community of Jefferiesburg among the forested hills of Franklin County. In the spring of 1846, a Jefferies officer had raised a local company for Colonel Alexander Doniphan's regiment and glory, while another relative served in the epic Mexican War expedition into northern Mexico. Fulfilling a dream through industry and toil on the rich soil, the clan prospered on the bountiful land.

Hurt, a farmer, was well acquainted with the Jefferies family. Orphaned at an early age, the twenty-two-year-old Hurt had been adopted and raised by the hard-working family. As soldiers in the Missouri State Guard, both Lieutenant George Warren and Hurt were captured together near Springfield, Missouri, in late 1861. The two cavalry lieutenants escaped before imprisonment, however. Hurt would die in battle before the war's conclusion.[153]

The exploits of the Fifth Missouri Confederates at Port Gibson became well known throughout the Western army and the entire South. Indeed, the reputation of Colonel McCown's Missourians was on the rise. As Colonel Cockrell stated: "Too much praise cannot be bestowed on the private soldiers of this brigade for their coolness, discretion, patient endurance, and chivalrous bearing during all these memorable events — under the fire of the enemy's iron-clads at close range, in the rapid march to the field of strife and duty; the Third and Fifth Regiments in fearlessly charging a division of the Federal Army, and engaging such fearful odds so long."

By any measure, the Confederate effort at Port Gibson as orchestrated by General Bowen had been masterful. General Pemberton paid a fitting tribute: "Confronted by overwhelming numbers, the heroic Bowen and his gallant officers and men maintained the unequal contest for many hours with a courage and obstinacy rarely equaled, and though they failed to secure a victory, the world will do them the justice to say they deserved it." But at least the Fifth Missouri's sacrifice in killed, wounded, and captured at Port Gibson had not been wasted as in the past. In playing a key role in helping to save the day at Port Gibson, Colonel McCown's regiment suffered the highest loss of any Confederate unit on May 1.[154]

Another group of young men from the Fifth Missouri would never return to their homes on the west side of the Mississippi: Adjutant Greenwood, Captain Stokely, Lieutenant Fincher, Sergeants Lee and Auren G. McCormack, Corporal Parks, Privates Momon, Childers, James H. Myers, John A. Priddy, William Thomas Ballard, William Seney, William B. Miller, Moses James, Halstead, and James Bunass. Claiborne County, Mississippi, had now become a permanent home for these members of the Fifth Missouri who made the ultimate sacrifice hundreds of miles from their Union-occupied homeland without achieving victory. Throughout the history of the Fifth Missouri, this tragic fate of the Missouri exiles of Colonel McCown's regiment would never change.[155]

# VI

## ALMOST WINNING IT ALL
## AT CHAMPION HILL

Secure on the safe side of Bayou Pierre behind a light line of earth-works, the soldiers of the Fifth Missouri prepared for Grant's expected at-tack. Besides the Fifth Missouri, two of Cockrell's other infantry regiments, Captain Guibor's Missouri battery, and a Virginia battery held the line across the bottoms of Bayou Pierre. As a thin pall of gray mist rose through the cypress overhanging the bayou on May 2, a threatening line of blue skirmishers began advancing as if they meant business and started popping away. More Yankee regiments began pouring through the woodlands bordering the south bank, while explosions "cover[ed] us with splashes of ooze and dirt," recalled one of McCown's officers.[1]

Again the hardy Celts of Company F advanced and skirmished before the defenses, holding at bay the attackers, including some Missourians in blue. A hot fire fight escalated across the bayou for most of May 2. Both sides remained cautious, exchanging fire and not advancing. The Unionists, nevertheless, hunted for a weakness in Bowen's line. Hoping in vain, General Bowen prayed for Loring's troops to arrive for another effort to strike Grant's beachhead in one last desperate bid to negate the Unionists' gains. But Bowen received startling information that Federal troops had forded Little Bayou Pierre to Port Gibson's east on the afternoon of May 2. This development forced Bowen to order an immediate withdrawal or once more face being "completely cut off." Mad about missing another chance to tangle with Grant and reverse his gains, the sullen Missourians again swung northward in the darkness without breakfast and with even less hope. A desperate race for the upper ferry of Big Black River began, with much at stake.[2]

The rising sun of May 3 found Colonel McCown's soldiers plodding onward, covering the withdrawal of Bowen's weary forces. During the dash to the Big Black River, wrote one Missouri soldier, "the Feds were close after us all the way and therefore we were marched very hard night and day." Outflanked by Grant's Port Gibson success, Bowen correctly reasoned that Grand Gulf had to be evacuated and was determined to save as much supplies and munitions as possible for the difficult days and challenges ahead. With muskets on shoulders, the Missouri Confederates swung north toward Vicksburg, leaving beind a doomed Grand Gulf. Explosions to the southwest during the previous night had indicated to McCown's veterans the demolition of the fortress's magazines and the evacuation of Grand Gulf. Now only Port Hudson and Vicksburg stood as Rebel strongholds along the Mississippi.[3]

To guard the Rebel column's western flank, Captain Canniff's men of Company F skirted the forested ridges above the narrow dirt road leading to Vicksburg. Some of General Loring's forces had belatedly linked with Bowen, and Loring now led the retrograde movement. But Loring had only one brigade with him; once again Confederate reinforcements were too little and too late: a recurring theme during the ill-fated Vicksburg campaign. Skirmishing with the pursuing bluecoats intensified during the race north through the woodlands of western Mississippi. To ensure a safe withdrawal, Cockrell ordered a defensive stand to be made before the Big Black River crossing at Hankinson's Ferry. With his usual skill, Colonel Cockrell deployed his regiments across the road. Once known as "the praying captain," Colonel Cockrell stretched his gray formations along the high ground near and above sluggish Kennison Creek. Time had to be won for the slow-moving Confederate troops and the wagon trains overflowing with Grand Gulf's supplies to pass to the river's north side and eventually to Vicksburg.[4]

Along with a company of the Second Missouri, Colonel Cockrell sent the Missouri Brigade's finest company of skirmishers forward to perform yet another mission to slow down the advancing Unionists. With a shout of defiance, Captain Canniff's Irishmen of Company F leaped into action, hustling off the ridge and pushing forward to meet the Federals. After racing about 200 yards ahead of the main line, Canniff spied a perfect position for orchestrating an ambush. Captain Canniff fanned out his soldiers on the high ground behind Kennison Creek, which flowed north toward Big Black River. Irish wharf workers and Kerry Patchers of humble origin from St. Louis and Emerald Islanders from the rural areas of Missouri camouflaged themselves in underbrush along the wooded crown of the hill.[5] With a clattering of gear, a long column of blue troopers soon appeared. From the hill above the narrow road snaking up from Kennison Creek, Captain Canniff and his Catholic and Protestant Celts silently gripped their muskets and watched as the Federal horsemen rode farther into the well-conceived ambush of Company F.

With the Union cavalrymen within a stone's throw, the Irish captain from St. Louis bellowed, "Fire!" A sheet of flame poured down the slope, toppling a handful of Yankees from their saddles and causing the blue column to retire.[6] In addition, Captain Landis's Missouri cannoneers pounded the advancing Union infantry formations in the creek's environs. To ascertain Cockrell's position and strength, a brigade of hardy Union soldiers from Minnesota, Wisconsin, and Indiana charged across Kennison Creek with flags flying and bugles blaring. On the double, the Rebels of Company F retired to the main line as the Federals arrived in force, falling back in order and discipline.[7]

After delaying the Union pursuit on May 3, Colonel Cockrell led the final Confederate brigade now alone on the south side of Big Black onward during the withdrawal. The Missourians in gray hurried across a flatboat bridge spanning Big Black at Hankinson's Ferry with the distinction of being the last Rebel troops to cross the river. So vigorous was the Union pursuit that the Confederates were unable to destroy the wooden structure before the Yankees could use it. Always where he would ask others to go, Bowen was engaged in the dismantling of the bridge when the rapid approach of the Yankees forced the abandonment of the attempt. Supervising the destruction of the bridge, General Bowen barely escaped himself before the Federals swarmed over the bridge.[8]

While Grant's units consolidated to overrun the next objective, Pemberton also concentrated his forces. He hastily made new defensive dispositions to safeguard Vicksburg on the east, or rear. The Confederate withdrawal north toward the Mississippi River citadel was one of the most trying experiences for the Fifth Missouri. Maintaining their usual high discipline, Colonel McCown's soldiers trudged behind the 140 wagons of Bowen's division, sweating under the blistering sun and eating dust along the route roughly paralleling Big Black. Heat, sore feet, fatigue, and empty canteens resulted in much straggling among the Fifth Missouri's soldiers.[9]

Colonel McCown's troops reached Bovina on the evening of May 4, after a more than 50-mile withdrawal via Vicksburg. Near the railroad line that linked Jackson to Vicksburg, the Missourians encamped along Clear Creek east of Vicksburg and finally gained some much needed rest. A brief respite in the Bovina area allowed the healing of blistered feet and bruised spirits of the Fifth Missouri Rebels. To protect the railroad line and the main approaches to Vicksburg, General Pemberton had assembled a defensive line which jutted northeastward from Warrenton, south of Vicksburg on the Mississippi, to Big Black River, directly east of the fortress. After pushing farther eastward on May 6, McCown's soldiers encamped near the bridges across Big Black River, occupying a strong defensive position on Pemberton's left.[10]

The dawning of the first day at the new encampment offered no rest for the Fifth Missouri Confederates. McCown's men immediately started erecting earthworks across the flat cotton fields lying in a wide bend east of the river. Gangs of slaves from nearby Warren County plantations

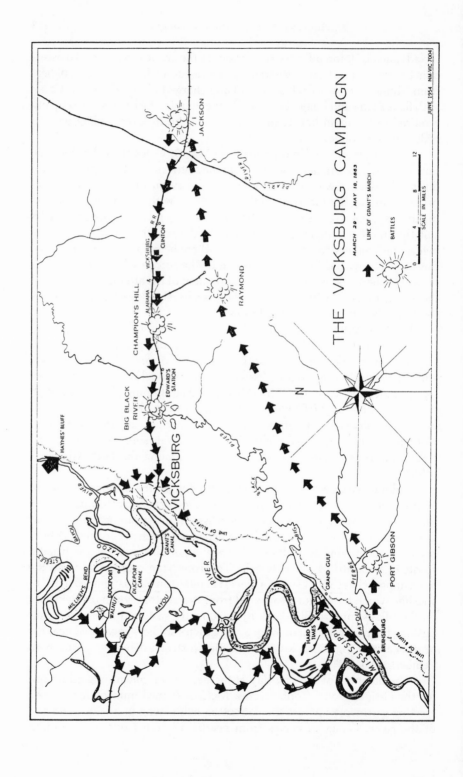

THE VICKSBURG CAMPAIGN

MARCH 29 - MAY 18, 1863

⬆ LINE OF GRANT'S MARCH

☁ BATTLES

SCALE IN MILES
0    4    8    12

JUNE 1954  NM VIC 7004

worked beside the exiles in gray. The soldiers' cursing of Mississippi mud, menial labor, and General Pemberton grew longer and louder as the sun inched higher into the hot Mississippi sky. In less than three weeks, ironically, these muddy trenches of Big Black would save the lives of Fifth Missouri Rebels during yet another crisis in the lifetime of the Confederacy.[11]

Despite the daily shoveling of mud and the building of cotton-bale breastworks, Colonel McCown's laborers savored a period without marching or fighting. Last-minute preparations were now made by the Fifth Missouri to meet the wily General Grant, whose legions could not yet be pinpointed without enough cavalry to gather the vital intelligence. Consequently, cautious General Pemberton was staying close to Vicksburg, keeping his forces near the Confederacy's most important citadel in the West. Reorganizations and new appointments in companies were now necessary to fill vacancies for those Fifth Missouri soldiers killed and wounded at Port Gibson.

Taking Adjutant Greenwood's place was the popular Lieutenant Crow, age thirty, who had been born in the Kentucky Bluegrass region. Formerly a clerk working with his brother and father at their family-owned store in St. Louis, "Will" Crow had been a member of the prewar militia company of St. Louis, the City Guards. John S. Bowen had been the captain of his company. Crow had marched to the border with the Missouri Volunteer Militia of St. Louis during the Southwest Expedition in 1860. While in the uniform of a Missouri State Guard private, Crow had danced an "Irish jig" upon the grave of General Nathaniel Lyon, after Lyon was killed leading a charge at the battle of Wilson's Creek in August of 1861.[12]

Colonel McCown returned to rejoin the Fifth Missouri during this quiet period. After having evidently taken a furlough for illness that had caused him to miss the battle of Port Gibson, he returned in good spirits and ready for action. McCown was even more eager than usual to encounter the Yankees on the next Mississippi battlefield because he knew that his large family had been driven from their Warrensburg home by the hated Missouri Unionists. Then their house had been burned to the ground as the inhabitants, his wife and five children, were pushed out into the bitter cold of a wintry night. Such stirrings for revenge kept Colonel McCown at the head of the Fifth Missouri, where he fought until the end of the war.[13]

With Captain Stokely mortally wounded at Port Gibson, Lieutenant Atkinson, the Johnson County merchant, once more took command of Company A. He would win official promotion to captain in June 1863. The young businessman from Hazil Hill township, just north of Warrensburg, would lead the former Johnson Guardsmen for most of the conflict.[14]

Opposite: The Vicksburg Campaign (courtesy: National Park Service).

Company G was in shambles after the slaughter at Port Gibson. Captain Coale and Lieutenant Fincher were both left in the bloody ravine with Yankee bullet holes through them. The first of these fine officers had been wounded, and the other was dead. To fill the void, Andrew Jackson Lee was elected lieutenant. The enterprising Lee had founded a community near Tebo Creek in 1854. Demonstrating his mercantile talents, Lee opened a general store on the sprawling grasslands of eastern Henry County. The business seed that young Lee planted had thrived amid the prairies of western Missouri, just north of the Ozark highlands.[15]

Lee's civic duties later increased when he became postmaster for the small agricultural community on the Western frontier. The town's expansion had beckoned other opportunistic citizens to participate in the boom times. Another individual who gambled on starting a new life in Lee's community enterprise was Fifth Missouri commissary officer William H. Murrell, whose abilities had landed him a berth as Lee's business partner. And Henry C. Herndon, a twenty-year-old Company G soldier, destined to be killed in less than two weeks, had clerked at Lee's store. Lee also had sold town plots, anticipating a railroad line that would ensure permanent prosperity and more money. This thriving community was appropriately named Leesville after its founding father.[16]

When war clouds darkened, Lee had been chosen by the people of Henry County as their state convention delegate. He advocated secession in early 1861, according to the wishes of the people of western Missouri. Indeed, the entire area around Leesville had been a hotbed of secessionist feeling, and its population with its Southern roots provided the nucleus for Company G, Fifth Missouri. Among these zealous volunteers were two brothers, Corporal George Washington Parks, who was mortally wounded at Port Gibson, and Sergeant Wade D. Parks. Other recruits hailing from the Leesville area were the Fifth Missouri's oldest member, Private John A. Pigg, age sixty, and his teenage son.[17] Lieutenant Lee was a primary driving force behind Company G, providing both leadership and inspiration to the men in the ranks. The former Missouri State Guard sergeant had recently recovered from a Corinth wound. A fine leader by any measure, Lieutenant Lee, age thirty, would perish of disease in barely five months.[18]

Captain Canniff was the only Fifth Missouri captain to retain command during the ten months since the regiment's organization at Saltillo. Ironically, Canniff had always been in the most exposed position as the commander of the Missouri Brigade's best skirmish company, leading his men almost recklessly in practically every clash with the Yankees. For years, the Irish captain would inspire his skirmishers to meet each new challenge as if he were leading a charmed life, while dozens of others were cut down in battle around him.[19] The Irishman's good fortune would continue until a November 1864 afternoon.

New color Sergeant Walton had carried the regimental flag with distinction at Port Gibson after Sergeant Stark fell on the field. Having no fear of the bluecoats, Walton had long been accustomed to risks. When war fever swept Polk County in 1861, the young man had worked as a laborer on the Hart family farm. What had made this situation precarious was that the Illinois-born Walton slept in the same house as old man Hart and his four teenage daughters, who were known for their attractiveness. Walton had learned that facing minié balls brought no more fear than did old man Hart's wrath when he tried to keep the young man away from his pretty daughters.[20]

May 7 saw the unexpected arrival of a 165-man Missouri company, which was stranded on the Mississippi's east side. Recently exchanged in Virginia, these exiles from the home state had banded together into a cavalry company bound for the Trans-Mississippi theater. Most of these Missouri Rebels had been captured in Missouri and now wanted to return and settle old scores with the Missouri Federals. This cavalry unit had left Petersburg, Virginia, in mid–April, on the journey to help reclaim Missouri. But the cavaliers in gray had been almost captured by Colonel Grierson's raiders at Newton Station, Mississippi.[21] Barely escaping Grierson's Illinois troopers, these Rebels finally reached Jackson safely on May 1. Colonel Cockrell's heavy losses at Port Gibson guaranteed that these stranded men would not cross the Mississippi or ever see Missouri again as a unit. Seemingly a timely godsend to reinforce the Missouri Brigade, which was cut off from the manpower pool in Missouri, the ill-fated cavalry company was ordered to join General Bowen's command.[22]

Sixty-five of the newcomers from the Eastern theater considered "long arm" duty preferable to infantry duty after they learned of the nightmarish fighting at Port Gibson. Consequently, these men enlisted in Bowen's Missouri batteries. The remaining 100 soldiers went to the Fifth Missouri, which had lost more men than any other Confederate regiment at Port Gibson. Perhaps to avoid the red tape of such an unorthodox and improper addition, Colonel McCown designated the ex-cavalrymen as Company H besides Captain Grant's Company H.[23]

Leading the new Company H was Captain Harvey G. McKinney. He had been captured during the always dangerous duty of recruiting in Union-occupied north Missouri. Like most of his followers, Captain McKinney had been a yeoman of the Boone's Lick country along the Missouri River near Rockeport in mid–Missouri, which was part of a sprawling area mostly bordering the Missouri River that was known as "Little Dixie" because of its Southern roots, heritage, and culture. The former tiller of Boone County soil had left behind a young wife and an infant daughter to join the struggle and fight for what he believed to be right. McKinney would never see them again.[24]

One of the first and foremost revolutionaries of the Boone's Lick region, McKinney had organized a company known as the Blackfoot Rangers who hailed from the rich and productive area along the Missouri River.[25] The fiery Ranger leader had first gained prominence at the battle of Wilson's Creek, when he led his cheering Rebels over Oak Hill and took possession of General Lyon's dead body. He had protected the general's remains against a howling mob of soldiers wanting revenge. Some Missourians wanted to desecrate the body of one of the men most responsible for saving Missouri for the Union. Consequently, they were eager to "cut his damned heart out."[26] The last sizable reinforcements that the Fifth Missouri would ever receive, Colonel McCown's 100 "volunteers" were welcome additions, especially at the beginning of a decisive campaign. Morale and spirits among the Fifth Missouri men rose because the newcomers included relatives and former neighbors, who brought joyful news from loved ones. Unfortunately, they also told of new outrages committed by Union occupation forces in Missouri.[27]

Also arriving on May 7 were crates of imported Enfield rifles from Britain. As never before, the Fifth Missourians' fighting prowess was enhanced by the superior firearm, which was the finest import the Confederacy could provide its troops. A universal relief came with the casting aside of the cumbersome and bulky .69 caliber smoothbores that kicked like mules and fouled easily. Lighter than the Federals' Springfield rifled-muskets at under nine pounds, the sleek and finely crafted Enfield rifled-musket was more reliable, accurate, and durable than the Springfield: a Fifth Missouri infantryman's dream come true. Crafted in Enfield, England, the 1853 or 1858 models were the best pieces McCown's troops would be issued. It was most timely that these guns were received immediately before the most decisive engagement of the Vicksburg campaign, in which the Missouri Brigade was destined to play the leading role on the Confederate side.[28]

The smoothbore's ball and buckshot at close range had cut down a good many Union cannoneers within Battery Powell and made the Port Gibson gully more formidable, but the marksmen from Missouri needed a rifled-musket for longer ranges. With its higher velocity and greater accuracy, the Enfield bullet could strike down a Yankee at 700 yards. The new rifles also had good balance. These guns were easier to draw to the shoulder and lighter in touch. Run through the Union blockade from Britain, these imports embodied the finest nineteenth-century firearm technology. But by far their best feature was the advantages of the .577 caliber ammunition. Now if they found themselves without ammunition and at the mercy of the Federals as during the holocausts of Corinth and Port Gibson, Colonel McCown's graycoats could gather rounds from the cartridge boxes of Union dead. Indeed, the bullets for the United States .58 caliber Springfield could now be used in the new Enfield muskets whenever the cartridge boxes of Fifth Missouri soldiers were emptied. Ironically, Abe Lincoln was now guaranteed to be a supplier of bullets for McCown's boys for years to come. Never again would Fifth Missouri troops be slaughtered with unloaded muskets in their hands and empty cartridge boxes as at Corinth and Port Gibson.[29]

Strategic developments, meanwhile, were taking shape in the campaign for Vicksburg. As usual, Grant wasted little time in the all-important campaign to gain Vicksburg's rear. General Joseph E. Johnston, in overall command of Confederate forces in Mississippi, remained busy trying to meet Grant's threat as best he could. He concentrated his forces around Jackson, forty-five miles east of Vicksburg. But, as throughout this decisive campaign, Grant was always one step ahead of his less aggressive and less capable adversaries. First and foremost, General Grant planned to strike quickly and to confuse his opponents by rapid and bold maneuver before "Old Joe" united with Pemberton, who manned the defensive lines round Big Black east of Vicksburg.

To achieve Grant's goal, Federal columns slashed northeastward along the east side of Big Black. With characteristic boldness, Grant embarked upon the improbable, striking deep into Confederate territory in a gamble to whip Johnston and sever the Southern Railroad of Mississippi, Vicksburg's strategic lifeline to the eastern Confederacy. More important, this rail-line linked the state capital, Jackson, to the great Confederate fortress, Vicksburg.[30]

Pouring his bluecoat legions parallel to Big Black into the rolling agricultural lands between Johnston and Pemberton before mid–May, Grant neared his all-important goal of placing his command between the two Rebel forces with each passing hour. To the west, meanwhile, Pemberton's troops remained immobile and stationary, playing into Grant's unorthodox strategy during a campaign in which mobility would determine the winner. General Pemberton, who had concentrated his forces around Bovina two miles west of Big Black, failed to ascertain Grant's plan, thanks in part to Union probes toward Vicksburg. With most of his Rebel cavalry chasing Colonel Grierson's raiders toward Baton Rouge in a futile romp through the Mississippi countryside, Pemberton now had insufficient means to determine if Grant wanted Vicksburg or Jackson. But Pemberton was inclined to believe the former. General Grant, as he had planned, thus obtained the initiative and time to cut across Mississippi at will, while Pemberton's impotent divisions protected Vicksburg.[31]

Only after much time had slipped away did the Confederate high command at last understood that the bluecoats intended to smash the railroad. General Pemberton consequently shifted troops to parry the threat to Vicksburg's supply line. However, Grant now altered his plan of hitting the tracks at Edwards Station and turned on Johnston's forces, making

Jackson his target. After beating a Rebel force at Raymond, Mississippi, on May 12, the Unionists won another victory on May 14 at Jackson, the key communication center, supply depot, and arsenal that funneled tons of supplies westward into the Mississippi River citadel.[32]

As Grant had envisioned, Jackson fell quickly. General Johnston evacuated the capital before overwhelming numbers of encroaching Unionists. But more important, Grant scattered a budding army, Johnston's force, which was badly needed if Vicksburg were to be saved for the Confederacy. To cut the jugular vein of Vicksburg and protect his rear before moving west toward Vicksburg, Grant destroyed Confederate installations and railroad tracks to disrupt the Confederate logistical network. The capture of Jackson knocked another pillar out of the foundation that supported Vicksburg.[33]

While the Unionists were striking at Jackson, Pemberton cautiously inched forth to locate Grant on May 13. Intent on making contact with the elusive Unionists, the long Rebel columns pushed over the Big Black River and ventured eastward. After passing through Edwards Station, McCown's troops swung southward near sunset, marching silently through the darkening forests before halting for the night. With the savvy of veterans, the Fifth Missouri soldiers immediately threw up rail breastworks just in case of an attack, after they encamped along the Telegraph Road. Somewhere in the dark woodlands to the east lurked perhaps the best fighting machine of Lincoln's armies commanded by the North's most capable general, Grant. As if they knew as much, Colonel McCown's Rebels huddled around smoking campfires behind their works, frying strips of bacon and no doubt praying there would be no engagement in these blackened forests. But there would be no fighting tonight, because General McClernand's corps had retired and hastened toward Raymond after a bold front.[34]

Pemberton's search for the Unionists ended on May 14 when a recent dispatch to Pemberton from Johnston now altered the situation. These orders told Pemberton to hit the Federals concentrated around Clinton, two-thirds of the way from Big Black to Jackson, in order to rescue Jackson. Pemberton thought that such a move would result in disaster, however. Concerned with the safety of Vicksburg, he realized that such a movement farther eastward would increase the vulnerability of the Mississippi River citadel. Dealing intelligently with ever-changing circumstances and without knowing it was too late to save Jackson, Pemberton ignored his superior's directive.[35]

However, subordinates eager for action complicated Pemberton's stance. Such leaders had argued against the cautious, but wise, strategy of waiting for the invaders behind Big Black's fortifications closer to Vicksburg. In a heated council of war, Pemberton's chief lieutenants, enraged that Grant was marching roughshod over Mississippi and destroy-ing anything he wanted at will, clamored for the Clinton strike.

An old Seminole and Mexican War veteran, General Loring offered a compromise. In order to cut Grant's alleged supply line which seemingly had to link to his Mississippi River base at Grand Gulf, Loring proposed advancing southeastward down the Raymond Road. Pemberton and his lieutenants agreed, proposing to strike ten miles southeast of Edwards Sta-tion and just west of Raymond. The march to cut Grant's supply line was to begin immediately. Pemberton's objective did not exist, however, for Grant's forces had abandoned the supply link to the Mississippi River base of Grand Gulf and were living off the land.[36]

With the fate of Vicksburg in its hands, Pemberton's army moved out to accomplish great things. However, the strength of the command was diminished by almost 10,000 Confederate troops of two full divisions which remained west of Big Black to guard Vicksburg. The rising sun of May 15 found Colonel McCown's Missourians in full marching gear and standing in ankle-deep mud which filled the roads. Here they waited for ammunition to be distributed, while resting under dreary, rain-filled skies. Confederate plans for a dawn march had gone awry in the rain and the sea of mud. Strewn out for miles, Southern columns could not move out until rations and cartridges arrived by rail from Vicksburg. While mud puddles in the narrow Raymond Road reflected rows of stacked muskets, McCown's boys sat on the damp ground and waited for the order to move out. Stiff and sore from the recent hard marching, the grayclad soldiers smoked pipes, chewed tobacco, and wondered what the hell had gone wrong with Confederate leadership and the army ordered to save Vicks-burg.

As the Missourians' chatter and tobacco smoke drifted across the soggy fields, a cold rain continued to fall on the already saturated land, soaking the Fifth Missouri Rebels, whose blankets were left in wagons miles away. While Pemberton was stuck in the mud and rain during an ill-advised effort to break the supposed supply line, General Grant meanwhile concentrated more than 30,000 Yankees and advanced westward upon Ed-wards Station. After having already routed the forces of General Johnston, Grant now closed in on Pemberton.[37]

Not until the afternoon did Fifth Missouri captains finally shout orders for their companies to form in column, after rations were cooked and Enfield rounds were distributed to the regiment. In a downpour of rain, McCown's soldiers shouldered their new Enfield rifles beside the dripping trees and wet brush. Confederate officers, couriers, and generals' staffs galloped along the road, splashing water and mud on McCown's stand-ing soldiers. The lengthy Rebel column finally slogged forward through the mire, moving out slowly in the dampness. Regiments, brigades, and divisions of Pemberton's army soon piled up in a mammoth traffic jam, however. In a short time, many Confederate munitions wagons and artillery caissons sank up to their wheel-hubs in the oceans of mud. Motionless files of cursing graycoats, meanwhile, stood idle in the clinging mud as the rain pelted down. Colonel McCown's wet Missourians remained in formation for hours, waiting for the massive Confederate jam-up to unclog.[38]

The Rebel blunders and mistakes of May 15, ironically, were a blessing in disguise for Pemberton. Striking southeastward to cut Grant's supply line that had already been abandoned and marching away from General Johnston's forces was not exactly an ideal tactical move. Indeed, if Vicksburg were to be saved, Pemberton and Johnston had to unite as soon as possible. Hopes for a successful effort were dimmed with the news that the Baker's Creek Bridge two miles southeast of Edwards Station had been washed out by torrential rains. The avenue to the Federals' supposed supply line was now barred. But Pemberton refused to forsake the scheme, as if he were spurred on by events beyond his control. More valuable time slipped away, with the Southerners waiting for the waters to recede while Grant's troops marched ever closer. Colonel McCown's troops fell out of formation to rest in the wet fields and woodlands of Hinds County.[39]

General Grant, in contrast, made the most of the time and opportunity which he had won with flexibility, imaginative tactics, and bold maneuver. In their drive west toward Vicksburg, the Federals encountered few of the delays and confusion that plagued the Rebels. The Army of the Tennessee flowed onward, moving across the Mississippi countryside with a will of its own like the fine-tuned fighting machine. As throughout this campaign, superior Yankee ability and competence once again stayed one step ahead of the blundering States' Righters, who seemingly would do nothing right during this campaign before the most decisive engagement for Vicksburg. More than 30,000 Unionists, with full bellies and cartridge boxes and supreme confidence in themselves and their leaders, spilled along the narrow roads twisting towards Edwards Station at a pace that would surprise Pemberton.[40]

With the Raymond Road out of service, Pemberton learned that the Jackson Road bridge was still standing across Baker's Creek to the north. Southern columns, therefore, plodded along the creek's west bank by late afternoon to gain the crossing. After passing over the bridge and slogging forward a short distance, the Confederates pushed southwestward. Up before dawn and again out of rations, the Fifth Missouri Rebels trudged through the morass which filled the Plantation Road. This ribbon of mud led to the Raymond Road, slicing across the Sidney S. Champion farm, an obscure place soon to become the grim killing fields and place of death for many young men in both blue and gray.

The miserable, wet trek in the inky darkness ended around eleven o'clock. Finally the wide detour by the Confederates to regain the Raymond Road had concluded for the night. Just north of the Ratliff brothers' plantation, General Bowen called a halt to the night march. Like the good commander he was, Bowen refused to take any unnecessary chances, especially after spying a faint shimmer of Yankee campfires glowing above the black forests to the east.[41]

Knowing only too well of Grant's habit of performing unexpected feats at the most improbable time, Bowen deployed his crack division in battle array. As never before, Pemberton's army was vulnerable on May 15, scattered for miles down muddy roads and worn out. Indeed it would have been wise for Pemberton to have placed Baker's Creek between him and Grant. To prevent surprise, a gray line of Fifth Missouri pickets, without sleep for more than 24 hours, slipped more than 100 yards eastward through the dark woodlands. The last scenario any of McCown's soldiers wanted now was to run headlong into the Yankees and fight a confusing night skirmish that might spark a big battle.[42]

While Pemberton's weary army slept, the string of pickets of Company F splashed forward through the rain-fresh thickets, staying on the lookout for Yankees. It soon became apparent to Captain Canniff and his scouts that the Federals were not advancing through the wet Mississippi forests on the eve of the campaign's major action. The well-fed Union army was resting for the climactic engagement on May 16, while hundreds of tired and mud-splattered Fifth Missouri Rebels lay in line of battle without blankets or overcoats. Most of the night a steady drizzle dropped through the trees, pelting on the leaves covering the forest's floor. The night of May 15 was miserable for Colonel McCown's soldiers, and the twinkle of Federal campfires glowing on the eastern horizon only reminded them of the hard fighting that lay ahead.[43]

Captain Canniff's skirmishers, meanwhile, remained picketed to the east for some time, trying to stay awake and warm in the cold dampness. No doubt the mournful calls of whippoorwills echoed through the sombre pine thickets, offering eerie premonitions of death which seemed to linger forever in the haunting mists of the early morning hours. Many of McCown's soldiers reflected upon their fates, which would be determined with the sunrise. Hundreds of young men and boys would fall the next day on this same ground. A chilling rain, meanwhile, filtered down from black skies, drenching the fields and forests which would soon become a mass killing ground. As fate would have it, the Confederates of the Fifth Missouri, without blankets, luck, or fires, were soaking wet and exhausted on the night before the largest and most decisive battle of their lives.[44]

Fateful May 16 dawned warm and clear with little promise of more rain or inactivity. Sunrise was accompanied by high humidity, setting the mood for one of the hottest days of the year. The Missouri Confederates

stirred early on May 16, gray cotton trying to dry their uniforms by standing close to campfires and attempting to find something to eat before continuing the push toward Raymond. Hardly had the sun eased up over the
horizon when gunfire crackled to the south, alerting the worn Rebels that
the bluecoats had arrived in force. Blue horsemen of the Federals' vanguard
clashed with gray pickets along the Raymond Road, and skirmishing intensified. Behind the Yankee troopers marched long blue infantry columns of
Grant's rapidly advancing army.[45]

Before meeting the threat, Pemberton learned by courier of the capture
of Jackson. General Johnston stated in his dispatch that the two Southern
forces should link together north of the railroad to strike the invaders in
a united effort. As Grant's army closed in on Edwards Station from the east,
consequently, Pemberton ordered his command to reverse its course. Confederate units turned back north up the Plantation Road to recross Baker's
Creek to gain the Jackson Road and the railroad. The decision made good
sense to Pemberton, for the native Pennsylvanian wanted to avoid being
caught by Grant's army with too few troops amid the forests and rough terrain drained by Baker's and Jackson creeks. Ironically, Pemberton's
original desire had been to make a defensive stand behind Big Black's fortifications to avoid the present situation.[46]

General Grant was determined not to let the Rebels slip through his
grasp, having them where he wanted them. Capitalizing on the information
of Confederate plans from a captured Johnston dispatch, seven Federal
divisions raced westward toward Pemberton. The blue juggernaut poured
forward along the Jackson, Middle, and Raymond roads leading east toward
Edwards Station and Pemberton. The swelling sound of musketry soon indicated Grant's success in preventing Pemberton and Johnston from linking. As fate and General Grant would have it, the Confederate Army now
lay directly in the path of the advancing Union forces. A wave of sharp skirmishes exploded through the woodlands like wildfire, threatening to erupt
into a full-blown contest before most of the Southern columns moved out.
Reports filtered into headquarters of Yankees swarming everywhere, approaching rapidly from the east in overwhelming numbers. Pemberton correctly ascertained that he now confronted the whole of "Grant's victorious
army returning, exultant and eager for more prizes, from the capture of
Jackson." In only a few hours, Vicksburg's fate would be decided in the
wilderness of mid-eastern Mississippi on May 16.[47]

Forced to fight one of the most decisive battles of the war on short
notice, Pemberton canceled the reverse march and prepared to make a
stand on the best available defensive ground that he could find. He would
have to adjust to the tactical situation and make the best of it. The West
Pointer (Class of 1837) hurriedly deployed his command on the high
ground overlooking Jackson Creek, a watercourse angling northward and

parallel to the Plantation Road. This natural position on good ground was strong defensively, but unfortunately for Confederate fortunes no officer had bothered to halt the long train of the army's munitions wagons. Last in line before the about-face order, the supply train, now first in line, would be west of Baker's Creek far from the battleground when the storm burst over Champion Hill. While Pemberton consolidated his three divisions east of Baker's Creek, the Confederates' ammunition wagons continued to amble across Baker's Creek and beyond. But worst of all, two Southern divisions of almost 10,000 men — two-fifths of Pemberton's army — were many miles to the west and idle. These Confederates who would be so badly needed that day at Champion Hill were in the trenches guarding Vicksburg, while the most important battle of the campaign and one of the most decisive engagements of the war was about to erupt more than twenty miles to the east in Hinds County.[48]

As Loring's troops skirmished to the south along the Raymond Road, Bowen hurriedly formed the two brigades of his division in the line's center near the Ratliff brothers' house. Along the low range of hills overlooking the ravines which cut eastward toward the valley of Jackson Creek, the grayclad Missourians hustled into formation east of the Ratliff home. Holding a key flank position, Colonel McCown's soldiers aligned to Green's left, taking position behind a sheltering knoll. The army's line on the left and farther to the north meanwhile took shape. Here, Pemberton's remaining division, under General Carter L. Stevenson, deployed while the gunfire to the south escalated in the morning's heat.[49]

Redeploying to a better defensive position, the Fifth Missouri boys double-quicked over to a fallow field, where they formed in a long battle-line under a heavy bombardment. To stop the blue swarm pouring across Jackson Creek and to silence the roar of the angry Union cannon, fourteen pieces of Captains Guibor's, Wade's and Landis's Missouri batteries unlimbered along the ridge commanding the valley.[50] But the Missouri guns only acted as magnets that drew a heavier artillery response upon the infantrymen of the Missouri Brigade. While more shells exploded in the field, Colonel McCown's Johnny Rebs hugged the ground under the storm of projectiles.[51]

Confidence lifted among the rank and file when Colonel Cockrell came galloping down the line. Mounted and wearing a fine double-breasted uniform, Cockrell spoke encouragement to the enlisted men while shells exploded nearby. He challenged his Missourians to uphold their hard-earned reputation as the hardest and most reliable fighters in the West during the upcoming action. The Missouri Brigade commander, who in battle carried a Bible in one pocket and *Hardee's Tactics* in the other, leaped off his horse and directed the fire of one of Wade's artillery pieces. To the cannoneers' disbelief, the infantry colonel from Warrensburg helped aim a field piece which fired and exploded a Federal artillery caisson. May 16 would be Colonel Cockrell's finest day, ensuring a general's rank.

To protect his division, General Bowen reasoned that a five-company skirmish battalion needed to be pushed forward to ensure the safety of his position if the Federals attacked out of the valley. Therefore, Cockrell shortly ordered each regiment of the Missouri Brigade to supply its best company for skirmish duty. Colonel McCown, of course, picked the elite Celtic skirmishers of Company F. As they had done during prewar militia service in St. Louis, Company F's musicians instantly blew bugles and whistles in the humid air of early afternoon. The clear notes cutting across the valley signaled the division's prize skirmishers of Company F, Fifth Missouri, to prepare for more hazardous duty before the main line.[52]

The lieutenant colonel of the Third Missouri, Finley Lewis Hubbell, assembled the battalion within minutes. Battalion skirmishers consisted of hardy frontiersmen from the Bootheel region swamps to the north Missouri prairies which spread into Iowa and Nebraska. With a cheer and clattering of accoutrements, Captain Canniff's Irishmen and battalion members raced through the grain fields east of the Plantation Road, trampling down the young stalks that stood motionless in the windless heat. Across good ground at the headwaters of two branches above Jackson Creek, the five Missouri companies fanned out 400 yards before the Missouri Brigade.[53]

With considerable skill, General Pemberton completed the disposition of his forces along an overly extended three-mile front. But the overextension of the Confederate line allowed the Southerners to occupy the highest ground in the area, including Champion Hill, which was held by Stevenson. This sharp elevation on the Sid Champion Plantation was nearly 150 feet higher than the surrounding terrain. If General Grant were not advancing in force, then Pemberton planned to hasten his army northeastward toward the strategic crossroads where the Jackson Road turned westward toward Edwards Station.

Indeed, while the northernmost Confederate units plodded onward to unite with Johnston, one of Grant's strongest columns closed in from the northeast via the Jackson Road. This blue mass neared Pemberton's vulnerable left in overpowering numbers. But the Unionists' aggressive thrusts up the Raymond and Middle roads caused the Southerners to overlook the disaster brewing along the Jackson Road, which was the avenue leading to the Rebel left flank and rear.[54] The Confederates had already lost the initiative on May 16. Led by an inexperienced and cautious commander, the Southern army was tentative and groping and seemed to be waiting for something to happen. This was the type of opportunity that a leader of Grant's ability would soon exploit to the fullest.[55]

As the Confederate army prepared to continue to withdraw northward, three Union divisions hovered near the exposed Rebel flank northeast of the Champion house. Here some of Grant's best troops, including Hovey's division, prepared to slam into the unwary Southerners. Grant understood that the crossroads where the Jackson and Plantation, or Ratliff, roads intersected was one of the battlefield's keys. Equally important was the commanding elevation of the area, Champion Hill. This eminence dominated the farm lands and hilly terrain of the Champion Plantation. A strategic reality was clear to Grant on May 16: Yankee troops atop Champion Hill or at the crossroads would spell disaster for Pemberton and perhaps Vicksburg.

By late morning, thousands of Unionists were poised and stood perpendicular to the Confederate line on the northeast: an ideal situation and a supreme tactical advantage for Grant's forces. Most of Pemberton's soldiers, meanwhile, faced eastward toward the Jackson Creek threat, oblivious to their precarious position and the imminent danger. Without enough grayclad cavalry to reconnoiter, Pemberton was unaware of the massive Union build-up on the northeast.[56]

Captain Canniff's skirmishers and the skirmish battalion meanwhile had run into a hornet's nest. After picking their way several hundred yards down the brushy terrain leading into Jackson Creek, these advanced graycoats had encountered large numbers of Unionists and consequently returned on the double. Colonel Hubbell reformed his skirmishers in a gully bordering the field, where Bowen's busy artillerymen kept their cannon roaring at a steady pace. In this natural shelter, Canniff's Irish soldiers lay low under the shell-fire and found shelter from the storm.[57]

About two hours after the artillery duel subsided, a division of Federals crossed Jackson Creek and advanced west of the watercourse. The Celts of Company F braced for this threat. Generals Pemberton and Bowen were convinced that the Unionists had concentrated for a major attack in this sector. To parry this threat, the Missouri skirmish battalion again dashed east to slow the expected Yankee attack in the Missouri Brigade's front. Colonel Hubbell deployed his Confederates on good defensive ground to await developments. Meanwhile, the accurate fire of Bowen's artillery deterred a strike upon Pemberton's center throughout May 16.[58]

As Hovey's blue formations aligned in the rye fields and thick woodlands around the Champion house, General Stevenson shifted his troops northeastward to counter the threat. But no new dispositions could compensate for the large numbers of Unionists. A confident Pemberton now calmly awaited the expected assault from the southeast that would never come, while more than 10,000 bluecoats of two divisions had assembled to attack from the opposite direction at the north end of the Confederate battle-line. Equally as blind, the Missouri Rebels waited in vain for the expected Federal onslaught from the valley of Jackson Creek. As throughout the Vicksburg campaign, the absence of cavalry and timely intelligence continued to keep the Confederates guessing.[59]

As fate would have it, General Stevenson and his men on the north were in a bad fix. His appeals for support to Pemberton went ignored, and his troops were spread too thinly across a wide area. With Pemberton's left flank dangling in mid-air, the blue tidal wave rolled forward on the north around 10:30 A.M. Positioned in a line running along Champion Hill, the bald hilltop 800 yards southwest of the Champion house, Stevenson's defense did not stand a chance. General John A. Logan's division on the right swung wide to strike Stevenson's left. Meanwhile, the hard-hitting Yankees of Hovey's division swarmed down the Plantation Road, ripping into the thin gray lines. Attacking with abandon, McGinnis's brigade on the right side of the road and Slack's brigade to the left chewed up everything in their paths. McGinnis's troops soon overran the crest of Champion Hill, capturing four Alabama and Virginia cannon.[60]

Stevenson's two Georgia, one Tennessee, and one Alabama brigades were buried under the Yankee avalanche. After Stevenson's left was shattered, only a thin line of Georgians and four Alabama and four Mississippi guns stood at the strategic crossroads, 400 yards southwest of Champion Hill's crest, braced for the fast-approaching blue tornado. The crossroads defense was hastily patched together and was the last hope to blunt the drive of the victorious Yankees. But nothing in the world could stop the Federal juggernaut from steamrolling onward. After charging through a wide cornfield, Slack's brigade poured over the crossroads like a flood. Cheering Iowa farm boys bayoneted and clubbed down Rebel cannoneers around the four field pieces, taking possession of the trophies. The whole Confederate left was destroyed by the powerful blow delivered by the Unionists, and Champion Hill and the crossroads were captured by one o'clock. Pemberton's army, the principal force defending Vicksburg, now tottered on the verge of annihilation.[61]

Rushing to the scene, Pemberton attempted to rally the panic-stricken mob streaming rearward. After much effort, he stabilized the Fifty-Sixth and Fifty-Seventh Georgia, which had been routed from the crossroads. A new Rebel defensive line was hastily patched together across the Plantation Road just north of the Isaac Roberts house, Pemberton's headquarters, about 600 yards south of the crossroads. The Unionists had not only smashed the Confederate left but also charged into Pemberton's rear. Thus Grant had gained one of the Southerners' primary escape routes across Baker's Creek. The Confederates now were cut off from their Vicksburg base and reinforcements. Grant's powerful onslaught barreling southward down both sides of the Plantation Road threatened to sweep over Pemberton's headquarters and completely roll up the vulnerable battle-line of the reeling Confederate army.[62]

The growing racket of battle to the north had convinced General Bowen to ignore Pemberton's noon orders to push the Unionists out of the bottoms of Jackson Creek. Bowen wisely reasoned that the smartest move was to make no move at all. To meet the new threat, Pemberton now ordered Bowen's division to reinforce Stevenson. But by this time, the situation in the Missouri Brigade's front had become more serious. An increasing amount of Union pressure gradually built up after nearly three hours of silence. The Missouri skirmish battalion had opened fire on the advancing bluecoats, but the skirmishers were under heavy pressure and could give way at any moment. Under this, intensifying threat, General Bowen, a brilliant leader who thought for himself, reasoned that he could not abandon his position despite his commander's directive.[63]

To reemphasize his order, Pemberton personally urged his finest lieutenant, General Bowen, forward to Stevenson's aid on the "double quick [to] retake those [captured] guns." Bowen sprang into action, and the Missourians instantly shifted direction to meet the threat to the north. Cockrell's buglers blew the notes of calls for maneuvers practiced on a hundred drill fields, and the gray ranks quickly formed with precision into echelon, a step-like formation with each regiment slightly to the left-rear of the foremost unit. Shortly after, Cockrell's units dashed forward with war-cries to save the day. While they were en route toward the left on the double, Pemberton redirected his fast-moving frontier exiles to shift east to the crossroads.[64]

Colonel McCown's soldiers sprinted eastward through the grain fields west of the Roberts house. Since the Fifth Missouri had been positioned on the right of the original line, Colonel McCown's regiment now led the advance. These grayclads headed straight into the eye of the storm where musketry crackled like thunder. The Missourians' alignment remained tight as McCown's formations pushed swiftly across the rows of green rye plants and cornstalks. Double-quicking with Enfields on their right shoulders, the Missouri infantrymen contemplated the grim work ahead as the cheers of victorious Unionists and musketry crashed louder around the crossroads.

Behind the onrushing Rebel ranks came the fast-moving guns of Wade's, Guibor's, and Landis's batteries in the tradition of the "flying artillery" of Mexican War fame. These guns were the Missouri Brigade's guardian angels, a role especially demonstrated to be true on May 16. One of these artillery pieces advancing forward to join the counterattack was appropriately named the "Lady Bowen," in honor of the general's wife. Colonel Cockrell's troops faced their greatest challenge that day, engaging in their most decisive battle to date. Union victory seemed inevitable by early afternoon with Pemberton's left hurled back nearly a half-mile, losing thousands of prisoners and sixteen artillery pieces.[65]

Colonel McCown's graycoats were eager to reverse the day's fortunes;

"[We were] moving faster the nearer we approached the firing," wrote one soldier. Drenched in sweat under the broiling Mississippi sun, the Fifth Missouri Rebels now saw an unnerving spectacle. Thousands of panicked Southerners were fleeing rearward across the steaming farm lands, running for their lives before the Yankee onslaught. After having been caught facing the wrong direction, east instead of north, the Confederate army now faced complete destruction by early afternoon.[66]

As the Fifth Missouri soldiers pushed eastward, they saw General Pemberton vainly attempting to rally Stevenson's fleeing throng along the Plantation Road. Before the Missouri Brigade swarmed a blueclad mass, charging onward with a will of its own and smashing everything before it. Colonel McCown's troops, nevertheless, dashed ahead to "redeem the day from utter disaster," recalled one Rebel.[67]

Some Fifth Missouri Confederates were shaken by the unforgettable sight around the crossroads: countless Federals of Slack's division charged through the smoke-laced woods and fields, unleashing volleys and bayoneting and clubbing down Southern soldiers. The grim scene was too much for Private Joshua M. Poe, age twenty-one. Dropping out of Company G's ranks, the former Macon County laborer threw down his musket and joined the panicked hordes of beaten Southerners. Other Fifth Missouri Confederates probably followed Private Poe's example, heading for the rear to escape from the most Yankees that they had ever seen. One Rebel would never forget the sight of Cockrell's cheering troops rushing into the fray with drill-field precision and battle flags waving: the crack "Missourians to the rescue."[68]

The greater distance that Colonel Cockrell's troops raced forward through the fields, the more routed Southern troops they met. In the words of one Fifth Missouri soldier, this defeated Rebel mob poured through "our ranks without imparting their own alarm or disarranging our files." Nearing the crossroads, Colonel Cockrell screamed above the crashing guns for the Missouri Brigade to swing "left by file into line." This complicated maneuver was performed flawlessly as if on a parade ground, while the attacking Federals "opened a galling fire on the right flank of our unformed brigade." Here, northwest of the Roberts house, around 300–400 yards to the crossroad's south, Colonel McCown began to deploy the Fifth Missouri for battle. As fate would have it, McCown's command was the first Missouri regiment in column and the first unit to feel the wrath of the howling tide of charging Unionists.[69]

At the last moment, General Pemberton had successfully rallied the two Georgia regiments across the Plantation Road before the Roberts house. A shaky line upon which Colonel McCown hoped to align his regiment took shape. With minié balls whistling all around, McCown frantically tried to align troops to the Fifty-Sixth Georgia's left, performing the

maneuver in record time. The gamecocks of the Fifty-Sixth Georgia continued fighting spiritedly against overwhelming numbers, while holding a
gully just to the road's left. Snug in their natural trench, the Peach Staters
anchored the right of the new Confederate line which had been patched
together from scratch in the midst of battle. But if the Georgians broke as
they had done earlier in the day, these deploying units of the Missouri
Brigade would be rolled up and smashed to bits.[70]

By this time, Colonel Cockrell had recalled Hubbell's skirmishers. This
reinforcement would be timely, because five additional companies might be
enough to decide the success of the upcoming counterattack. Lieutenant
Colonel Hubbell and his couple hundred skirmishers now followed on the
Missouri Brigade's heels during its advance. When they raced past Pemberton, the general encouraged them forward to help reverse the day's fortunes. At the Roberts house, a group of women inspired the Missouri
skirmishers onward with a chorus of "Dixie." Captain Canniff and his
breathless soldiers of Company F unleashed Rebel yells in response.[71]

Slack's Iowa, Indiana, and Ohio soldiers meanwhile continued charg-
ing forward in a slashing assault that had already chewed up a third of the
Rebel army. The victorious Federal throng pushed onward through the
sprawling grain fields east of the Plantation Road. Rushing past and
enfilading the gully on the right, Slack's bluecoats shot down Fifty-Sixth
Georgia boys with ease. Under the pounding, the Georgians' line collapsed.
The hard-hit Georgia boys poured out of the cut, running to the rear before
Colonel McCown could complete the dispositions of the Fifth Missouri on
the Fifty-Sixth Georgia's left.[72]

McCown's regiment, on the Missouri Brigade's right and nearest the
Plantation Road, where the Unionists had made the most headway, suddenly found itself in serious trouble. The cheering Fifth Missouri soldiers,
nevertheless, kept moving forward to align near where the Georgians had
once stood. But nothing now existed on Colonel McCown's right except
"the heavy, strong lines of the enemy, rapidly advancing and cheering,
flushed with their success and the capture of our guns." Dangerously exposed in an open field, the right flank of the Fifth Missouri offered an ideal
target for the attackers. And unlike other Missouri regiments deploying to
the west, McCown's Confederates did not have the advantage of the shelter
of the sunken road. Slack's veterans quickly exploited McCown's vulnerability, striking hard with a vengeance. Hundreds of Federals turned their
fury on the newly arriving Confederates of the Missouri Brigade, but no
unit took more punishment than the badly exposed Fifth Missouri.[73]

South of the crossroads and nearest the Plantation Road on the Fifth
Missouri's extreme right, Company C was the first unit attacked and the
hardest hit by the raging blue tide.[74] With smoke draping the field like a
blanket, Captain Bradford and his Polk County men failed to see the

Georgians melting away to their right. Consequently, Bradford's soldiers were surprised when Bluecoats suddenly poured through the smoky haze only ten feet away. Recovering from the shock, some Company C Rebels got off snap shots at the nearest Unionists, but nothing could now stop the fierce onslaught of the attackers.

Indeed, the Yankees had caught sight of Company C first. Scores of Federals responded with a point-blank volley, raking the Polk County boys of Company C with a vicious fire. Caught in the worst fire he had ever seen, Captain Bradford had no time to bark out new orders to realign his men to meet the threat before his company was enfiladed by the blistering fire. More than any other company of the Fifth Missouri, Company C's ranks wavered under the impact of the withering fire.

Raked and hard hit by the murderous fire, Captain Bradford's unit had never been placed in such a deadly quandary. Not only were they cut to pieces by an enfilade fire, the Rebels also started falling after being hit by musketry from the rear. Indeed, the Unionists had charged beyond McCown's right flank to turn and shoot the Fifth Missouri boys from behind. Being struck by a close-range musketry from three sides, Company C seemingly would be wiped out within minutes if something were not done soon. Bradford now took action without orders, relying upon the well-honed battle instincts and savvy of a veteran commander. Above all, he knew that he had to get his men out of the murderous crossfire before it was too late. Captain Bradford yelled above the din for his survivors to fall back. This was the first time Fifth Missouri soldiers had ever relinquished ground with full cartridge boxes. [75]

With decisive victory in sight, Colonel Slack's overwhelming numbers continued to pour down the Plantation Road en masse, threatening to sweep everything before them. After gaining McCown's right and rear, the surging blue tide also opened flanking fires on the other companies of the Fifth Missouri stretching through the open fields to the west. Punished severely by the withering volleys, additional companies of Colonel McCown's regiment besides Company C were thrown into disarray. The once neat double lines of Fifth Missouri Confederates soon turned into a mass of milling soldiers who had been hit harder than ever before. Point-blank, scorching volleys ripping down the length of the formation from right to left were too much to take even for McCown's elite veterans from the Western frontier. [76]

The right portion of the Fifth Missouri grudgingly surrendered ground, falling back to escape the terrible fire. On the left of McCown's right-center company, the regimental color guard and flag fell back along with the survivors of Company I. The enfilade fire had riddled Company I before it could fully deploy in a battle-line. With McCown's right rapidly dissolving, the left of the Fifth Missouri now lay isolated and exposed in an open field in the face of the Union onslaught. It was not long before the regiment's left also retired to escape the enfilade fire. The entire Fifth Missouri headed rearward without having had the time to form a line of battle. But despite this severe punishment, McCown's regiment continued to maintain organization and composure during the withdrawal, which was no small feat under the ferocious Federal attack.[77]

To Colonel McCown's left, meanwhile, the Third Missouri's right companies also fell back. Colonel Gause's left was sheltered in the sunken Middle Road, bordered by high split-rail fences as it spanned westward. While the rail fence protected the Third Missouri to some extent, their Fifth Missouri comrades were vulnerable in the open fields. These neat formations of the Third Missouri were soon forced to give way, however, under the relentless pressure from the attackers to the east.[78]

Farther to the left, or westward and under less pressure, the "Fighting Sixth" Missouri and Second Missouri maintained their positions. But, the Fifth Missouri Rebels losing their lives on the far right had bought time for these veteran regiments to align.[79] However, it seemed quite likely that the Missouri Brigade's whole line might yet be crumpled and rolled up before its formation could be completed. McCown's officers could do nothing to keep their soldiers turning rearward on their own to save themselves and escape slaughter.

Backtracking a short distance across the field to escape the worst punishment, the hard-hit Rebels of the Fifth Missouri scrambled behind a split-rail fence with the instinct of soldiers who knew exactly when and where to make a stand and fight. The regimental flag flying along the fence line served as a rallying point. Colonel McCown's veterans had fallen back to a better defensive position on better ground, where they could make a stand against one of the most successful Union attacks of the war to date. Here, behind the fence's cover, the Fifth Missouri was fully intact and ready to fight after instinctively regrouping at a better position.[80]

After hurriedly biting off cartridges and ramming down bullets, Colonel McCown's Confederates lay low and rested their rifles on rails to blast away into the blue legions charging toward them. The battered right of the Third Missouri had also taken cover beside the fence and stabilized the defense on the Fifth Missouri's left.[81] Fifth and Third Missouri soldiers were determined not to be whipped by Slack's warriors, who had beaten them barely two weeks before at Port Gibson. Minié balls shattered rails, sending splinters flying through the air to cut the hands and faces of McCown's men, who were holding firm. Most important, the Missouri Brigade's right had been rallied. But the crisis had only begun on May 16.

In order for Cockrell's brigade to counterattack and stem the raging blue tide, the bloodied Fifth Missouri and at least several Third Missouri companies also pinned down behind the fence had to advance to their original positions. The Missouri Brigade alignment had to be completed before an effective counterstroke could be launched to save the day. Around 2,000 First Missouri Brigade soldiers were now all that stood between the attacking Unionists and the annihilation of Pemberton's army. The fate of Vicksburg hung in the balance around the Roberts house south of the crossroads by midafternoon.[82]

Behind the high rail fence with his largely Macon County unit, Lieutenant Johnston was the senior officer of Company I. At this critical moment, neither Johnston nor anyone else could yet "tell whether [the Fifth Missouri's and, consequently, the Missouri Brigade's line as well] would stand or run" during this crisis. Nearly 400 Fifth Missouri Rebels were huddled behind the fence on the field's edge, maintaining a scattered fire and knowing that they could relinquish no more ground. It appeared, however, as if nothing could stop the blue avalanche from steamrolling over them and destroying Pemberton's army.[83]

Holding their ground, Colonel McCown's Rebels behind the zigzagging rails meanwhile kept their heads down in the storm. Only occasionally did Confederates pop up on their knees to shoot back at their tormentors. The unbeatable élan and fighting spirit which had enabled McCown's command to maul Grant's flank at Port Gibson had seemingly disappeared. More Missourians probably now threw down muskets and dashed rearward, forsaking the fight and seeking safety. Pemberton's shock troops had seemingly lost their spunk after running head-on into Grant's buzz saw and taking the worst beating of their lives.

Just when it seemed that most sensible Rebels had given up hope for winning a victory and that a crushing defeat seemed inevitable, one Company I private thought differently on May 16; however, Private John D. Dale, the farm boy from the prairies of northeast Missouri who was one of the last-stand defenders of Port Gibson's gully, did not like the idea of taking punishment and giving none back. Now occurred the type of individual initiative and action that verified the military axiom "the position of a brigade, the strength of a company, the command of a detachment, may affect and decide the whole outcome of a battle." Private Dale was now angry at the bitter prospect of the third consecutive loss for the Fifth Missouri in barely six months in Mississippi.[84] While bullets whistled by and grayclads seemed glued to the fence line, Private Dale suddenly decided to do something about the situation. He stood up on his own, forsaking the shelter of the fence. The enlisted man in dirty gray from Randolph County reasoned that it was now time for a ragged private to take the initiative and not some fancy West Point–trained general.

The fiery Private Dale swung over the fence in one bound while his comrades looked on in disbelief. With hundreds of Slack's cheering Westerners swarming over the field like a locust plague, Dale sprang forward and charged ahead alone. Exposed in an open field, Private Dale suddenly halted and turned around to challenge the men of Company I who remained pinned down behind the fence. Dale screamed at the top of his lungs, "Come on, Company I, we can whip the God Damn Yankees sons-of-bitches!" The effect of the private's dare on the Missourians was electric. Immediately, the soldiers of the northeast Missouri company snapped back to life and cheered. Color bearer Walton sprinted from the left of Company I into the field, waving the dark blue regimental flag for all to see.[85]

Inspired by Private Dale's one-man attack and the sight of the Latin cross-adorned banner flapping before the line, entire Fifth Missouri companies spilled over the fence. Colonel McCown's advancing Confederates spontaneously unleashed their high-pitched yelps from the Western frontier: the old esprit de corps of the Fifth Missouri had returned. Now the Rebels poured over the cleared land, rushing forward with renewed spirit and energy. Howling attackers of McCown's unit soon hurled back the foremost Unionists and, most important, took their former positions several hundred yards south of the crossroads and to the left, or west, of Plantation Road. With McCown's regiment surging ahead with a new determination, the right companies of the Third Missouri joined the Fifth Missouri's advance to reclaim the lost ground. Accomplishing in only a few minutes what seemed impossible only a short time before, the soldiers of the Fifth Missouri had advanced to realign in their former position and now held firm in the face of the Union onslaught. The Missouri Brigade's alignment once again was almost complete.[86]

To bolster the yet vulnerable right flank of the Fifth Missouri, Colonel Cockrell hurled Colonel Amos Camden Riley's First and Fourth Missouri (consolidated) into the fray near the Plantation Road. The arrival of Riley's troops could not have been at a better time nor in a more desperate situation. Here, was General Bowen, who was directing alignment and inspiring his troops. Fittingly, during the most decisive engagement of his life, Bowen was beside his old regiment that he had organized nearly two years before. During this new crisis on the Missouri Brigade's right, General Bowen sought desperately to stabilize the shaky Rebel lines. In retaking the ground of the open field abandoned earlier, the Fifth Missouri was once again placed in a dangerous and enfiladable position, paying a high price for its recent resurgence.[87]

Meanwhile, the blue legions continued charging down the Plantation Road area and sent a stinging flank fire sweeping down the gray formations of Colonel McCown's regiment, inflicting considerable damage. The First and Fourth Missouri now found itself in the identical dilemma that the Fifth Missouri had faced earlier: a severe enfilade fire pouring forth from the attackers less than 40 yards distant from the right flank. Nevertheless, Colonel

Riley's veterans now prevented the Fifth Missouri from perhaps suffering a repeat of its earlier fate. Hundreds of Riley's St. Louisans and southeast Missouri Bootheelers gamely waded into the raging storm with their distinctive war cries and bayonets flashing in the bright sunlight of early afternoon.[88]

Rescuing the Fifth Missouri, the First and Fourth Missouri Rebels charged forward, following their blue silk flag, which was decorated with a tigress with cubs and the warning "Beware." One Confederate wrote that Colonel Riley's soldiers "poured a volley of musketry into them and prevented them from flanking us, which they were doing rapidly." To meet this crisis, Colonel Riley, trained in the Kentucky Military Institute, adjusted to face the Union attack and the blistering flank fire by hurriedly turning his two right companies at right angles to the Missouri Brigade's line. After the Rebels of the First and Fourth Missouri, now aligned in a V-shaped formation, had delivered two punishing volleys, the Federal pressure diminished enough to enable the Missouri Brigade to complete its alignment. Then Colonel Riley's troops charged forward a short distance to hurl back the foremost Union attackers and solidify the Missouri Brigade's right flank.[89]

In addition, the prospects for a counterattack increased with the arrival of Green's Missouri and Arkansas Brigade. These veteran Western troops, including former First Missouri Brigade units, reached the field with Rebel yells. Colonels McCown's and Riley's efforts on the Missouri Brigade's right now allowed Green's brigade to deploy on Cockrell's right. Ignoring the stream of bullets, General Bowen made sure that his 3,500-man division was properly aligned for the counterattack. No one felt more confident than General Bowen that the potential gap near the road between the two Confederate brigades of his division had been bridged and that the weakest links had been stabilized by an elite regiment which he had led into the storms of Shiloh and Corinth.[90]

In the next few minutes, additional preparations were made before launching the counterattack. Fast-moving volunteers, including some Fifth Missouri boys, darted across the fields to tear down the zigzagging rail fences in the Missouri Brigade's front. Then, Colonel Cockrell and Colonel Gates, whose First Missouri Cavalry (dismounted) anchored Green's left, met and shook hands amid the drifting smoke of battle and rifle fire: a sight giving more confidence to Bowen's soldiers. This dramatic meeting between the two most popular Missouri Brigade commanders took place before the lengthy Confederate formations and in the face of the Unionists' onslaught. Now, at long last, Bowen's two brigades were linked and ready to strike back. The two commanders from western Missouri had fought side by side since early Missouri State Guard days and risen through the ranks by natural ability and tactical skill to become Bowen's two top lieutenants.

Now Colonels Cockrell and Gates, two of the most experienced officers in the Vicksburg army, stood side by side, preparing to reverse Confederate fortunes. But the odds hardly favored a successful Rebel counterattack. In the words of one Southern officer, the fight was now largely "the Missouri Confederates against Grant's army."[91]

Finally, the long, double lines of grayclads were in position, ready to deliver some punishment of their own. Never had the Fifth Missouri been in better fighting shape than now. Every available soldier was in Colonel McCown's formation. Private Dyson stood in line when he should have been in the infirmary. Ordered to stay with the baggage that morning, Dyson had ignored the directives of Assistant Surgeon Atwood and gamely kept up with the regiment during the long dash to meet the day's greatest crisis. Perhaps the ex-teacher wanted to avenge the death of former students who had been killed at Port Gibson. And the black servant of Lieutenant Colonel Bevier again had to be practically dragged out of line so eager was he to fight the Yankees. One-armed Rebels of the Fifth Missouri, such as Privates Doyle, Hicks, and Tipton, were also in formation and ready to do their part.[92]

The Missouri lines stretched for hundreds of yards across the open fields, while the Unionists continued to charge forward. Blue Latin cross–decorated banners flapped above the Rebel ranks in the warm sunshine. McCown's officers galloped down the ranks and spoke words of encouragement around 2:30 on this hot afternoon. As they waited for the long-expected order to finally lash out at their tormentors, the men of the Fifth Missouri may have recalled Colonel Cockrell's inspiring challenge that "by our acts we will avenge" the deaths of regimental members slain at Port Gibson.[93] These fallen comrades included Adjutant Greenwood, the alternating cynic and romantic; Captain Stokely, the respected leader from the Bootheel region; the handsome teenager, Sergeant Lee, and many other regimental members who were now only a memory.[94]

With sunlight sparkling off the bayonets of hundreds of Fifth Missouri soldiers, Colonel Cockrell, in the words of one Missourian, "rode down the lines; in one hand he held the reins and a large magnolia flower, while with the other he waved his sword." Before the order came to attack, Captain Canniff and his panting Emerald Islanders of Company F at last reached the Fifth Missouri and hustled into line. Finally, the Fifth Missouri, along with the Missouri Brigade and Bowen's division, was ready to deliver one of the hardest-hitting counterattacks of the war. Pointing his saber toward the Union masses swarming forward, Cockrell galloped to the front and roared, "Charge!" Like a gray tidal wave, all five Missouri regiments rolled forward.[95]

Hundreds of McCown's attackers "gave them the Missouri yell, and gave them a charge in Missouri Rebel style," wrote Sergeant Ruyle. The

Missourians' peculiar scream echoed over the fields and forests of the Sid Champion Plantation. The Rebel yells of Colonel McCown's soldiers now competed with the roar of Captains Wade's, Guibor's, and Landis's cannon. With a grasp of the psychological value of their fierce battle-cry, McCown's men valued the effect of the Rebel yell on their Port Gibson antagonists, who "knew the sound of [our] yell." To save Pemberton's army, Bowen's division — "the best combat unit in either army" — had to meet its greatest challenge. With Cockrell's brigade charging west of the Plantation Road and Green's brigade east of it, the Confederacy's most accomplished troops in the Deep South advanced side by side with a determination to reverse the day's fortunes.[96]

McGinnis's troops, mostly to the road's west, were the first to be hit by the Missourians' fierce onslaught. The Bluecoats recoiled when stunned by Cockrell's and Green's slashing attack, which slammed into them like a thunderbolt. With battle flags waving above the advancing ranks, Colonel McCown's formations swarmed to the road's left, charging across the grain fields south of the crossroads. McGinnis's and Slack's mob was riddled with a point-blank volley delivered by the Missourians, who gained revenge. But these stubborn opponents in blue stood their ground before the crossroads until they were overwhelmed by the onrushing Missouri tide, fighting tenaciously.[97]

Here, in a nightmarish struggle on an afternoon that no one would ever forget, blue and gray tangled face to face. Close fighting erupted with men swinging rifle-butts and jabbing with bayonets in the afternoon heat. Keen-eyed Missourians concentrated their fire on Union officers and color bearers, demonstrating the effectiveness of their new Enfields. With a savage fury, the Fifth Missouri tore into the Unionists in the Roberts orchard, just south of the crossroads. Both sides traded volleys and death in the orchard, which became a place of slaughter. Bodies began piling up around the fruit trees among the colorful blossoms. Along with other soldiers of Company H, Captain McKinney tumbled mortally wounded to the ground when a minié ball whistled through his lungs.[98]

A smoky haze blanketed the ground and drifted up through the fruit trees, giving the orchard a surreal appearance. Streams of bullets clipped leaves from limbs and sent branches tumbling to earth. Colonel McCown's soldiers blasted away and their ear-piercing screams rose higher during the wild surge which gradually gained more momentum. Now, wrote one Company F soldier, the "ground was contested inch by inch," while the Federals were pushed rearward. The gray ranks swept onward through the orchard with blue banners waving and bayonets gleaming. In Sergeant Hogan's words, McCown's Rebels now continued to smash "through the enemy's lines, the ground strewn with their dead." Howling Confederates closely pursued the retreating Federals, as the chase continued across terrain which gently sloped upward and northward through the hot forests of Mississippi.[99]

After charging forward several hundred yards, the victorious Confederates neared the crossroads. Here, Colonels McGinnis and Slack had assembled a formidable defense around four guns of an Alabama battery at the crossroads, which had been captured earlier. Two heavy blue lines, one solidly entrenched behind the sunken road, awaited the Missourians, who were screaming and converging on the crossroads. For Bowen's counterattack to succeed, the strategic crossroads had to be taken at all costs.[100]

After stopping to quickly form a line, these well-disciplined Confederates soon unleashed one volley which dropped a good many of McGinnis's and Slack's defenders. Before the smoke had cleared, the Missourians raised a battle cry and then swept onward to take the crossroads with battle flags waving through the layers of drifting smoke. A fierce struggle raged around the captured artillery. During this savage clash, hand-to-hand combat swirled along the chest-high rail fences lining the roads, beside the guns, and in the sunken roadbed. Only after a nightmarish melee of vicious fighting did the Yankees give way. Leaving blue bodies and dead artillery horses in bloody piles, the Federals bitterly contested the ground as they retired northward.

One Missouri Confederate bragged, "We engaged them in hand to hand conflict and finally drove them off, re-capturing [Captain James F. Waddell's Alabama Battery]." Against the odds, the crossroads was finally captured by the Missourians, which was the beginning of the reversing of the tide. But the price was high, for "men lay dead in heaps" and blood ran like water on the ground, recalled one Missouri Brigade soldier. Resuming the attack, Colonel McCown's elated troops continued onward with yells of victory to destroy more Federals and reverse the hands of fate on May 16.[101]

At the edge of the woods just beyond the crossroads, Fifth Missouri leaders implored their men forward through the choking smoke. Attacking Rebels made the belt of forest ring with their war cries from the frontier. The densely wooded terrain now rose steadily northward toward the crest of Champion Hill, 600 yards distant. Under the relentless pounding of the Missourians' attack, the mauled Union forces retired deeper into the dense forest, continuing to fight back. Groups of bluecoats rallied in ravines and thickets, and sheets of flame erupted from pockets of resistance, mowing down some of the onrushing Confederates, who never knew what had hit them.

The cheering Fifth Missouri Rebels swarmed through the trees, loading and firing on the run. In the haste of biting off cartridges and hurriedly loading on the move, soldiers had black powder smeared on faces and spilled in mouths, which increased thirst on this hot day. All alignment of the attackers evaporated in the confused fighting amid the tangled woodlands and deep ravines. As the advancing gray ranks fragmented, some Missourians kept charging, while others took cover in the underbrush and behind trees and returned fire. Thousands of muskets from both sides roared incessantly, filling the forest with blinding smoke and noise.[102]

Nightmarish duels broke out when Confederates overran hollows filled with blue defenders. Then McCown's soldiers pressed onward with shouts to the next ravine, stabbing their opponents with bayonets and clubbing them with muskets. Few orders or shouts among the attackers could be heard in the tempest engulfing the woodlands covered with blossoming magnolias. Despite staggering losses, the punished Yankees fought stubbornly up the brushy slopes. After unleashing close volleys, the Unionists leap-frogged rearward to the next ravine or thicket and again prepared to greet the next assault of onrushing Missourians. This vicious battle in the forests dissolved into an enlisted man's fight. Despite so many officers shot down, the common soldiers of the Fifth Missouri continued forward dodging from tree to tree and overrunning narrow, Union-held hollows with bayonets to finish the tough job of wiping out the next band of defenders.[103]

During the nonstop fighting for hundreds of yards, many cartridge boxes of the charging Rebels of the Fifth Missouri were empty. McCown's Confederates had expended nearly 40 rounds in the forests of Sid Champion. A few regimental leaders galloped to the rear to find ammunition and to hurry up reinforcements: futile efforts. Consequently, the struggle for Champion Hill would have to be decided in the ravines and tangled thickets along the southern slope with bayonets, sabers, musket-butts, and fists. Victory in the forests could only be measured by the soldier's yardstick of swinging a musket butt with sufficient force to crush an opponent's skull or lunging a bayonet deeply into a bluecoat's body. Success today at Champion Hill would be determined by the number of Yankees that could be killed.[104]

The relentless Rebel surge toward the crest exacted a high toll on the attackers. Amid the summerlike foliage, the onrushing Confederates ran head-on into hidden groups of Unionists. As the thick battle smoke drifted up through the trees, lines of Federals suddenly seemed to appear out of nowhere to unleash volleys from only a few feet away. Yellow and red flames lashed out of the greenery from multiple directions. Despite the punishment inflicted upon them, Colonel McCown's soldiers continued charging through the body-littered woodlands, with yells and battle flags waving in the palls of smoke.[105]

Having survived the Port Gibson delaying action, Private Allen Marion Edgar went down when a bullet ripped through his thigh. His son, Private John Henry Edgar, continued forward with Company I. Another Company I hero of the last stand also fell in the smoke-laced forests of Champion Hill, the irrepressible Sergeant Moore who had commanded the delaying party at Port Gibson. Attempting to hurriedly patch together a defensive line near the crest and calling for reinforcements to meet the Missourians' sweeping charge, McGinnis would never forget how "at this point occurred one of the most obstinate and murderous conflicts of the war." The woodlands of the Champion Plantation were turned into a boiling cauldron as the contest raged in unprecedented fury.[106]

The officer corps of the Fifth Missouri was decimated during the wild surge toward the crest of Champion Hill. Lieutenant William Jasper Hickman, a twenty-one-year-old Bootheel farmer of Company K, dropped with three wounds. But few of McCown's soldiers halted to assist fallen comrades on May 16, for the assault must not falter. There was little taking of prisoners because no time or manpower could be lost if this attack were to succeed. The animal instincts of kill or be killed took over and consumed Colonel McCown's men during the tenacious struggle in the snarled tangles of oaks, pines, cedars, and magnolias.

Catching a glimpse of the enemy before he saw you and firing a quick shot in a hazy thicket meant the difference between life or death for many Fifth Missouri Rebels on this afternoon in hell. Those Fifth Missouri infantrymen loading the fastest or finding the best cover on Champion Hill managed to survive the most bitter contest anyone had ever seen. Around regimental colors, cursing men in blue and gray hacked savagely with rifles, punched adversaries, and snatched at flag staffs. Throughout the attack, Sergeant Walton kept the Fifth Missouri's banner out of the hands of the Unionists and securely in his possession.[107]

Along the commanding crest of Champion Hill, "Dad" McGinnis saw his fine Indiana and Wisconsin Brigade crushed by the Missourians' onslaught. The slashing assaults of Cockrell, to the road's west, and Green, east of the road, had virtually destroyed Hovey's division. In desperation, McGinnis called for artillery to try to stop the Missouri Brigade's charge, but it was too late to halt the gray avalanche rolling onward with a will of its own. Emplaced along the crest, two Sixteenth Ohio artillery pieces hurled double loads of canister into the charging ranks of the howling Missouri Confederates. An Ohio gunner was shocked at the daredevil abandon of the attacking Missouri soldiers, for "though the slaughter was appalling," they continued charging forward in suicidal fashion. Seemingly nothing could now stop Cockrell's fierce counterattack. Realizing as much, Colonel McGinnis ordered the captured Virginia and Alabama guns spiked before they could be captured by the Missourians.[108]

Besides being supported by more artillery, McGinnis's troops were bolstered by infantry reinforcements in the thick forests. This timely support resulted in more stands being made by the Unionists along the rough terrain, ensuring more hard fighting. Additional Fifth Missouri soldiers, therefore, were cut down in the face of the tenacious defense. Captain

Spicer implored Company K onward until a minié ball crashed through his neck. Fighting swelled to levels not seen previously in this war, rolling in crackling waves through the dark woodlands. "Under the most galling fire [most had] ever witnessed," McGinnis's Twenty-fourth Indiana was one unit decimated by the Missouri Rebels, who inflicted more than 200 casualties, the highest loss suffered by any Union regiment at Champion Hill. Just when the Missouri soldiers were about to capture the colors of the Twenty-fourth Indiana, the lieutenant colonel of the Indiana regiment retrieved it. He then "waved them with cheers in the very face" of the Confederates. An immediate Rebel volley riddled the colonel, and he dropped dead. The flag of the Indiana regiment was evidently captured by Cockrell's men in their relentless drive toward the crest.[109]

Blinded by the smoke, rugged terrain, and dense forest, few Confederates could see more than a few yards during their surge up Champion Hill. Amid the tangled woodlands, stalking graycoats outflanked Union-occupied positions and then stormed down hollows to shoot and bayonet Yankees from behind. Unable to believe his eyes, Slack saw his crack brigade wrecked by Bowen's onslaught during a vicious struggle that "finds but few parallels in the history of civilized warfare."[110]

The Rebels' push for the crest continued through the woodlands strewn with bodies of both blue and gray. For what seemed an eternity, the charge of McCown's grayclad warriors steamrolled onward, covering hundreds of yards. Occasionally, Missourians caught their breath for a few moments when they knelt or rested their Enfields against trees for well-aimed shots. More Confederates fell in the attack as it poured northward. Along with so many others, the former schoolteacher Private Dyson went down with a wound he later described to his Franklin County wife: "[A bullet] entered my right breast and passing directly through my right lung and coming out under my right shoulder blade, I actually thought I had received my death stroke."[111]

The desperate struggle amid the blooming magnolias and tall pines escalated to levels seldom seen. Loading and firing on the move, one group of Polk County infantrymen sprinted through the woods to strike a Union band holding a deep ravine choked with underbrush. The Company C soldiers advanced frontier-style, keeping low in the brush, following advantageous terrain, and "crawling on them until we got, in many places within ten paces of them," according to Sergeant Ruyle. Then the Confederates spilled into the bluecoats' position with screams and slashing bayonets for more hand-to-hand combat. In one duel, Sergeant Guthrie, just recovered from a Port Gibson wound, received a scar across his face. Even a veteran commander like General Hovey declared in horror, "I never saw fighting like this." Struggling tenaciously all the way, McGinnis's troops continued retiring up the southern slope of Champion Hill, with the onrushing Missouri Rebels close behind.[112]

A hard-fighting Irishman from St. Louis, Private Monahan raced far ahead of Company F to wage his own personal war. This hardened veteran "darted away, and through a depression in the ground, approached a large log, which was being used as a shelter by a squad" of Federals. Private Monahan slipped down a ravine, inching ever closer to the Unionists behind their log parapet. Consumed with the desire to obtain revenge for the suffering inflicted upon civilian friends, the Irish warrior sprang from the hollow, while gripping his Enfield like a war club. Bounding over the log in Celtic rage, Private Monahan "commenced striking right and left, with mad energy, while a thousand bullets, from both sides, whistled around him. His long hair streaming in the wind, the Herculean blows he made, and the [curses] with which he accompanied each one, gave him the appearance of being some avenging [angel of death]," as a Fifth Missouri officer who never forgot the scene recalled.[113] Using a musket butt like an ax and chopping away with wild abandon, the private finished off each bluecoat who fell under his wrath.[113]

Through such individual acts of daring, the Fifth Missouri attackers gained more ground in their wild surge for the crest. Onrushing Third Missouri soldiers on the left and First and Fourth Missouri troops on the right of the Fifth Missouri were intermingled in the thickets and ravines with McCown's troops during the charge west of the road. One natural leader of the Fifth Missouri who was killed was Sergeant Rumpf, the St. Louisan of German ancestry. As fate would have it, he had rejoined the regiment only nine days earlier after a prison camp internment.[114]

General Hovey's Yankee troops continued to stubbornly retire, "contesting with death every inch of the field they had won." The high ground of the Sid Champion Plantation had now become the "hill of death." Heavy pressure was maintained by the attacking Missourians against the Federals' disintegrating lines all across the body-littered slopes. With hands and faces black as coal from the stains of gun powder in rapidly loading, McCown's charging Rebels raced through the sulfurous woodlands in their desperate bid to win the day. Another member of the Port Gibson's delaying action, Private Elias Taylor Barton, dropped when a minié ball shattered both his thighs. Decimated by volleys, Fifth Missouri, the Unionists' ranks "soon gave way in wild disorder," wrote Sergeant Ruyle, and "we again gave the Missouri yell and took after them."[115]

For more than a half mile Bowen's fierce charge gained momentum, driving the Federals rearward. According to a Sergeant Hogan letter, "the farthest the enemy was away from us during that time was not over 25 yards." With high-pitched screams, McCown's soldiers attacked through the smoke with a "careless, almost joyous look," ironically, on a day which would be the last for so many Missourians in dirty gray. While surging for the summit, two of the Mitchell boys went down with wounds. Company C also lost a primary leader of the Polk County unit when Lieutenant Benjamin Looney Mitchell, who would never grip his saber again, had three fingers mangled. In addition, he received a "hole in his hip" from a hail of projectiles. Despite the fall of these relatives, the Mitchell clan's remainder continued attacking through the smoke-filled forest to reach the strategic crest of Champion Hill.[116]

As a result of almost continuous firing, shortages of cartridges grew more serious each passing minute. As the struggle raged "with unabated and almost unparalleled [sic] fury," the Missouri Rebels began filling cartridge boxes with rounds from the cartridge boxes of the multitudes of dead. Sergeant Hogan later described how he "fired forty-five rounds during the charge, which was about the hardest one hour's work that I ever done." On bloody May 16, the dominating crest of Champion Hill had to be taken at all costs, even with bayonets and musket butts.[117]

Efforts of McCown's officers to secure more ammunition proved futile with the army's ammunition wagons on the west side of Baker's Creek. Now "one unbroken deafening roar of musketry was all that could be heard," wrote one Missouri Rebel. Such firing meant that a serious shortage of rounds was inevitable on this afternoon in hell. Amid the blinding woodlands, noted another Missourian, "we were so hotly engaged that it was impossible to do anything but shoot, shoot. Point your gun in almost any direction and you could see a blue-coat to shoot at."[118]

On the bald crest of Champion Hill, nearly 200 feet higher than Baker's Creek, Colonel McGinnis's shattered units rallied, demonstrating how well these fine troops could perform despite the punishment. Crossing hard-earned ground, the Fifth Missouri soldiers passed over hollows and rises blanketed with ugly clumps of blue bodies, the best indicators of Confederate success on May 16. The wreckage of Grant's best division caused McCown's attackers to scream louder, shoot faster, and run harder toward the crest as they could now sense an unprecedented success in the West. Victory lay just ahead and up the timbered slope to the Union infantry and artillery-lined summit, which rose to more than 350 feet.[119]

This commanding hill dominated the surrounding area and was one of the highest points in Hinds County, the key to the battleground. The charging grayclads brushed aside the last of McGinnis's defenders before the crest. Under fire and narrowly escaping death twice, General Grant had seen Hovey's division mauled and all but destroyed today. Thanks to Bowen's counterattack, the Union army's center was now near complete collapse.[120]

Striking open ground after finally emerging from the smoke-laced forests, the Missourians converged on the crest of Champion Hill like a locust plague. Demonstrating frontier marksmenship with deadly effectiveness,

McCown's Rebels shot down Ohio cannoneers and horses, dropping them in bloody clumps along the crest. Utilizing frontier instincts, Missouri soldiers piled into the last ravine before Champion Hill's summit and took cover to escape the blasts of canister and bullets and to catch their breath before the final rush. From this natural shelter, Cockrell's men raked the Sixteenth Ohio Light Artillery, which was exposed in the field atop the crest and around the Champion Plantation's slave cabins and a log smokehouse. Here the Fifth Missouri sharpshooters obtained revenge, blasting away at the battery that had wiped out so many of their regimented members at Port Gibson. A concentrated Rebel volley was leveled upon the battery commander, dehorsing and mortally wounding the officer. McCown's men were inflicting severe damage in becoming familiar with their New Enfield rifles.[121]

After firing at targets they could hardly miss, some Missouri Rebels darted past the log cabins and rushed the Union artillerymen with bayonets to finish the job. Federal battery officers dropped the first attackers with pistol shots or sabers, but they could not slow the gray tide vomiting out of the ravine. Forcing McGinnis's last infantry defenders to abandon the battery and flee, swarming Fifth Missouri men, "yelling like Indians," bayoneted and clubbed down the remaining Buckeye gunners. A mob of Rebels overran the summit, howling and cheering their success. Here, Colonel McCown's men captured "two of the enemy's Napoleon guns" of the Sixteenth Ohio Light Artillery. Only the swiftness of the battery's horses spared the remaining Ohio cannon from being captured by the Missourians.

In addition, two Southern field pieces taken earlier by the Unionists were among the prizes won by the Missouri Brigade when the crest was captured. But the captured Federal guns could not be taken off the field by the Rebels because so many artillery horses had been killed. At last, the crest of Champion Hill had fallen to the Missouri Confederates, who had reversed the day's fortunes, taking the momentum and initiative away from General Grant, a feat not often accomplished in this war. After achieving the impossible, Bowen's hard-fighting division now held the key to the battlefield. Grant's finest troops had been smashed in less than an hour by the fury of Bowen's counterattack.[122]

On the hilltop commanding the surrounding area, the Missourians cheered their success. But the life-or-death struggle for Champion Hill had only begun. Now "compelled to depend intirely [sic] on the amunition [sic] found on the enemy's dead," wrote one Missourian, these veteran Rebels gathered rounds from the cartridge boxes of the stacks of Federal bodies. Indeed, the Springfield rifle-musket rounds could be loaded into Enfields. Meanwhile, surviving Missouri officers quickly reformed their lines across the open ground atop the hill. While standing in formation, McCown's exhausted soldiers caught their wind and made last-minute preparations before the final drive to exploit their amazing success.

After taking the dominant high ground, McCown's Confederates and other Missouri Brigade troops along the crest could look before them and not see a blue formation on the grain fields topping the elevation. Up ahead the terrain was more wooded and the brush heavier on the hill's northern slope before it dipped into a low spot. From this low point, the land then continued northward to rise up another dominant hill upon which stood the Champion house. Less steep and less high than Champion Hill, this elevation was the last high ground before Baker's Creek and was covered in timber near the top.[123]

After Bowen's troops had pushed Hovey's division back three-fourths of a mile during some of the most bitter fighting of the war, decisive success had seemingly been won by the Missourians. The farm boys from Missouri, wrote one soldier, were now the undisputed "masters of the field as far as our own front was concerned." As on no other battlefield, Sergeant Hogan felt elated by this most improbable victory in Hinds County, "for one mile [we had] advanced through the enemy's lines" during one of the fiercest onslaughts of the war.[124]

Indeed, Cockrell and Green had punched a hole into Grant's center and had the Northern army reeling. To exploit the opportunity, McCown's officers assembled as many men as possible for the final push to complete the victory before Grant recovered from the shock of Bowen's counterattack. As the thick smoke of battle hovered over the ground, a thin line of Missouri soldiers in soiled gray and butternut stood poised and ready to resume the attack to widen the wedge driven deep into Grant's center. Some Missourians, determined to win victory that day at any cost, ignored multiple wounds to align in formation for the last attempt to split Grant's army in half and win the day.[125]

Rallied Georgians, who had broken earlier to uncover the Fifth Missouri's right flank, now filled a gap between Bowen's two brigades, making up in part for the Missouri Brigade's high losses. Also bolstering the ranks, two Alabama infantry regiments rallied on Bowen's formations "as if by magic," after watching the Missourians' charge sweep by. But these reinforcements could not make up for hundreds of Missouri casualties left behind in the orchard, the woodlands, and the fields of the Champion Plantation.

Additionally bolstering Bowen's battle-lines were the three Missouri batteries of Bowen's division. After ax-wielding cannoneers had chopped paths through the tangled forests, Captains Wade's, Guibar's, and Landis's caissons and guns had galloped behind the Missouri Brigade's surging ranks to support the charging infantrymen.

The veteran gunners of these batteries now unlimbered on the open ground atop the summit of Champion Hill, which was littered with "Piles of

Federals," penned one Missouri gunner in his diary. These artillery pieces now provided a solid anchor on the Missouri Brigade's right, strengthening the position. Deploying to guard the Missouri Brigade's left flank was Captain Guibor's cannon, now under the able command of Ireland-born Lieutenant William Corkery. The St. Louis officer had been taught artillery tactics by Colonel Bowen during the prewar Southwest Expedition for just such an important day as this. With casualties high among the artillery and replacements nonexistent, Father Bannon quit attending to casualties and joined the fray as at Pea Ridge. The fiery Irish chaplain picked up a sponge-staff to serve on the gun crew of one of the Missouri artillery pieces.[126]

Just 600 yards northeastward around the Champion house atop the opposite hill could be seen Grant's large supply and ammunition wagons. This was another prize that needed to be captured to deliver yet another severe blow to Grant's army. One of Cockrell's men later recalled the extent of the success which had been equaled on few battlefields to date: "the federal forces gave way before us, abandoning batteries and leaving us almost in possession of their ammunition train. The drivers were whipping up their mules and making every effort to escape. We had broken Grant's centre and felt the day ours."[127]

Extra rounds and scattered Missouri Confederates were quickly gathered for the final push northward, which might save Vicksburg and perhaps the Confederacy. Since the war's beginning, a dozen battles, hundreds of miles marched, and countless comrades' deaths were all in preparation for such an opportunity to win a decisive victory. In addition, here was a chance to end the meteoric rise of the North's most promising general. Gaining just a few hundred more yards on this hot day in late spring might mean the fulfillment of a dream. Only a short distance and directly ahead lay one of the Confederacy's best chances to reverse the war's fortunes in the ill-fated West.

With a complete success so near, Bowen's two depleted brigades again would have to fight without substantial reinforcements or munitions, as at Corinth and Port Gibson. Pemberton had repeatedly ordered Loring and his division to Bowen's aid, but Loring continued to balk for fear of the threat in his front. Loring's 6,500 troops therefore stood idle while Bowen prepared for the final advance off Champion Hill to complete the defeat of Grant and to win glory. As at Grand Gulf and Port Gibson, Bowen's division was once again largely on its own.[128]

Resuming the counterattack, Colonel McCown led his skeleton regiment down through the forests along the northern slope of Champion Hill with Rebel yells and banners flowing in the smoke-filled air. Cockrell's brigade surged forward on the left of Bowen's division with "a terrific [resounding] yell and charge," remembered one Rebel. General Green's troops meanwhile advanced to the Missouri Brigade's right, rushing forward to

complete the victory. The gray waves surged onward to break the back of
Grant's Mississippi invasion. Hit by the Confederate tide, battered
fragments of Union regiments were pushed through the woods and into the
fields beyond. By this time, all substantial Union resistance had ceased on
Champion Hill, and the attacking Missourians at long last held decisive victory within their grasp, or so it seemed.[129]

But the dream of decisive victory and ending the career of General
Grant was not to be. Indeed, wrote one Fifth Missouri officer of the critical
turning point, "we were masters of the field in our front for a short time only."
Saving the day, Brigadier General Marcellus M. Crocker's 4,000-man division spilled from the woodlands and the open ground along the adjacent
hilltop in overwhelming numbers. A seemingly endless stream of heavy
blue formations deployed across the open fields until covering the southern
slope. The mystical path leading to victory and the Union-occupied
homeland was barred by thousands of fresh veteran Yankees who were
ready for the Missouri Brigade's challenge.

With drummer boys pounding away and battle flags waving in the
heat and humidity of mid–May, the Missouri Rebels pushed forward
through the dense forests to the edge of the field on the northern slope
of Champion Hill. While the cheering Missourians surged past, one
Confederate asked another officer what troops were charging madly
against impossible odds at this critical moment in an attempt to yet win the
day. The veteran officer replied: "They are Missourians going to their
deaths."[130]

After deploying amid the cotton fields south of the Champion house,
Colonel George B. Boomer's veteran brigade charged forward to thwart the
Missourians steamrolling toward them. One Iowa soldier waded into the
onslaught of the Missouri Confederates and never forgot facing Pemberton's shock troops for the first time: "We saw a solid wall of men in gray,
their muskets at their shoulders blazing into our faces and their batteries
of artillery roaring as if it were the end of the world. Bravely they stood
there." More carnage resulted as the killing resumed in earnest. Shaken by
the Rebels' counterattack, General Grant continued to try to plug the hole
in his center before it was too late.[131]

Boomer's Illinois, Iowa, and Missouri troops stood face to face with
the crack troops of Cockrell's brigade. Both sides blasted away, and it seemed
that neither would ever break on this bloody afternoon in Mississippi.
From the same counties, towns, and neighborhoods, Missourians in blue
and gray exchanged a blistering fire, killing each other as fast as they
could. Here in the belt of woods on the north slope of Champion Hill, the
Missouri Confederates again returned to their frontier ways of fighting,
loading, and firing from behind trees. As at Port Gibson, the Western frontiersmen in gray had the advantage of cover in the woodlands. In addition,

they held higher ground and more advantageous terrain than did their attackers, who suffered under a plunging fire.

One bluecoat recalled how the Missourians in gray "kept their line like a wall of fire" for hours, firmly standing their ground. While the antagonists exchanged a blistering fire through the palls of smoke, the right of the Missouri Brigade not only held its own but also resumed the offensive. Colonel Riley's First and Fourth Missouri, anchoring the Missouri Brigade's right, was joined by some Fifth Missouri troops as well in attacking downhill and out of the woods at the gullied northern base of Champion Hill.[132]

With Rebel yells, the elated Missourians now poured down both sides of the road and through the trees at the hill's base. This desperate charge gained momentum as these Missouri soldiers advanced out of the forest and continued across the open corn and cotton fields filling the small valley between the two hills, past Sid Champion's cotton gin, and then uphill toward Boomer's left flank. Colonels McCown's and Riley's Rebels charged onward with battle flags waving and the desire to win it all that day. This last determined Confederate push of the day surged along both sides of the deeply cut road, which sliced 10 to 15 feet into the soft soil of Hinds County. The narrow road turned sharply northwestward after leaving Champion Hill and then dropped into the slight valley before ascending the elevation upon which stood the Champion house. Here, deep in Mississippi, the dirt road now led uphill to what might be a decisive victory for these onrushing Missouri Confederates. The initiative won by the Missourians with so much blood and desperate fighting now seemed destined to yet propel the attackers over the last high ground south of Baker's Creek and to achieve decisive victory.[133]

Punished by the Rebel onslaught pouring down Champion Hill, Boomer's regiments on the left wavered and then were shattered by the hard-hitting Missouri boys. Going for broke on a day that decisive victory could be won, the cheering Confederates ripped savagely into their antagonists. Colonel Riley's troops, together with some of Colonel McCown's men, slammed into the Unionists with a vengeance. "[They] poured through the gap and were already firing into our rear and yelling to us to surrender," recalled one horrified Yankee.[134]

With large numbers of Crocker's troops fleeing, the Missourians continued forward in a desperate bid to win the day. Yelping Confederates charged forward like men possessed, knowing that it was now or never. The St. Louis Irishmen of the Fifth Missouri fought not only for their Union-occupied home state, but also for the honor of their native Ireland thousands of miles away. The Missouri Brigade spearhead thrust even deeper into the Union lines by Bowen's center again seemed to threaten to sweep everything before it. Colonel Riley's regiment, and perhaps the Fifth

Missouri as well, attacked the hill of the Champion house three times in a desperate effort to turn Boomer's left flank.

Another objective of these relentless attacks was Grant's wagon train, which had hurried to safety just beyond the hill. The foremost Missouri attackers fought hand-to-hand with the Federals, including some wounded soldiers and guards, after overrunning an ambulance train and striking deep behind the Yankee lines. Some of Cockrell's soldiers battled their adversaries among some Union supply wagons, so far had these Rebels penetrated into Grant's rear.[135]

Overwhelmed by the hard-hitting capabilities of the Missouri Confederates, Colonel Boomer finally had enough of tangling with the shock troops of the Vicksburg army and yelled to a superior, "The enemy are too strong for my brigade." More of Boomer's soldiers were swept rearward.

General Bowen's troops, incredibly, now appeared to be on the verge of defeating Grant's reinforcements as well. But just when it looked as if General Grant were on the ropes for good, the ever-resourceful General Hovey rose to the fore. Anticipating that Bowen's onslaught could not be stopped, Hovey massed the Sixth Wisconsin — the Missourians' nemesis at Corinth — and the First Missouri (Company A) batteries and the remaining Sixteenth Ohio guns in an open field atop a commanding rise southeast of the Champion house. In the meantime, General Grant viewed the shocking spectacle of Colonel Boomer's routed troops streaming rearward, reliable veterans that Grant knew were among the last forces which could stop Bowen's onslaught. Calling for reinforcements at the last minute, Grant hurled everything he had into the raging storm in a desperate bid to stem the Missouri tide.[136]

Just when it appeared that Bowen's troops had won the day, the long rows of Union artillery pieces erupted like a volcano. Sixteen cannon pounded Cockrell's and Green's formations, inflicting terrible damage and throwing the attack into confusion. In addition, arriving Union infantry support and Hovey's troops, who had gamely rallied, reentered the contest at the critical moment. Blue hordes now seemingly converged from three sides upon the gray band, which was growing smaller by the minute and shorter of rounds and luck. Indeed, the punishment delivered by the massed Federal artillery broke the back of Bowen's last desperate gamble for victory. Bloodied and battered, Green's brigade fell back into the woodlands, after having lost almost 300 of its sons on May 16. Some Missouri Brigade elements intermingled with Green's brigade were likewise hurled rearward, retiring into the belt of forest that had become a graveyard in the wilderness.[137]

After more bitter fighting, Colonel Boomer's left was restored, and now the once-wide gap in Grant's line closed forever. In front of Cockrell's formations, meanwhile, the remainder of Boomer's brigade and reinforcements held the line, thwarting the full exploitation of the advantage won on Colonel Cockrell's right. The determined stand of the Federal reinforcements before the Missouri Brigade was the turning point of the war according to one veteran Federal officer.[138]

With bluecoats seemingly swarming everywhere, the Missouri Rebels now "imagined that another army was coming on them." Indeed, thousands of Unionists poured forward after the repulse of Green's brigade, rushing toward Cockrell's isolated regiments. With support on the right gone after Green's units were hurled back, the troops of Colonels Riley and McCown were soon raked with an enfilade fire. The punishment was too much for exhausted soldiers who had fought today without enough ammunition, support, or luck. After struggling more than two and a half hours, charging nearly a mile through the Union army, and reaching an advanced point just south of the Champion house, these foremost attackers had to give up when Green was pushed back. "We [were] forced to fall back for the want of support on our right," wrote one Missouri Rebel.[139]

The repulse of Bowen's May 16 attack, was Pemberton's best chance to win a decisive victory in this all-important campaign and "sound[ed] the doom of [Vicksburg and] Richmond." Instead of the Missouri Confederates winning it all, they had lost everything at Champion Hill. As one Missourian swore, "With any support, we would have followed [Colonel Cockrell] and pushed those Yankees clear into Alabama." Indeed, with adequate support, Bowen's counterattack might have turned the tide of the Western War. The hard-fighting Cockrell, nevertheless, still hoped that Loring might yet reinforce his heavily pressed lines before he was forced to give up the fight. The young colonel, therefore, refused to obey General Bowen's orders to withdraw until the possible last moment.[140]

But, as on other fields in the recent past, no support was forthcoming for the Missouri men facing impossible odds, and now the field had to be abandoned. Around four o'clock, a discouraged Colonel Cockrell finally choked out the order for withdrawal, and Colonel McCown relayed the painful directive to the survivors of the Fifth Missouri. As one soldier wrote, the powerful blue formations "were immediately threatening [our] rear [and] Bowen's position was compromised, and the dense gathering lines of the enemy threatened him on three sides." But fortunately Guibor's battery on the left and Landis's and Wade's guns on the right bellowed with all their might. The veteran cannoneers manning these guns held the Union legions at bay, buying time for a safe withdrawal. Despite the odds, the Missouri artillery kept the Federals from turning both flanks of the Missouri Brigade during this late afternoon crisis.[141]

But the greatest threat came to Bowen's right-rear, where heavy blue columns hastened westward down the Middle Road, driving toward the crossroads in overwhelming numbers. The Unionists had now advanced

almost to a position perpendicular to the Fifth Missouri's line. Without ammunition, or support, the withdrawing Missourians backtracked the way
they had come with "slow and sullen dignity" through the body-strewn
forests. The retrograde movement gained added purpose with the information of the Unionists' drive from the east, and a race to the crossroads ensued. Bowen's decimated division would have to fight its way out as it had
come into the Champion Hill sector. But now a third of the Missouri
Rebels, at least 600 Missouri Brigade soldiers, who had entered the action
with such high hopes for victory lay dead or wounded in the woodlands
around Champion Hill.[142]

For Colonel McCown's soldiers who had fought harder than ever
before that day, this was a painful journey rearward, especially passing so
many dead and wounded comrades. Throughout the forest sprawled the
sickening piles of the casualties of the badly mauled Fifth Missouri. Few of
the Fifth Missouri wounded could be taken rearward because escape was
now the top priority for the survivors. Corporal Stephen A. Barton refused
to desert his seriously wounded brother, Elias, however. Both of these fine
soldiers were captured. Clearly, the Company I brother team which had
won fame throughout the command because of the Port Gibson last stand
in the ravine could not be separated. Three of these seven delaying party
members of Company I were shot down at Champion Hill.[143]

Union artillery shelled the Fifth Missouri with a vengeance in the race
to the crossroads. When a blue column probed too close, Colonel McCown
deployed his unit. But enough rounds had been gathered by the men from
the cartridge boxes of the dead for one last defensive stand against their
relentless pursuers. A remaining handful of Fifth Missouri soldiers fired
their last volley of May 16 after the dream of decisive victory and reclaim-
ing Missouri had faded away.[144]

One of the best men of Company F, Sergeant Hogan wrote, "as it was,
we had half a mile to get out [of the entrapment] and then under the fire
of three of their batteries." Just barely missing being cut off, Bowen's troops
at last gained the crossroads. Again the Missouri batteries held the blue
legions at a safe distance with blasts of canister. Risking capture, Captain
Landis's artillery unit stayed in action until the last round was fired.

Wounded comrades, captured guns, and the dream of saving the Mississippi River for the Confederacy were left behind on ill-fated Champion
Hill by the survivors of the Fifth Missouri. But the race to the crossroads
had been won by Bowen's fast-moving soldiers. Eager to exploit their success, the Federals continued in their efforts to strike a deathblow to the reeling Confederate army. The Rebel withdrawal from the crossroads continued southward down Plantation Road. Shortly McCown's troops swung
more in a southwesterly direction, while shells rained down and took more
men out of the ranks.[145]

The dark, swirling waters of Baker's Creek had receded enough to allow an escape westward toward Edwards Station and the road to Vicksburg. Turning west after striking the Raymond Road, the Missourians finally crossed Baker's Creek. Here Bowen's units fell into line on the west bank to hold the crossing for General Loring's division. Again playing the role of the army's guardians, the Fifth Missouri boys took position within the Missouri Brigade's line, which was now much less lengthy than at any previous time.[146]

Not long thereafter, Union batteries shelled the Missourians' position, attempting to scatter Pemberton's last line of resistance. At this point, a quick inspection of their thinned ranks showed that around 100 of McCown's men had been cut down during the struggle for Champion Hill. The Missouri troops who survived the holocaust felt correctly that they had saved "the entire army by their valor [and with assistance] they could have cut the enemy to pieces." Official records indicate a Fifth Missouri loss of 4 killed, 49 wounded, and 37 missing at Champion Hill. But individual personnel records indicate 11 killed and 6 mortally wounded. Also, many more Fifth Missouri soldiers were wounded at Champion Hill than the inaccurate figures in the official records suggest. And at least 36 men of the Fifth Missouri were captured, which accounts for the high number of missing.

In obeying Pemberton's orders, General Bowen now risked encirclement by lingering too long at the Baker's Creek ford. However, he waited for troops that would never come. Indeed, General Loring's division had found another crossing. A cruel, never-ending pattern of sacrificing lives for nothing as victory again slipped away was becoming well-established in the service of the Fifth Missouri east of the Mississippi.[147]

Finally, Colonel Cockrell made his timely decision to abandon the creek crossing before it was too late. As the colonel explained, "seeing no other troops coming to cross (not even stragglers), and believing that the enemy probably occupied the road to Edward's Depot, I moved the brigade, leaving the road to Edward's Depot to my right, and after marching under cover of darkness through plantations, along and across ravines [struck the main road leading westward to Big Black River]."[148]

Letting decisive victory slip away, Pemberton's army had missed its best chance of the Vicksburg Campaign to beat Grant at Champion Hill. Indeed, the feeling lingered among McCown's survivors that perhaps the war's best opportunity to destroy Grant had vanished and would never come again. One of Bowen's followers caught the dark mood by writing in his journal that if adequate support had been sent to the Missouri Brigade's assistance, "We might have given the enemy a severe repulse." Indeed, such an opportunity to deliver the invaders a crushing blow would never come again in the Campaign for Vicksburg.[149]

While McCown's men trudged wearily West through the blackness for Big Black's fortifications, the nightmare had only started for scores of Fifth Missouri wounded left on the battlefield. Most of Colonel McCown's injured soldiers remained scattered in brushy hollows and thickets of bloody Champion Hill on the night of May 16. Without water or food and exposed to the weather, McCown's Johnny Rebs continued to perish at Champion Hill long after the roar of the guns ended.

General Grant lost nearly 2,500 men in winning the most important victory of the Vicksburg campaign. Not only did he lose the best opportunity to defeat Grant in this campaign, Pemberton also lost almost 1,300 soldiers more than Grant at Champion Hill. By any measure, Vicksburg's fate was sealed with the Confederate defeat at Champion Hill. Clearly, this engagement was one of the most decisive battles of the war. Ironically, while Gettysburg and Antietam have been endlessly romanticized and immortalized as the turning points of the war, the battle of Champion Hill has remained relatively obscure and forgotten despite its strategic importance.

Large numbers of the Fifth Missouri dead were found clumped around the Union artillery pieces, where the contest had been the most brutal. Days later, Federal soldiers threw shovel loads of dirt over the tangled mass of Confederate bodies, which had been thrown into a ravine by Union burial details. This hallowed ground of hundreds of the finest troops of Pemberton's Vicksburg army would be exposed by late summer when, in one Yankee's words, "the earth was washed away, and there stood or lay hundreds of half-decayed corpses. Some were grinning skeletons, some were headless, some armless, some had their clothes torn away, and some were mangled by dogs and wolves." This was a sad fate for the Fifth Missouri boys killed on the field, such as Captain McKinney, Sergeant Rumpf, Privates Jonathan W. Mills, Francis Marion Summers, William R. King, Pleasant Graves Rudd, Job L. Hammond, Perry W. Sears, Robert D. Donaldson, William W. York, and Henry C. Herndon. These soldiers so far from homes and families had nearly won it all at Champion Hill, with tenacity and hard fighting, but they had paid the ultimate sacrifice and had nothing to show for their supreme efforts on May 16 except for the ever-elusive dreams of victory now buried in the dark soil of Hinds County, Mississippi.[150]

# VII

## DISASTER AT
## BIG BLACK RIVER

After marching west ten miles in the blackness across the rugged countryside of Hinds County, the Missourians stumbled into the darkened valley of Big Black River around midnight. Far behind Colonel McCown's column rumbled wagon-loads of wounded Fifth Missouri. Men who had hobbled or been carried off the battlefield now rode in half-broken-down vehicles which jolted across the creeks and ravines along the hellish route toward Vicksburg. The screams and groans of the Rebel wounded rose from overloaded wagons like unearthly cries from hell, echoing eerily over the blackened forests and fields of Mississippi. Not until late on the night of May 16 did the long train of injured Confederates amble slowly across Big Black River and into Bovina, General Pemberton's headquarters about halfway between Vicksburg and Big Black's earthworks. Here the train of ambulances and wagons briefly ended its dismal journey.[1]

Hard-nosed Sergeant Ruyle, himself badly wounded at Champion Hill, now discovered other Company C boys, who he thought had been killed on Champion Hill. Relieved at finding many of his good friends yet alive, Ruyle noted in his diary: "Here I found Lt. J[ames] L. Mitchell [a nineteen-year-old] wounded severely in the side of the face, Lt. Ben L. Mitchell wounded in three fingers and the right thigh slightly, Corporal S[amuel] H. Tuck [an ex-farmer, age nineteen, who would be mortally wounded in a few weeks] was wounded in the hand [and] Sgt. Lane [was] missing and no doubt killed on the field."[2]

Upon reaching the defenses that they had helped build in May, Colonel McCown's troops filed behind the cotton-bale and dirt breastworks of Big Black River. The Missouri Brigade now filled the best defenses that it had ever fought behind in either Missouri, Arkansas, Mississippi or Louisiana. More than any other troops in the West, General Pemberton wanted these elite soldiers from Missouri who served as the ever-reliable "Old Guard" of Pemberton's Vicksburg army. "I knew that the Missouri troops, under their gallant leaders, could be depended upon," he said. Spirits lifted as General Bowen, in charge of the Big Black River defenses, deployed his two brigades in the strong network of fortifications and spoke inspiring words to invoke confidence. Without eating, weary from hard fighting, and without much ammunition, bone-tired Fifth Missouri Rebels instantly "sank heavily to rest" behind the earthworks. Here in the mile-long fortifications cutting across a horseshoe bend of Big Black River, General Pemberton decided to await the advance of his antagonists, who were flushed with the decisive victory won at Champion Hill. With Grant's army in pursuit, common sense now seemed to call for destroying the bridges across Big Black and for the Rebels making a stand on the high ground along the west bank of the river.[3]

But General Pemberton thought otherwise and allowed his combat inexperience and lack of confidence to dominate reason. He wanted to hold the fortified but vulnerable position in the lowlands in the vain hope that Major General Loring's division would rejoin the army at Big Black. As at Champion Hill, Bowen's Missourians would face overwhelming numbers and little chance for success because of the non-arrival of Loring's division. The position was especially vulnerable because two bridges spanning the chocolate-colored watercourse had caused Confederate engineers to erect defenses on the east side of Big Black rather than on higher and better defensive ground on the west bank. But worst of all, Loring's troops now marched away from Big Black to link with General Johnston. Consequently, the Fifth Missouri Confederates waited in damp earthworks for Southern troops who would never come.[4]

General Bowen's division and its twenty artillery pieces, a Mississippi infantry regiment, and Brigadier General John C. Vaughn's Tennessee brigade occupied a strong defensive network in the bottoms of Big Black. Intersected perpendicular through its center by the Southern Railroad of Mississippi, the network of fortifications had been carefully constructed. The reliable defenders of General Green's brigade held the line north of the railroad tracks. Anchoring the left, Green's position was fronted by an abatis-clogged bayou that presented a formidable obstacle. Also north of the railroad and protected by the bayou in their front, Vaughn's East Tennessee Mountaineers manned the center of the line.[5]

Because of geography the right of the line, held by the Missouri Brigade, was the most vulnerable. In front of the Fifth Missouri and beyond the bayou, the landscape was level and flat, an expanse of sprawling cotton fields. Here, south of the tracks and all the way to swampy Gin Lake, Bowen had aligned his most dependable defenders, the Missouri Confederates. Seemingly able to see into the mind of his former south St. Louis neighbor, General Bowen knew that Grant would probably strike where the Jackson Road and railroad cut through the works near the right-center.

This was the most obvious weak link visible to the Federals. No Confederate officer noticed this defensive deficiency more than Colonel Cockrell, and he ordered the Fifth Missouri to defend the most vulnerable sector. In large part, this compliment from Cockrell stemmed from the performance of the Fifth Missouri at Corinth, Port Gibson, and Champion Hill.[6]

Colonel McCown's defenders dozed on the cold ground in a worn stupor throughout the night. In only a few hours with the sunrise, the Missourians knew that they would again meet their old adversary, General Grant, who had learned and refined the art of war in Missouri in 1861. Hardly had the sun risen on May 17 when Grant arrived in force to finish the job started at Champion Hill, the destruction of Pemberton's army. Blue skirmishers swarmed over the barren cotton fields, popping away in the misty, half-light. Startled by the sudden musketry, the veterans of the Fifth Missouri awoke with empty stomachs, as well as with sore shoulders after most of these men had fired about 100 rounds the previous day. Intensifying gun-fire widened "eyes weary and bloodshot, [which now] were opened to respond to a new alarm," wrote one Fifth Missouri officer.[7]

Colonel McCown's defenders scrambled to their feet and out of the mud to grab their Enfields in the morning's chill. Grayclads hurriedly filed behind their cotton bales and prepared to meet the attack. Before McCown's soldiers stretched the river's floodplain, furrowed from the cotton rows of last summer and black with the fertility of the rich bottom soil. Through patchy ground fog, the Fifth Missouri Rebels could see the blue skirmishers darting over the fields, moving forward, and firing as if they meant trouble.

Alarmed by the Unionists' sudden appearance before the defenses, Sergeant Hogan and other defenders squinted at the brightness of the rising sun, while viewing the advancing Federal troops. The natural strength of the defenses, the bulk of the artillery of Bowen's division in line, and Tennessee troops fresh from garrison duty should have offered some optimism. But McCown's veterans felt pessimistic about the day's prospects, sensing a tactical vulnerability that was potentially disastrous. Indeed, despite the strong fortifications, two natural disadvantages for the defenders included the sun now in their eyes and a rain-swollen river to their backs. If any Confederates on the defensive line bolted on May 17, then Colonel McCown's exiles and other Missouri Brigade members on the line's southern end would be cut off and placed in grave danger.

In addition, all the artillery horses of Bowen's batteries had been ordered across the river three-fourths of a mile behind the fortifications. If Grant's troops broke through the lines, then Bowen's artillery could not escape and would be captured. General Pemberton's elite "Grenadier Guard," the Fifth Missouri and the First Missouri Brigade, now had moments of self-doubt as the drama of Confederate disaster unfolded along

the turbid Big Black River. In his diary, one Missouri infantryman summarized the commonsense frontier logic in regard to the defensive
weaknesses and the precarious situation of the Confederate artillery of
Bowen's division: "There was not a boy in our Company but what would
have exercised better judgment."[8]

Astride the Jackson Road to the Fourth Mississippi's right, McCown's
regiment would have to make the best of a bad situation if Grant suddenly
struck in their vulnerable sector. McCown's men were also uneasy because
not a single Confederate artillery piece stood in line to bolster the Fifth
Missouri's sector at the Jackson Road, which was the weak link in the Big
Black defensive line. Making one of the few sensible Confederate decisions
on May 17, the always vigilant General Bowen placed a section of Captain
Landis's Missouri guns atop the 60-foot-high bluff on the west bank of the
river, as if he were anticipating disaster at Big Black.

Also expecting trouble that day was the chief Confederate engineer,
Samuel H. Lockett. Acting on the portent of imminent disaster, he now
made preparations for the worst scenario along Big Black. Noting "signs of
unsteadiness in our men," the energetic engineer of considerable ability had
cotton and fence rails soaked with turpentine and strewn across the railroad
bridge. Then Engineer Lockett had barrels of turpentine placed aboard the
sunken steamboat *Dot*, now a make-shift foot-bridge of Jackson Road, in
preparation for setting the boat bridge afire. Such precautions might save
Bowen's forces if Grant broke through its defenses.[9]

Feeling confident that the Rebels could be defeated as they had in every
previous engagement during this campaign except at Grand Gulf, Grant's
soldiers closed in for the kill. Several Union batteries opened fire on
McCown's sector south of the railroad, seemingly indicating the Bluecoats'
intention to strike at this point. Direct hits by shells upon the breastworks
sent cotton and dirt flying through the air. But the sturdy cotton bales could
not be battered down by the artillery barrage, reminding some Missourians
of their ancestor's defense of New Orleans in 1815. Amid the exploding
shells, the tattered colors of the Fifth Missouri floated atop the fortifications
for all to see.[10]

The Union cannonade caused the situation to appear especially serious
around the Jackson Road sector. A concerned General Bowen and Colonel
Cockrell soon joined Colonel McCown and his defenders, explaining that
Grant's big push to overrun Big Black's defenses would soon be heading the
Fifth Missouri's way. Indeed, Bowen had placed the best regiment of the
elite Missouri Brigade in a key position in anticipation of such an emergency.

The long lines of blue skirmishers became more aggressive, swarming
ever closer with heavy infantry formations following close behind them.
The well-trained soldiers of the Fifth Missouri raised up as one with Colonel

McCown's order to unleash a volley. Stung by the exploding musketry, the blue lines rolled back a short distance, suffering from the marksmanship of the Fifth Missouri defenders. Then more hot skirmishing resumed after this initial repulse of the Unionists.[11]

Brigadier General Michael Lawler, a giant in size as well as in ability, formed his Iowa and Wisconsin troops in the thickets bordering Big Black on the north. In part, because Lawler was a tactically innovative, flexible, free-thinking Westerner, not a rigid West Pointer, he understood that a frontal assault across the flat cotton fields was suicidal. The Mexican War veteran, therefore, led his troops southward down a slight hollow cut by the river long ago, which ran parallel to the earthworks. When they had passed Green's front and were near the line's left-center, Lawler's entire Union brigade silently halted within almost a stone's throw of the unsuspecting Tennessee mountain boys.[12]

Charging out of the hollow in column, the Iowa and Wisconsin regiments smashed through Vaughn's left in minutes, losing only a few men to a ragged volley. Unable to contain the break, hundreds of Tennesseeans threw down their muskets to surrender or took to their heels. Vaughn's brigade disintegrated under the sudden bluecoat onslaught which seemed to come out of nowhere. A gaping hole was punched into Bowen's right-center before the Fifth Missouri defenders realized what had happened to their unfortunate Rebel comrades to the north. Aligned across the level terrain of the river's floodplain, McCown's soldiers failed to ascertain the disaster befalling their Confederate comrades to their left. The Missouri Rebels around Jackson Road meanwhile stood beside their cotton bales, not saying much, hoping for the best that day, and "munching hardtack and uncooked corned-beef," as one Fifth Missouri soldier later recalled.[13]

According to one of Colonel McCown's officers, "We were standing by our arms, idly waiting for something to do, when we were thunderstruck at the receipt of an order to 'retreat; we are flanked.'" Disbelieving the directive, Lieutenant Colonel Bevier climbed atop the earthworks to dispel the rumor. Now he could hardly believe his eyes: the soldiers of an entire Mississippi regiment on the Fifth Missouri's immediate left were pouring from the trenches and heading rearward. As far as the eye could see, the fortifications now "swarm[ed] with blue-coats [and] we had been flanked [and] were enfiladed both ways, and no alternative remained but to get away as fast as possible."[14]

With no alternative left, Colonel McCown finally gave the withdrawal order, and the Fifth Missouri Confederates attempted to escape. All the other Southern troops had left Cockrell's men once again on their own, and as so often in the past, "the Missourians were the last to leave" the field of strife, as one survivor of the fiasco wrote. Indeed, the other Rebel defenders of Big Black were now "running in wild disorder [which] caused a great many Missourians to get captured, who were disposed to stand their ground though the enemy completely flanked them." Colonel Elijah Gates's troops of the First Missouri Cavalry (dismounted) were quickly cut off and surrounded. Entire companies of Missouri Rebels, the blue regimental battle flags of the Missouri exiles, and the cannon captured by these troops at Pea Ridge were gobbled up by the victorious bluecoats. The gap ripped into the Confederate line rapidly extended to the left and right after feeble Southern resistance evaporated all along the front. Some of the best troops of Green's brigade, including Colonel Gates, were rounded up like sheep and hustled away as prisoners of war destined to endure the hell of northern prisons.[15]

To avoid such a fate, McCown's Rebels swarmed from the fortifications on the double and "in a jumbled crowd." Hundreds of Fifth Missouri men raced pell-mell for the bridges a mile distant to escape across the river: an ordeal for these exhausted Confederates who had fought one of the hardest battles of the war on May 16, had marched much of the previous night, and had had little food or sleep during the last couple of days. Sergeant Hogan wrote in a letter how he and his comrades dashed for the river "in regular Bull Run style — the devil take the hindmost being the order of the day." Even a Unionist who had faced Cockrell's troops before could not comprehend the scene before his eyes: the Confederacy's best Western troops "seeing the line all around them [give way] and being whipped 5 times in succession before, could not stand it. They broke and ran for the bridge, leaving everything," including artillery. Indeed, annihilation would have resulted if the Missouri Brigade had held its position.[16]

Rain had fallen the night before, and the fallow cotton fields were muddy and puddled with water. The fast-moving Missourians churned through the mire, but nothing could stop the wild dash for the bridges. Other Confederates gained the Jackson Road, which provided more solid footing in the race to escape a winter in disease-infested northern prisons. With "the enemy now being nearer [the] crossing than" the Fifth Missouri, Lieutenant Colonel Bevier was amazed at the newfound sprinting of his men: "the enemy were making a race with them, for the bridge, in an endeavor to cut them off, they 'let off,' and soon showed that they were as fleet-footed and expert in running as [in fighting]."[17]

Fifth Missouri boys raced through the fields under the hot sun, running for their lives as they poured past some slave cabins and over the levee. With "the foot race leaving no time for shooting," few of McCown's graycoats returned fire. After taking possession of the earthworks, the Federals opened with musketry and artillery, making the Rebels run a deadly gauntlet. But most of these Unionists fired too high in the excitement of having so many Southerners at their mercy. Some Fifth Missouri soldiers were cut down in the hail of bullets sweeping the river bottoms, however.

One dropping to the Yankees' fire was Private Calvin Clary, age twenty-three, who lay bleeding in the cotton field before he was captured. As the day before at Champion Hill, there was little time to help wounded comrades off the field.[18]

Unlike the infantrymen, many of Bowen's cannoneers refused to abandon their positions or their field pieces. On the high ground above and west of the river, a Missouri gunner felt pride as the artillerymen of Captains Guibor and Wade continued to stand their ground in the face of the Federal onslaught and serviced their cannon even as the Unionists overwhelmed them. A flood of jubilant Federals then turned the field pieces around, loading and hurling shells at the gray throng streaming rearward. But most of the projectiles sailed high over the retreating soldiers.[19]

Thousands of Yankees pursued their quarry, knowing that if they could beat the Confederates to the bridges, the capture of Bowen's forces — the best of Pemberton's army — would hasten Vicksburg's fall. In one Union officer's words, "onward [the troops] rushed, yelling, screaming like madmen, wild with excitement, and shaking the gleaming bayonet." Despite worn out from the long run in the heat, Colonel McCown's panting men, meanwhile, continued racing for the bridges oblivious to the hail of minié balls zipping by them in the muggy bottoms of Big Black.[20]

Finally gaining the bridges, surviving Fifth Missouri soldiers pushed their way across both the railroad bridge and the footbridge. Shell fragments and bullets occasionally dropped Southerners into Big Black like rocks, but most of the projectiles screamed overhead, slamming into the bluffs and causing no harm. Lieutenant Colonel Bevier, hobbled from falling after having three horses shot from under him at Champion Hill, floundered during the race for the bridges. Most of his men had long since passed him by, as he later recalled: "[I was] unable to keep up, so that from necessity alone I was nearly the last of the regiment to reach the safe side."

However, Private Edwin S. Johnson, who had been cited for bravery at Corinth, was slower than the lieutenant colonel and may have been wounded. One of Company E's most dependable soldiers, the twenty-five-year-old Johnson was cut off and surrounded by the Yankees. He soon would call the prison at Camp Morton, Indiana, his home. Johnson's impending prison term seemed all the more ominous because his younger brother, also of Company E, had already died of disease while incarcerated by the Yankees.[21]

Helping to save the day were Captain Landis's two cannon atop the bluffs. These Missouri guns roared at a furious pace and held back the Federals until most of the Confederates had crossed Big Black. Captain Guibor was also on the bluffs and helped maintain a solid defense during the crisis. He had escaped from the defenses with one gun and unlimbered it beside Landis's blazing artillery on the high ground along the river's west bank after his battery had been overwhelmed at the earthworks. Obtaining revenge, Captain Guibor now helped to work a cannon near the railroad bridge and assisted in repulsing the Union attack after almost all Southern resistance had evaporated.

Fortunately, two Confederate infantry brigades now helped solidify the defense on the west bank. The best service on the east side of Big Black came, however, from Colonel Riley's Missourians, who acted as an effective rear guard before the bridges. During this last stand, perhaps some of McCown's soldiers were among those stalwarts who risked capture to save their comrades. As at Pea Ridge, Port Gibson, and Champion Hill, the Missouri Brigade again played the key role in saving the day at Big Black River.[22]

The barking Missouri cannon also allowed Engineer Lockett to take final steps to help ensure the survival of Bowen's division. He later described his actions: "[After] waiting until all the Confederates in sight were across the river I touched a match to the barrel of turpentine [aboard the footbridge and] tipped it over. In a moment the boat was in a blaze. The railroad bridge was likewise fired, and all immediate danger of pursuit prevented."[23]

With the bridges a mass of yellow flames and billowing clouds of smoke, McCown's latecomers threw off their accouterments and swam across Big Black, while minié balls and fiery debris smacked in the muddy water beside them. According to one survivor: "It was a dreadful scene. Men shot down everywhere, others drowning in their attempt to swim the river." An unknown number of Fifth Missouri Rebels drowned in attempting to cross. As one soldier recalled, "'Lost at Black River,' was the only message that ever reached the home of many a Southern soldier [who fought] on that day."[24]

Other Missouri Confederates fled southward and followed the east bank until they found a shallow place to ford the river. Both bridges were consumed in flames before Grant's troops could cross Big Black. The worst of all fates now befell those Confederates shot down on the bridges, for "many of the poor wounded fellows were burned to death," penned one Missourian. As in every action in which it was engaged during the Vicksburg campaign, Bowen's division suffered the highest losses. Now General Bowen could count around 1,000 fewer soldiers in his division after the Big Black disaster. Most of those men captured were from Green's brigade. The Federals' rounding up of more than 1,700 Southerners helped buy time for McCown's survivors to escape, however. Almost all of the Missouri Brigade's artillery was captured as a result of the disaster at Big Black River. As lamented Sergeant Hogan in a letter to St. Louis, "This [was] the first artillery the 1st [Missouri] brigade has lost during the war." In total, Bowen's division lost fifteen artillery pieces as a result of the Big Black debacle, suffering a severe blow.[25]

The Missourians' reputation as the crack "Old Guard" troops of the Vicksburg army and the West was further enhanced on May 17. Indeed the Missouri Brigade's rearguard action allowed the destruction of the bridges and thus allowed Pemberton to make a safe withdrawal into fortress Vicksburg. No one understood the lost chance better than General Grant, who regretted the missed opportunity to destroy Bowen's elite division, which was Pemberton's best and most reliable unit: "But for the successful and complete destruction of the bridge[s], I have but little doubt that we should have followed the enemy so closely as to prevent [Pemberton's] occupying his defenses around Vicksburg," lamented Grant.

Becoming the North's most successful general, Grant had won another impressive victory at the cost of fewer than 300 casualties. Thanks to his own brilliance and Confederate blunders, Grant had set up the circumstances that now no longer made fortress Vicksburg a refuge for Pemberton's army. Instead, the lure of Vicksburg would prove to be fatal not for the Yankee army but for the Rebel army. The ill-starred soldiers of the Fifth Missouri had barely escaped Grant's grasp twice in less than twenty-four hours. But in the next meeting with Grant, there would no longer be an avenue left open for Colonel McCown's troops or any other Southerners to escape. Vicksburg was now looming before them not as a safe haven but as a fatal trap from which there would be no escape.[26]

# VIII
## FORTY-SEVEN DAYS
## IN HELL

Never before had Fifth Missouri's morale been so low as after the Confederates were swept out of Big Black's fortifications on the morning of May 17. By any measure, General Bowen's division had been lucky to survive the disaster at Big Black. Little time passed before the Unionists were laying pontoons across Big Black, the last natural obstacle before Vicksburg.[1]

Fifth Missouri soldiers lost their personal baggage during the withdrawal to Vicksburg. Knapsacks and other extra baggage had been set on fire at Bovina to prevent capture.[2] At sunset on May 17, McCown's infantrymen at last stumbled into the safety of the "hill city." The twelve-mile march westward into Vicksburg was most demanding for the survivors of the Fifth Missouri. After trudging down Graveyard Road to Vicksburg's north, McCown's troops were ordered to encamp near the city cemetery about halfway between the town and the fortifications. Here, north of Vicksburg, the Fifth Missouri Rebels finally gained some much-needed rest.

Now the stage was set for the struggle for the possession of the great Confederate fortress on the Mississippi River. By May of 1863, Vicksburg was the key to the Mississippi Valley. "If Vicksburg cannot be taken," predicted a Northern journalist, "the South has won the war." Americans, North and South, focused their attention during the late spring of 1863 upon the small but vital Mississippi River town.[3]

Bowen's division again earned the toughest job with assignment as a strategic reserve. This demanding duty now meant that Bowen's troops must always be in readiness to rush to any threatened sector on the north and east, above the railroad, of the city. One Confederate surgeon explained in his journal the rationale for employing Bowen's troops for this key assignment: "The two Missouri brigades; the first (1st) under the command of general [Colonel] Frank Cockrell and the second (2nd) under

General Martin E. Green, had acquired a reputation for steadfast reliability which they had justly earned [and therefore] were held in reserve behind any part of the line that might seem to need assistance." Indeed, by this time, the Missouri Brigade had won widespread acclaim from both friend and foe. It had become the finest brigade in either army, and the Fifth Missouri was the best regiment of this famous brigade.[4]

The first threat to Vicksburg came immediately from the Unionists, during the evening of May 18. With bluecoats closing the ring around Vicksburg, Missouri Brigade troops double-quicked across Mint Spring Hollow to assist General Martin L. Smith's division outside the works, which was making its way slowly into the citadel. North of town, McCown's Confederates advanced and skirmished before the main line, slowing down the approaching Unionists. The Missourians held the Yankees at bay before Mint Spring Bayou, allowing Smith's three brigades to reach the fortifications safely.

After Smith's troops gained the defenses, the Missourians shouldered their Enfield rifles and retired into the sanctuary after another job well done. Worn, sweaty, and covered in dust, the Fifth Missouri soldiers filed into the fortifications lining the ridge north of Mint Spring Bayou. Here, to the left of Baldwin's Mississippians, Colonel McCown's Rebels fought off both advancing Unionists and weariness, returning a hot fire until nightfall. But now one grim reality could no longer be denied by the Fifth Missouri's soldiers: the door had been slammed shut on Vicksburg. "On Sunday [May 17] the enemy appeared in sight, and by Monday [May 18] morning had us completely invested," wrote a dejected Sergeant Hogan in a letter.[5]

With as much silence as possible, Cockrell's and Baldwin's columns fell back at 3 A.M., pushing across Mint Spring Bayou to a better defensive position. This adroit shift took the Missouri command to better and higher ground along the main ridge that Fort Hill dominated. Spanning the second highest terrain between Memphis and New Orleans, this fortified line followed the high ground encircling Vicksburg. Colonel McCown's Confederates shortly moved into a strategic reserve position, retiring into a cane-filled hollow of a Glass Bayou tributary near the Green Riddle house. Here, to Baldwin's right-rear, the frontier exiles of the Fifth Missouri lay down to rest in a canebrake, gaining some much needed sleep.[6]

With the knowledge of veterans, the Fifth Missouri soldiers had already studied the strength of the fortifications they would call home for the next month and a half. Not even the considerable reserves of Warren County slave labor had been enough to complete the nine-mile arc of defenses that curved around the river community. Laid out by expert Confederate engineers, the fortifications stretched atop a line of bluffs and ridges which encircled the city limits of Vicksburg. So extensive was the network of redoubts, lunettes, rifle-pits, and redans that Vicksburg was known as the "Gibraltar of the Confederacy." The sprawling line of earthworks around the city was much too long, however, to be adequately defended by Pemberton's 32,000 troops against more than twice as many attackers. This explained the importance of Bowen's division in reserve and its readiness to meet any threat at any time, especially in the vital sector on the north.[7]

Indeed, the Fifth Missouri and Cockrell' brigade remained close to the all-important Stockade Redan, the strongest defensive bastion on the north, which guarded the Graveyard Road. Against this bastion, Major General William T. Sherman massed his corps of veteran Westerners, who had never known defeat in the West. Farther south, meanwhile, General Green's regiments were stationed in reserve positions above the Southern Railroad of Mississippi to cover Baldwin's Ferry Road on the right. The Fifth Missouri and the Missouri Brigade's role called for stabilizing any break in the lines from the Jackson road to the river on the left, while Green's troops were in reserve to protect those positions below the road.[8]

On the morning of May 19, Federal skirmishers poured from the ridges opposite the Rebel positions. To avoid a siege, General Grant formed two of his three corps to break Pemberton's northern sector. He had decided for sound political, domestic, and psychological reasons to gamble on a quick victory by launching a frontal assault on the afternoon of May 19.[9]

Thousands of Sherman's troops swarmed from the high ground with cheers, surging toward General John H. Forney's division, which defended the Stockade Redan complex sector. Striking hard from the north and east in converging attacks on the Stockade Redan complex to the Jackson Road's right, Blair's division rolled forward in the hope of taking Vicksburg by storm. Colonel McCown's men most of all wanted to face these Yankees, for they were the hated fellow-staters who had helped win Missouri for the Union.[10]

With three more of Cockrell's regiments rushing forward to reinforce defensive sectors, the Fifth Missouri troops raced eastward to bolster Florney's heavily pressured position. Colonel Cockrell led the Fifth and the First and Fourth Missouri on the double to reinforce the Thirty-Sixth Mississippi. As General Louis Hebert's Louisiana and Mississippi Rebels ran out of ammunition in blasting away at the swarms of attacking Yankees, Colonel McCown's cheering soldiers reached the defensive line with their distinctive Missouri war cries. The Fifth Missouri Rebels hurriedly filed into the trenches to the Thirty-Sixth Mississippi's left. On the double, the Fifth Missourians took up firing positions amid the swirling dust. Eager to punish the onrushing bluecoats, McCown's boys cocked hammers and took careful aim with Enfield rifles and on targets they could not miss. Bolstering the defenses at last moment, McCown's troops now anchored Hebert's right flank at the Stockade Redan, which was the main defensive

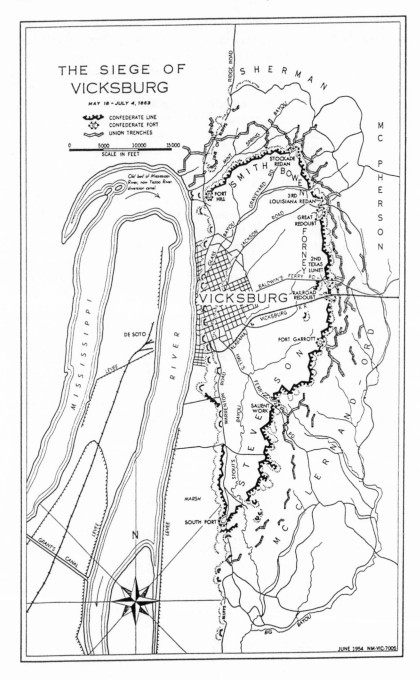

The Siege of Vicksburg (courtesy: National Park Service).

structure dominating the Graveyard Road. From the triangular-shaped earthwork atop a high hill commanding the road's approach into Vicksburg, Colonel McCown's Confederates took position on the east side of the redan. Before the defenders, General Blair's attackers surged up the road by the hundreds and as if nothing in the world could stop them.[11]

When the Unionists were close, Fifth Missouri soldiers opened with an accurate volley. The withering musketry of Colonel McCown's Rebs stabilized the Mississippians' heavily pressured flank. To impede the attackers, two deep valleys fronted the Stockade Redan on each side. But to the attackers, the Confederate-held ridge appeared deceptively vulnerable because of geography: intersected by a steep, perpendicular ridge leading from the Unionists' position and sloping upward toward the redan's middle like a giant earthen drawbridge, seemingly a natural avenue for an attack. With blaring bugles and beating drums, Federal columns charged up the road along the narrow strip of land in a compact target for the Missouri marksmen. Other masses of Unionists labored up the gorge-like valleys on each side, struggling through felled timber, underbrush, and cane while under a scorching fire. The alignment of the attackers fragmented when they encountered the rough terrain and met a barrage of bullets. Victims of encountered poor tactical planning by the highest levels of Northern leadership, the blue bodies soon piled up in the valley in ugly clumps.[12] Expert marksmen, Colonel McCown's men shot down the attackers of Colonel Giles A. Smith's brigade, which contained two Missouri regiments.[13]

Blair's Unionists charged straight into the blistering musketry. Federal officers encouraged their veteran Westerners forward to break Pemberton's line. The "Stars and Stripes" and regimental banners went down, only to pop back up in seconds. Devastated by the sheets of flame pouring from the defenses, the blue legions melted away within only 20–30 feet of the redan. The ridges and gorges were strewn with Grant's dead and wounded, demonstrating the folly of frontal assaults against fortifications. But other bands of attackers, such as the hated "renegades" of the Sixth Missouri Volunteer Infantry, U.S.A., continued onward against McCown's sector with the determination to do or die. Grayclad Missourians shot down their fellow staters with zeal. These Federals charged yet farther up the high and steep elevation upon which the works perched. Bluecoated Missourians and Illinoisans surged forward to the steep eastern face of the redan and then took shelter in the deep ditches surrounding the earthworks to escape the storm of lead.[14]

After regrouping, more cheering Unionists again swarmed out of the ravines by the hundreds to resume the attack. The noise of crackling gunfire, booming artillery, and Yankee hurrahs grew even louder. As the Federals charged closer to the earthworks, another crushing volley again

cut down more attackers like wheat before the scythe. Never had the Fifth
Missouri Rebels seen the Unionists charge so recklessly or with so much
courage as on bloody May 19. A strange respect, now emerged among Colonel McCown's fast-working defenders, even while they shot down
Yankees by the dozen on this hot Mississippi afternoon.[15]

Sustaining a wall of flame, the Fifth Missouri graycoats busily loaded
Enfields and passed them to soldiers on the firing steps. After the repulse
of the second Union assault, yet another attack pushed toward Colonel
McCown's sector, which held firm under the pounding. In the dusty trenches
of Company F was Sergeant Hogan, who described in a letter how he
helped to hurl back "three desperate attempts to carry out works by assault,
but [they were] driven back with great slaughter; they fought bravely and
desperately. There was no running from them trenches, as every man intended to die rather than surrender."[16] The futile charges continued in gory
repetition for some time, with more Yankees dying for no gain. Surviving
Federals took cover to escape the raging storm and to exchange fire for
hours. Both sides traded musketry as the sun lowered in a smoky sky.
Among those defenders in the trenches were the Fifth Missouri's drummer
boys, who put down their drums to pick up muskets.[17]

Grant's massed artillery meanwhile pounded the defenses without
mercy. Shell fragments rained down over the trenches, finding targets
among McCown's men. Ireland-born Private John Cunningham of Company H practically disintegrated when he took a direct hit from a
10-pounder Parrott shell. The gory remains of the ex-peddler, age thirty-
two, were scattered throughout the trench. With Unionists blasting away
at Rebel heads above the parapet, Sergeant Logan Rawlings, a farmer from
the Warrensburg region, dropped into the ditch after taking a bullet
through the head.[18]

The Fifth Missouri defenders continued to shoot at Yankees as darkness finally ended the slaughter. As could be expected from the folly of
launching frontal assaults against heavily fortified positions on the high
ground, the Union attackers were repelled at every point. Left behind were
hundreds of Federal dead and wounded strewn throughout the gorge-like
hollows. General Grant's ill-advised gamble and tactics cost him 1,000 men,
from primarily Illinois, Ohio, and Iowa. Pemberton lost only around 200
defenders on bloody May 19.[19] That night McCown's men scoured the
valleys of death in the darkness, taking anything of value. As in Missouri
State Guard days, the Fifth Missouri soldiers took shoes, ammunition, and
blue pants from the dead Federals. A proud Sergeant Hogan bragged in a
letter, "we took five stands of colors and any amount of muskets."[20]

With the mass killing at an end, the Fifth Missouri Rebels retired back to
a reserve position behind the Stockade Redan lines near Graveyard Road.[21]
On the morning of May 20, Union batteries advanced and unlimbered

closer to the defenses and opened a blistering fire. Federal sharpshooters also zeroed in on anything that moved, sending bullets whistling through the heads of unwary Confederates. As Fifth Missouri details regularly took shifts manning the defenses, casualties mounted with each passing day in the man-made hell of trench warfare. Teenage Private Thomas C. Mitchell was struck in the head with a minié ball and died before the siege's end.[22]

Life for McCown's soldiers was better in the reserve position. Here, one could at least attend to the calls of nature without getting shot by a sniper or blown to pieces by an exploding shell. But spent miniés dropped into the Fifth Missouri's protective ravine to ricochet with enough force to kill or cause a wound which would lead to infection and then death. And nothing could stop the endless stream of shells which were thrown into the encircled Confederates both day and night. For protection against projectiles and the scorching sun, McCown's soldiers constructed lean-tos from branches and cane stalks.[23]

The strategic river city of fewer than 4,500 citizens that had been given birth and vitality by the river now faced extinction because of it. Situated on bluffs rising 350 feet above the Mississippi, Vicksburg had thrived as the gateway to the fertile delta region which stretched into the state's interior. Once known as Walnut Hills, Vicksburg had long been the agricultural and commercial hub for the Mississippi and Yazoo river deltas. The bustling river town maintained the most complex economy of any community in the state of Mississippi. More than 100 mercantile establishments and two dozen industries were spread across the picturesque bluffs overlooking the mile-wide Mississippi.

From the beginning, the great river had been the town's lifeline and source of growth and wealth. Commodities from the vast farmlands of the West's "Valley of Democracy," including Missouri, which was now being destroyed by this war, had been transported down the Mississippi by keelboat and steamboat for decades. Prosperity had also naturally brought vice, especially along the major river of the republic. Some Fifth Missouri soldiers had visited the riverfront den of taverns, gambling, and whorehouses, finding this seedy life an escape from the horrors of war. Few Missouri farm boys had seen anything quite like the luxurious and decadent Home Sweet House at 15 China Street, which was one of the South's legendary bordellos. As if a victim of righteous retribution, the sin city on the Mississippi that had voted against secession in 1860 now found itself caught in Grant's vise, which was closing ever-tighter. It was an ironic fate for a populace which had cast Northerners adrift in the Mississippi on logs during prewar days. It would seem to some that it was because of this evil reputation that Vicksburg would endure one of the longest sieges of any American city in the nation's history.[24]

With his soldiers once again doing most of the hard fighting at

Vicksburg as throughout the campaign, General Bowen was angry about his troops serving and dying as the principal reserves of the Vicksburg army with no relief and no recognition for their sacrifice. After all, the Missouri troops had done most of the hard fighting and suffered the highest casualties during this decisive campaign. On May 21, therefore, Bowen demanded that his elite veterans be taken off reserve duty and maintained that each division should use its own reserves. Indeed, the Fifth Missouri had soldiers had more than their share of responsibilities, and many of these men doing double duty in reserve and in the trenches had been lost. McCown's troops had held Stockade Redan sectors since the attacks of May 19, for example.

Colonel Cockrell, also irritated by the exploitation of his soldiers, attempted to find relief for the Fifth Missouri and the First and Fourth Missouri but could not. The Fifth Missouri remained in the works at the front for several days, along with Colonel Riley's regiment. Clearly, Pemberton understood the importance of fully utilizing the best troops in the army of Vicksburg for the most difficult assignment of the siege, helping to buy Vicksburg more precious time for possible relief from General Johnston.[25]

Concerned about General Johnston to the east in his rear, Grant soon laid plans to assault Pemberton's defenses once more, hoping again for a quick victory to avoid a lengthy siege. But, ironically, Johnston would fail to mount a serious threat, considering the odds too great to relieve Vicksburg. Again, the Union general wasted little time. May 22 was set for an even greater effort to break Pemberton's lines and capture Vicksburg. Now the Army of the Tennessee massed to deliver a knockout blow to the surrounded defenders of Vicksburg. And this time the Southern fortifications would be softened up by every working gun in Grant's command.[26]

At sunrise on May 22, more than 200 Union cannon opened a furious cannonade, causing the earth to tremble under the pounding. Grant targeted the heaviest assault on the north, upon the Stockade Redan complex. In this sector, the attackers again had a natural avenue to hit the Southern works head-on via the Graveyard Road ridge, which thrust up into the midst of the redan complex. As the Federal guns roared to the north, the soldiers of the Fifth Missouri and Bowen's other reserves double-quicked to the front to meet yet another challenge. Through dust and heat, Colonel McCown's soldiers raced toward the Stockade Redan complex to parry the most serious threat to Vicksburg's life.[27]

Once more the Fifth Missouri Rebels rushed to the Thirty-Sixth Mississippi's right. On the complex's east and below, or south, of the main Stockade Redan, McCown's defenders piled into a small redan with a resounding cheer. Here, General Green would later be killed. Eventually named in General Green's honor, this redan stood as the dominant fortification protecting the right of the Stockade Redan complex. Colonel McCown, commanding the redan's defense, was assisted by Colonel Riley's St. Louisans of Company C and the Seventh Mississippi Infantry battalion. But the two-sided redan that pointed southeastward from the main line like a dagger where the attackers could be hit with enfilade fires would be primarily a Fifth Missouri bastion on May 22. In addition, Colonel McCown's left-most company, or perhaps as many two or three companies, held the rifle-pits north of the redan.

Just north of the Fifth Missouri's position ran the Graveyard Road along the ridge-top. To the right before McCown's regiment, the ground dipped down into a ravine-like valley. So steep did the land drop in McCown's front that the first attackers to climb out of the valley's depths would be practically atop the Fifth Missouri. It was almost inevitable that the foremost blue waves spewing out of this gorge would be cut to pieces by the massed fire of the Fifth Missouri Rebels atop the commanding ground in the redan. In this key sector, Confederate engineers had done a fine job, for the ground before the works could be swept with fire from several directions.[28]

During the intense bombardment, the parapet's head-logs and sections of the earthen embankment were blown to pieces by the cannonade. Shells hitting the trench top sent wooden splinters flying through the air like shrapnel, causing casualties in the Fifth Missouri.[29]

General Blair had organized a 150-man storming party, the "forlorn hope." With slim prospects for survival, these volunteers led the 10 A.M. onslaught up the Graveyard Road. Onrushing bluecoats carried ladders and boards to bridge the deep ditch and scale the high walls of the fortifications. In addition, they had orders to take positions close enough to the earthworks to pick off Confederate artillerymen and thus keep Rebel cannon from smashing the main attack. Scores of Union cannon pounded the Stockade Redan complex as thousands of Federals swarmed forward with the storming party leading the way. As the Fifth Missouri defenders lay low under the barrage, the foremost Unionists charged up the sunken road in a suicidal mission. While the colors of the Fifth Missouri fluttered from the redan's walls, not one Southerner along the fortified line could be seen by the attackers as they neared the defenses.[30]

As dirt from exploding shells rained over them, Fifth Missourians hugged the parapet with fixed bayonets and cocked muskets. Nerve-racking minutes slowly passed while the charging Federals of the "forlorn hope" storming party, containing many Missouri Yankees, drew closer. The defenders eagerly awaited the signal to fire, for the attacking bluecoats were Blair's Missourians. Before turning left upon entering the complex's primary redan, the Graveyard Road rose higher up on more elevated terrain, rising out of a deep cut within easy gunshot range.[31]

When the attacking Federals emerged from the road's cut and were exposed on the high and open ground as never before, several hundred Fifth
Missourians, the Mississippians, and the First and Fourth Missouri company members rose as one, appearing like a long gray wall. This stonewall
of "Old Guard" Missourians could not be knocked down today by the blue
battering ram. These veteran Rebels poured a blistering volley into the
Federal ranks, hitting targets that they could not miss at such a close range.
One Unionist never forgot how the Fifth "Missourians, which garrisoned
this part of the lines, stood up, and the parapet fairly blazed." When the
smoke after the initial volley cleared, a high percentage of the storming
party's volunteers were stacked dead and wounded in the narrow roadbed
like cordwood.[32]

But General Blair's survivors continued to advance in the face of the
scorching fire and soon placed foot-bridges across the ditch, laying a foundation for the troops following to charge over the top. Continuing up the
road on the run, most Federal volunteers veered away from the punishment
delivered by McCown's regiment and piled into the ditches fronting the
main Stockade Redan sector. On the heels of the "forlorn hope" came hundreds of cheering infantrymen in blue who were determined to break
through Pemberton's line and capture Vicksburg. Rebels cut down entire
formations of Westerners who were some of Lincoln's best troops. Despite
comrades falling before them, more Unionists surged forward into the hail
of lead: "it was much like marching men to their graves in line of battle,"
noted one Yankee who never forgot the slaughter. Never before had Grant's
troops been butchered at such a high rate as on fatal May 22.[33]

After charging through the sheets of flame, Union soldiers gained the
ditches before the Fifth Missouri's redan in more than one sector. One party
of Ohioans planted their colors on the earthworks just to the left of the Fifth
Missouri. Close range firing ensued across the parapet, with deadly exchanges dropping more soldiers on both sides. Some Unionists silenced the
Confederate artillery by shooting exposed graycoats through the head. Hit
by a bullet, Corporal Edward Fitzgerald, a twenty-seven-year-old Warrensburg laborer of Company H, spun to the ground dying.[34]

Dense formations of Federals continued storming forward with renewed vigor in last-ditch efforts to win the day, as Missouri Confederates
stood up by the hundreds and delivered sweeping volleys over the field.
Colonel McCown's troops cheered and taunted the Yankees to come and
get them while they rapidly loaded and fired, decimating every Union attack thrown against them. Young James Holtzhouser, an Illinois-born
private of German ancestry, fell dying in the ranks of Company K.[35]

Fifth Missouri soldiers in the rifle-pits north of the redan helped to turn
the tide as well. Before the advancing blue masses could join their comrades
pinned down in the ditch before the earthworks for an united surge over

the Stockade Redan, McCown's men on the left turned their muskets northward and opened a destructive fire on the Unionists. The Polk County soldiers of Company C and perhaps others regimental members blasted into the left flank of the Unionists. The enfilade musketry struck some of the pinned down Yankees from behind as well. Colonel McCown's musketry slaughtered those trapped not only in the ditches before the works, but also those Unionists jumbled up in the sunken road. Federal parties to the right, or southeast, of Stockade Redan's salient also took Fifth Missouri lead and suffered high losses.[36]

Not only were they decimated by the Fifth Missouri's flank fire, the Unionists clinging to their position at the base of the main redan also fell victim to a grim innovation. Some Missourians obtained shells from artillery limbers and cut fuses short to make homemade hand grenades. After lighting the fuses, Cockrell's defenders hurled the shells into the Unionists' midst. Explosions from these homemade hand grenades wiped out many of Blair's foremost men around the bloody perimeter of Stockade Redan.[37]

With special eagerness, the Fifth Missouri soldiers decimated the Sixth and Eighth Missouri Volunteer Infantrymen who were struggling and dying across the open slopes. Revenge was now won by McCown's Rebels upon the "renegade" Missourians in blue. After charging to within 25 yards of the flaming defenses, the hard-hit soldiers of Colonel Giles A. Smith's brigade retired around 75 yards to dig shallow rifle pits and shoot back at their Missouri tormentors.[38] Both sides continued exchanging gunfire and death for the remainder of this bloody afternoon. Private Benjamin Franklin Mitchell, an ex-preacher from the Little Sac River country of Polk County, dropped severely wounded. The young, blond-haired private of Company C died from the wound within a month. At last, the law of percentages was catching up with the Mitchell clan.[39]

As on May 19, the battle subsided at dark. Hard-fighting Billy Yanks, "victims of their own bravery [and the] folly of others," vanished back to their ridges after the worst beating they had ever taken, losing more than 3,000 on a "day [when] the Missourians saved the town," according to one Southerner. General Grant learned another bitter lesson of the folly of frontal assaults on May 22. He would never again attempt to take the defenses of Vicksburg with a massive frontal attack all along the line.[40]

After the bloody repulse, Colonel McCown led his reservists back to their ravine at the upper reaches of Glass Bayou behind the Stockade Redan complex. The two Union assaults upon Vicksburg had added yet another grim chapter to of this brothers' war. Indeed, Missourians in blue and gray had killed one another hundreds of miles from their home state with a savagery seldom seen. Only one other state, Illinois, had more of her sons at Vicksburg than Missouri. But unlike any other state, Missouri could claim more than 40 units on both sides at Vicksburg.[41]

The recent reversals convinced Grant to strangle Vicksburg's garrison into submission with a long siege. Since the campaign's beginning, Grant had been assisted in his bid to capture Vicksburg by a confused and disjointed effort by the Richmond government to manufacture an adequate defense of Vicksburg and the Mississippi Valley. The North's success during this decisive summer of 1863 was also made possible by a never-ending stream of Federal reinforcements. Union forces would swell to 77,000 men before the siege's conclusion. After the repulses of May 19 and 22, siege warfare commenced in earnest. A Federal gunboat fleet along the Mississippi hammered the defenses day and night from the west. An arsenal of Union cannon, meanwhile, echoed relentlessly from the north, east, and south as well, pouring an endless stream of shot and shell upon the doomed defenders of Vicksburg.[42]

Duty for the Fifth Missouri as a strategic reserve continued along with a regular manning of the fortifications. Usually from one to several companies of Fifth Missouri soldiers marched daily to the trenches and held various sectors north of the Jackson Road. Throughout most of the siege, the Missouri reservists had more responsibilities and held more vital sectors than any of Pemberton's troops. While stationed in their redan on May 24, the Fifth Missouri men became well acquainted with their opponents, who had already dug quite close to the defenses. One Federal wrote, "our soldiers are calling over to the rebels and conversing aloud with them. The 1st Mo., 5th Mo. and others made themselves known."[43]

Yet while still in the danger zone, McCown's soldiers lounged during off-duty hours in their hollow refuge. At first, the hillsides along the environs of Glass Bayou at first were thick with summer growth and plenty of shade against the Mississippi sun. But a constant barrage of shells and bullets soon defoliated the thickets. The area surrounding the encampment of the Fifth Missouri was soon turned into a winter-like landscape denuded of cover and foliage, where even officers' horses would starve to death. At the siege's beginning, plentiful supplies of bacon and cornbread existed for McCown's soldiers, but such provisions would shortly disappear. Each passing day brought more casualties among the Fifth Missouri along with smaller amounts of rations and less likelihood of relief. A Union marksman leveled his sights on Georgia-born Private Archibald Offett, age nineteen and of German ancestry, and shot him dead on May 26. Like so many others, young Offett was just another almost unnoticed death in the defense of the "hill city" and in the dusty trenches that knew no glory.[44]

As the Unionists continuously dug closer to the fortifications in parallels, Colonel McCown's losses increased. Each new sunrise revealed freshly excavated lines dug by the Federals, who worked day and night. The slits in the ground drew ever closer to the position of the Fifth Missouri. These encroaching parallels were filled with sharp-eyed Yankee snipers who made sport of riddling Rebel heads with minié balls. Grant's multitudes were tightening the noose around the city and securing a death grip which would never be released. Tragedy struck Company I on May 28 when Private James R. Ramsey, age twenty-one, was killed. The young man from Johnson County, who hailed from a Columbus family which owned eight slaves and 320 acres on the rolling prairies of western Missouri, had several relatives in Company I to carry on the family's tradition without him.[45]

But the Macon County unit suffered a greater blow on May 28 when Lieutenant Johnston was killed in action. The officer of Scotch descent and Virginia and Kentucky antecedents had left for war in 1861 only days before the birth of the son whom he would never see. He had led the company with distinction at Port Gibson and Champion Hill in Captain Guthrie's absence. Like so many others, Johnston was laid in a lonely grave at Vicksburg which today is known only to God. Having recently recuperated from a Corinth wound, Lieutenant John P. Harmon now took charge of Company I.[46]

As the siege progressed and casualties mounted ever higher, the Fifth Missouri's sheltering ravine, the 150-foot deep hollow of Glass Bayou, fell under heavier bombardment. Now death could strike as quickly in McCown's encampment as in the trenches. Also hazardous was the city hospital on the northern outskirts of town. Shells tore regularly into the infirmary, further injuring those men, including Fifth Missouri soldiers, who were already wounded.[47]

Union dead and wounded from the May 22 assaults lay rotting before the fortifications until a May 25 truce was declared. Some men of the Fifth Missouri had carried some injured Yankees to Confederate infirmaries after the slaughter, but most of the fallen bluecoats had lain for days under the sun, bloating and turning black. During the cease-fire, Johnny Rebs and Yankees came out of their defenses to trade insults with and yell taunts at each other.[48]

Colonel McCown's exiles, who might have killed relatives in blue during the assaults on May 19 and 22, discovered kinfolk among the Unionists. A Southern chaplain recorded how the "Missouri Regiments from each side begin to inquire for friends & relatives. Old friends, once friends, now meet & extend the welcome hand. A brother meets a brother — bound by such ties which no relations in life can sever." Some meetings between brothers were cordial, with an exchange of letters from home. But not all encounters between Missouri brothers from opposing sides were friendly. After bartering coffee for Confederate whiskey, another set of Missouri siblings parted with one promising to kill the other on the following day.[49]

Spirits among the Fifth Missouri Rebels lifted during the last week of May with mail delivery. The last link of an elaborate mail service, two men from Missouri had floated down the Yazoo River at night and slipped into

the Mississippi and Vicksburg with their cargo. At sunrise, the letter-car-
riers were escorted triumphantly into the Missouri camps. One mail runner
was a former Missouri Brigade member, Absalom C. Grimes who had
fought as a horseman in Colonel Gates First Missouri Cavalry. More than
3,000 letters were brought to the Missourian graycoats in a carnival-like at-
mosphere. A network of women had gathered mail from across Missouri
at considerable risk to boost the morale of those boys fighting in the far-
away Deep South. But hundreds of letters went unclaimed after so many
recent deaths of the best men and officers of the Fifth Missouri and the
Missouri Brigade. Hearing the names of the deceased Greenwood, McKinney, Stokely, Lee, and so many other Fifth Missouri soldiers go unan-
swered no doubt brought back memories of those comrades killed at Port
Gibson and Champion Hill.[50]

Another morale booster came from the efforts of Amada Bowen, who
had been banished from Missouri for her Southern sympathies. As an exile
in Mississippi who evidently had either a husband or brothers in the
Missouri Brigade and now trapped inside the city, Bowen developed an innovative scheme to deliver medicines through Grant's choke-hold on
Vicksburg. A large horse was killed, cleaned out, and the insides lined with
oiled silk. The animal's body cavity was then crammed full with precious
medicines in short supply in Vicksburg and sewed up. After word had been
relayed to those besieged inside Vicksburg, the carcass was cast adrift into
the Mississippi. Confederate lookouts in skiffs intercepted the invaluable
medical shipment where the current swung close to Vicksburg's bluffs.[51]

On May 27 the Fifth Missouri and two other Missouri Brigade regiments moved to support Forney's defenses on the east and farther south.
The following day Colonel McCown's troops at last settled down in a
permanent reserve position around the magazine near the headwaters of
Stouts Bayou, which ran roughly parallel to and south of Glass Bayou. But
the new reserve position was dangerous because the huge munitions depot
was located nearby in a wooden house about halfway between the Baldwin's Ferry and Jackson Roads.[52]

Casualties among the Fifth Missouri from Yankee guns and disease
mounted during the first week of June as temperatures soared to the highest
levels of the year. Sanitation, never good to begin with, now became worse
among McCown's defenders. Trash and waste gathered in the trenches. Not
only soiled with dirt, body filth, and grease, cotton uniforms became little
more than rags, literally falling apart in some cases after one of the hardest
campaigns of the war. Instead of the clean-shaven faces which had
distinguished the soldiers of the Missouri units, dirt-smeared features and
beards were now commonplace.[53]

Inside the hellish fortifications of Vicksburg, dust stood ankle-deep
and rain water gathered in pools at the bottom of trenches. Swarms of flies,

ticks, mosquitoes, and lice tormented Colonel McCown's defenders, who could do nothing to stop them. Muddy river water, moldy bread, and rancid pork, caused bouts of diarrhea throughout the Fifth Missouri. Such an unhealthy diet sent Colonel McCown's men to the hospitals and shallow graves by the dozen. Disease proved more fatal than projectiles. By the beginning of June, the Fifth Missouri soldiers were haggard-looking, diseased, and worn by fatigue from weeks of campaigning.[54]

Field hospitals and the city infirmaries had been overcrowded since the start of the siege, and soon the wounded fell prey to epidemics which swept hospitals like wildfire. Assistant Surgeon Goodwin's field hospital probably located in the same hollow of Stouts Bayou as was the regimental encampment. Here the ever-growing number of Fifth Missouri sick and wounded lay under ad hoc shelters in the relative safety of the ravine. Injured and ill soldiers were routinely visited by Chaplains Atwood and Bannon, but spiritual uplifting could no longer help many of these men.

Scorching 100-degree weather and humidity added to Vicksburg's misery. Horse flies and other insects buzzed through the regimental hospital tents, lighting on bandages of stricken Rebels and laying eggs in festering wounds. The nightmare of swarming maggots in the wounds of Fifth Missouri soldiers was added to the long list of the siege's horrors.[55] With Goodwin becoming the senior physician of the Fifth Missouri during the siege in Surgeon Dysart's absence, Private James M. Lemmon, age twenty-one, took over assistant surgeon duties. He now put his Missouri Medical College degree, Class of 1860, to good use, assisting more suffering humanity than he could have possibly imagined when he was a young medical student in what now seemed like another lifetime.[56]

A directive from Pemberton's headquarters which restricted Confederate return fire because of a percussion cap shortage caused widespread discontent among the Fifth Missouri boys. But the order had to be obeyed to conserve percussion caps in case Grant launched another massive assault. Frustration in the trenches increased while friends and relatives in gray fell on each side, and McCown's Rebels could only watch and not fire back. As he wrote in a bitter letter, Sergeant Hogan was incensed by the "useless saving of ammunition during the siege. Had our men been allowed to keep a fire on the Federal lines, they could never have approached to within thirty yards of our line, much less have erected forts that close to us." This opinion was also shared by Grant's veteran officers.[57]

The Fifth Missouri lost Private Jasper Lieb, age twenty-one, to a marksman's bullet in early June. The Osage County farmer was one of the German-born Fifth Missouri soldiers. Indeed, the Civil War in Missouri divided the German community with more rural than urban Germans wearing gray. Other rebels of German birth were "Doctor" Henry A. Wolfe and Private Henry Leonhart, a young Macon County baker. These German immigrants had planted roots in rural Missouri, assimilating into local society and culture more easily than did the city-dwelling "Dutch," who had banded together in ethnic communities that preserved a separate cultural identity at the cost of isolation. These Fifth Missouri Confederates of German ancestry had compiled distinguished records in the service for the South. On May 19, for instance, one German Rebel of the First and Fourth Missouri captured the regimental colors of the largely German Eighth Missouri. As with the St. Louis Irish, sectional divisions had existed in St. Louis's large German community as well.[58]

The first eight days of June cost more lives in the ever-dwindling ranks of the Fifth Missouri. The weather was steamy, with a scorching sun blistering the battle-scarred land of Warren County like an oven. Sergeant George R. Duncan, a twenty-two-year-old farmer from the Leesville area, took a mortal wound during this period. Other Fifth Missouri Confederates died in the steady bombardment. Private Edmund S. Wilks, a young farmer from Macon County, was another victim. Approaching Union parallels were leading to more Fifth Missouri deaths than the repulse of the May 19 and 22 attacks. By late June, holding Bowen's decimated Division in reserve was no longer feasible. Now, according to one Rebel, "there had been so many casualties, and there were so many sick on account of wretched diet, that there were no reserves" left available to meet any new crisis. General Pemberton could no longer afford the luxury of a strategic reserve at Vicksburg.[59]

Colonel McCown's troops struck back whenever the chance arose. On such one occasion, a Fifth Missouri officer spied a Union officer against a distant tree-line. The Rebel called for six of the regiment's best riflemen, presenting them with their greatest challenge. This group of McCown's finest marksmen probably included Private William Walker Morrow, a sniper par excellence. All six sharpshooters fired a volley that toppled the Federal officer at hundreds of yards. The Enfields had again proved their worth, and the grim art of killing was little more than amusement and business as usual at Vicksburg.[60]

Chaplain Atwood's work never ended during the siege. With morale and hope sinking each day, the spiritual role of the man of God in gray was more crucial than ever before. The Presbyterian clergyman spent much time at the hospital and front, caring for the wounded and dying and instilling faith. Swearing, card playing, and other forms of sin diminished as the siege lengthened. Indeed, there were few atheists in the Fifth Missouri at Vicksburg. As if anticipating death in Mississippi, some Missourians not only prayed longer and harder but also went to H. D. Gurney's photographic studio on Washington Street to have their pictures taken. Some of McCown's men hoped that their daguerreotypes, tintypes, and cartes de visites might one day reach home, even if they never saw Missouri again.[61]

Father Bannon repeated Atwood's role within the Fifth Missouri. Father Bannon's many accomplishments were absent from the annals of Civil War historiography for more than 130 years. It long had been a common sight to see Bannon at Captain Canniff's tent, bestowing communion and listening to confessions.

The St. Louis Irish Catholics of the Fifth Missouri found inspirational shelter from the storm not only with Bannon but also at St. Paul's Church, the second most dominant structure on the Vicksburg skyline. More than once Bannon refused to stop his services even as shells tore through the church, but continued his Mass calmly as if at his St. John's Church.[62]

But two other Company F men found no solace at St. Paul's Church — Privates Andrew and John Fine, two Jewish brothers from St. Louis. Perhaps during the siege the two brothers discovered spiritual refuge with Vicksburg's large — by Southern standards — Jewish community. If so, the former tobacco merchants were probably welcomed in the homes of Jewish families, who held their services at their own private residences.[63]

More Fifth Missouri soldiers turned away from gambling and blasphemy much to the amazement of Chaplains Atwood and Bannon. As the weather grew rainy on June 10, more of McCown's veterans were reading the Bible and hoping to embrace a sufficient amount of religion before their own judgment day on the banks of the Mississippi. One Missourian, for example, fully understood the importance of religion on Sunday, June 14, when he wrote in his diary: "May God's blessing abide with us through this day and soon deliver us from the foe, that is endeavoring to dispoil [sic] our homes and wrench from us those rights so dear to the human heart — freedom and independence." Superstition also became more commonplace. Feeling that survival depended more upon fate, and luck, than God, strange rituals and quirks dominated much of the activity of Fifth Missouri Rebels who were living like animals in the trenches week after week.[64]

Insult was added to injury on June 18, when the Missourians' siege guns captured at Grand Gulf and the field pieces captured at Big Black River now joined Grant's vast artillery arsenal. These pieces, along with Bowen's Missouri guns captured at Big Black River [more than two dozen cannon] added their fury to the bombardment.[65]

The siege became a waiting game Grant's masses could pour out of the parallels at any moment, day or night. There was now only one strategy left for Vicksburg's defenders: remain prepared for the next emergency and lose as few men as possible, while enduring a nightmarish life as the "caged birds" of Vicksburg. Close calls were commonplace each day. Spent minié balls, splinters from head logs, and shell fragments repeatedly hit McCown's Rebels. In some instances, Fifth Missouri defenders continued to man the fortifications despite being recently wounded.[66]

Often the bluecoats' wrath increased for no apparent reason. One such day came on June 20, when Union batteries pounded the fortifications with more intensity than usual. Cited for gallantry at Corinth, Private Ira French took a mortal wound. A favorite throughout the regiment, the popular drummer boy, age nineteen, was known as "Ben." The bombardment also fatally cut down on this day Privates James F. Reinhart, a twenty-five-year-old farmer of German ancestry who was born in North Carolina, and Tyler A. Mason, a Macon County farmer of twenty. With little hope or rations remaining for the trapped Confederates, the situation was becoming more bleak for Vicksburg's ever-shrinking garrison. By this period, Bowen's elite division had been reduced to the strength of a single brigade. The Fifth Missouri's strength had dwindled to only several full companies.[67]

Hunger became one of Grant's chief allies as the siege progressed. Food supplies continued to decrease in the hot weather, as the summer lengthened. First, daily rations were slashed by one-half. Pork, beef, rice, sweet potatoes, and other delicacies had lasted for only the first few days of the siege. A foul-tasting pea bread that was baked from cow peas [animal fodder] or black-eyed peas became a staple for McCown's defenders. With typical frontier humor, one Missourian swore that a chunk of pea-bread "might have knocked down a full-grown steer." An odd-tasting bean coffee was tolerated by the Fifth Missouri men after the end of the trading.[68] Rabbits caught in snares added variety to the diet of McCown's Rebels, who were likewise trapped in a snare from which there would be no escape. Shoots of cane gathered along the bottoms of Stouts and Glass Bayou were boiled and eaten by the Westerners in gray.[69]

Survival in the fortifications depended upon luck. Union artillerymen cut fuses to the correct length for shells to explode directly over the defenses. Well-directed shots bursting in midair hurled death from above, usually hitting a grayclad's head and shoulders. No matter how close McCown's Confederates hugged the trenches, "all were struck time & again," as one soldier noted.[70]

Coping with constant and high levels of stress and fear both day and night took various forms. Child-like psychological comfort could only be gained with long periods of sleep for some defenders whose spirit and faith had vanished. Other Fifth Missouri soldiers became reckless, accepting danger as nonchalantly as the scorching Mississippi sun, Yankee snipers, or biting lice. Death no longer brought fear. Four Fifth Missouri soldiers, wrote one officer, were "engaged in a friendly game as 'Seven-up' [a game of colonial antecedents as popular as poker in 1863] in the trenches, when a Minie bullet struck down one of them, and while a second ran for an ambulance corps, the other two moved their positions slightly, and seeking another partner, renewed their sport with unabated zest."[71]

With Missouri occupied, most of the Fifth Missouri Rebels were determined to hold out until the end for the loss of Vicksburg would practically end the dream of Missouri's "liberation." The struggle for McCown's soldiers could not end as long as Federal troops occupied Missouri soil. One soldier exemplifying this never-say-die attitude was Private William Walker Morrow, the hard-fighting teenager of Company I. He hailed from a College Mound, Macon County, family which prospered on the rich land of north central Missouri. Migrating from Tennessee, the Morrow clan were some of the region's earliest settlers. Private Morrow's ancestors had thrived so well that an entire region of the fertile prairie lands was christened "the Morrow Settlement."[72]

Private Morrow never contemplated surrender because letters from his relatives of the "Morrow Settlement" revealed the harsh reality of warfare on the home front and vividly described the ugly side of Union occupation in Macon County. Morrow's pro–Southern community had been hit hard by Illinois troops and local Home Guards who considered all pro–Southern citizens to be the enemy. In the opinion of Surgeon Dysart, Private Morrow was "one of the best soldiers in the Southern Army."[73] The young man won a well-earned reputation during the siege as a sharpshooter who never missed his targets. According to Surgeon Dysart, Private Morrow "killed more Yankees at Vicksburg than any other soldier there." Morrow would survive the siege. But even as he shot down more Federal soldiers in the bloody trenches day by day, the early stages of typhoid fever slowly sapped his strength and destroyed his health. The disease was destined to do what no Yankee bullet could do: Private Morrow died not long after the siege.[74]

Colonel McCown, a horse lover and a Missouri State Guard cavalry officer in 1861, suffered a personal blow when his prized horse starved to death. This was the fate of the horses of Fifth Missouri officers during the siege of Vicksburg. Animals forced to live off hillsides, which now resembled deserts from the damage of thousands of projectiles, could not survive the long siege. Colonel McCown was supported throughout the siege, however, by his young son, James Sanford McCown, who shared the same dangers. James would be at his father's side from the war's beginning to its end, serving as an unofficial private of the Fifth Missouri.

For those defenders trapped inside Vicksburg, the last hope fell upon God's mercy and General Johnston's relief column, but not exactly in that order. But the best that Johnston could now do would be to draw off enough bluecoats so that Pemberton might be able to break through Grant's ever-tightening web. As so often in the Western war, the Richmond government could largely be blamed for the almost inevitable loss of Vicksburg and the Mississippi. The Confederacy on both sides of the Mississippi had failed to galvanize the resources and manpower and the coordination of effort necessary to either repulse Grant's invasion or relieve Vicksburg.

Instead President Davis had allowed General Lee to invade the North in the futile hope of winning victory in Maryland or Pennsylvania and drawing Union forces away from the Deep South and Vicksburg. It was a tragic mistake in strategic planning which cost the Confederacy dearly and may have resulted in the South's defeat. Perhaps only veteran troops from the Army of Northern Virginia could have relieved the besieged Rebels of Vicksburg, and General Lee out-ruled that possibility. Ironically, now thousands of Confederates of the Army of Northern Virginia were marching confidently toward a rendezvous with destiny and defeat at a small town in Pennsylvania called Gettysburg. Meanwhile, day after day the siege's deadly monotony was the same: blistering heat, endless dust and lice, and omnipresent death hovering over the fortifications like a dark cloud.[75]

The third week of June saw not only cloudy weather threatening rain but also the death of Private Presley J. Duvall, a twenty-five-year-old carpenter from Newtonia, Newton County. Another Fifth Missouri soldier falling during this period was Private Henry Rich. During the prewar years, he had migrated across the Mississippi from Illinois and had fashioned a home from the cypress forests and swamps around St. Luke, Stoddard County. Rich, a twenty-two-year-old farmer, met his fate on June 22. Like so many other Fifth Missouri soldiers, both Privates Duvall and Rich would find final resting places in unidentified graves among the hills and ravines of Vicksburg.[76]

The powerful Third Louisiana redan, "Fort Beauregard," to the left of the Jackson Road was the dominant fortification in the "little confederacy" of Vicksburg. Built atop a hill to command the nearby road as it entered the earthworks, the V-shaped redan had to be taken if Grant wanted Vicksburg before the end of summer. These reliable Third Louisiana troops had fought beside these same Missouri Rebels at Wilson's Creek and Pea Ridge. Perhaps Private James M. Bedicheck of French ancestry found kindred spirits among the French-speaking Louisiana Confederates with names like LaPlante, Pettit, and LaBlanc.[77]

While the Louisiana troops guarded the strategic redan, the ominous sounds of the Unionists' picks and shovels burrowing underneath them could be heard by the increasingly nervous defenders. Forsaking frontal assaults, Grant now had his blueclads tunneling to place hundreds of pounds of black powder under the entrenchment. If the Third Louisiana redan, the key to Vicksburg, could be blown up by the mine, then the blue legions might roll through the Jackson Road sector and take Vicksburg by storm.

But these vigilant Confederates were prepared for the new Yankee stratagem. While Unionists mined under the redan, a second Rebel line was constructed behind the bastion to meet the anticipated emergency. In addition,

Rebel countermines were sunk to intercept the opponent's tunnels, but these were futile efforts. The most encouragement for the Louisianans came, however, with the knowledge that "the Fifth and Sixth Missouri Infantry were close at hand, held in reserve [and] the Louisianans needed no better assistants." The veteran soldiers of the Fifth Missouri knew that the great explosion was drawing ever closer with each passing day. As early as mid–June the Missourians in this sector, wrote one soldier, "could distinctly hear them spading and throwing out dirt not more ten feet from us" and contemplated the worst.[78]

The early morning hours of June 25 were muggy and hot. The siege's first rains had soaked the scorched and battered land during the night, but the rising sun heralded the same blistering weather which had characterized this hellish summer in Mississippi. Hardened Louisiana soldiers from Natchitoches, Baton Rouge, and the Red River country slept peacefully in their targeted redan, while 2,200 pounds of black powder, "a huge powder-magazine," lay only a few feet directly below them. The night of June 24-25 had been the last night's sleep for many Rebel defenders who were about to be blown into another world. The springing of the great Union mine had been set for the following day.[79]

June 25 was hot, with high humidity. A hint of more rain lingered on the horizon, which was hazy with summer heat. A blazing sun inched higher, emerging through a thin layer of clouds. In a living hell that Confederate leadership had created, this was the 38th day of the siege. Temperatures shortly soared to more than 100 degrees in the shade on the day that might determine the fate of the besieged Rebel "Republic of Vicksburg."[80]

Around three o'clock the situation looked bleak to the ill-fated defenders at the doomed Third Louisiana redan. To these savvy veterans in gray, the Unionists appeared close to exploding the mine. Telltale signs of an imminent explosion were louder noises beneath the fort and then an unusually long silence which spoke loudly to these experienced soldiers. Consequently, the Louisiana troops wisely abandoned the redan and deployed behind the second line. A half-hour later the whole redan suddenly exploded, as one witness recorded: "So terrible a spectacle is seldom witnessed. Dust, dirt, smoke, gabions, stockades, timber, gun-carriages, logs — in fact, everything connected with the fort — rose hundreds of feet into the air." To add to the devastating impact of the mine's blast, rows of Union artillery opened fire on the redan area just after the massive blow-up.[81]

The Forty-Fifth Illinois Volunteer Infantry, known as the "Washburn Lead Mine Regiment," led the wild charge into the hole torn into Pemberton's line by the great blast. Hundreds of blueclad veterans raced forward. The explosion of the mine, dug with the help of some bluecoated Missourians, had blown up the vortex of the redan. Colonel Cockrell instantly met the challenge with his reserves encamped near the head of Stouts Bayou. Colonel Erwin led his Sixth Missouri, the closest unit to the blast, toward the bellowing smoke clouds within minutes of the eruption. A huge gap, a 20 foot deep and 50 foot diameter crater, stood open and wide enough for the swarming of attackers to pour through and split Pemberton's army in half. The path to Vicksburg was now wide open.[82]

After a long run through the heat and humidity, Colonel Erwin's cheering troops piled behind the second retrenchment to assist the Third Louisiana. As more Unionists charged into the crater, Colonel Erwin understood that this was the battle's turning point. To stabilize the defense, the young colonel jumped atop the parapet, waving his saber and yelling encouragement to his men. Yankees instantly turned their rifled-muskets on the unbelievable sight: a finely uniformed Confederate colonel, Henry Clay's grandson no less, attempting to lead a counterattack and offering himself as a target that could not be missed. A close volley riddled the aggressive Erwin, who was making a desperate effort to launch a counterattack into the crater-hell to blunt the Union onslaught. As the dying colonel tumbled backward, the Rebel defense wavered in the face of the Yankee charge and a barrage of hand grenades. Inspired by Colonel Erwin's example, the Johnny Rebs from Missouri now stood their ground and held firm beside their fallen colonel. Against the odds, the hard-hit gray ranks solidified after Erwin's death and inspiration.

A point-blank struggle raged across the crater at a distance of less than thirty feet with a ferocity seldom seen. The determined Federals could not break through the second line, although Union leaders hurled additional troops into the crater. Among those attacking Yankees that day were the St. Louis Irishmen in blue of the Seventh Missouri Volunteer Infantry, U.S.A. Captain Canniff and his St. Louis Celtic boys were especially eager to shoot down these hated "renegade" Irish Yankees from the Emerald Isle and St. Louis.[83]

With the battle escalating to new levels, Cockrell ordered the Fifth Missouri forward so that the break in Pemberton's line could not be exploited. Colonel McCown's troops sprinted forward with cheers, wading into the storm with a determination to plug the hole in Pemberton's line.[84] Yipping the well-known fox-hunt yells from the Western frontier, the Fifth Missouri Rebels joined their Sixth Missouri and Third Louisiana comrades struggling against the raging blue tide. Shocked by the horror, Sergeant Hogan saw how the massive explosion buried "some of our men alive; they [the Yankees] assaulted the position, thinking to force their way through in the confusion."

Exploding shells from Grant's artillery savagely tore into the Southern ranks around the redan. Ripping apart the Missouri formations, great blasts hurled Rebels to the ground like rag dolls. After deploying his troops in a ragged line amid the tumult and confusion, Colonel McCown roared, "Fire!" From behind the mounds of yellow earth that had once been a parapet, Fifth Missouri soldiers swept the smoldering pit with a point-blank volley. Milling Yankees crammed in the crater's depths and scaling its steep wall were easy targets to these frontier marksmen. Hit by the hail of bullets, more Unionists rolled down into the sides of the crater dead or wounded. While the tattered regimental colors flapped above them, McCown's defenders furiously rammed down rounds and shot Federals as fast as they could in the choking smoke and dust.

Thinking that Colonel Erwin's counterattack had been launched into the hellish depths of the crater, some Missouri Confederates charged into the crater during the confusion. These ghostly looking figures in gray emerged from the blinding smoke and attacked down the crater's lip. In the resulting hand-to-hand contest, Missouri soldiers lunged with bayonets, clubbed with musket butts, and snatched muskets out of opponents' hands. A few desperate Rebel defenders heaved bayoneted rifles like harpoons into the midst of the jumbled mob of Federals to impale their victims.[85]

To break the back of the Union charge, cases of shells were passed along the Rebel line. After being lit, dozens of shells were rolled down into the crater among the Yankees. A good many projectiles exploded in the midst of the blue masses, causing much damage. Bursting shells blew some Federals to bits and deterred others from advancing further. The vicious struggle for the crater roared to new levels of intensity, for "the firing [was now] more terrific than any battle-field ever the gory field of war has witnessed." Private James H. Ring of Company H fell with an arm completely blown off by one explosion.[86]

When able to see through the drifting smoke, the soldiers of the Fifth Missouri were enraged by the sight of the flag of the Forty-Fifth Illinois floating on the opposite side of the crater. Corporal Samuel H. Tuck of Company C fell into the debris with a mortal wound, while the air was filled with the drifting smoke of battle and a shower of Ketchum hand grenades thrown by the Unionists. The finned, elongated missiles exploded when they struck the ground, spraying death in sweeping arcs among the defenders. Risking a horrible death, some graycoats picked up and then hurled back the unexploded grenades to cause havoc among the Federals. Grenades burst in every direction, blowing holes in the ever-thinning Confederate ranks. Dead and wounded Confederates piled high behind the retrenchment line with the fading day. The crater now became the "slaughter pen" of Vicksburg.[87]

The Rebels tossed more lit 12-pounder shells over the parapet and into the crater's abyss. Grenades thrown by the Unionists continued to be hurled back in return. Private Benjamin Franklin Mitchell, a former Methodist preacher and another member of the Company C clan from the Little Sac River valley, dropped mortally wounded.[88]

Colonel McCown's soldiers fired rapidly and shouted for the attacking Unionists to come and get them if they dared. As the sun dimmed on the smoky horizon, the tenuous position of the Fifth Missouri, Third Louisiana, and Sixth Missouri behind the retrenchment remained in jeopardy. More than two hundred Union cannon pounded the line with a vengeance. In addition, the Federals unleashed a more concentrated and heavier fire after being reinforced by fresh troops. Corporal John Patten Denny, an eighteen-year-old farmer from Polk County, was killed by the hurricane of fire. In the tempest, Sergeant Ruyle spun rearward from the explosion of a grenade. He took an iron fragment through his hand, and his musket was snapped in half by the blast which exploded practically atop him.[89]

The throwing and rolling of shells into the crater by the Rebels began at last to turn the tide. One Union officer watched in horror as an avalanche of projectiles "made sad havoc amongst my men, for, being in the crater of the exploded mine, the sides of which were covered by the men, scarcely a grenade was thrown without doing damage, and in most instances horribly mangling those they happened to strike." Caught in a bad fix, the Federals countered by passing logs forward and erecting a parapet. If successfully implanted on the crater's slope, the logs could stop incoming shells and help establish a permanent bridgehead in an advanced position. And if a solid log breastwork and artillery emplacement took shape, then Grant would have a salient in Pemberton's line which could be exploited. Then for greater gains more blueclads could then be hurled forward to roll over the thin line of Louisiana and Missouri defenders at the hard-pressed retrenchment.[90]

With the threat more serious than ever before, Confederate resistance stiffened just when it looked as if it might collapse. More Rebels heaved shells down into the fiery crater and the resulting explosions destroyed more Yankee lives and chances for success. Meanwhile additional defenders fell to the attackers' unceasing fire. Private Elijah E. Thompson of Company C had his arm severed by a grenade which practically landed on top of him and then exploded. Despite the Unionists' tenacity, a fortified salient was not to take shape on the crater's wall. As so often in the past, the bitter fighting had not altered the strategic situation or the fate of Vicksburg.[91]

In the half-light of the dropping sun, the Fifth Missouri's flag waved atop the retrenchment amid the drifting smoke, while the fighting continued with unabated fury. Union banners, meanwhile, flapped from the parapet's opposite side only a few feet away. No tragedy better exemplified the contest's severity than the deaths of the colonels of the Sixth Missouri and the Forty-Fifth Illinois, who fell near the same spot. The price of plugging the gap was high. Near the Jackson Road, McCown's regiments lost nineteen men during the crater struggle of June 25–26.[92]

The killing did not end with the darkness. Now the Fifth Missouri defenders aimed at muzzle flashes as the fighting continued. Meanwhile, McCown's men helped a steady stream of wounded comrades to Surgeon Goodwin's hospital. The exchanges of musketry and death in the darkness continued throughout the night. During a night of frantic loading and firing and, no sleep, the Fifth Missouri soldiers held their exposed position from sundown to sunup, losing more men in the haunting blackness.[93]

The dawn of June 26 unveiled smoke hanging over the crater, clumps of dead of both armies, and the Missourians clinging to their precarious position. Fighting again swelled with the growing light. The struggle for the crater's possession resumed with a ferocity comparable to the day before. More boxes of artillery shells were distributed among the Rebels, who were becoming experts at this type of warfare. Additional shells were thrown over the trench-top and rolled down the steep slope of the crater to destroy the latest threat to Vicksburg's life.[94]

Rebel casualties again mounted as the struggle swirled around the giant hole blown in the ground. One of the first to fall this second day of the crater fight was Private Hiram Karrison Joyce. During a distant time which now must have seemed like a dream, he had been one of Private Absalom Dyson's students back in Japan, Franklin County. Private Joyce was the second of three Company E brothers destined to die with his company. Throughout the day, the Federals tried to additionally fortify the crater and to sink another mine shaft under the redan, while maintaining a heavy fire. The struggle around the bloody crater raged throughout June 26.[95]

Determined to contain the threat at all costs, Colonel Cockrell arrived at the retrenchment with a special detail. The colonel brought enough cases of shells with him to put a permanent end to the Unionists' designs. Late in the evening, the Missourians threw more shells into the crater's bowels than ever before, and scores of explosions rocked the advanced position of the Yankees. Dozens of projectiles exploded in the Federals' midst, causing more casualties. Still, however, the Unionists' fought back with determination. In Company E, Private L. W. Burr, age twenty-eight and cited for gallantry at Corinth, was killed. The crisis finally passed for the moment, after the vicious twenty-four-hour contest for possession of the crater at last diminished in intensity.[96]

June 27 once again saw the siege resume its familiar pattern, with sharpshooting and shelling steadily taking defenders from the ranks. Skies darkened with rain-filled clouds, and winds picked-up indicating that a natural storm would soon join the man-made storm which had settled over Vicksburg for more than a month. The bluecoats, meanwhile, continued to cling tenaciously to their precarious toehold by the destroyed redan. For the next two days, the Fifth and Sixth Missouri took turns manning the parapet opposite the crater, while resuming the exchange of musketry. Meanwhile, this position around the crater continued to be the most dangerous sector in Vicksburg. With a guarantee of more fighting, Colonel McCown's soldiers occupied the line in six-hour shifts from noon to 6 P.M. and from midnight to 6 A.M. Now to meet any sudden emergency more effectively, the Fifth Missouri had been ordered to encamp closer to the redan in a ravine directly behind the redan at the head of Stouts Bayou, which was formerly occupied by the Sixth Missouri.[97]

The fortieth day of the siege was an especially bad one for the Fifth Missouri. "[We] continued fighting at our Parapet [retrenchment line] all day, sharp shooting and throwing hand grenades. 3 of our Regt was shot through the head, Lieut Woodard of Polk Cty, Mo. was killed," scribbled one soldier in his diary. The Unionists' closeness and accurate fire guaranteed instant kills on June 27. Federal marksmen only a few yards away fired at targets that they could not miss and sent bullets whizzing through Rebel heads as if at a shooting gallery. Young Lieutenant James W. Woodard, age twenty-two, would never again see his Polk County home near Bolivar and his eleven siblings, who had grown up with one slave on a middle-class farm on the Western frontier.[98]

Incessant musketry also dropped Sergeant William Donaldson. When confident of a quick victory over the "Black Republicans," the young man had enlisted in Captain Grant's Canton Guards in the early days of the war. The Illinois-born Donaldson had laid his school books aside and left Christian University, overlooking the Mississippi like Vicksburg, to pick up a musket and go to war. Sergeant Donaldson, age twenty-one, had fired rapidly and with spirit from the earthworks until "a minnie [sic] ball passed through [his] brain," in the words of one soldier. Likewise hit from the deadly sniper fire was Private John Henry Garth. The Macon County soldier, age twenty-one, died shortly in the sweltering trenches.[99]

At sectors other than the crater area, the situation was equally dangerous for the defenders. Union sharpshooters became more effective as the miles of parallels snaked ever closer to the Confederate fortifications. Parallels soon stood only several yards away from the Rebels in some sectors. Ammunition supplies among the Southerners had dwindled despite standing orders to conserve rounds. As a result, the surrounded grayclads increasingly felt the frustration and inner rage of not being able to return fire while more comrades and relatives died beside them.[100]

Each night at Vicksburg the sky was lit up and streaked with the glow of the lighted fuses of a seemingly endless stream of projectiles which rained down upon the defenders. Porter's fleet poured forth a barrage of shells into the battered city of death. General Johnston's 40,000 troops to the east had left Pemberton on his own. Considering Vicksburg's relief to be an impossibility, General Johnston could only give the ill-fated Vicksburg garrison advice instead of help: abandon the "hill city" and escape from Grant's death grip. Vicksburg was on its own.[101]

Despite its vital importance, Vicksburg had been forsaken and left to die by Richmond, Johnston, and trans–Mississippi forces. Confederate strategic errors and mismanagement and inadequate manpower from the outset that Grant's brilliant generalship and maneuvering would eventually overwhelm the strategic city on the Mississippi. Supplies for the garrison dwindled. One Rebel complained when already meager rations were cut to "one small biscuit and one or two mouthfuls of bacon per day." Hundreds of malnourished Southerners fell victim to diseases for which there were no cures. Sleep loss, suffocating heat, and filthy water further weakened the worn Fifth Missouri Rebels who had been fighting continuously for six weeks. Even the detested pea-bread rations ran low, but this caused no widespread complaining among the ever-dwindling band of Fifth Missouri survivors. Employing frontier know-how, Colonel McCown's famished men gained some nutrition from wild blackberries, watercress, cottonwood bark, and greens from the woodlands, including grass, sassafras tea, and wild parsley. But such efforts to secure nourishment would come too late for many of the stricken Fifth Missouri soldiers in the hospitals of Vicksburg. According to a letter written by Sergeant Hogan, "we were living on less than quarter rations [and soon] we had nothing to eat but mule meat."[102]

Indeed, regimental butcher Henry C. Mullins, age thirty, learned new tricks of his trade by carving mule steaks for the boys. But even the mule meat destined for tin plates was not from "fat mule[s], either, but [from] one[s] that had lived among the shells and minie balls during the siege, and [were] by no means in good order." Although it was stingy and greasy, the mule cuisine tasted like good grade beef after McCown's Rebels had been choking down pea-bread for the past six weeks.[103]

But when the mule meat ran out, more extreme measures were taken. As a Missouri surgeon of Bowen's division wrote in his journal: "Rats, the largest, finest, sleekest rats I ever saw, were here in large numbers when the siege began; they had lived on the sugar, here stored in large quantities: but the market price of one dollar for each soon caused their extermination." And tales circulated of hungry Missourians dining on rodents, mice, rats, and household pets, including dogs and cats. During one of the longest sieges of American history, Vicksburg's cuisine was as unique as it was varied.[104]

The churches of Vicksburg suffered in the ceaseless bombardment. On June 28, Sergeant Hogan hobbled on crutches through the devastated town and along streets torn up with shell holes the size of wagons. Running the gauntlet of shell-fire was worth the risk for Hogan to hear the Sunday Mass of Father Bannon as he had done in St. Louis before the war. St. Paul's Catholic Church was the "most salient feature of Vicksburg's skyline." After much effort, Sergeant Hogan reached the church, and he later wrote in a letter what happened then: "[I] had just gotten inside the door when a 132-pound parrott shell, from the batteries on the [De Soto] peninsula struck the railing outside the church, taking off the arm of a citizen who was coming in . . . another shell as Father Bannon was commencing mass, went in one side and out the other of the church, however, hurting nobody but badly frightening the women, who all left." As much of a soldier as a chaplain, Father Bannon calmly continued the six o'clock Mass as if nothing had happened.[105]

General Green's death on June 27 had left a sense of gloom throughout Bowen's division. Not even a June 25 wound had slowed down the gray-haired general and former Missouri Brigade commander, who left the hospital to personally reconnoiter the front from the redan on the right of the Stockade Redan complex, where the Fifth Missouri had repulsed the May 22 attacks. To inspire confidence, General Green had bragged to his men that "a bullet has not been molded that will kill me." This boast was ill-timed. The northeast Missouri general had just grabbed a musket to take a shot from the trenches when a bullet struck him in the head. As fate would have it, Green would be the only general killed during the siege.[106]

On June 28, the First and Fourth Missouri joined the Fifth and Sixth Missouri at the defenses around the crater. Another unit now included in the two regiment's twelve-hour rotating shifts allowed for more rest and fewer casualties among McCown's exhausted defenders. From their crater breachhead, the Unionists continued to burrow another mine under the Missourians' defenses. The noise of clanging picks and shovels beneath the band of Rebels continued day after day. Another gigantic explosion such as that of June 25 could come at any moment. The Federals' freshly dug excavations could be seen within only ten feet of the retrenchment.[107]

The Fifth Missouri's eight-hour duty shifts with sixteen hours off was a deadly game in Russian roulette. No longer was it a question of when or where General Grant might unleash his next attack. Indeed, it was only a matter of time before either the Fifth, Sixth, or First Missouri and Fourth Missouri would be blown up by the mine explosion. The next day the Second Missouri joined the shift duty near the crater. The Fifth Missourians' odds for survival increased with the timely arrival of these troops. Duty for the men of the Fifth Missouri now consisted of one six-hour stint per day. The Third Louisiana, meanwhile, also held a point in this sector, and its veteran soldiers served as reliable comrades for the Missourians.[108]

On June 30, a giant Missouri blacksmith, perhaps from McCown's regiment, lifted and "threw among them to-day, a keg containing one hundred pounds of powder, with a fuse in it" to stop the mining. The huge explosion failed to sway the Yankees, however, who continued digging under the retrenchment. Hence the waiting game continued. More than two hundred Union cannon hammered the encircled city more fiercely than ever. Going down at this time with wounds were two cousins from Polk County, Sergeant James M. Perryman, a twenty-year-old farmer, and Private James Perryman, also age twenty. Both of these members of a Company D band of four Perryman soldiers would survive the siege.[109]

On June 29, Private William Palmer, a Macon County farmer of Company I, dropped mortally wounded. By this time Pemberton had lost around 10,000 troops during the siege. A third of his force had been killed, wounded, or were sick in hospitals. Despite the grim prospects for Johnston's relief, most of Colonel McCown's troops were determined to hold out to the end. In one soldier's words, the men of the Fifth Missouri "were eager to contest the ground until the last mule was consumed and our ranks thinned so that it would be impossible to man the works."

The last day of June and the forty-third day of the siege was marred by the death of Lieutenant Peter W. Coale. Having left his Henry County farm before his daughter had reached her first birthday, the Company G officer, unlike many regimental members, at least died with the peace of mind of knowing that a brother would care for his young family. Rotting his life away at Johnson's Island Prison after his Port Gibson capture, another brother, Captain Coale, had been spared the agony of witnessing Peter's death in the trenches of Vicksburg.[110]

At the hellish crater, the Fifth Missouri Rebels continued to light and hurl shells at the encroaching blueclads. When no shells were available, the Missourians threw sun-hardened chunks of clay over the fortifications in desperate attempts to impede the Unionists' mining and relieve pent-up frustration. Meanwhile, the second mind which the Federals had dug under the northeast side of the redan was almost ready to explode by the end of June. Rotating shifts with three other ill-fated Missouri Brigade regiments, Colonel McCown's troops risked a one-in-four chance of getting blown sky-high by the inevitable blast. Now the hundreds of pounds of powder stacked beneath the Johnny Rebs from Missouri "requir[ed] only a spark of fire to hurl them into eternity." Sleeping above the Union mine was not easy for the nervous Confederate defenders, who could now only look to God for deliverance.[111]

On the afternoon of July 1, the hot, sun-baked landscape around the Jackson Road began to cool at last. The usual patter of rifle and cannon fire had inexplicably ceased before three o'clock: clearly, Colonel McCown's savvy veterans could sense that something was about to happen. Scant rations of pea bread—"hard enough to kill a dog"—and mule meat were passed around to the Missouri boys at the front. Here two Sixth Missouri companies held the retrenchment line. An ominous stillness not heard since the siege's beginning settled over the city of so much destruction. The doomed soldiers of the Sixth Missouri stayed under the shade in the sweltering trenches, hoping the mine would not blow them out of this world and into the next.[112]

The Sixth Missouri Rebels, most of whom came from western Missouri, did not realize that nearly a ton of powder had just been lit only a few feet directly beneath them. Some veteran soldiers of the Sixth Missouri sensed impending doom but now could do nothing except pray and hope for the best. In their hollow in the environs of Stouts Bayou, the weary Fifth Missourians had their muskets stacked and were resting. Some of Colonel McCown's soldiers were preparing for their six-hour shift at the retrenchment. Few Fifth Missouri Confederates felt good about going back to the front at 6 P.M. on this fateful Wednesday along the Mississippi.[113]

A low-sounding growl suddenly erupted under the Third Louisiana redan. The deep moan grew louder and angrier, shaking the whole retrenchment line before the crater like a leaf. Then the entire hilltop vibrated and lurched violently, arching and swelling upward from the great eruption caused by 1,800 pounds of powder, as the redan and those luckless graycoats in it blew skyward.[114]

During an explosion that seemed to shake all of Warren County one Missourian wrote: "All at once a sound as the rolling of many thunders broke in harshly upon the calm. The whole hill trembled [and] the air was filled with dust clouds and bursting bombs." Caught in the vortex of an erupting volcano, more than a score of Sixth Missouri boys were hurled high into the air. Many were never seen again after being buried alive. Six of the airborne Rebels were blown eastward and landed inside the Union line. One Johnny Reb rose to such heights above the redan that he later claimed he "could see Joe Johnston in the rear!"[115]

Immediately after the huge blast, Union artillery pounded the area around the Jackson Road sector. Another deep crater and gaping hole was now torn in Pemberton's line. The explosion leveled much of the remaining redan. Where once there had been a powerful Confederate redan, there was now only a larger crater. Grant seemingly now had another open avenue leading over the debris and bodies to Vicksburg.[116]

Colonel Cockrell and his Second Missourians were knocked off their feet and hurled over the brow of the high ground behind the retrenchment by the blast. Hundreds of Johnny Rebs were sent tumbling into the depths of the hollow in a jumbled pile, with rifles, blanket-rolls, and hats flying through the air. The Second Missouri Rebels rallied amid the clouds of smoke and dust choking the hollow.[117]

As so often in the past, Colonel Cockrell rose to the challenge. On July 1, despite badly bruised by the blast that had sent him high into the air, the former Warrensburg lawyer rallied his dazed soldiers. The Second Missouri soldiers quickly grabbed their rifles and charged forward without orders, meeting Cockrell on the way, who encouraged his old regiment onward into the tempest. Cockrell also ordered the First and Fourth Missouri forward on the double. Now the crack troops of both the Second Missouri and the First and Fourth Missouri hastened toward the smoky breach. The Third Louisiana also advanced to meet the attackers, and Colonel Cockrell encouraged the Fifth Missouri onward to plug the hole in the lines, which now threatened the life of Vicksburg.[118]

But Grant threw no troops into the breach, having learned the June 25–26 lesson. Upon arriving at the crater, Colonel McCown's breathless soldiers could hardly believe the sight. "Men buried alive in the heap of ruins that lay scattered around and mangled bodies of brave veterans who had, since the siege, acted a noble part, there met our eyes," recalled one Missourian. Soldiers frantically dug out half-alive comrades by hand as shells exploded around them.[119]

The shaky gray line could yet snap under the pressure, but the cheering Fifth Missourians soon arrived to restore confidence. Providing timely support, Colonel McCown's troops hurriedly scrambled into line with the Second, First and Fourth, and Sixth Missouri and the Third Louisiana. A Cromwellian-type, Colonel Cockrell now made one last appeal to his band of defenders, declaring that at all costs the Missouri Brigade must hold this point. Every man would have to be sacrificed if necessary to stop the attack.[120]

To patch up a twenty-foot-wide gap in the retrenchment and prepare for the expected Union onslaught, the Rebels began throwing up earthworks. Holes were blown into the gray ranks with greater frequency as Federal artillery zeroed in on targets. Private Frederick Byersdorf, of German antecedents commended for bravery at Corinth, fell dying. Homemade Union wooden mortars delivered severe punishment upon the Fifth Missourians. These mortars were charged with just enough powder to lift and drop shells into the Confederates' mist. Positioned in trenches only 50–75 yards distant, the hand-carved mortars were fashioned from sweet gum trees and Yankee ingenuity. Practically every shell from the "devil's mortars," as one Missourian called them, exploded in the ranks, dropping defenders in bunches.[121]

The task of rebuilding the parapet during the cannonade was impossible. So furious was the bombardment, wrote one Rebel, that "the earth was swept away by the storm of missiles faster than it could be placed in position. We tried sand-bags, but they, too, were torn to shreds and scattered." Only by filling canvas wagon-tops and tents with earth were the Missourians finally able to erect a parapet across the gorge. Meanwhile, the bitter struggle raged fiercely across the crater as on bloody June 25–26. Some of the most vicious fighting of the siege now took place around the crater.[122]

Some desperate Johnny Rebs threw shovelfuls of dirt over the parapet to blind the eyes of Yankee marksmen only a few feet away. But the slaughter continued, with the little wooden mortars spreading death with each shell. According to one Missouri soldier, these shells "burst immediately in our faces, killing and disabling the men, and almost covering us with earth [but the Fifth Missourians retained] the determination to hold the parapet or die in its defence [sic]." Not even darkness ended the killing at the crater. Union batteries, including Missouri artillery pieces, continued pounding away at the retrenchment line during the night.[123]

As a result of this ongoing bombardment, Missouri and Louisiana boys continued to die long after sunset. The Union tree-mortars tossed projectiles with uncanny accuracy throughout the night's remainder, but the crisis had been successfully met once again by the defenders. As before, the Fifth, First and Fourth, Second, and Sixth Missouri rotated six-hour shifts at the reconstructed retrenchment, which had become Vicksburg's primary bone of contention.[124]

The July 1 success in rallying and standing firm at the crater was of no strategic consequence in terms of altering Vicksburg's fate for those Confederates trapped inside Vicksburg. It was now clear that relief would not be coming either from the Trans-Mississippi theater to the west or from Johnston to the east. But the possibility yet existed for the Southerners to perhaps break out of the blue anaconda that was strangling the life out of the Vicksburg garrison. If a Confederate attack could punch a hole in Grant's line, then the Rebels could yet make a dash for Big Black River and Johnston. General Pemberton therefore asked each division commander about the feasibility of such a gamble. All of Pemberton's top lieutenants felt that the attempt could not succeed. Even the hard-fighting General Bowen, Pemberton's "right-arm," thought that his Old Guard Missouri troops could not both fight and escape eastward in their decimated condition. But the normally aggressive Bowen was racked with exhaustion, malnutrition, and the dysentery which would shortly take his life. General Pemberton now contemplated what had been unthinkable only a short time before, the surrender of fortress Vicksburg.[125]

Despite the gloomy assessments from the army's highest ranking officers, many Missourians refused to consider capitulation at this late date. Even while standing half-naked in watery trenches with only rag strips of carpet for protection against the rain and knowing their fates were sealed, most Fifth Missouri Rebels never "dreamed of surrender." Colonel McCown's veterans were determined to keep struggling "as long as there was a cartridge or a ration of mule or horse [left]."[126]

But the leading Southern officers at Vicksburg had lost faith in themselves and their troops after more than a month and a half of siege warfare and a campaign of successive defeats. Thanks to General Grant's brilliance and Confederate incompetence, defeatism had now consumed the besieged at Vicksburg. Disagreeing with Bowen, Colonel Cockrell was the highest ranking officer who advocated making the attempt to charge out of Vicksburg. He proposed to lead the attack himself with the Missouri Brigade. With "the last morsels of mule meat and dog meat in the haversacks," Colonel McCown's survivors stood ready to slash through Grant's chokehold on Vicksburg if Pemberton gave the order, but it would never come.[127]

A Missouri Brigade's soldier summarized in his diary the general feeling among the rank and file, for they prayed only "to be massed at some point on the line and cut our way through: it would have been feasible with such men as ours; but fate decided against us." Dirty white flags popped up on the Rebel parapets during the morning of July 3. Colonel McCown's Confederates, meanwhile, laid low in their trenches, unknowing that capitulation would soon be discussed.[128]

Dressed in a fine gray uniform, General Bowen rode down the Baldwin's Ferry Road with Pemberton's request for terms. After performing more brilliantly than any Southern general during the Vicksburg campaign, Bowen had been assigned the most painful mission of his career, even now while losing the battle for his life with disease, "the result of severe mental and physical exertion" of the recent campaign.[129]

In the sweltering trenches around the crater on the Jackson Road sector, the Fifth Missouri Confederates were curious as to why the firing suddenly ceased. White handkerchief-flags at the tip of ramrods on the fortifications along the Jackson Road caused McCown's defenders to speculate that Pemberton must be stalling for time or establishing a truce to evacuate citizens or bury more dead. After all, Colonel McCown had already passed word along the trenches that Colonel Cockrell would lead the attack to cut out of Vicksburg on the night of the Fourth of July. Cartridge boxes of the Missouri Confederates contained enough bullets for one last charge.[130]

The negotiations to determine Vicksburg's fate continued as Bowen tried to obtain the best terms. Since General Grant "had been a neighbor of Bowen's in Missouri, and knew him well and favorably," Bowen had the best chance of securing the most liberal terms of a general parole rather than prison terms for a manpower-short nation in a war of attrition. General Bowen gambled that Grant would bestow "liberal terms of capitulation." A lull settled over the doomed river city upon which the whole nation had riveted its eyes during this climatic summer in western Mississippi. Filthy and lice-covered Fifth Missouri soldiers crawled out of the defenses to stretch atop the parapet and rest in peace for the first time in weeks.[131]

Hundreds of bluecoats also climbed out of their holes. Former neighbors in blue from Missouri, the renegades, were seen by McCown's grayclads who had fought some of these men in Missouri. Taking advantage of the opportunity, Southern boys ambled into the open with bags of tobacco to trade for Yankee newspapers and coffee. Jokes were exchanged between fellow Americans who had been trying to kill one another only a few minutes before. Unlike the highest ranking Rebels at Vicksburg, Vicksburg's women remained defiant to the bitter end. Since the siege's beginning, they had served as nurses day and night, saving untold lives and inspiring hope. Indeed, wrote one Southerner, "had the women of Vicksburg had their way the city would still be under siege."[132]

But the unthinkable finally came true: word filtered down the next morning that Vicksburg would be surrendered. The final all-out effort to slash through Grant's lines was never launched. Worst of all, the surrender ceremony would occur on the Fourth of July. News of the capitulation came as a severe blow to the long-suffering men of the Fifth Missouri. McCown's soldiers wept or cursed while Union batteries and gunboats fired victory salutes to honor one of the North's greatest victories of the war. Outbursts of Federal cheering rang around Vicksburg, and Yankee brass bands struck up lively music. But Sergeant Hogan wrote in a letter that the Missouri Confederates "felt, and were in no wise whipped, conquered, or subjected."[133]

Just after 10 A.M. on the hot morning of Independence Day, Colonel McCown formed his ragged band of survivors in column for the capitulation ceremony. The soldiers of the Fifth Missouri, diseased, lice-infested, and wearing dirty rags which had once been uniforms, marched from the defenses and halted just north of the Jackson Road. Feeling that they had been forced to surrender only to "General Starvation" and not to General Grant, the Missouri Rebels held their heads high on the day of their greatest humiliation. Now Colonel McCown's vanquished went through their final maneuvers. Impressed by what he saw, one Unionist felt that "they are as good as [sic] looking set of Reb. troops as we have seen."[134]

Here along the dusty Jackson Road, a victorious General Grant watched while 276 survivors of McCown's decimated regiment stacked Enfield rifles: the final act in a bloody drama at Vicksburg which had lasted for more than a month and a half. Sun-bronzed and dirty, a good many of the Rebels of the Fifth Missouri choked with emotion as Sergeant Walton laid the regimental colors along a stack of muskets. Across the shredded fabric were stitched the names of the battles in the Deep South — Iuka, Corinth, Grand Gulf, Port Gibson, Baker's Creek, and Big Black River — which had been fought in a futile attempt to deny the North such a day as this. Fourth of July, 1863 when more American soldiers surrendered than ever before, more than 29,000 men would never be forgotten by McCown's survivors.[135]

Taking advantage of Grant's desire to celebrate his success on the national holiday, Bowen had played the key role in securing liberal surrender terms for Vicksburg's garrison from "Unconditional Surrender" Grant. Now most of these Confederates, including the Missourians, would not have to endure the hell of northern prisons and could be exchanged at a future date. But good feelings about gaining parole for Vicksburg's defenders dimmed when Grant's legions marched triumphantly into "impregnable Vicksburg."[136]

Nevertheless, blue and gray intermingled freely after the surrender with few violent incidents. Sympathetic Unionists gave bacon and hardtack to McCown's famished men. The soldiers of both sides maintained respect for their adversaries, producing an odd camaraderie and empathy not long after some of the hardest fighting of the war. Thereafter, like the rest of the garrison, the Fifth Missouri Rebels remained in their encampment, and this helped defuse a potentially volatile situation. By far the most angry Rebels in Vicksburg were the Irishmen of Company F, for Celtic tempers could not be soothed by signing parole papers. Even Father Bannon was in a fiery rage over the humiliation of surrender.[137]

The deadly effects of the siege lingered on for weeks and even months as McCown's boys steadily died from wounds and disease. While United States brass bands blared and Yankees cheered their great victory on July 4, Lieutenant Charles G. Selby, one of Captain McKinney's ex-horsemen, died of pneumonia. His nurse Private Samuel J. Hodge, also of Company H, was likewise ill-fated. Hodge signed a parole and would be captured in Missouri and fall victim to a fatal sickness. The high price of Vicksburg's defense continued to be exacted on the "Old Guard" Fifth Missouri long after the siege. Those men of McCown's regiment who were hit by bullets and shells during the siege would continue to perish across the Deep South. Among these mortally wounded men was Private William Henry Murley, age twenty, a farmer of Company B.[138]

The Fifth Missouri had been decimated during the Vicksburg Campaign. One of McCown's officers lamented that the "regiment had been reduced to a mere handful of men" by July 1863. Official records indicate that the Fifth Missouri lost 20 killed and 52 wounded during the siege of Vicksburg, a total of 72. But more detailed search of individual soldier's records sets the loss at 24 killed and another 19 who were mortally wounded or died of disease at Vicksburg. Indeed at least 43 Fifth Missouri soldiers met their Maker during the forty-seven-day siege. And the number of wounded was much higher than the official records indicate, for nearly every soldier of McCown's regiment, swore one officer not long after the siege, had been hit once, twice, or more.[139]

Losses among the "Grenadier Guard" Missourians had indeed been devastating. More than a third of the Missouri Brigade became casualties during the siege alone. And during the entire Vicksburg campaign, the Missouri Brigade lost more than one-half of its strength. Bowen's Division had been virtually annihilated since May 1. This elite division took unparalleled losses of nearly 2,300 men, the highest casualties of any division on either side during the Vicksburg campaign. Perhaps it was fitting that like a captain going down with his ship, division commander Bowen, along with many of his soldiers, would not survive the Vicksburg campaign. After his division's destruction in Port Gibson and Champion Hill and at Big Black River and Vicksburg, perhaps General Bowen indeed "died of grief." But a physician's diagnosis would lay the blame on dysentery.[140]

The Vicksburg campaign had virtually destroyed the Fifth Missouri and the Missouri Brigade as well. Of the 432 Fifth Missourians ready for duty on the morning of May 1, at least 262 had been killed or wounded in barely two months by the conclusion of the siege, amounting to a loss of more than 60 percent. The Missouri Confederates had once more paid in blood for their lofty reputation as Pemberton's most dependable troops and best fighters. From the beginning of the campaign, Pemberton had skillfully employed the frontier exiles as his army's shock troops. He later swore, "If I had 10,000 more Missourians I would have won and carried the war." Indeed, the Missouri Brigade had been badly overused and exploited by Confederate leadership during the past campaign. No one realized more than an embittered Colonel Cockrell that "a few more engagements will almost annihilate them."[141]

The last pitiful drama was played out on July 11. Sullen Rebels fell into column for the march east to their Alabama parole camp. Union officers checked the Fifth Missouri Confederates' parole papers and haversacks for weapons. As a condition of parole, Colonel McCown, Major Waddell, Captain Canniff, and other officers carried their sabers and pistols by their side on the march out of the fallen fortress. Finally, black servants, only about half a dozen in McCown's unit, had won their long-desired freedom. Some African Americans who had been raised with families in Polk or Johnson County found the separation hard. One not eagerly embracing emancipation was Shad, the lieutenant colonel's servant who loved fighting beside the Fifth Missouri. But Shad's case was probably the exception. The vast majority of officers' slaves relished the liberty granted them by the men in blue.[142]

As much as Confederate defeat at Gettysburg, Vicksburg's capitulation proved to be one of the most decisive turning points of the conflict, hastening the death of the Confederacy. Cutting the Confederacy in half and winning control of the Mississippi knocked another pillar out of the shaky foundation of Southern nationalism. The possibilities for Rebel success dimmed to new lows after the fall of the South's mighty Gibraltar. The golden dream of independence had slipped farther away during the disastrous summer of 1863. "That year," wrote Lieutenant Colonel Bevier, "had been great with mighty events; and our Missouri Brigade had been no ignoble participants. Like rugged mountains, looming through the eddying mists of an Alpine Valley, stand forth the stricken fields of our bloodiest battles, and on three occasions our command had lost more than half its men."[143]

President Lincoln's grand objective of cutting the Confederacy in half and controlling the Mississippi, solidified with Port Hudson's fall a few days later, had been won by hard fighting, imaginative and bold tactics, and Grant's brilliant generalship. Now the depleted South would be forever denied the crucial manpower, resources, and materiel from the rich Trans-Mississippi states of Texas, Louisiana, Arkansas, Missouri, and the Indian Territory. With the all-important "Father of Waters" finally cleared of Confederate guns and armies, the Southern heartland was now more wide open to invasion than ever before. There would be many more sanguinary battles in the struggle for the possession of the mid–South, but the conquest of not only the Mississippi River but also the Mississippi Valley was ensured with the loss of Vicksburg.[144]

# EPILOGUE

For those Fifth Missouri Confederates who had survived the murderous first half of the war, the fateful years 1864 and 1865 brought only greater odds and challenges for them to face, more suffering and death, and fewer chances for success than ever before. As the conflict turned increasingly brutal and destructive, it became something more horrible than these naive, innocent young men from Missouri could possibly have imagined in the exciting summer of 1861. Indeed, thousands more of the common soldiers — Johnny Reb and Billy Yank — would be slaughtered during the bloody years 1864–65. As a cruel fate ordained, the Missouri Brigade's losses in the upcoming 1864–65 engagements across the South continued to be higher and more out-of-proportion to their numbers than any other Confederate brigade. After the nightmarish fighting of the Vicksburg campaign, the possibility that Southern independence would be won was a fast-fading dream for the outnumbered ghosts in gray.

After exchange and consolidation in mid–September 1863, Colonel McCown's soldiers became members of the Third and Fifth Missouri Confederate Infantry (Consolidated) and continued to serve with distinction in the First Missouri Confederate Brigade. Unlike many Southern troops surrendered at Vicksburg, the former Fifth Missouri Rebels continued struggling to the bitter end. They met General Sherman's forces during the Meridian Mississippi Campaign during January 1864. After joining General Joseph E. Johnston's Army of Tennessee, they fought well at New Hope Church and Latimer's House and repelled one of Sherman's principal attacks on Kennesaw Mountain, Georgia, during the Atlanta Campaign. They were among the last Confederate troops to march through a burning Atlanta, and they recaptured Jonesboro, Georgia, with aggressiveness on a hot September day in 1864. In the mountainous wilderness of northwest Georgia, they assaulted impregnable fortifications atop the heights of Allatoona and almost captured one of Sherman's largest supply depots. During a suicidal assault on a bloody November afternoon in Tennessee, they charged headlong into the holocaust of Franklin with the Missourians suffering the highest loss of any brigade on either side during the war. Fighting from the trenches with their backs to Mobile Bay, they faced the unstoppable, blue assault waves near the Gulf of Mexico on the day that General Robert E. Lee surrendered his Army of Northern Virginia at Appomattox. Here at Fort Blakeley the remaining band of a few hundred Missouri Confederates were surrounded and captured deep in Alabama on the Gulf of Mexico.

In more key situations in more important battles more often than any other Missouri Brigade troops, the elite soldiers of the Fifth Missouri helped the Missouri Brigade compile an unparalleled epic in the annals of Civil War historiography. Indeed, the Missouri Brigade established a combat record more distinguished than that of the most legendary fighting brigades on either side during the Civil War, including the Union's Iron and Irish brigades and the Confederacy's Stonewall, Orphan, and Texas brigades.

By the fateful spring of 1865, Colonel McCown's men had little left but shattered dreams, and the tattered gray uniforms on their backs. After the end of the war, however, the hardened Fifth Missouri veterans of Iuka, Corinth, Grand Gulf, Port Gibson, Champion Hill, Big Black River, and Vicksburg also took with them to their Missouri homes not burned down by Jayhawkers and Union Militia a lifetime of memories never to be forgotten. Indeed, they had overrun Battery Powell and Fort Richardson, seizing more than 40 pieces of artillery in an attack that nearly captured Corinth. The cheering Celtic Rebels of Company F charging on battlefields across the South, while dueling with the Union skirmishers. The survivors would always remember how the long-haired Captain Canniff had shouted orders in his thick, Irish brogue, inspiring his sons of Erin to push onward through a hail of lead. Their memories would include Captain Canniff and his rough-hewn Emerald Islanders bowing their heads in prayer in ragged and dirty gray uniforms, while Father Bannon met their spiritual needs before they entered another bloody engagement. Colonel McCown and Generals Cockrell and Bowen leading the howling tide of elated Fifth Missouri attackers through the drifting smoke of battle during some of the most decisive clashes of the Vicksburg campaign. At Port Gibson, the Fifth Missouri soldiers attacking with abandon through the dense canebrake against impossible odds to help save a Confederate force on a hot spring day in Mississippi. Seven determined Company I volunteers holding the Union forces at bay in a body-strewn ravine with audacity and only a handful of rounds. During one of the most desperate charges of the war, the Missourians overrunning Union battle-lines and capturing Federal artillery, almost splitting Grant's army in half, and nearly winning it all in the woodlands and fields of Sid Champion. McCown's men would always remember charging more than a mile and making the tangled woodlands of Champion Hill ring with the cries of victory during the near-successes that almost reversed the Civil War's outcome. They had fought against fate in Vicksburg's sweltering trenches while subsisting on pieces of mule and rat meat in a futile effort to save the South's great fortress in the West. One of their most heart-wrenching memories was of laying the grayclad bodies of friends and relatives in long burial trenches while choking with emotion.

The bullet-shredded, red battle flags that Colonel McCown's veterans had followed faithfully for years were finally captured by the victorious Federals on April 9, 1865. These battle-inscribed banners were never to be seen again except in the lingering memories and dreams of the handful of remaining survivors of the Fifth Missouri. Dreams of a new nation had slipped away like so many elusive battlefield victories in the Deep South.

But most of all, the men of the Fifth Missouri would never forget the hundreds of comrades who had died in vain during four years of sacrifice. After they had experienced the most crushing defeat ever suffered by any Americans in the nation's history, the deeds and accomplishments of the Fifth Missouri Confederates would be forgotten in the national epic, fading away like so many dreams. But the visions of the countless heroics and the long list of Fifth Missouri dead would remain alive in the memories of Colonel McCown's band of survivors for the rest of their lives.

Coming home to a war-ravished Missouri, confiscated properties, and families which had become victims to a greater extent than those in any other section of the country, the veterans of the Fifth Missouri had to adjust to a hostile environment and to a life as second-class citizens who faced a bleak future. Indeed, in 1865, Colonel McCown's battle-scarred veterans were among the most completely defeated Americans in the republic's history: men without a country, with few expectations, and with only lost dreams with which to face an uncertain future.

The Fifth Missouri Confederates who had come so close to bringing decisive victory at Corinth, Port Gibson, and Champion Hill could best cope with the harsh reality of life after Appomattox and the loss of so many Fifth Missouri neighbors and relatives by offering a solitary prayer. This prayer stemmed from the haunting guilt and pain that lingered for Colonel McCown's survivors once they returned home after leaving so many comrades in untended and unmarked graves across Missouri, Arkansas, Mississippi, Louisiana, Georgia, Tennessee, and Alabama.

Indeed, Colonel McCown's survivors prayed that God would bless and acknowledge the final resting places of the scores of Fifth Missouri dead by bestowing a small clump of wild flowers in the area near to the many unknown graves along the narrow ridge-top of Corinth, Port Gibson's brushy ravine, the haunted thickets of Champion Hill, and the hills of Vicksburg. Psychologically for the survivors, this final solemn prayer for a natural and spiritual recognition of the many Fifth Missouri comrades in far-away Dixie who never returned home helped to honor those who had fallen in vain even though a new American nation would neither honor or remember them or what they did.

Perhaps today on some rain-fresh spring morning in Missouri, Arkansas, Mississippi, Louisiana, Georgia, Alabama or Tennessee a sprinkling of colorful wild roses or jasmine may yet be found blossoming in some unlikely place amid a lonesome clump of pines, atop a briar-covered knoll, or along an obscure, brush-choked ravine that had been significant enough in 1862-63 for these young soldiers of the Fifth Missouri Confederate Infantry to forfeit their lives so long ago for what they believed to be right.

# NOTES

## Chapter I

1. Compiled Service Records of Confederate Soldiers Who Served in Organizations from the State of Missouri, Record Group 109, National Archives, Washington, D.C.; Sandie Murdock to John W. Ross, 8 Oct. 1905 letter, William Skaggs Collection of Confederate Veteran Letters, box 2, folder 12, Arkansas History Commission, Little Rock, Arkansas; Robert Bevier, *History of the First and Second Missouri Confederate Brigades, 1861–1865 and from Wakarusa to Appomattox, a Military Anagraph* (St. Louis: Bryan, Brand, 1879), p. 333; Francis Marion Cockrell Scrapbook, Missouri Historical Society, St. Louis; Bell Irvin Wiley, *The Life of Johnny Reb: The Common Soldier of the Confederacy* (Baton Rouge: Louisiana State University, 1978), pp. 234–35; *The War of the Rebellion: A Compilation of the Official Records of the Union and Confederate Armies*, 128 vols. (Washington, D.C. 1880– 1901), vol. 17, ser. 1, pt. 1, p. 382.

2. Compiled Missouri Service Records; John McElroy, *The Struggle for Missouri* (Washington, D.C.: National Tribune Co., 1909), p. 320; Ephraim McDowell Anderson, *Memoirs: Historical and Personal, Including the Campaigns of the First Missouri Confederate Brigade* (St. Louis: Times Printing Co., 1868), pp. 144–45, 148, 152–53, 165, 169–71; Brauckman Scrapbook, Missouri Historical Society, St. Louis. *Union and Confederate Annals: The Blue and Gray in Friendship Meet, and Heroic Deeds Recite* 1, no. 1 (Jan. 1884): p. 70.

3. Compiled Missouri Service Records; Bevier, *History of the First and Second Missouri Confederate Brigades*, pp. 79, 116–17; George W. Warren Diary, George W. Warren, IV, Montpelier, Virginia; William A. Ruyle Memoir, Dee Ruyle, Bolivar, Missouri, pp. 5, 11; Francis Marion Cockrell to Skaggs, 3 April 1914, Skaggs Collection, box 1, folder 3.

4. Compiled Missouri Service Record; Jay Monaghan, *Civil War on the Western Border, 1854–1865* (New York: Bonanza Books, n.d.), p. 158; Donald J. Stanton, Goodwin F. Berquist, Jr., and Paul C. Bowers, "Missouri's Forgotten General: M. Jeff Thompson and the Civil War," *Missouri Historical Review* 70, no. 3 (April 1976): 248–49; Emory M. Thomas, *The Confederacy as a Revolutionary Experience* (N.J.: Prentice-Hall, 1971), pp. 109–13; Clement Eaton, *A History of the Southern Confederacy* (New York: Free Press, 1954), p. 111.

5. Ruyle Memoir, p. 11; Bevier, *History of the First and Second Missouri Confederate Brigades*, p. 83; Compiled Missouri Service Records; *Portrait and Biographical Record of Johnson and Pettis Counties, Missouri* (Chicago: Chapman, 1895), p. 345; McCown Family Papers, in private collection of Garland McCown of Garland, Texas, and Frank D. McCown, Fort Worth, Texas; *Official Records*, vol. 3, ser. 1, p. 26; Warren Diary; Francis Marion Cockrell to Skaggs, 9 May 1911, Skaggs Collection, box 1, folder 3.

6. *Portrait and Biographical Record of Johnson and Pettis Counties, Missouri*, p. 345; Eighth Census of the United States, Johnson County, Missouri, 1860; Walter B. Stevens, *Centennial History of Missouri (The Central State): One Hundred Years in the Union 1820–1921*, 5 vols. (Chicago: S. J. Clarke, 1921), vol. 2, pp. 344–45; Francis Marion Cockrell to Skaggs, 9 May 1911, Skaggs Collection, box 1, folder 3.

7. *Portrait and Biographical Record of Johnson and Pettis Counties, Missouri*, p. 345; *History of Johnson County, Missouri* (Kansas City: Historical Company, 1881), pp. 218, 232–34, 275, 402, 415; Francis Marion Cockrell to Skaggs, 9 May 1911; *The United States Biographical Dictionary*, Missouri volume, p. 723.

8. The 1860 Johnson County, Missouri, Census Records; *Portrait and Biographical Record of Johnson and Pettis Counties, Missouri*, p. 346; *History of Newton, Lawrence, Barry and McDonald Counties, Missouri* (Chicago: Goodspeed, 1988), p. 329; Lois Stanley, George F. Wilson, and Mary Helen Wilson, *Death Records from Missouri Newspapers: The Civil War Years, January 1861–December 1865* (Decorah, Mo.: Anundsen, 1983), p. 59.

9. *Portrait and Biographical Record of Johnson and Pettis Counties, Missouri*, p. 346; Compiled Missouri Service Records; Bruce Nichols, "The Civil War in Johnson County, Missouri," (Master's thesis, "Central Missouri State University: Warrensburg, Missouri 1974), p. 35; 1860 Johnson County, Missouri, Census Records; Francis Marion Cockrell to Skaggs, 9 May 1911; *Weekly Standard*, Warrensburg, Missouri, 22 July 1865; *Bulletin of the Johnson County Historical Society* (April 1976), p. 3; *The Golden Years: 50th Anniversary: Johnson County Historical Society, 1920–1979* (Clinton, Mo.: The Printery, 1970), pp. 74–75.

10. Bevier, *History of the First and Second Missouri Confederate Brigades*, pp. 278, 287–91; Compiled Missouri Service Records.

11. Compiled Missouri Service Records; *History of Johnson County, Missouri*, p. 108; 1860 Johnson County, Missouri, Census Records; Bevier, *History of the First and Second Missouri Confederate Brigades*, pp. 321–22, 356–57; *St. Louis Missouri Republican*, 10 Oct. 1885.

12. Compiled Missouri Service Records; Ewing Cockrell, *History of Johnson County, Missouri*, p. 108; Bevier, *History of the First and Second Missouri Confederate Brigades*, p. 302; Brigadier General H. M. Duffield, Introduction to *Deeds of Valor, From Records in the Archives of the United States Government: How American Heros Won the Medal of Honor* (Detroit: Perrien Keydel, 1906), vol. 1, pp. 14–15.

13. The 1860 Johnson County, Missouri, Census Records; Cockrell, *History of Johnson County, Missouri*, pp. 634–35; Compiled Missouri Service Records; George Greenwood Service Record, Adjutant General of Missouri Records, Adjutant General Office, Jefferson City, Missouri.

14. Compiled Missouri Service Records; "Dr. Benjamin Givens Dysart," *Confederate Veteran* 12, no. 4 (April 1904), p. 190; *History of Randolph and Macon*

*Counties, Missouri* (St. Louis: National Historical Company, 1884), pp. 397–98, 1108–9; *History of Randolph and Macon Counties, Missouri*, pp. 673–77; Alexander H. Waller, *History of Randolph County, Missouri* (Topeka, Kans.: Historical Publishing Company, 1920), p. 404; *History of Monroe and Shelby Counties, Missouri* (St. Louis: National Historical Company, 1884), pp. 546–47; Bevier, *History of the First and Second Missouri Confederate Brigades*, pp. 310–11; Laura V. Balthis, ed., *Early Recollections of George W. Dameron: Biographical Sketches of Log Cabin Pioneers* (Huntsville: Herald Print Company, 1898), pp. 50–51; *General History of Macon County, Missouri* (Chicago: Henry Taylor, 1910), p. 249; Catalogue of the Officers and Students of McGee College, 1854–1855, Missouri Historical Society, St. Louis.

15. *History of Monroe and Shelby Counties, Missouri*, pp. 546–47; *History of Macon and Randolph Counties, Missouri*, pp. 1108–9; Paul Alexander, ed., *The Chronology of a County Editor: The Writings of T. V. Bodine* (n.p., n.d.).

16. Compiled Missouri Service Records; Adjutant General of Missouri Records.

17. Compiled Missouri Service Records; Mitchell Family Papers, William F. Moore, Redstone, Alabama; *Bolivar Courier*, 14 Jan. 1860; Ruyle Memoir, pp. 2, 4; *History of Hickory, Polk, Cedar, Dade and Barton Counties, Missouri* (Chicago: Goodspeed, 1889), p. 343.

18. *History of Polk County, Missouri*, p. 331; 1850 and 1860 Polk County, Missouri, Census Records; Maxine Dunaway, *1840 Polk County Census* (Springfield, Mo.: Maxine Dunaway, 1978), p. 91; *History of Hickory, Polk, Cedar, Dade and Barton Counties, Missouri*, p. 331; Mitchell Family Papers; *History of Hickory, Polk, Cedar, Dade and Barton Counties, Missouri*, p. 758.

19. Compiled Missouri Service Records; Avington Wayne Simpson Diary, Western Historical Manuscript Collections, State Historical Society of Missouri, Columbia, Missouri; Mitchell Family Papers; Reverend Benjamin Looney Mitchell, "A Confederate Participant Describes the Battle of Wilson Creek," *Ozark Mountaineer* 7 (Feb. 1959): 6.

20. Compiled Missouri Service Records; Mitchell Family Papers; Boyce Scrapbook, Missouri Historical Society, St. Louis; *History of Polk County, Missouri*, p. 696; Simpson Diary.

21. Mitchell Family Papers; Warren Diary; Bevier, *History of the First and Second Missouri Confederate Brigades*, pp. 326–27; Compiled Missouri Service Records; Mitchell Family Papers; Ruyle Memoir, p. 6; Simpson Diary.

22. Compiled Missouri Service Records; *History of Randolph County, Missouri*, p. 675; Dysart to Fannie Sharp, 18 Nov. 1863; Adjutant General of Missouri Records.

23. Compiled Missouri Service Records; 1860 Henry County, Missouri, Census Records; Simpson Diary; Albert Herman Norton, *Rebel Religion: The Story of Confederate Chaplains* (St. Louis: Bethany, 1961), p. 115.

24. The 1860 Henry County, Missouri, Census Records; Uel W. Lamkin, *History of Henry County, Missouri* (Topeka, Kans.: Historical Publishing Company, 1919), pp. 134–36; Compiled Missouri Service Records; Mrs. Mary E. Owen to Skaggs, 9 Nov. 1914, Skaggs Collection, box 3, folder 20; Warren Diary; Thomas Hogan to Father, 22 July 1863, Civil War Collection, box 3, Missouri Historical Society, St. Louis.

25. Adjutant General of Missouri Records; Compiled Missouri Service

Records; 1860 and 1850 Johnson County, Missouri, Census Records; *History of Johnson County, Missouri*, pp. 668–69, 879; Thomas L. Connell and Barbara L. Bellows, *God and General Longstreet: The Lost Cause and the Southern Mind* (Baton Rouge: Louisiana State University Press, 1982), p. 2.

26. Howard Michael Madaus and Robert D. Needham, *The Battle Flags of the Confederate Army of Tennessee* (Milwaukee: Milwaukee Public Museum, 1976), pp. 133–37; 1860 United States Population Census, pp. 286–87; Compiled Missouri Service Records; Bevier, *History of the First and Second Missouri Confederate Brigades*, pp. 308–9.

27. Compiled Missouri Service Records; Nichols, "The Civil War in Johnson County, Missouri," p. 15; *Official Records*, vol. 24, ser. 1, pt. 1, p. 669.

28. Compiled Missouri Service Records; *History of Johnson County, Missouri*, pp. 107–8, 194; W. H. King, "Early Experiences in Missouri," *Confederate Veteran* 17, no. 10 (Oct. 1909): 502–3; Reverend George Miller, *Missouri's Memorable Decade 1860–1870: An Historical Sketch — Personal — Political — Religious* (Columbia, Mo.: E. W. Stephens, 1898), p. 41; Cockrell, *History of Johnson County, Missouri*, pp. 710, 723.

29. Compiled Missouri Service Records; Milton D. Rafferty, *Historical Atlas of Missouri* (Norman: University of Oklahoma, 1981), plate no. 12.

30. Compiled Missouri Service Records; Simpson Diary; *History of Hickory, Polk, Dade, Cedar and Barton Counties, Missouri*, p. 277; Maxine Dunaway, *1862 Rebel List of Polk County, Missouri, including Slave Owners from 1861 Tax Assessment Book* (Springfield: Maxine Dunaway, 1984), p. 72; *Bolivar Weekly Courier*, 28 Jan. 1860, 25 Feb. 1860, 22 Dec. 1860, and 4 May 1861; Herbert Aptheker, *American Negro Slave Revolts* (New York: International, 1974), p. 353; Mitchell Family Papers; "Polk County Rangers," *The Résumé: Newsletter of the Historical Society of Polk County, Missouri* (Jan. 1991).

31. *History of Vernon County, Missouri* (Chicago: Goodspeed, 1911), vol. 1, p. 258; *Bolivar Weekly Courier*, 14 July 1860; John P. Shield to John F. Snyder, 11 May 1861, John F. Snyder Papers, box 2-3, 1860–69, Missouri Historical Society, St. Louis.

32. Mitchell Family Papers; *Bolivar Weekly Courier*, 14 July 1860; *St. Louis Daily Evening News*, 28 Nov. 1860; *Bolivar Weekly Courier*, 29 Sept. 1860; *Daily Missouri Democrat*, 14 December 1860; John Knapp Collection in the Camp Jackson Papers, Missouri Historical Society, St. Louis; R. I. Holcombe to John F. Snyder, 2 Nov. 1886; Compiled Missouri Service Records.

33. James Bradburn to Skaggs, April 1923, Skaggs Collection, box 1, folder 3; Simpson Diary; Ruyle Memoir, p. 1; *History of Hickory, Polk, Dade, Cedar and Barton Counties, Missouri*, p. 318.

34. Compiled Missouri Service Records; Ruyle Memoir, pp. 1, 3; Simpson Diary.

35. Compiled Missouri Service Records; 1860 Polk County, Missouri, Census Records; Lemmon Family Papers, Joe Lemmon, Bolivar, Missouri; *History of Hickory, Polk, Cedar, Dade and Barton Counties, Missouri*, pp. 318–19; Boyce Scrapbook; *The United States Biographical Dictionary, Missouri*, pp. 612–13; Adjutant General of Missouri Records; Simpson Diary; *Official Records*, vol. 45, ser. 1, pt. 1, p. 1235.

36. Warren Diary; Compiled Missouri Service Records; Bevier, *History of the First and Second Missouri Confederate Brigades*, p. 340; 1860 Franklin County, Missouri, Census Records.

37. Warren Diary; Compiled Missouri Service Records; Bevier, *History of the First and Second Missouri Confederate Brigades,* p. 340.

38. Warren Diary; Warren to Father, 10 Jan. 1863, in private collection of Warren letters in possession of Ellen R. Deremer, Alexandra, Virginia; Herman Gottlieb Kiel, *The Centennial Biographical Directionary of Franklin County, Missouri* (Washington, D.C.: H. G. Kiel, 1925), p. 94; Compiled Missouri Service Records; *History of Franklin, Jefferson, Washington, Crawford, Gasconade Counties, Missouri* (Chicago: Goodspeed, 1888), p. 338; Warren Collection.

39. Compiled Missouri Service Records; 1860 St. Louis, Missouri, Census Records; Kennedy's St. Louis City Directory of 1860, p. 71; Warren Diary.

40. Joseph Boyce, Introduction to the Hogan letters to Father, Missouri Historical Society, St. Louis; *St. Louis Missouri Republican,* 4 Dec. 1884; Compiled Missouri Service Records; Camp Jackson Papers, Missouri Historical Society, St. Louis; Joseph Boyce, "Military Organizations of St. Louis," pp. 22, 68, 71–73, Missouri Historical Society, St. Louis; Babcock Scrapbook, Missouri Historical Society, St. Louis; Anderson, *Memoirs,* p. 32.

41. Compiled Missouri Service Records; 1860 St. Louis, Missouri, Census Records; Boyce, "Military Organizations," pp. 73–76; Michael McGrath to Marie L. Dalton, 12 May 1905, Civil War Papers 1900–1962, Missouri Historical Society, St. Louis; Basil Duke, *Reminiscences of Basil Duke* (New York: 1969), p. 52; 1860 St. Louis, Missouri, Census Records; Martin G. Towey, "Kerry Patch Revisited: Irish Americans in St. Louis in the Turn of the Century Era," in Timothy J. Meagher, ed., *Irish-American Communities in the Turn of the Century Era 1880–1920* (New York: Greenwood, 1986), pp. 143–45.

42. Towey, "Kerry Patch Revisited," p. 5; *From Kerry Patch to Little Paderhorn: A Visit in the Irish-German Communities of Nineteenth Century St. Louis* (St. Louis: Landmarks Association of St. Louis, 1966), pp. 4–6, 142.

43. Compiled Missouri Service Records; 1860 St. Louis, Missouri, Census Records; John O' Hanlon, *Life and Scenery in Missouri: Reminiscences of a Missionary Priest* (Dublin: James Duffy, 1890), pp. 141, 224–25; Albert C. Danner, Historical Memorandum, Dorothy Danner Tribets, Mobile, Alabama, p. 20; James Neal Primm, *Lion of the Valley: St. Louis, Missouri* (Bolder, Colo.: Pruett, 1981), p. 173; Reverend John Joseph Horgan, *On the Mission in Missouri 1857–1868* (Kansas City: John A. Heilmann, 1892), p. 38; Bevier, *History of the First and Second Missouri Confederate Brigades,* pp. 307, 330.

44. *St. Louis Missouri Republican,* 5 Dec. 1884; Boyce, "Military Organizations," p. 77; Michael K. McGrath to Marie L. Dalton, 12 May 1905.

45. Compiled Missouri Service Records; 1860 St. Louis, Missouri, Census Records; William Barnaby Faherty, *Better the Dream, Saint Louis: University and Community, 1818–1968* (St. Louis: St. Louis University, 1968), p. 101; Stanley, Wilson, and Wilson, *Death Records,* p. 178; Meagher, ed., *Irish-American Communities,* pp. 143–45.

46. Bevier, *History of the First and Second Missouri Confederate Brigades,* p. 313; St. John's Evangelist Church Archives, St. Louis, Missouri; 1860 St. Louis, Missouri, Census Records; Babcock Scrapbook; Kennedy's 1859 St. Louis City Directory Appendix, pp. 38–39; Michael McEnnis to Joseph Boyce, 22 July 1907, Camp Jackson Papers; Meagher, ed., *Irish-American Communities,* p. 155; Billion Scrapbook, 2, Missouri Historical Society, St. Louis; Boyce, "Military Organizations," p. 71; Martin G. Towey and Margaret Lopiccolo Sullivan, "The Knights of

Father Mathew: Parallel Ethnic Reform," *Missouri Historical Review* 75, no. 2, (Jan. 1981): p. 172.

47. John Bannon Diary, Yates Snowden Collection, South Caroliniana Library, University of South Carolina, Columbia, South Carolina; Billion Scrapbook, 2; St. John's Evangelist Church Archives.

48. Warren to Father, 21 June 1863; Compiled Missouri Service Records; *St. Louis Missouri Republican*, 5 Dec. 1884; 1860 St. Louis, Missouri, Census Records; Seumas MacManus, *The Story of the Irish Race* (New York: Devin-Adair, 1944), p. 532; Mark Wyman, *Immigrants in the Valley: Irish, Germans and Americans in the Upper Mississippi Country 1830–1860* (Chicago: Nelson-Hall, 1984), pp. 20–25; William Barnaby Faherty, *The Catholic Ancestry of Saint Louis* (St. Louis: Bureau of Information, Archdiocese of Saint Louis, 1965), p. 27.

49. Joseph M. Hernon, Jr., "The Irish Nationalists and Southern Secession," *Civil War History* 12, no. 1 (March 1966): 43–48; McElroy, *Struggle for Missouri*, p. 38; Babcock Scrapbook; Camp Jackson Papers; Boyce, "Military Organizations," p. 68; *Daily Missouri Democrat*, 12 Dec. 1860.

50. *Daily Missouri Democrat*, 23 Feb. 1858.

51. St. Louis Directory, 1854–1855, p. 28; 1860 Kennedy's St. Louis City Directory, p. 87; 1860 St. Louis, Missouri, Census Records; Camp Jackson Papers.

52. Edward Edwards, *History of the Volunteer Fire Department of St. Louis* (St. Louis: Veteran Volunteer Fireman's Historical Society, 1906), pp. 130–31; A. B. Lampe, "St. Louis Fire Department 1820–1850," *Missouri Historical Review* 62, no. 3 (April 1968): p. 236.

53. Duke, *Reminiscences*, p. 52; 1860 St. Louis, Missouri, Census Records; 1860 Kennedy's St. Louis City Directory, p. 91; Boyce, "Military Organizations," pp. 71, 92–93; Compiled Missouri Service Records.

54. 1859 Kennedy's St. Louis City Directory Appendix, p. 47; William B. Faherty, *Dream by the River: Two Centuries of Saint Louis Catholicism, 1766–1967* (St. Louis: Piraeus, 1973), pp. 81–83; G. Engelmann to Soulard, 24 Nov. 1854, Antonine P. Soulard Papers, Missouri Historical Society, St. Louis; John C. Schneider, "Riot and Reaction in St. Louis, 1854–1856," *Missouri Historical Review* 68, no. 2 (Jan. 1974), pp. 171–85; Primm, *Lion of the Valley*, p. 173; Harrison Anthony Trexler, *Slavery in Missouri 1804–1865* (Baltimore: Johns Hopkins Press, 1914), p. 19.

55. McElroy, *The Struggle for Missouri*, p. 38; Neal Primm and Steven Rowan, Introduction to *Germans for a Free Missouri: Translations from the St. Louis Radical Press 1857– 1862* (Columbia: University of Missouri Press, 1983), p. 228.

56. Earl F. Niehaus, *The Irish in New Orleans 1800–1860* (Baton Rouge: Louisiana State University Press, 1965), p. 158; *St. Louis Missouri Republican*, 5 March 1861; John Coleman, Jr., "The Riots at St. Louis, Missouri—1861," p. 2, Camp Jackson Papers.

57. Babcock Scrapbook; William C. Breckenridge Papers, p. 8, Western Historical Manuscript Collection, State Historical Society of Missouri, Columbia, Missouri.

58. *St. Louis Missouri Republican*, 5 Dec. 1888; Compiled Missouri Service Records; *St. Louis Missouri Republican*, 5 Dec. 1884; McNamara, "An Historical Sketch of the Sixth Division, Missouri State Guard," p. 29, Missouri Historical Society, St. Louis.

59. Compiled Missouri Service Records; Bannon Diary; Danner, "Historical Memorandum," p. 20; Anderson, *Memoirs*, p. 51.

60. Boyce Scrapbook; Bevier, *History of the First and Second Missouri Confederate Brigades*, p. 406; *Official Records*, vol. 38, ser. 1, pt, 3, p. 919; Compiled Missouri Service Records; *St. Louis Missouri Republican*, 5 Dec. 1884.

61. Compiled Missouri Service Records; 1860 St. Louis, Missouri, Census Records; 1860 Kennedy's St. Louis City Directory, p. 247; 1859 Kennedy's St. Louis City Directory, p. 236; Thomas Hogan to Ellen, 1 May 1864, and Hogan to Father, 22 July 1863, Missouri Historical Society, St. Louis.

62. Compiled Missouri Service Records; Bevier, *History of the First and Second Missouri Confederate Brigades*, pp. 2, 401, Appendix; 1860 Henry County, Missouri, Census Records; Mrs. Mary E. Owen to Skaggs, 9 Nov. 1914, Skaggs Collection, box 3, folder 20; Miscellaneous Paper of the John Stevens Bowen Collection, Missouri Historical Society, St. Louis.

63. Compiled Missouri Service Records.

64. Compiled Missouri Service Records; Brauckman Scrapbook, Missouri Historical Society, St. Louis.

65. Compiled Missouri Service Records; *Portrait and Biographical Record of Ralls, Marion, Pike and Randolph Counties, Missouri*, p. 1895; Rafferty, *Historical Atlas of Missouri*, plate no. 11; *History of Randolph and Macon Counties, Missouri*, pp. 1160–61; *General History of Macon County, Missouri*, p. 299; Walter Williams, *History of Northeast Missouri*, 3 vols. (Chicago: Lewis, 1913), vol. 3, p. 1450.

66. *General History of Macon County, Missouri*, pp. 178–79, 300; *History of Randolph and Macon Counties, Missouri*, pp. 1160–61; R. C. Ewing, *Historical Memoirs: Containing a Brief History of the Cumberland Presbyterian Church in Missouri and Biographical Sketches of a Number of Ministers Who Contributed to the Organization and the Establishment of that Church in the Country West of the Mississippi* (Nashville: Cumberland Presbyterian Board of Publication, 1874), pp. 267–70; *General History of Macon County, Missouri*, p. 300; Williams, *History of Northeast Missouri*, vol. 3, p. 1449; *Portrait and Biographical Portrait of Ralls, Marion, Pike and Randolph Counties, Missouri*, p. 1895; *History of Randolph and Macon Counties, Missouri*, p. 1161.

67. Williams, *History of Northeast Missouri*, vol. 3, p. 1449; *General History of Macon County, Missouri*, pp. 178, 300–1; M. W. Barton to Benjamin Eli Guthrie, 13 Aug. 1864, Bedford Family Papers, folder no. 14, Western Historical Manuscript Collection, State Historical Society of Missouri, Columbia, Missouri; Compiled Missouri Service Records; *History of Randolph and Macon Counties, Missouri*, p. 1162; List of First Missouri Brigade Recruiters in Warren Collection of Ellen Warren.

68. Douglas, *History of Southeast Missouri*, pp. 559, 836; Compiled Missouri Service Records; "Colonel David Young Pankey," *Confederate Veteran* 18, no. 4 (April 1910); p. 179; Floyd C. Shoemaker, *Missouri and Missourians: Land of Contrasts and People of Achievements* (Chicago: Lewis, 1943), vol. 4, p. 475; Mary F. Smyth-Davis, *History of Dunklin County, Missouri, 1845–1895* (St. Louis: Nixon-Jones, 1896), p. 232; Pankey Family Papers in possession of Mrs. Mary Pankey, Cardwell, Missouri.

69. Douglas, *History of Southeast Missouri*, pp. 309, 836–38; 1860 Dunklin County, Missouri, Census Records; Pankey Family Papers; *History of Southeast*

*Missouri* (Chicago: Goodspeed, 1888), pp. 308–9; *Campbell's Gazetteer of Missouri* (St. Louis: R. A. Campbell, 1874), p. 199.

70. Roy Godsey, "Southeast Missouri: An Agricultural Empire," *Monthly Bulletin of the Missouri State Board of Agriculture* 21, no. 10 (Oct. 1923), pp. 3–5; Miles Horner, *History and Genealogy of Buffalo Township, Cardwell, Missouri 1843–1972* (Kennett, Mo.: Guy Derby, 1973), pp. 3–4; Compiled Missouri Service Records; Douglas, *History of Southeast Missouri*, p. 309; Smyth-Davis, *History of Dunklin County*, pp. 232–33.

71. Organization and Status of Missouri Troops in Service During the Civil War, p. 266; *Daily Avalanche*, Memphis, Tennessee, 24 June 1861; Charles Chaney to Skaggs, 8 March 1913, Skaggs Collection, box 1, folder 3; Godsey, "Southeast Missouri," pp. 3–6.

72. Godsey, "Southeast Missouri," pp. 4, 5, 8; Edison Shrum, *The History of Scott County, Missouri; Up to the Year 1880* (Sikeston: Standard Printing Company, Scott County Historical Society), p. 116; Trexler, *Slavery in Missouri*, p. 26; Duane Meyer, *The Heritage of Missouri — A History* (St. Louis: State Publishing Company, 1973), pp. 317, 377; Compiled Missouri Service Records; 1860 Dunklin County, Missouri, Census Records.

73. Smyth-Davis, *History of Dunklin County*, p. 234; *History of Southeast Missouri*, pp. 506–7; Pankey Family Papers; *St. Louis Missouri Republican*, 8 Dec. 1861; Jay Monaghan, *Swamp Fox of the Confederacy: The Life and Military Services of M. Jeff Thompson* (Tuscaloosa: Confederate Publishing Company, 1956), pp. 30–50; Douglas, *History of Southeast Missouri*, p. 309; Monaghan, *Swamp Fox of the Confederacy*, p. 32; Stanton, Berquist, and Bowen, "Missouri's Forgotten General," p. 249; Monaghan, *Civil War on the Western Border*, p. 158.

74. Jay Carlton Mullen, "Pope's New Madrid and Island Number Ten Campaigns," *Missouri Historical Review* 59, no. 3 (April 1965): 330–32, 340–43; Stanton, Berquist, and Bowen, "Missouri's Forgotten General," pp. 249–50; Compiled Missouri Service Records; Douglas, *History of Southeast Missouri*, p. 309; Compiled Missouri Service Records; Robert H. Forister, *History of Stoddard County, Missouri*, (n.p.: Stoddard County Historical Society, n.d.), p. 29; Warren Diary.

75. Compiled Missouri Service Records; Felix Snider and Earl Collins, *Cape Girardeau: Biography of a City* (Cape Girardeau, Mo.: Ramfire, 1956), p. 39; Horner, *History and Genealogy of Buffalo Township*, p. 4; Duke, *Reminiscences*, pp. 80–84; Compiled Missouri Service Records.

76. *Daily Missouri Democrat*, 14 Dec. 1860.

77. Compiled Missouri Service Records.

78. 1860 Johnson, Polk, and Macon County, Missouri, Census Records.

79. *General History of Macon County, Missouri*, pp. 248–49; Trexler, *Slavery in Missouri*, p. 26n; 1860 United States Population Census, pp. 286–87; *History of Randolph and Macon Counties, Missouri*, p. 740n; R. Douglas Hurt, *Agriculture and Slavery in Missouri's Little Dixie* (Columbia: University of Missouri Press, 1992), pp. 80–82, 87, 102.

80. Compiled Missouri Service Records; 1860 Polk, Macon, and Johnson County, Missouri, Census Records; Snead, *The Fight for Missouri*, p. 239; Charles M. Wiltse, *The Jeffersonian Tradition in American Democracy* (New York: Hill and Wang, 1960), pp. 96, 98–99, 102–3, 127–28, 139–44, 250–51; Merrill D. Peterson, *The Jefferson Image in the American Mind* (New York: Oxford University Press, 1960), pp. 81–85, 216–18; Henry C. Dethloff, ed., *Thomas Jefferson and American*

*Democracy* (Lexington, Mass.: D. C. Heath, 1971), pp. vii, viii, x, 4–5, 9–10, 39–58; Karl Lehmann, *Thomas Jefferson: American Humanist* (New York: MacMillan, 1947), pp. 205–6.

81. Compiled Missouri Service Records; Francis Marion Cockrell to Mrs. Stamp, 7 June 1853, Western Historical Manuscript Collection, State Historical Society of Missouri, Columbia, Missouri; Francis Marion Cockrell Scrapbook, 7; Ewing, *History of the Cumberland Presbyterian Church*, p. 39; Bob Priddy, *Across Our Wide Missouri*, 2 vols. (Independence: Providence Press, 1982–84), vol. 1, pp. 65–66, 117–19; Stevens, *Centennial History of Missouri*, vol. 2, pp. 41–42; *History of Macon County, Missouri*, pp. 144–45; *History of Lewis, Clark, Knox and Scotland Counties, Missouri* (Chicago: Goodspeed, 1887), pp. 176–79; Historic Homes of Missouri Scrapbook, 9, Missouri Historical Society, St. Louis.

82. Compiled Missouri Service Records; Bevier, *History of the First and Second Missouri Confederate Brigades*, p. 13.

83. William Henry Kavanaugh Memoir, 2, unpublished memoir in the Western Historical Manuscripts Collection, State Historical Society of Missouri, Columbia, Missouri; Snead, *The Fight for Missouri*, pp. 93–94; Russell L. Gerlach, *Settlement Patterns in Missouri: A Study of Population Origins* (Columbia: University of Missouri Press, 1986), pp. 19–23; Rafferty, *Historical Atlas of Missouri*, plate no. 36; Compiled Missouri Service Records; *Richmond Enquirer*, 22 June 1861; Anderson, *Memoirs*, p. 12; 1860 Polk, Macon, and Johnson County, Missouri, Census Records; Bevier,*History of the First and Second Missouri Confederate Brigades*, p. 276.

84. Thomas A. Harris, "Speech of the Hon. Thomas A. Harris Delivered at the Camp of the First Missouri Brigade, C.S.A., April 30th, 1864, near Tuscaloosa, Alabama," (Cleveland: Western Reserve Historical Society, n.d.); Arthur R. Kirkpatrich, "Missouri's Delegation in the Confederate Congress," *Civil War History* 5, no. 2 (June 1959), p. 197; James Payne "Early Days of War in Missouri," *Confederate Veteran* 37, no. 2 (Feb. 1931), p. 58.

85. Babcock Scrapbook; Snead, *Fight for Missouri*, p. 112; C. Vann Woodward, *American Counterpoint: Slavery and Racism in the North-South Dialogue* (Boston: Little, Brown and Company, 1971), p. 22; Boyce, "Military Organizations," pp. 25–26, 93; Compiled Missouri Service Records; State of Missouri House of Representatives Journal, Twenty-First Assembly, First Session, Appendix, p. 762.

86. Bevier, *History of the First and Second Missouri Confederate Brigades*, p. 307; Kavanaugh Memoir, p. 9.

87. Charles W. Ramsdell, "The Natural Limits of Slavery Expansion," in Edwin C. Rozwenc, ed., *The Causes of the American Civil War* (Boston: D. C. Heath, 1961), pp. 160–62; *Bolivar Weekly Courier*, 5 Sept. 1857.

88. Rafferty, *Historical Atlas of Missouri*, plate no. 36; George Wilson Pierson, "The Frontier and American Institutions, A Criticism of the Turner Theory," in George Rogers Taylor, ed., *The Turner Thesis, Concerning the Role of the Frontier in American History* (Boston: D. C. Heath, 1956), p. 59; Howard Wight Marshall, *Folk Architecture in Little Dixie: A Regional Culture in Missouri* (Columbia: University of Missouri Press, 1981), p. 7.

89. Reverend George Miller, *Missouri's Memorable Decade*, pp. 33–34; *History of Randolph and Macon Counties, Missouri*, p. 720; C. Vann Woodward, "The Southern Ethnic in a Puritan World," in Patrick Gerster and Nicholas Cords,

eds., *Myth and Southern History: The Old South* (Chicago: Rand McNally, 1974), p. 719.

90. William J. Cooper, Jr., *Liberty and Slavery: Southern Politics to 1860* (New York: Knopf, 1983), pp. 267–71; Grady McWhiney and Robert Wiebe, eds., *Historical Vistas: Readings in United States History* (Boston: Allyn and Bacon, 1963), p. 34; Dethloff, *Thomas Jefferson and American Democracy*, pp. 39–58; Cooper, *Liberty and Slavery*, pp. 282–85.

91. Lamkin, *History of Henry County, Missouri*, pp. 134–36.

92. Robert E. Shalhope, "Eugene Genovese, The Missouri Elite and Civil War Historiography," *Bulletin of the Missouri Historical Society* 26, no. 4, pt. 1 (July 1970): 277–78.

93. *Bolivar Weekly Courier*, 18 May 1861; Warren to Father, 10 Jan. 1863; Edward C. Robbins to Sister, 5 June 1862, Mercantile Library Archives, St. Louis; James Kennerly to Sister, 8 Aug. 1864, Kennerly Family Papers, Missouri Historical Society, St. Louis; *Bolivar Weekly Courier*, 14 April 1861.

94. Warren Diary.

95. *Bolivar Weekly Courier*, 15 Dec. 1860; Drew Gilpin Faust, *The Creation of Confederate Nationalism: Ideology and Identity in the Civil War South* (Baton Rouge: Louisiana State University Press, 1988), pp. 14–15; Alice E. Cayton to Alexander Badger, 12 May 1861, Badger Collection, Missouri Historical Society, St. Louis; Bevier, *History of the First and Second Missouri Confederate Brigades*, p. 14; Warren Diary; *Organization and Status of Missouri Troops in Service During the Civil War*, (Washington, D.C.: U.S. Government Printing Office, 1902), p. 294; *Bolivar Weekly Courier*, 18 May 1861; J. Cutler Andrews, *The South Reports the Civil War* (Princeton, N.J.: Princeton University Press, 1970), p. 247; Anderson, *Memoirs*, p. 47.

96. Frank Moore, ed., *The Rebellion Record*, II vols. (New York: n.p., 1862–1868), pp. 66–67, 480; *Bolivar Weekly Courier*, 18 May 1861; Compiled Missouri Service Records.

97. Warren Diary; *Organization and Status of Missouri Troops*, p. 293; Absalom Roby Dyson to wife, no date, Absalom Roby Dyson letters, Western Historical Manuscript Collection, University of Missouri–St. Louis; Dysart to Fannie Sharp, 18 Nov. 1863, in Compiled Missouri Service Records; Dyson to Mrs. Robertson, 3 Feb. 1864; Dyson to Mrs. Robertson, 23 Dec. 1863.

98. Cockrell, *History of Johnson County, Missouri*, p. 220.

99. King, "Early Experience in Missouri," pp. 502–3; Francis Marion Cockrell, 12 Sept. 1863 report to General Samuel Cooper, Virginia Historical Society, Richmond, Virginia; Francis Marion Cockrell Scrapbook; *St. Louis Missouri Republican*, 30 Jan. 1886; Warren Diary; *Organization and Status of Missouri Troops*, pp. 293, 298; Warren to Father, 21 June 1863.

100. Snead, *Fight for Missouri*, p. 239; 1860 Johnson, Macon, and Polk Counties, Missouri, Census Records; Meyer, *Heritage of Missouri*, p. 317; Ruyle Memoir, p. 2; Trexler, *Slavery in Missouri*, p. 18.

101. Trexler, *Slavery in Missouri*, p. 19; D. R. Hundley, *Social Relations in Our Southern States* (New York, Henry B. Price, 1860), p. 197; Hurt, *Agriculture and Slavery*, pp. 215–17, 238–42.

102. *Bolivar Weekly Courier*, 25 Feb. 1860; Joel Williamson, *New People: Miscegenation and Mulattoes in the United States* (New York: New York University Press, 1984), pp. 24–25, 65.

103. Trexler, *Slavery in Missouri*, p. 173; William E. Parrish, *A History of Missouri, 1860–1875*, 3 vols. (Columbia: University of Missouri, 1973), vol. 3, pp. 6–7; Compiled Missouri Service Records; 1860 Johnson County, Missouri, Census Records; Adjutant General of Missouri Records.

104. 1860 Franklin County, Missouri, Census Records; *History of Hickory, Polk, Cedar, Dade and Barton Counties, Missouri*, p. 275; 1860 Polk County, Missouri, Census Records.

105. Bevier, *History of the First and Second Missouri Confederate Brigades*, pp. 276–77, 351–53; Bell Irvin Wiley, *The Life of Billy Yank: The Common Soldier of the Union* (Baton Rouge: Louisiana State University Press, 1978), pp. 315, 327–28; 1860 Polk, Macon, Franklin, and Johnson Counties, Missouri, Census Records; Trexler, *Slavery in Missouri*, p. 19; Compiled Missouri Service Records.

106. Douglas, *History of Southeast Missouri*, pp. 559, 836; Joe Lemmon, Bolivar, Missouri, 15 Sept. 1987 interview by author; H. Riley Bock, New Madrid, Missouri, 18 Nov. 1987 interview by author, concerning his ancestor, Colonel Amos Camden Riley; Adjutant General of Missouri Records; Robert E. Acock to Major B. F. Robinson 9 Jan. 1858, Robert E. Acock Papers, 1854–1866, Collection No. 2166, Western Historical Manuscript Collection, State Historical Society of Missouri, Columbia, Missouri.

107. Bevier, *History of the First and Second Missouri Confederate Brigades*, pp. 352–53.

108. Compiled Missouri Service Records.

## Chapter II

1. George W. Warren Diary, George W. Warren, IV, Montpelier, Virginia; Avington Wayne Simpson Diary, Western Historical Manuscript Collections, State Historical Society of Missouri, St. Louis; Allan Nevins, *Ordeal of the Union, The War for the Union: War Becomes Revolution 1862–1863*, 8 vols. (New York: Charles Scribner's Sons, 1960), vol. 2, pp. 113, 152–53; Stanley Horn, *The Army of Tennessee*, (Norman: University of Oklahoma Press, 1952), pp. 172–73.

2. Warren Diary; Compiled Service Records of Confederate Soldiers Who Served in Organizations from the State of Missouri, Record Group 109, National Archives, Washington, D.C.

3. Robert Underwood Johnson and Clarence Clough Buel, eds., *Battles and Leaders of the Civil War*, 4 vols. (New York: Thomas Yoseloff, 1956), vol. 2, pp. 725–30; Warren Diary.

4. Warren Diary; Simpson Diary; *History of Johnson County, Missouri*, (Kansas City: Historical Company, 1881), p. 635.

5. Warren Diary; Compiled Missouri Service Records.

6. Warren Diary; Ben Earl Kitchens, *Rosecrans Meets Price: The Battle of Iuka, Mississippi* (Florence, Alabama: Thornwood, 1985), pp. 22–23; Compiled Missouri Service Records; Bevier, *History of the First and Second Missouri Confederate Brigades*, p. 397.

7. Albert Castel, *General Sterling Price and the Civil War in the West* (Baton Rouge: Louisiana State University, 1968), p. 97; Simpson Diary; Warren Diary; Kitchens, *Rosecrans Meets Price*, p. 26; John K. Bettersworth, *Confederate*

*Mississippi: The People and Policies of a Cotton State in Wartime* (Baton Rouge: Louisiana State University Press, 1943), pp. 188–89; Compiled Missouri Service Records; William A. Ruyle Memoir, Dee Ruyle, Bolivar, Missouri, pp. 17, 19, 21.

8. Simpson Diary; Compiled Missouri Service Records.

9. Warren Diary; Edwin Hedge Fay, *This Infernal War* (Austin: University of Texas Press, 1958), p. 132; Compiled Missouri Service Records; Simpson Diary; Ruyle Memoir, p. 14; Castel, *General Sterling Price*, p. 97; Johnson and Buel, eds., *Battles and Leaders*, vol. 2, pp. 730–31; Little Diary, U.S. Army Military Historical Institute, Carlisle, Pennsylvania.

10. Warren Diary; Johnson and Buel, eds., *Battles and Leaders*, vol. 2, pp. 730–31; *Richmond Enquirer*, 7 Oct. 1862.

11. Warren Diary; Simpson Diary; Kitchens, *Rosecrans Meets Price*, pp. 57–58; Anderson, *Memoirs*. p. 218; *Richmond Enquirer*, 7 Oct. 1862; Compiled Missouri Service Records; Bevier, *History of the First and Second Missouri Confederate Brigades*, p. 332.

12. Bevier, *History of the First and Second Missouri Confederate Brigades*, pp. 332–33.

13. Johnson and Buel, eds., *Battles and Leaders*, vol. 2, pp. 730–31; Castel, *General Sterling Price*, pp. 96–98.

14. Ulysses S. Grant, *Personal Memoirs of U.S. Grant* (New York: Century, 1903), pp. 211–13; Johnson and Buel, eds., *Battles and Leaders*, vol. 2, p. 731.

15. Little Diary; Johnson and Buel, eds., *Battles and Leaders*, vol. 2, pp. 731–32; Simpson Diary; Warren Diary; Ruyle Memoir, p. 17; William H. Tunnard, *A Southern Record: The History of the Third Regiment Louisiana Infantry* (Dayton: Morningside, 1970), p. 187; *Richmond Enquirer*, 10 Oct. 1861; Kitchens, *Rosecrans Meets Price*, pp. 67–68.

16. Warren Diary; Simpson Diary; Compiled Missouri Service Records; Mrs. Howard W. Woodruff, *Polk County Marriage Records, 1836–1959* (Kansas City: Mrs. Howard W. Woodruff, 1970), book A; Grant, *Memoirs*, p. 213; Castel, *General Sterling Price*, pp. 100–1; Johnson and Buel, eds., *Battles and Leaders*, vol. 2, pp. 731–32; Kitchens, *Rosecrans Meets Price*, p. 72; Francis V. Greene, *The Mississippi, Campaigns of the Civil War* (New York: Charles Scribner's Sons, 1885), vol. 8, p. 39.

17. Simpson Diary; Warren Diary; Ruyle Memoir, p. 18.

18. Greene, *The Mississippi*, p. 39; Grant, *Memoirs*, p. 213.

19. Greene, *The Mississippi*, pp. 39–40.

20. Greene, *The Mississippi*, p. 40; *Richmond Enquirer*, 7 Oct. 1862; Jack W. Gunn, "The Battle of Iuka," *The Journal of Mississippi History* 24, no. 3 (July 1962): 154; Johnson and Buel, eds., *Battles and Leaders*, vol. 2, p. 732; *Richmond Enquirer*, 7 Oct. 1862; Grant, *Memoirs*, p. 214; Warren Diary.

21. Greene, *The Mississippi*, pp. 39–42; Little Diary; Johnson and Buel, eds., *Battles and Leaders*, vol. 2, pp. 732–33; *Richmond Enquirer*, 7 Oct. 1862; Grant, *Memoirs*, p. 214; *Richmond Enquirer*, 7 Oct. 1862; Castel, *General Sterling Price*, pp. 101–2; Bannon Diary, Little Diary, Bannon's entry concerning Little's death; Bevier, *History of the First and Second Missouri Confederate Brigades*, pp. 130, 333; Lyla Merrill McDonald, *Iuka's History Embodying Dudley's Battle of Iuka* (Corinth: Rankin Printery, 1923), p. 18.

*History Embodying Dudley's Battle of Iuka* (Corinth: Rankin Printery, 1923), p. 18.

22. Bevier, *History of the First and Second Missouri Confederate Brigades*, p. 333; James Bradley, *The Confederate Mail Carrier* (Mexico: n.p., 1894), p. 70; Warren Diary; McDonald, *Iuka's History*, p. 18.

23. Bevier, *History of the First and Second Missouri Confederate Brigades*, p. 333; Warren Diary; Kitchens, *Rosecrans Meets Price*, p. 189.

24. Simpson Diary; Compiled Missouri Service Records; *History of Hickory, Polk, Cedar, Dade and Barton Counties, Missouri,* (Chicago: Goodspeed, 1889), p. 313; "The Blue and the Grey," John F. Snyder Papers, Missouri Historical Society, St. Louis; James W. Goodrich, "Robert Eaton Acock: The Gentleman from Polk," *Missouri Historical Review* 73, no. 3 (April 1979): 281–85.

25. Compiled Missouri Service Records; Bevier, *History of the First and Second Missouri Confederate Brigades*, p. 425; Phyllis E. Mears, *Macon County, Missouri, Obituaries 1889–1903* (Decorah, Mo.: Anundsen, 1987), pt. 1, p. 222.

26. Warren Diary; Anderson, *Memoirs*, pp. 222–23; Bevier, *History of the First and Second Missouri Confederate Brigades*, pp. 130, 333–34.

27. Compiled Missouri Service Records; Bevier, *History of the First and Second Missouri Confederate Brigades*, p. 334.

28. Anderson, *Memoirs*, pp. 224–25; Kitchens, *Rosecrans Meets Price*, pp. 142–43; Bevier, *History of the First and Second Missouri Confederate Brigades*, pp. 334–35.

29. Bevier, *History of the First and Second Missouri Confederate Brigades*, p. 334; Compiled Missouri Service Records; Warren Diary.

30. Compiled Missouri Service Records; Bevier, *History of the First and Second Missouri Confederate Brigades*, pp. 334–35.

31. Compiled Missouri Service Records; Ruyle Memoir, p. 18; Bevier, *History of the First and Second Missouri Confederate Brigades*, p. 334; Warren Diary; Ruyle Memoir, p. 18; Johnson and Buel, eds., *Battles and Leaders*, vol. 2, pp. 731–33; *Daily Picayune*, New Orleans, Louisiana, 11 Aug. 1901; Tyler to Yancy, 15 Oct. 1862, Western Historical Manuscript Collections, State Historical Society of Missouri, Columbia, Missouri; *Richmond Enquirer*, 10 Oct. 1861 and 7 Oct. 1862; Greene, *The Mississippi*, p. 41.

32. Johnson and Buel, eds., *Battles and Leaders*, vol. 2, pp. 733–34; *Richmond Enquirer*, 7 Oct. 1862; Kitchens, *Rosecrans Meets Price*, pp. 152–53; Bannon Diary; *Daily Picayune*, 11 Aug. 1901; Bevier, *History of the First and Second Missouri Confederate Brigades*, pp. 334–35; Warren Diary; John J. Fuller to Mary McEwen, 27 Sept. 1862, McEwen Papers, Missouri Historical Society, St. Louis.

33. Bevier, *History of the First and Second Missouri Confederate Brigades*, p. 335; Anderson, *Memoirs*, p. 225; Warren Diary; Compiled Missouri Service Records; *St. Louis Missouri Republican*, 5 Dec. 1884; J. H. Parker to Skaggs, 26 March 1912, Skaggs Collection, Arkansas History Commission, Little Rock, Arkansas.

34. Warren Diary; Bevier, *History of the First and Second Missouri Confederate Brigades*, pp. 136, 335–36; Kitchens, *Rosecrans Meets Price*, pp. 157–58; Compiled Missouri Service Records; Castel, *General Sterling Price*, pp. 103–4; *General History of Macon County, Missouri* (Chicago: Henry Taylor, 1910), p. 145.

35. Warren Diary; Compiled Missouri Service Records; Bevier, *History of the*

*First and Second Missouri Confederate Brigades,* p. 335; 1860 Kennedy's St. Louis City Directory, p. 444.

36. Warren Diary; Warren Letters, Private collection of Ellen R. Deremer, Alexandria, Virginia; Bevier, *History of the First and Second Missouri Confederate Brigades,* p. 336.

37. Compiled Missouri Service Records; Bevier, *History of the First and Second Missouri Confederate Brigades,* p. 336; Warren Diary.

38. Johnson and Buel, eds., *Battles and Leaders,* vol. 2, pp. 733–34; Warren Diary; Compiled Missouri Service Records.

## Chapter III

1. Warren Diary; Tyler to Yancy, 15 Oct. 1862, Western Historical Manuscript Collections, State Historical Society of Missouri, St. Louis; *Richmond Enquirer,* 18 Oct. 1862.

2. Tyler to Yancy, 15 Oct. 1862; Robert C. Black, III, *The Railroads of the Confederacy* (Chapel Hill: University of North Carolina Press, 1952), p. 139; George Edgar Turner, *Victory Rode the Rails: The Strategic Place of the Railroads in the Civil War* (New York: Bobbs-Merrill, 1953), pp. 120, 126–27, 226–27; Dabney H. Maury, "Recollections of Campaign against Grant in North Mississippi in 1862–1863," *Southern Historical Society Papers* 13 (Jan.–Dec. 1885): 292; Francis W. Greene, *The Mississippi, Campaigns of the Civil War* (New York: Charles Scribner's Sons, 1885), vol. 8, pp. 42–43.

3. Maury, "Recollections of Campaign Against Grant," pp. 286–87, 292–93; Robert G. Hartje, *Van Dorn,* (Nashville: Vanderbilt University Press, 1967), pp. 215–16; Thomas L. Connelly, *Civil War Tennessee: Battles and Leaders* (Knoxville: University of Tennessee Press, 1979), p. 54.

4. Warren Diary; William E. Parrish, "The Palmyra 'Massacre': A Tragedy of Guerilla Warfare," *Journal of Confederate History* 1, no. 2 (Winter 1988): 243–64; *Official Records,* vol. 8, ser. 1, pp. 908–10; Compiled Service Records of Confederate Soldiers Who Served in Organizations from the State of Missouri, Record Group 109, National Archives, Washington, D.C.; Maury, Recollections of Campaign Against Grant," p. 293.

5. Warren Diary.

6. William A. Ruyle Memoir, Dee Ruyle, Bolivar, Missouri, p. 18; Compiled Service Records.

7. Tyler to Yancy, 15 Oct. 1862; *St. Louis Missouri Republican,* 6 Sept. 1884; *Richmond Enquirer,* 18 Oct. 1862.

8. Warren Diary; Hogan to Father, 12 Oct. 1862, Missouri Historical Society, St. Louis; Ruyle Memoirs, p. 19.

9. Warren Diary; Bannon Diary; Bevier, *History of the First and Second Missouri Confederate Brigades,* p. 337; Ruyle Memoir, Introduction; *Richmond Enquirer,* 17 Oct. 1862.

10. Compiled Missouri Service Records; Hogan to Father, 12 Oct. 1862; Daniel Steele Durree, *An Illustrated History of Missouri* (Cincinnati: R. Clarke, 1876), p. 547; Michael K. McGrath to Marie L. Dalton, 12 May 1905, Missouri Historical Society, St. Louis; *St. Louis Missouri Republican,* 2 July 1888; Necrologies Scrapbook, vols. 6 and 7, pp. 1, 4, Missouri Historical Society, St. Louis.

11. Johnson and Buel, eds., *Battles and Leaders*, vol. 2, p. 760.

12. Johnson and Buel, eds. *Battles and Leaders*, vol. 2, p. 743; Grant, *Memoirs*, pp. 215–16; Tyler to Yancy, 15 and 18 Oct. 1862; Bannon Diary; *Richmond Enquirer*, 18 Oct. 1862; "Diary of Lieutenant Colonel Hubbell of 3d Regiment Missouri Infantry, C.S.A.," *The Land We Love* 6, no. 2, p. 99; Compiled Missouri Service Records.

13. *The War of the Rebellion: A Compilation of the Official Records of the Union and Confederate Armies*, 128 vols. (Washington, D.C., 1880–1901), vol. 17, ser. 1, pt. 1, pp. 160, 166–67, 457; Monroe F. Cockrell, ed., *The Lost Account of the Battle of Corinth and the Court Martial of Gen. Van Dorn* (Jackson: McCowart Mercer, 1955), p. 63; Tyler to Yancy, 15 Oct. 1862.

14. William M. Lamers, *The Edge of Glory: A Biography of Gen. William S. Rosecrans, U.S.A.* (New York: Harcourt, Brace and World, 1961), p. 133; Maury, "Recollections of Campaign Against Grant," p. 294; Kenneth P. Williams, *Lincoln Finds a General: A Military Study of the Civil War*, 5 vols. (New York: MacMillan, 1949–1959), vol. 4, p. 86; Bevier, *History of the First and Second Missouri Confederate Brigades*, p. 337; Tyler to Yancy, 15 Oct. 1862; Bannon Diary.

15. Victor M. Rose, *Ross' Texas Brigade* (Louisville: Courier Journal, 1881 ), p. 72; Tyler to Yancy, 15 Oct. 1862; Maury, "Recollections of Campaign Against Grant," p. 294; *Richmond Enquirer*, 18 Oct. 1862; Edward C. Robbins to Sister, 16 Oct. 1862, Mercentile Library, St. Louis.

16. Bevier, *History of the First and Second Missouri Confederate Brigades*, pp. 148, 337; Tyler to Yancy, 15 Oct. 1862; *Richmond Enquirer*, 18 Oct. 1862; Johnson and Buel, eds., *Battles and Leaders*, vol. 2, pp. 744–45; *Richmond Enquirer*, 18 Oct. 1862.

17. Bevier, *History of the First and Second Missouri Confederate Brigades*, pp. 148–49, 337; Compiled Missouri Service Records; Babcock Scrapbook, Missouri Historical Society, St. Louis; Hogan to Father, 12 Oct. 1862; Stanley, Wilson, and Wilson, *Death Records from Missouri Newspapers: The Civil War Years, January 1861–December 1865* (Decorah, Mo.: Anundsen, 1983), p. 178; Calkins, Homer L., ed., "Elkhorn to Vicksburg: James H. Fauntelroy's Diary for the Year 1862," *Civil War History* 2 (Jan. 1956): 34; Robbins to Family, 16 Oct. 1862.

18. Bevier, *History of the First and Second Missouri Confederate Brigades*, pp. 148–49; Tyler to Yancy, 15 Oct. 1862; Ruyle Memoir, p. 19.

19. Ruyle Memoir, p. 19–20; Robbins to Family, 16 Oct. 1862; Bevier, *History of the First and Second Missouri Confederate Brigades*, pp. 149, 337–38.

20. Anderson, *Memoirs*, pp. 232–33; Bevier, *History of the First and Second Missouri Confederate Brigades*, pp. 149–50, 337–38; *Richmond Enquirer*, 18 Oct. 1862; Robbins to Family, 16 Oct. 1862, Mercentile Library, St. Louis, Ruyle Memoir, p. 20; Hogan to Father, 12 Oct. 1862.

21. Hogan to Father, 12 Oct. 1862; Bevier, *History of the First and Second Missouri Brigades*, pp. 151–53; Anderson, *Memoirs*, p. 234.

22. Bevier, *History of the First and Second Missouri Confederate Brigades*, pp. 151–52; Compiled Missouri Service Records; Hogan to Father, 12 Oct. 1862; 1860 Kennedy's St. Louis City Directory, p. 247.

23. Anderson, *Memoirs*, p. 234; Bevier, *History of the First and Second Missouri Confederate Brigades*, p. 151; Hogan to Father, 12 Oct. 1862; Compiled Missouri Service Records; St. Louis 1860 Census; *Official Records*, vol. 17, ser. 1,

pt. 1, pp. 262, 273; Johnson and Buel, eds., *Battles and Leaders*, vol. 2, p. 273; Boyce, "Military Organizations of St. Louis," pp. 72–73, Missouri Historical Society, St. Louis.

24. Ruyle Memoir, p. 20; Avington Wayne Simpson Diary, Western Historical Manuscript Collections, State Historical Society of Missouri, Columbia, Missouri. Compiled Missouri Service Records.

25. Anderson, *Memoirs*, pp. 234–35; Bevier, *History of the First and Second Missouri Confederate Brigades*, pp. 151–52; Hogan to Father, 12 Oct. 1862.

26. Bevier, *History of the First and Second Missouri Confederate Brigades*, pp. 338–40; *Organization and Status of Missouri Troops in Service During the Civil War*, p. 273; *Richmond Enquirer*, 17 Oct. 1862.

27. John B. Bannon, "Experiences of a Confederate Army Chaplain," *Letters and Notices of the English Jesuit Province* (Oct. 1867): pp. 3–4, 201–2. Bannon Diary; Compiled Missouri Service Records; Anderson, *Memoirs*, pp. 234–35; Hogan to Father, 12 Oct. 1862.

28. Bevier,*History of the First and Second Missouri Confederate Brigades*, pp. 140–41, 152, 338–39; Johnson and Buel, eds., *Battles and Leaders*, vol. 2, p. 748; Tyler to Yancy, 15 Oct. 1862; *Official Records*, vol. 17, ser. 1, pt. 1, pp. 415–16, 421–23; Hogan to Father, 12 Oct. 1862; Robbins to Family, 16 Oct. 1862; *Richmond Enquirer*, 18 Oct. 1862; Bannon Diary.

29. Bevier, *History of the First and Second Missouri Confederate Brigades*, pp. 338–39.

30. Bevier, *History of the First and Second Missouri Confederate Brigades*, p. 339; *Richmond Enquirer*, 7 Oct. 1862 and 18 Oct. 1862; Hartje, *Van Dorn*, pp. 226–28; Castel, *General Sterling Price*, pp. 113–14; *Official Records*, vol. 17, ser. 1, pt. 1, pp. 421–23.

31. Anderson, *Memoirs*, pp. 235–36; *Official Records*, vol. 17, ser. 1, pt. 1, pp. 262, 266, 273; Bevier, *History of the First and Second Missouri Confederate Brigades*, pp. 152–53; Alonzo Brown, *History of the Fourth Regiment of Minnesota Infantry Volunteers During the Great Rebellion* (St. Paul: Pioneer Press, 1892), p. 113; William Henry Kavanaugh Memoir, pp. 26–27, Western Historical Manuscripts Collection, State Historical Society of Missouri, Columbia, Missouri; Cockrell, *The Lost Account of the Battle of Corinth*, map; Johnson and Buel, eds., *Battles and Leaders*, vol. 2, p. 749.

32. Bevier, *History of the First and Second Missouri Confederate Brigades*, p. 341; Hogan to Father, 12 Oct. 1862; Johnson and Buel, eds., *Battles and Leaders*, vol. 2, p. 741; Claude Gentry, *The Battle of Corinth* (Baldwyn: Magnolia, 1976), p. 30; *Richmond Enquirer*, 17 Oct. 1862; Evert Augustus Duychinck, *National History of the War for the Union* 3 vols. (New York: Johnson, Fry, 1861–1865), vol. 2, pp. 623–24; *Official Records*, vol. 17, ser. 1, pt. 1, pp. 215, 238, 240–41, 391; Kavanaugh Memoir, p. 27; Anderson, *Memoirs*, pp. 236–37; Joseph E. Chance, *The Second Texas Infantry: From Shiloh to Vicksburg* (Austin: Eakin, 1984), p. 70; *Richmond Enquirer*, 17 Oct. 1862; William Hyde and Howard L. Conrad, *Encyclopedia of the History of St. Louis*, 4 vols. (St. Louis: Southern Historical Company, 1899), vol. 4, p. 2441.

33. Castel, *General Sterling Price*, pp. 114–15; Tyler to Yancy, 15 Oct. 1862; *Richmond Enquirer*, 18 Oct. 1862.

34. Maury, "Recollections of Campaign Against Grant," p. 296; Greene, *The*

*Mississippi,*, p. 49; Tyler to Yancy, 15 Oct. 1862; *Official Records*, vol. 17, ser. 1, pt. 1, pp. 379, 387; James Gordon, "The Battle and Retreat from Corinth," *Mississippi State Historical Society Publications*, 4 (1901): 67; Lamers, *The Edge of Glory*, vol. 4, p. 155; Williams, *Lincoln Finds a General*, p. 85.

35. Compiled Missouri Service Records; Bannon, "Experience of a Confederate Chaplain," p. 202.

36. Bevier, *History of the First and Second Missouri Confederate Brigades*, pp. 152–53; *Official Records*, vol. 17, ser. 1, pt. 1, pp. 190, 262, 273–74, 391; Kavanaugh Memoir, p. 27; Compiled Missouri Service Records; Brown, *History of the Fourth Regiment*, p. 113; A. M. Bedford to Mary Bedford, 14 Nov. 1862, Collection 2610, folder 8, Bedford Family Papers, Western Historical Manuscript Collection, State Historical Society of Missouri, Columbia, Missouri.

37. Tyler to Yancy, 15 Oct. 1862; Kavanaugh Memoir, p. 27; Bevier, *History of the First and Second Missouri Confederate Brigades*, p. 337.

38. Compiled Missouri Service Records; Howard Michael Madaus and Robert Needham, *The Battle Flags of the Confederate Army of Tennessee* (Milwaukee: Milwaukee Public Museum, 1976), pp. 37–42; Hogan to Father, 12 Oct. 1862; 1859 Kennedy's City of St. Louis Directory, p. 495; Stanley, Wilson, and Wilson, *Death Records*, p. 178.

39. Tyler to Yancy, 15 Oct. 1862; William Snyder to Parents, 25 Nov. 1862, William Snyder Letters, New Madrid Historical Museum, New Madrid, Missouri.

40. Bevier, *History of the First and Second Missouri Confederate Brigades*, pp. 340–41; Greene, *The Mississippi*, pp. 49–50; Tyler to Yancy, 15 Oct. 1862; *Richmond Enquirer*, 18 Oct. 1862; Maury, "Recollections of Campaign Against Grant," p. 296; James Bradley, *The Confederate Mail Carrier* (Mexico: n.p., 1894), p. 73.

41. Tyler to Yancy, 15 Oct. 1862.

42. Compiled Missouri Service Records; Johnson and Buel, eds., *Battles and Leaders*, vol. 2, p. 744; *Official Records*, vol. 17, ser. 1, pt. 1, p. 240; Johnson and Buel, eds., *Battles and Leaders*, vol. 2, pp. 741, 759; Charles F. Hubert, *History of the Fiftieth Illinois Infantry* (Kansas City: Western Veteran, 1894), p. 142; *Official Records*, vol. 17, ser. 1, pt. 1, pp. 238, 240, 258–60, 759.

43. Calkins, ed., "Elkhorn to Vicksburg," p. 35; Henry M. Alden and Alfred H. Guernsey, eds., *Harper's Pictorial History of the Civil War* (New York: Fairfax, n.d.), p. 317; Bradley, *Confederate Mail Carrier*, p. 73; Bevier, *History of the First and Second Missouri Confederate Brigades*, pp. 153, 341–42; Kavanaugh Memoir, p. 27; Hogan to Father, 12 Oct. 1862; *Official Records*, vol. 17, ser. 1, pt. 1, p. 259.

44. Hyde and Conrad, *Encyclopedia of the History of St. Louis*, vol. 4, p. 2441; Greene, *The Mississippi*, p. 50; *Official Records*, vol. 17, ser. 1, pt. 1, pp. 390–91; Robbins to Family, 16 Oct. 1862.

45. Bevier, *History of the First and Second Missouri Confederate Brigades*, p. 167; Compiled Missouri Service Records; Gordon, "The Battle and Retreat from Corinth," p. 68; Official Proceeding of the Sixth Annual Reunion of Missouri Division, United Confederate Veterans, 9–12 Sept. 1902 (St. Joseph: Combe, 1902), p. 48.

46. Tyler to Yancy, 15 Oct. 1862; Ruyle Memoir, pp. 20–21; Bevier, *History of the First and Second Missouri Confederate Brigades*, pp. 154, 341; Pankey Family

Papers, Mrs. Mary Pankey, Cardwell, Missouri; Ruyle Memoir, p. 20; Compiled Missouri Service Records; Kavanaugh Memoir, p. 27.

47. Greene, *The Mississippi*, p. 50; *Official Records*, vol. 17, ser. 1, pt. 1, pp. 227, 273–74, 390–91; Robbins to Family, 16 Oct. 1862; Bevier, *History of the First and Second Missouri Confederate Brigades*, p. 294; Ruyle Memoir, pp. 20–21; Greene, *The Mississippi*, pp. 48–49; Johnson and Buel, eds., *Battles and Leaders*, vol. 2, p. 748; Thomas W. Knox, *Campfire and Cotton-Field: Southern Adventure in Time of War* (Philadelphia: James Brothers, 1865), p. 215; Compiled Missouri Service Records.

48. Greene, *The Mississippi*, p. 50; Johnson and Buel, eds., *Battles and Leaders*, vol. 2, pp. 741, 744, 749; Cockrell, ed., *The Lost Account of the Battle of Corinth*, p. 66; Louis Philippe Albert D'Orléans, Comte de Paris, *The Civil War in America*, 4 vols. (Philadelphia: Joseph H. Coates, 1876), vol. 2, pp. 411–12; *Official Records*, vol. 17, ser. 1, pt. 1, pp. 273–74; Hogan to Father, 12 Oct. 1862; Bevier, *History of the First and Second Missouri Confederate Brigades*, pp. 341–42, 443.

49. Anderson, *Memoirs*, p. 237; Tyler to Yancy, 15 Oct. 1862; *Richmond Enquirer*, 18 Oct. 1862; *Official Records*, vol. 17, ser. 1, pt. 1, p. 259.

50. *Official Records*, vol. 17, ser. 1, pt. 1, pp. 206, 230, 238, 240; Compiled Missouri Service Records.

51. Compiled Missouri Service Records; Johnson and Buel, eds., *Battles and Leaders of the Civil War*, vol. 2, p. 749; *Official Records*, vol. 17, ser. 1, pt. 1, pp. 206, 215, 227, 231, 240, 259, 268–69, 272, 275–76; James E. Payne, "The Sixth Missouri at Corinth," *Confederate Veteran* 36, no. 12 (Dec. 1928): 465; Tyler to Yancy, 15 Oct. 1862.

52. Tyler to Yancy, 15 Oct. 1862; Bevier, *History of the First and Second Missouri Confederate Brigades*, p. 153; *Official Records*, vol. 17, ser. 1, pt. 1, pp. 206, 226–27, 231, 238–40, 260, 273–74, 391.

53. *Official Records*, vol. 17, ser. 1, pt. 1, pp. 240, 259; *Richmond Enquirer*, 18 Oct. 1862; Maury, "Recollections of Campaign Against Grant," p. 296.

54. *Official Records*, vol. 17, ser. 1, pt. 1, pp. 240, 259.

55. Compiled Missouri Service Records; Bevier, *History of the First and Second Missouri Confederate Brigades*, p. 340; Dyson to wife, 14 Oct. 1862, Western Historical Manuscript Collection, University of Missouri, St. Louis; Ruyle Memoir, p. 21.

56. Bevier, *History of the First and Second Missouri Confederate Brigades*, p. 342; Compiled Missouri Service Records; Kavanaugh Memoir, p. 27; *Official Records*, vol. 17, ser. 1, pt. 1, p. 238; Simpson Diary; Rule Memoir, p. 21.

57. Bevier, *History of the First and Second Missouri Confederate Brigades*, pp. 153, 341–42; Compiled Missouri Service Records; Lemmon Family Papers, Joe Lemmon, Bolivar, Missouri; Simpson Diary; Ruyle Memoir, p. 21; *Official Records*, vol. 17, ser. 1, pt. 1, pp. 215, 231, 238, 240; Anderson, *Memoirs*, pp. 174, 231, 237, 240.

58. *Official Records*, vol. 17, ser. 1, pt. 1, pp. 215, 231, 238, 240, 273–74; *Richmond Enquirer*, 17 Oct. 1862 and 18 Oct. 1862; Bevier, *History of the First and Second Missouri Confederate Brigades*, p. 342.

59. Bevier, *History of the First and Second Missouri Confederate Brigades*, pp. 341–42; Compiled Missouri Service Records; Simpson Diary; Ruyle Memoir,

pp. 21–22; Greene, *The Mississippi*, pp. 49–50; Tyler to Yancy, 15 Oct. 1862; Robbins to Family, 16 Oct. 1862.

60. Compiled Missouri Service Records; Ruyle Memoir, p. 21; *Richmond Enquirer*, 18 Oct. 1862; Johnson and Buel, eds., *Battles and Leaders*, vol. 2, pp. 749, 759; Robbins to Family, 16 Oct. 1862; Tyler to Yancy, 15 Oct. 1862; Anderson, *Memoirs*, p. 237; *Official Records*, vol. 17, ser. 1, pt. 1, pp. 206, 237–38, 241, 271, 391; Hubert, *History of the Fiftieth Illinois Infantry*, p. 142; Bevier, *History of the First and Second Missouri Confederate Brigades*, pp. 153–54, 341; "The Diary of Lieut. Col. Hubbell," p. 101; *Richmond Enquirer*, 10 Oct. 1862 and 18 Oct. 1862.

61. Anderson, *Memoirs*, p. 237; Bevier, *History of the First and Second Missouri Confederate Brigades*, pp. 341–42; Ruyle Memoir, p. 21; Tyler to Yancy, 15 Oct. 1862; Robbins to Family 16 Oct. 1862; Oscar Lawrence Jackson, *The Colonel's Diary* (Sharon: n.p., 1922), pp. 83–84; *Official Records*, vol. 17, ser. 1, pt. 1, pp. 206, 238, 241, 259–60; Duychinck, *National History*, vol. 2, pp. 623–25.

62. Bevier, *History of the First and Second Missouri Confederate Brigades*, p. 153; Greene, *The Mississippi*, pp. 49–50; Johnson and Buel, eds., *Battles and Leaders*, vol. 2, p. 749; D'Orléans, *The Civil War in America*, vol. 2, pp. 411–12; Alden and Guernsey, eds., *Harper's Pictorial History*, p. 317; *Official Records*, vol. 17, ser. 1, pt. 1, pp. 209, 238, 241, 274; Hubert, *History of the Fiftieth Illinois Infantry*, p. 142.

63. Lamers, *Edge of Glory*, pp. 149, 155; *Official Records*, vol. 17, ser. 1, pt. 1, pp. 215, 238, 259; *Richmond Enquirer*, 18 Oct. 1862.

64. M. O. Frost, *Regimental History of the Tenth Missouri Volunteer Infantry* (Topeka, Kan.: Frost, 1892), pp. 36–37; *Official Records*, vol. 17, ser. 1, pt. 1, pp. 206, 227, 231, 238, 241, 259; Alden and Guernsey, *Harper's Pictorial History*, p. 317; *Richmond Enquirer*, 17 Oct. 1862; Robbins to Family, 16 Oct. 1862; Tyler to Yancy, 15 Oct. 1862; Hubert, *History of the Fiftieth Illinois Infantry*, p. 147.

65. *Official Records*, vol. 17, ser. 1, pt. 1, p. 206; Tyler to Yancy, 15 Oct. 1862; Alden and Guernsey, *Harper's Pictorial History*, p. 317, Bevier, *History of the First and Second Missouri Confederate Brigades*, pp. 341–42; Johnson and Buel, eds., *Battles and Leaders*, vol. 2, p. 749; Duychinck, *National History*, vol. 2, p. 625.

66. *Official Records*, vol. 17, ser. 1, pt. 1, pp. 206, 238, 274–75; Tyler to Yancy, 15 Oct. 1862.

67. *Official Records*, vol. 17, ser. 1, pt. 1, p. 206; Ruyle Memoir, p. 21; Johnson and Buel, eds., *Battles and Leaders*, vol. 2, p. 750; *Richmond Enquirer*, 18 Oct. 1862; Bevier, *History of the First and Second Missouri Confederate Brigades*, pp. 215, 341–42; Hogan to Father, 12 Oct. 1862.

68. Hogan to Father, 12 Oct. 1862; Gordon, "The Battle and Retreat from Corinth," p. 68; Ruyle Memoir, p. 21.

69. Tyler to Yancy, 15 Oct. 1862; Ruyle Memoir, p. 22; *Richmond Enquirer*, 18 Oct. 1862; Dyson to wife, 28 Oct. 1862; Compiled Missouri Service Records; 1850 and 1860 Franklin County, Missouri, Census Records.

70. Ruyle Memoir, p. 22; Tyler to Yancy, 15 Oct. 1862; *Official Records*, vol. 17, ser. 1, pt. 1, pp. 391, 402.

71. Bevier, *History of the First and Second Missouri Confederate Brigades*, p. 342; *Official Records*, vol. 17, ser. 1, pt. 1, pp. 401–2.

72. Tyler to Yancy, 15 Oct. 1862; *Richmond Enquirer*, 18 Oct. 1862; Bevier, *History of the First and Second Missouri Confederate Brigades*, p. 343.

73. *Official Records*, vol. 17, ser. 1, pt. 1, pp. 206, 227–28, 231, 238, 251, 260, 274, 401–2; Johnson and Buel, eds., *Battles and Leaders*, vol. 2, pp. 750–51; *History of Randolph and Macon Counties, Missouri*, (St. Louis: National Historical Company, 1884), pp. 855–58; Compiled Service Records of Union Soldiers Who Served in Organizations from the State of Missouri, Record Group No. 94, National Archives, Washington, D.C.; Frost, *Regimental History*, pp. 36–37; Bevier, *History of the First and Second Missouri Confederate Brigades*, pp. 341–42.

74. Bevier, *History of the First and Second Missouri Confederate Brigades*, pp. 154, 341–42; George Elliott Journal, p. 22, Tennessee State Library and Archives, Nashville, Tennessee; *Richmond Enquirer*, 18 Oct. 1862; Ruyle Memoir, p. 21; "Sandie" Murdock to John Ross, 8 Oct. 1905, Skaggs Collection, box 2, folder 12, Arkansas Historical Commission, Little Rock, Arkansas; Maury, "Recollection of Campaign Against Grant," p. 297.

75. Compiled Missouri Service Records; Bevier, *History of the First and Second Missouri Confederate Brigades*, pp. 34041; *Official Records*, vol. 17, ser. 1, pt. 1, p. 402.

76. Bevier, *History of the First and Second Missouri Confederate Brigades*, pp. 341–42; Ruyle Memoir, p. 42; James Harrison Wilson, *The Life of Ulysses S. Grant, General of the Armies of the United States* (Springfield: Gurdon Bill, 1968), p. 155; Hyde and Conrad, *Encyclopedia of the History of St. Louis*, vol. 4, p. 2441.

77. *Official Records*, vol. 17, ser. 1, pt. 1, pp. 207, 228, 231, 233, 238; Frost, *Regimental History*, pp. 36–37; Alden and Guernsey, *Harper's Pictorial History*, p. 137; J. V. Frederick, ed., "An Illinois Soldier in North Mississippi: Diary of John Wilson, February 15–December 30, 1862," *The Journal of Mississippi History* 1, no. 3 (July 1939): 190; Tyler to Yancy, 15 Oct. 1862; Johnson and Buel, eds., *Battles and Leaders*, vol. 2, pp. 749–50.

78. Compiled Missouri Service Records; Bevier, *History of the First and Second Missouri Confederate Brigades*, p. 342; Robert Dunlap Diary, John B. Sampson, DeKalb, Missouri.

79. Frost, *Regimental History*, p. 37; Tyler to Yancy, 15 Oct. 1862; *Richmond Enquirer*, 18 Oct. 1862; Compiled Missouri Service Records; Simpson Diary; Ruyle Memoir, p. 22.

80. Tyler to Yancy, 15 Oct. 1862; *Richmond Enquirer*, 18 Oct. 1862; Frederick, ed., "An Illinois Soldier," p. 190.

81. *Official Records*, vol. 17, ser. 1, pt. 1, p. 231; Frost, *Regimental History*, p. 37; Bevier, *History of the First and Second Missouri Confederate Brigades*, p. 155; William L. Webb, *Battles and Biographies of Missourians* (Kansas City: Hudson-Kimerly, 1903), pp. 124–25; Hyde and Conrad, *Encyclopedia of the History of St. Louis*, vol. 4, p. 2441.

82. Ibid., p. 263; Ruyle Memoir, p. 21; Hogan to Father, 12 Oct. 1862. Compiled Missouri Service Records; Michael K. McGrath to Marie L. Dalton, 12 May 1905.

83. Bevier, *History of the First and Second Missouri Confederate Brigades*, p. 343; Frost, *Regimental History*, p. 37; Williams, *Lincoln Finds a General*, vol. 4, pp. 94–95; Greene, *The Mississippi*, p. 51; Maury, "Recollection of Campaign Against Grant," p. 305.

84. Robbins to Family, 16 Oct. 1862; *Richmond Enquirer*, 18 Oct. 1862; Compiled Missouri Service Records; Warren Diary; *History of Monroe and Shelby*

Counties, Missouri, (St. Louis: National Historical Company, 1884), p. 547; Connelly, *Civil War Tennessee*, pp. 55–57; Thomas Lawrence Connelly, *Army of the Heartland: The Army of Tennessee, 1861–1862* (Baton Rouge: Louisiana State University Press, 1967), pp. 279–80.

85. *Official Records*, vol. 17, ser. 1, pt. 1, p. 382; Ruyle Memoir, p. 21; Bevier, *History of the First and Second Missouri Confederate Brigades*, pp. 341–42, 443; Compiled Missouri Service Records; *Official Records*, vol. 17, ser. 1, pt. 1, p. 382.

86. Adjutant General of Missouri Records, Adjutant General Office, Jefferson City, Missouri; Compiled Missouri Service Records; 1860 Johnson County, Missouri, Census Records; Brauchman Scrapbook, Missouri Historical Society, St. Louis.

87. Compiled Missouri Service Records; Bevier, *History of the First and Second Missouri Confederate Brigades*, p. 342; Ruyle Memoir, pp. 21–22; Simpson Diary; Johnson and Buel, eds., *Battles and Leaders*, vol. 2, p. 760.

88. Bevier, *History of the First and Second Missouri Confederate Brigades*, p. 343; *Official Records*, vol. 17, ser. 1, pt. 1, p. 382; Compiled Missouri Service Records.

89. Compiled Missouri Service Records; Dyson to wife, 24 Nov. 1862; Stanley, Wilson, and Wilson, *Death Records*, p. 178.

90. Wilson and Wilson, *Death Records*, p. 178; Compiled Missouri Service Records; Warren Diary; 1860 St. Louis, Missouri, Census Records; Bevier, *History of the First and Second Missouri Confederate Brigades*, p. 148.

# Chapter IV

1. Compiled Service Records of Confederate Soldiers Who Served in Organizations from the State of Missouri, National Archives, Washington, D.C.; Absalom Roby Dyson to Mrs. Robertson, 7 April 1864; Warren to Father, 10 Jan. 1863, Warren Letters, Private Collection of Ellen R. Deremer, Alexandria, Virginia.

2. Compiled Missouri Service Records; Frank E. Vandiver, "The Confederacy and the American Tradition," pp. 133–34 in William E. Parrish, ed., *The Civil War: A Second American Revolution?* Dyson to Wife, n.d.

3. Warren Diary; Bevier, *History of the First and Second Missouri Confederate Brigades*, pp. 346–47.

4. George Elliott Journal, Tennessee State Library and Archives, Nashville, Tennessee, p. 35; Simpson Diary; Compiled Missouri Service Records; Robbins to Sister, 19 Oct. 1862, Mercentile Library, St. Louis; Bevier, *History of the First and Second Missouri Confederate Brigades*, pp. 107, 114, 165.

5. Compiled Missouri Service Records.

6. Bevier, *History of the First and Second Missouri Confederate Brigades*, p. 307; Babcock Scrapbook, Missouri Historical Society, St. Louis; *St. Louis Daily Evening News*, 1 Nov. 1860.

7. Newspaper clipping, n.d., Edwin L. Miller Papers, Western Historical Manuscript Collection, Historical Society of Missouri, Columbia, Missouri; Dunbar Rowland, ed., *Jefferson Davis, Constitutionalist: His Letters, Papers and*

Speeches, 6 vols. (Jackson: Mississippi Department of Archives and History, 1923), vol. 6, p. 412; *Official Records*, vol. 24, ser. 1, pt. 1, p. 267.

8. Compiled Missouri Service Records; 1860 Johnson County, Missouri, Census Records; Wheatley Family Papers, Mr. Carlos W. Bowman, San Carlos, California.

9. *History of Johnson County, Missouri*, pp. 64, 808; Adjutant General of Missouri Records, Adjutant General Office, Jefferson City, Missouri; Compiled Missouri Service Records; 1860 Johnson County, Missouri, Census Records; Nichols, "Civil War in Johnson County, Missouri," p. 20.

10. Compiled Missouri Service Records; Author's interview with historians of the Johnson County Historical Society, Warrensburg, Missouri, in May and June of 1977.

11. *History of Johnson County, Missouri*, p. 808; Wheatley Family Papers; 1860 Johnson County, Missouri, Census Records; Author's interview with Johnson County Historical Society historians in May and June of 1977; Compiled Missouri Service Records; Nichols, "Civil War in Johnson County, Missouri," Appendix B, pp. v, 109.

12. *Official Records*, vol. 17, ser. 1, pt. 2, pp. 759–61; *St. Louis Missouri Republican*, 6 Sept. 1884; Simpson Diary; Castel, *General Sterling Price*, pp. 128–31, 138.

13. Clement Eaton, *Jefferson Davis* (New York: Free Press, 1977), pp. 131, 132–39, 188–89; Warren Diary; Bevier, *History of the First and Second Missouri Confederate Brigades*, p. 359; Simpson Diary.

14. Bevier, *History of the First and Second Missouri Confederate Brigades*, pp. 166–67; Warren Diary.

15. Castel, *General Sterling Price*, pp. 132–34; Thomas C. Reynolds, "General Sterling Price and the Confederacy," pp. 46–48, Missouri Historical Society, St. Louis; Robert E. Miller, "One of the Ruling Class, Thomas Caute Reynolds: Second Confederate Governor of Missouri," *Missouri Historical Review* 80, no. 4 (July 1986): 422–23, 432; Dyson to Wife, n.d.; Warren to Father, 10 January 1863; Compiled Missouri Service Records.

16. Dyson to Wife, 29 Nov. 1862.

17. Ruyle Memoir, pp. 25–26; Simpson Diary.

18. Bevier, *History of the First and Second Missouri Confederate Brigades*, pp. 348, 351.

19. Dyson to Wife, 29 Nov. 1862.

20. Warren Diary; Elliott Journal, p. 36.

21. Warren Diary.

22. Bevier, *History of the First and Second Missouri Confederate Brigades*, pp. 352, 359, 414–15.

23. *Ibid.*, p. 359.

24. Compiled Missouri Service Records; Bevier, *History of the First and Second Missouri Confederate Brigades*, p. 359; Warren Diary.

25. Warren Diary.

26. Ruyle Memoir, p. 26; Archer Jones, *Confederate Strategy from Shiloh to Vicksburg* (Baton Rouge: Louisiana State University Press, 1961), pp. 123, 131; Bevier, *History of the First and Second Missouri Confederate Brigades*, p. 166; Compiled Missouri Service Records.

27. Warren Diary; Simpson Diary; *General History of Macon County,*

Missouri (Chicago: Henry Taylor, 1910), pp. 144–45; Catalogue of the Officers and Students of McGee College, 1854–1855, Missouri Historical Society, St. Louis.

28. Warren Diary.

29. Warren Diary; Simpson Diary; Compiled Missouri Service Records; Edwin L. Miller Scrapbook, 1888–97 volume; Castel, *General Sterling Price*, pp. 130–34.

30. Compiled Missouri Service Records; Simpson Diary; Warren Diary.

31. Warren Diary.

32. Jones, *Confederate Strategy*, pp. 123, 131; Compiled Missouri Service Records; Warren Diary; Grant, *Memoirs*, pp. 364–65; J. F. C. Fuller, *The Generalship of Ulysses S. Grant* (New York: Da Capo, 1991), p. 131; Robbins to Sister, 24 Jan. 1863, Mercentile Library, St. Louis.

33. Warren Diary; Ruyle Memoir, p. 26.

34. Warren Diary; Compiled Missouri Service Records; Jones, *Confederate Strategy*, p. 131; Canton, Mississippi, Confederate Cemetery, Notes on Confederate Soldier's Burials at the Canton Cemetery.

35. Bevier, *History of the First and Second Missouri Confederate Brigades*, p. 330; Sidney J. Romero, *Religion in the Rebel Ranks* (Lanham: University Press of America, 1983), p. 35; Billon Scrapbook, 2, Missouri Historical Society, St. Louis.

36. Bevier, *History of the First and Second Missouri Confederate Brigades*, pp. 330, 425; Romero, *Religion in the Rebel Ranks*, p. 35; Primm, *Lion of the Valley*, p. 174.

37. Compiled Missouri Service Records; Kennedy's 1860 St. Louis City Directory, p. 99; 1860 St. Louis City Census Records; Warren Diary; Brauckman Scrapbook, Missouri Historical Society, St. Louis.

38. Warren Diary; Glenn Tucker, *Zeb Zance: Champion of Personal Freedom* (Indianapolis: Bobbs-Merrill, 1965), pp. 12–13, 169, 171.

39. John C. Pemberton, *Pemberton, Defender of Vicksburg* (Chapel Hill: University of North Carolina Press, 1942), p. 65; Warren Diary; Compiled Missouri Service Records; Allan Nevins, *Ordeal of the Union, The War for the Union: War Becomes Revolution 1862–1863*, 8 vols. (New York: Charles Scribner's Sons, 1960), vol. 3, p. 48.

40. Warren Diary.

41. Ibid.

42. Warren Diary; Ruyle Memoir, p. 27; Compiled Missouri Service Records; *Official Records*, vol. 24, ser. 1, pt. 3, p. 614; Bevier, *History of the First and Second Missouri Brigades*, p. 167–68; Adjutant General of Missouri Records.

43. Warren Diary; Castel, *General Sterling Price*, p. 138; Bevier, *History of the First and Second Missouri Confederate Brigades*, pp. 167–68; Ruyle Memoir, pp. 4, 27.

44. Compiled Missouri Service Records; Robbins to Brother, 17 May 1862; List of First Missouri Brigade Trans-Mississippi Recruiters, Warren Collection.

45. Compiled Missouri Service Records; Warren Diary; James Bradley, *The Confederate Mail Carrier* (Mexico: n.p., 1894), p. 90; Mary Ann Loughborough, *My Cave Life in Vicksburg* (New York: D. Appleton, 1864), pp. 185–86.

46. Bevier, *History of the First and Second Missouri Confederate Brigades*, pp. 397–400.

47. Ruyle Memoir, p. 28; Bowen to Major R. W. Memminger, 27 March 1863, General John Stevens Bowen Letterbook, Virginia Historical Society, Richmond, Virginia; Bevier, *History of the First and Second Missouri Confederate Brigades*, pp. 168–69; Rowland, *History of Mississippi*, vol. 2, pp. 702–3; Thomas S. Hawley to Parents, 18 May 1863, Missouri Historical Society, St. Louis; *Missouri Republican*, 17 July 1886; Rowland, *History of Mississippi*, vol. 2, pp. 702–3; William C. Wright, *The Confederate Magazine at Fort Wade, Grand Gulf, Mississippi Excavations, 1980–1981* (Jackson: Mississippi Department of Archives and History and the Grand Gulf State Military Monument, 1982), p. 3; Edwin C. Bearss, "Grand Gulf State Military Monument, 1982), p. 3; Edwin C. Bearss, "Grand Gulf's Role in the Civil War," *Civil War History* 5 (1959): 14–15.

48. Compiled Missouri Service Records; "Sketch—General Bowen's Life," pp. 3, 5, (General) John Stevens Bowen Papers, Missouri Historical Society, St. Louis; Simpson Diary; *The Battle of Shiloh and the Organizations Engaged* (Washington, D.C., Government Publication, 1902), pp. 87–88; *Daily Missouri Democrat*, 4 Dec. 1860; John Stevens Bowen Genealogy, Georgia Historical Society, Savannah, Georgia; U.D.C., *Reminiscences of the Civil War*, p. 226; Anderson, *Memoirs*, pp. 365–66; Mary Preston Kennerly-Bowen Obituary, Kearny-Kennerly Scrapbook, 2, 1888–1932, Missouri Historical Society, St. Louis; Kennerly Papers, Missouri Historical Society, St. Louis.

49. Ruyle Memoir, p. 28; Bowen to Memminger, no. 18, Bowen Letterbook, Virginia Historical Society, Richmond; Bevier, *History of the First and Second Missouri Confederate Brigades*, p. 406; Grand Gulf State Military Monument historian's interview with author, 30 Jan. 1988.

50. Bevier, *History of the First and Second Missouri Confederate Brigades*, p. 406; Leslie Anders, "Men from Home: Missouri Volunteers in the Pacification of Mobile, Alabama, 1865–1866," *Missouri Historical Review* 69, no. 3 (April 1975): 253; Bell Irvin Wiley, *The Life of Billy Yank: The Common Soldier of the Union* (Baton Rouge: Louisiana State University Press, 1978), p. 114.

51. Bevier, *History of the First and Second Missouri Confederate Brigades*, p. 406; Jon L. Wakelyn, *Biographical Dictionary of the Confederacy* (Westport: Greenwood, 1977), p. 103; Bowen to Memminger, 2 April 1863; Compiled Missouri Service Records.

52. Bevier, *History of the First and Second Missouri Confederate Brigades*, pp. 146, 406–7.

53. Bowen to Memminger, 2 April 1863; R. R. Hutchinson memo to Bowen, 21 March 1863; Bowen to Memminger, 27 March 1863.

54. *St. Louis Missouri Republican*, 17 July 1886; John S. Bowen Letterbook, Aug. 1862–Nov. 1863; Reports no. 9, 11, War Department Collection of Confederate Records, chap. 2, vol. 274, National Archives, Washington, D.C.

55. *St. Louis Missouri Republican*, 17 July 1886; Ruyle Memoir, p. 28.

56. Ruyle Memoir, pp. 28–29; Bevier, *History of the First and Second Missouri Confederate Brigades*, p. 403; Mike Casey to Family, 6 April 1863, Robbins Collection.

57. Bevier, *History of the First and Second Missouri Confederate Brigades*, pp. 414, 425.

58. Grant, *Personal Memoirs*, vol. 1, pp. 380–81, 388–89.

59. David D. Porter, *The Naval History of the Civil War* (New York: Sherman, 1886), p. 313; Carondelet Historical Society Archives, Carondelet, Missouri; William P. Barlow, "How Guibor's Battery Was Transformed to Heavy Artillery," Boyce Scrapbook, Missouri Historical Society, St. Louis; Bowen to R. W. Memminger, 27 March 1863; Compiled Missouri Service Records.

60. Barlow, "How Guibor's Battery Was Transformed to Heavy Artillery"; Boyce Scrapbook; Bevier, *History of the First and Second Missouri Confederate Brigades,* pp. 402–3; Compiled Missouri Service Records; *Official Records,* vol. 24, ser. 1, pt. 1, p. 486.

61. Bowen to Pemberton, 17 March 1863; *Official Records,* vol. 24, ser. 1, pt. 3, p. 797; Jones, *Confederate Strategy from Shiloh to Vicksburg,* pp. 188–90.

62. Bevier, *History of the First and Second Missouri Confederate Brigades,* pp. 400, 414; Warren Diary; Dyson to Louisa, 30 Aug. 1863.

63. Bevier, *History of the First and Second Missouri Confederate Brigades,* pp. 400–1; Compiled Missouri Service Records.

64. Compiled Missouri Service Records; Appler Diary, p. 12, Missouri Historical Society, St. Louis.

## Chapter V

1. Jones, *Confederate Strategy from Shiloh to Vicksburg,* pp. 188–90; Phillip Thomas Tucker, "Reconnaissance in Tensas Parish, April 1863: Missouri Confederates in Louisiana," *Louisiana History* 31, no. 2 (Spring 1990): 193–206.

2. Clifford Dowdey, *Experiment in Rebellion* (Garden City, N.J.: Doubleday, 1946), pp. 244–52.

3. Ibid., pp. 244–52, 271, 275–82.

4. Michael B. Ballard, *Pemberton: A Biography* (Jackson: University Press of Mississippi, 1991), pp. 116–17.

5. Ibid., p. 120.

6. Dowdey, *Experiment in Rebellion,* pp. 280–81.

7. Ballard, *Pemberton,* pp. 116–17.

8. Dowdey, *Experiment in Rebellion,* pp. 244–52, 280–81.

9. Compiled Service Records of Confederate Soldiers Who Served in Organizations from the State of Missouri, National Archives, Washington, D.C.

10. David D. Porter, *The Naval History of the Civil War* (New York: Sherman, 1886), p. 314; *Official Records,* vol. 24, ser. 1, pt. 1, p. 575.

11. Greene, *The Mississippi,* p. 124; Porter, *Naval History,* p. 317; Fletcher Pratt, *Civil War on Western Waters* (New York: Henry Holt, 1956), p. 164; *Official Records,* vol. 24, ser. 1, pt. 1, pp. 48, 575.

12. Hogan to Father, 22 July 1863, Missouri Historical Society, St. Louis; William P. Barlow, "How Guibor's Battery Was Transformed to Heavy Artillery," Boyce Scrapbook, Missouri Historical Society, St. Louis; "Partnership Agreement Between Wade, Stille, Osborne and D. M. Frost," 29 April 1853, Fordyce Collection, Missouri Historical Society, St. Louis; Compiled Missouri Service Records; William Wade to Governor Robert M. Stewart, 23 Feb. 1860, Western Historical

Manuscript Collection, State Historical Society of Missouri, Columbia, Missouri; Camp Jackson Papers, Missouri Historical Society, St. Louis; Bevier, *History of the First and Second Missouri Confederate Brigades*, pp. 173–74; Johnson and Buel, eds., *Battles and Leaders*, vol. 3, pp. 240, 494–95; Ruyle Memoir, p. 29; George Elliott Journal, p. 57, Tennessee State Library and Archives, Nashville; James E. Payne Account, Vicksburg National Military Park.

13. Samuel Carter III, *The Final Fortress: The Campaign for Vicksburg 1862–1863* (New York: St. Martin's, 1980), p. 182; Johnson and Buel, eds., *Battles and Leaders*, vol. 3, pp. 477–78, 549–50; *Official Records*, vol. 24, ser. 1, pt. 3, pp. 792–93.

14. Ulysses S. Grant to William T. Sherman, 27 April 1863, William K. Bixby Collection, Missouri Historical Society, St. Louis; Bruce Catton, *Grant Moves South* (Boston: Little, Brown, 1960), p. 426; John C. Pemberton, *Pemberton, Defender of Vicksburg* (Chapel Hill: University of North Carolina Press, 1942), p. 111; *Official Records*, vol. 24, ser. 1, pt. 1, pp. 141, 257, 328.

15. Johnson and Buel, eds., *Battles and Leaders*, vol. 3, pp. 495–96; John Hebron Moore, "Railroads of Antebellum Mississippi," *Journal of Mississippi History* 41, no. 1 (Feb. 1979): 66–67; Dunbar Rowland, *History of Mississippi* vol. 2, p. 702; *Official Records*, vol. 24, ser. 1, pt. 1, p. 48.

16. Johnson and Buel, eds., *Battles and Leaders*, vol. 3, 496; D. Alexander Brown, *Grierson's Raid: A Cavalry Adventure of the Civil War* (Urbana: University of Illinois Press, 1962), p. 157; R. R. Hutchinson to Col. Adams, 15 March 1863, Bowen Letterbook, Virginia Historical Society, Richmond; *Official Records*, vol. 24, ser. 1, pt. 1, p. 663.

17. *Official Records*, vol. 24, ser. 1, pt. 1, pp. 663, 672; Bowen to R. W. Memminger, 2 May 1863; Bowen Letterbook, Report No. 52; Edwin C. Bearss, *Grant Strikes a Fatal Blow*, (Dayton, Ohio: Morningside, 1986), pp. 348–49.

18. Johnson and Buel, eds., *Battles and Leaders*, vol. 3, p. 496; *Official Records*, vol. 24, ser. 1, pt. 1, pp. 663, 672; Bearss, *Grant Strikes a Fatal Blow*, pp. 349, 405.

19. *Official Records*, vol. 24, ser. 1, pt. 1, pp. 658–59, 663; Howard P. Nash, Jr., *A Naval History of the Civil War* (New York: A. S. Barnes, 1972), p. 28; Brown, *Grierson's Raid*, p. 154.

20. Camp Jackson Papers; "Sketch — General Bowen's Life," Bowen Papers, Missouri Historical Society, St. Louis; *Official Records*, vol. 24, ser. 1, pt. 1, pp. 663–64.

21. *Official Records*, vol. 24, ser. 1, pt. 1, pp. 663–64, 655, 657, 659–60; Bearss, *Grant Strikes a Blow*, pp. 405, 407; John T. Simon, *The Papers of Ulysses S. Grant, April 1–July 6, 1863* (Carbondale: Southern Illinois University Press, 1979), p. 147; Bowen to Memminger, 6 April, 1863.

22. Bowen to Memminger, 2 May, 1863; Bowen to Memminger, 4 June 1863.

23. Bowen to Memminger, 2 May, 1863; Johnson and Buel, eds., *Battles and Leaders*, vol. 3, p. 496; *Official Records*, vol. 24, ser. 1, pt. 1, pp. 634–35; Bowen to Memminger, 4 June, 1863; Compiled Missouri Service Records.

24. Bevier, *History of the First and Second Missouri Confederate Brigades*, p. 177.

25. *Official Records*, vol. 24, ser. 1, pt. 1, pp. 658–59.

26. Bowen to Memminger, 4 June, 1863; Compiled Missouri Service Records;

Appler Diary, p. 15, Missouri Historical Society, St. Louis; Bowen to Memminger, 6 June 1863.

27. *Official Records*, vol. 24, ser. 1, pt. 1, p. 668; Compiled Missouri Service Records; William F. Swindler, "The Southern Press in Missouri 1861-1864," *Missouri Historical Review* 35, no. 3 (April 1941): 400; Bevier, *History of the First and Second Missouri Confederate Brigades*, p. 414.

28. Bevier, *History of the First and Second Missouri Confederate Brigades*, pp. 414-15.

29. Bevier, *History of the First and Second Missouri Confederate Brigades*, pp. 402-3, 414-15; Compiled Missouri Service Records; Bevier, *History of the First and Second Missouri Confederate Brigades*, pp. 414-15.

30. Compiled Missouri Service Records; Dyson to Wife, 8 June 1863.

31. Compiled Missouri Service Records; Dyson to Wife, 8 June 1863; *Official Records*, vol. 24, ser. 1, pt. 1, p. 668.

32. *Official Records*, vol. 24, ser. 1, pt. 1, pp. 675, 688; Bevier, *History of the First and Second Missouri Confederate Brigades*, p. 415.

33. Bowen to Memminger, 4 June, 1863; *Official Records*, vol. 24, ser. 1, pt. 1, pp. 663-64; Bearss, *Grant Strikes a Fatal Blow*, p. 367; Bowen to Memminger, 4 June 1863.

34. Compiled Missouri Service Records; *Official Records*, vol. 8, ser. 1, p. 313; "Colonel Eugene Erwin," *Confederate Veteran* 4, no. 8 (Aug. 1896): 264.

35. Sheridan A. Logan, *Old Saint Jo: Gateway to the West 1799-1932* (n.p.: John Sublett Foundation, 1979), p. 293; Landis Family Papers, Walter A. Landis, Jr., Faucett, Missouri; Henry Hance to Eve, 15 June 1864, Robbins Collection, Mercentile Library, St. Louis; Compiled Missouri Service Records; "The Storey [sic] of Guibor's Battery, C.S.A.," box no. 1, Civil War Papers, Missouri Historical Society, St. Louis; *Official Records*, vol. 24, ser. 1, pt. 1, p. 664.

36. Bearss, *Grant Strikes a Fatal Blow*, pp. 363-67; Bowen to Memminger, 2 May 1863.

37. *Official Records*, vol. 24, ser. 1, pt. 1, pp. 256, 661, 664, 670, 673-76; Bearss, *Grant Strikes a Fatal Blow*, p. 382; Edwin C. Bearss, Battle of Port Gibson-Troop Movement Map, United States Department of the Interior National Park Service, Division of Design and Construction Prepared by Eastern Office, region 1, sheet 1 of 4, Arlington, Virginia.

38. *Official Records*, vol. 24, ser. 1, pt. 1, pp. 576, 664, 668, 675-76; Bowen to Memminger, 2 May 1863; Johnson and Buel, eds., *Battles and Leaders*, vol. 3, p. 496; Bearss, *Grant Strikes a Fatal Blow*, p. 382; Bearss, Battle of Port Gibson Map, sheet 2 of 4.

39. Bearss, *Grant Strikes a Fatal Blow*, pp. 384-85; Bearss, Battle of Port Gibson Map, region 1, sheet 3 of 4; *Official Records*, vol. 24, ser. 1, pt. 1, pp. 664, 668, 675-76; Bearss, *Grant Strikes a Fatal Blow*, p. 385; Bevier, *History of the First and Second Missouri Confederate Brigades*, p. 415.

40. Bearss, Battle of Port Gibson Map, region 1, sheet 3 of 4; Brauckman Scrapbook, Missouri Historical Society, St. Louis, Missouri; Bearss, *Grant Strikes a Fatal Blow*, pp. 384-85, 389; Compiled Missouri Service Records.

41. Bearss, *Grant Strikes a Fatal Blow*, pp. 387-89; Compiled Missouri Service Records; *Official Records*, vol. 24, ser. 1, pt. 1, pp. 676-77; Mark M. Boatner, III, *The Civil War Dictionary* (New York: David McKay, 1959), p. 525.

42. *Official Records*, vol. 24, ser. 1, pt. 1, pp. 659, 664, 667, 669; Bearss, *Grant Strikes a Fatal Blow*, pp. 384–85.

43. Bearss, *Grant Strikes a Fatal Blow*, pp. 389–90.

44. Bowen to Memminger, 4 June 1863.

45. William Roscoe Livermore and John Codman Ropes, *The Story of the Civil War: A Concise Account of a War in the United States of America Between 1861 and 1865*, 4 vols. (New York: G. P. Putnam's Sons, 1904–1913), vol. 2, p. 275; Bevier, *History of the First and Second Missouri Confederate Brigades*, pp. 415–16; *Official Records*, vol. 24, ser. 1, pt. 1, pp. 664, 670–71, 673–74; William C. Thompson, "From Shiloh to Port Gibson," *Civil War Times Illustrated* 3, no. 6 (Oct. 1964): 23; James E. Payne, "Skylarking Along the Line," *Confederate Veteran* 38, no. 3 (March 1930): 96; George Elliott Journal, pp. 57–58, Tennessee State Library and Archives, Nashville; Compiled Missouri Service Records.

46. Elliott Journal, pp. 57–58; James A. Payne, "From Missouri," *Confederate Veteran* 38, no. 9 (Sept. 1930): 366; Edgar J. Erickson, ed., "With Grant at Vicksburg: From the Civil War Diary of Captain Charles E. Wilcox," *Journal of the Illinois State Historical Society* 30, no. 4 (Jan. 1938): 474; Boatner, *Civil War Dictionary*, pp. 75, 538; Bearss, *Grant Strikes a Fatal Blow*, pp. 368–72; *Official Records*, vol. 24, ser. 1, pt. 1, p. 659; Bowen to Memminger, 4 June 1863; Bevier, *History of the First and Second Missouri Confederate Brigades*, p. 416.

47. Bevier, *History of the First and Second Missouri Confederate Brigades*, p. 416; Compiled Missouri Service Records; Camp Jackson Papers; *Official Records*, vol. 24, ser. 1, pt. 1, pp. 675–76; William Pit Chambers, "My Journal: The Story of a Soldier's Life Told by Himself," *Publications of the Mississippi State Historical Society* 5 (1925): 264.

48. *Official Records*, vol. 24, ser. 1, pt. 1, p. 664; Ezra Warner, Jr., *Generals in Gray: Lives of the Confederate Commanders* (Baton Rouge: Louisiana State University Press, 1959), pp. 271–72.

49. Bowen to Memminger, 4 June 1863; Bevier, *History of the First and Second Missouri Confederate Brigades*, pp. 414–15; "Consolidated Provision Return for First Brigade, May 1–May 10, 1863," Roster sheet in National Archives; Isaac Vincent Smith Memoir, p. 27, Western Historical Manuscript Collection, State Historical Society of Missouri, Columbia, Missouri; Jefferson Davis, *The Rise and Fall of the Confederate Government* (New York: D. Appleton, 1881), p. 398.

50. Bearss, *Grant Strikes a Fatal Blow*, p. 391; Bevier, *History of the First and Second Missouri Confederate Brigades*, p. 416.

51. Jon L. Wakelyn, *Biographical Dictionary of the Confederacy* (Westport: Greenwood, 1977), p. 103; Bearss, Battle of Port Gibson Map, sheet 3 of 4; *Official Records*, vol. 24, ser. 1, pt. 1, p. 668; Bevier, *History of the First and Second Missouri Confederate Brigades*, p. 416; Bearss, *Grant Strikes a Fatal Blow*, p. 391.

52. *Official Records*, vol. 24, ser. 1, pt. 1, pp. 603–4, 668, 676; Bevier, *History of the First and Second Missouri Confederate Brigades*, p. 416; Bearss, *Grant Strikes a Fatal Blow*, pp. 384–85, 391.

53. Compiled Missouri Service Records; Anderson, *Memoirs*, p. 298; Herschel Schooley, *Centennial History of Audrain County, Missouri* (Mexico: McIntyre, 1937), pp. 79, 127; Schooley, *Centennial History*, p. 87.

54. *Official Records*, vol. 24, ser. 1, pt. 1, pp. 603–4; Charles A. Dana, *Recollections of the Civil War* (New York: Collier Books, 1963), p. 75.

55. Dana, *Recollections of the Civil War*, p. 75; *Official Records*, vol. 24, ser. 1, pt. 1, pp. 583, 604–5; Bearss, Battle of Port Gibson Map, sheet 3 of 4.

56. *Official Records*, vol. 24, ser. 1, pt. 1, pp. 604–5, 612; Bearss, Battle of Port Gibson Map, sheet 3 of 4; Frances H. Kennedy, ed., *The Civil War Battlefield Guide* (Boston: Houghton Mifflin, 1990), p. 138.

57. Bearss, Battle of Port Gibson Map, sheet 3 of 4; *Official Records*, vol. 24, ser. 1, pt. 1, pp. 604, 668.

58. Bevier, *History of the First and Second Missouri Confederate Brigades*, pp. 178, 416–17.

59. Bearss, *Grant Strikes a Fatal Blow*, p. 391; Topographical Map of the United States Department of the Interior Geological Survey for Claiborne County, Mississippi; Bearss, Battle of Port Gibson Map, sheet 3 of 4; Bevier, *History of the First and Second Missouri Confederate Brigades*, p. 178.

60. Bearss, *Grant Strikes a Fatal Blow*, pp. 390–91; Topographical Map for Claiborne County, Mississippi; Anderson, *Memoirs*, p. 298.

61. Anderson, *Memoirs*, p. 298; Bevier, *History of the First and Second Missouri Confederate Brigades*, pp. 178, 416–17; Bearss, Battle of Port Gibson Map, sheet 3 of 4.

62. Bevier, *History of the First and Second Missouri Confederate Brigades*, p. 416; *Official Records*, vol. 24, ser. 1, pt. 1, pp. 583, 605; Smith Memoir, p. 27.

63. Smith Memoir, p. 27; Bevier, *History of the First and Second Missouri Confederate Brigades*, pp. 177–78, 416–17; *Official Records*, vol. 24, ser. 1, pt. 1, p. 604.

64. *Official Records*, vol. 24, ser. 1, pt. 1, pp. 605, 610–11; Topographical Map of Claiborne County, Mississippi.

65. Bevier, *History of the First and Second Missouri Confederate Brigades*, pp. 146, 178, 414–16; Bearss, *Grant Strikes a Fatal Blow*, p. 391; *Official Records*, vol. 24, ser. 1, pt. 1, pp. 605, 668–69; Topographical Map of Claiborne County, Mississippi; Smith Memoir, p. 27; "Consolidated Provision Return for First Brigade"; Hogan to Father, 22 July 1863.

66. *Official Records*, vol. 24, ser. 1, pt. 1, pp. 583, 605–7, 611; Bearss, Battle of Port Gibson Map, sheet 3 of 4; Bearss, *Grant Strikes a Fatal Blow*, p. 392; Bowen to Memminger, 2 May 1863.

67. Smith Memoir, p. 27; Anderson, *Memoirs*, p. 298; *Official Records*, vol. 24, ser. 1, pt. 1, pp. 602–3; Bevier, *History of the First and Second Missouri Confederate Brigades*, p. 416.

68. *Official Records*, vol. 24, ser. 1, pt. 1, pp. 583, 605; Bearss, *Grant Strikes a Fatal Blow*, pp. 391–92; Johnson and Buel, eds., *Battles and Leaders*, vol. 1, pp. 537–38.

69. Topographical Map of Claiborne County, Mississippi; *Official Records*, vol. 24, ser. 1, pt. 1, pp. 583, 605.

70. Bevier, *History of the First and Second Missouri Confederate Brigades*, p. 353.

71. Smith Memoir, p. 27; Compiled Missouri Service Records; Bowen to Memminger, 4 June 1863; *Official Records*, vol. 24, ser. 1, pt. 1, p. 607; Bearss, *Grant Strikes a Fatal Blow*, pp. 178, 394–95.

72. Hogan to Father, 22 July 1863; Bevier, *History of the First and Second Missouri Confederate Brigades*, pp. 178–79; Compiled Missouri Service Records; Bearss, *Grant Strikes a Fatal Blow*, p. 391; Smith Memoir, p. 27.

73. Bearss, *Grant Strikes a Fatal Blow*, pp. 391–92; *Official Records*, vol. 24, ser. 1, pt. 1, pp. 611, 613; Bevier, *History of the First and Second Missouri Confederate Brigades*, pp. 179, 417; Boatner, *Civil War Dictionary*, p. 763.

74. *Official Records*, vol. 24, ser. 1, pt. 1, pp. 606–7, 611; Bearss, *Grant Strikes a Fatal Blow*, pp. 391–92; Bevier, *History of the First and Second Missouri Confederate Brigades*, pp. 178–79, 416.

75. Bevier, *History of the First and Second Missouri Confederate Brigades*, p. 179.

76. Bearss, Battle of Port Gibson Map, sheet 3 of 4; *Official Records*, vol. 24, ser. 1, pt. 1, pp. 603, 611; Colonel William H. Raynor Diary, Vicksburg National Military Park, National Park Service Archives, Vicksburg, Mississippi; Bearss, *Grant Strikes a Fatal Blow*, p. 392.

77. Bevier, *History of the First and Second Missouri Confederate Brigades*, pp. 178–79; *Official Records*, vol. 24, ser. 1, pt. 1, p. 611.

78. *Official Records*, vol. 24, ser. 1, pt. 1, p. 611; Compiled Missouri Service Records.

79. *Official Records*, vol. 24, ser. 1, pt. 1, pp. 611–12; Howard Michael Madaus and Robert D. Needham, *The Battle Flags of the Confederate Army of Tennessee* (Milwaukee: Milwaukee Public Library, 1976), p. 44.

80. Bevier, *History of the First and Second Missouri Confederate Brigades*, pp. 179, 353.

81. Hogan to Father, 22 July 1863; T. B. Cox, "Gen. Pettus Escapes Johnson's Island," *Confederate Veteran* 13, no. 1 (Jan. 1905): 19; Bevier, *History of the First and Second Missouri Confederate Brigades*, p. 353.

82. Compiled Missouri Service Records; Bevier, *History of the First and Second Missouri Confederate Brigades*, pp. 179, 353.

83. Compiled Missouri Service Records; Dysart to Fannin Sharp, 18 Nov. 1863, Compiled Missouri Service Records; Smith Memoir, p. 27.

84. Bearss, *Grant Strikes a Fatal Blow*, p. 392; *Official Records*, vol. 24, ser. 1, pt. 1, p. 605.

85. Bearss, Battle of Port Gibson Map, sheet 3 of 4; Bearss, *Grant Strikes a Fatal Blow*, p. 392; *Official Records*, vol. 24, ser. 1, pt. 1, pp. 606–8; Bevier, *History of the First and Second Missouri Confederate Brigades*, p. 167.

86. Bevier, *History of the First and Second Missouri Confederate Brigades*, pp. 416–17; Compiled Missouri Service Records; *Official Records*, vol. 24, ser. 1, pt. 1, p. 669.

87. *Official Records*, vol. 24, ser. 1, pt. 1, pp. 607–13, 626–27; Bearss, Battle of Port Gibson Map, sheet 3 of 4; Bearss, *Grant Strikes a Fatal Blow*, p. 392; Bevier, *History of the First and Second Missouri Confederate Brigades*, p. 417.

88. Bevier, *History of the First and Second Missouri Confederate Brigades*, p. 179; Anderson, *Memoirs*, p. 298; *Official Records*, vol. 24, ser. 1, pt. 1, pp. 605, 611–12.

89. Bevier, *History of the First and Second Missouri Confederate Brigades*, p. 179; Hogan to Father, 22 July 1863.

90. Bevier, *History of the First and Second Missouri Confederate Brigades*, pp. 179, 416; *Official Records*, vol. 24, ser. 1, pt. 1, p. 612.

91. Bearss, *Grant Strikes a Fatal Blow*, p. 393; Smith Memoir, p. 27; *Official Records*, vol. 24, ser. 1, pt. 1, pp. 607, 612; Bearss, Battle of Port Gibson Map, sheet 3 of 4; Emily Crawford to Elizabeth Lewis, 11 June 1863, Charles Sullivan, Perkinston, Mississippi; Edgar L. Erickson, ed., "With Grant at Vicksburg: From the Civil War Diary of Captain Charles E. Wilcox," *Journal of the Illinois State Historical Society* 30 (Jan. 1938): 474; Bearss, *Grant Strikes a Fatal Blow*, p. 392.

92. Bevier, *History of the First and Second Missouri Confederate Brigades*, p. 417; Bowen to Memminger, 4 June 1863.

93. *Official Records*, vol. 24, ser. 1, pt. 1, p. 612; Bevier, *History of the First and Second Missouri Confederate Brigades*, p. 417.

94. Raynor Diary; *Official Records*, vol. 24, ser. 1, pt. 1, p. 603; *Official Roster of the Soldiers of the State of Ohio in the War of the Rebellion 1861-1866* (Akron: Werner Printing Co., 1887), vol. 5, p. 83; Compiled Missouri Service Records.

95. *Official Records*, vol. 24, ser. 1, pt. 1, pp. 607-8, 613; David I. McCormick, comp., and Mrs. Mindwell Crompton Wilson, ed., *Indiana Battle Flags: And a Record of Indiana Organizations in the Mexican, Civil and Spanish American Wars* (Indianapolis: n.p., 1929), pp. 182-83; Bearss, *Grant Strikes a Fatal Blow*, p. 392.

96. Bearss, *Grant Strikes a Fatal Blow*, p. 392; *Official Records*, vol. 24, ser. 1, pt. 1, pp. 582-85, 606, 613, 627.

97. Erickson, ed., "With Grant at Vicksburg," p. 472; *Official Records*, vol. 24, ser. 1, pt. 1, pp. 605, 613.

98. *Official Records*, vol. 24, ser. 1, pt. 1, pp. 659, 668; Bowen to Memminger, 4 June 1863; James Bradley, *The Confederate Mail Carrier* (Mexico: n.p., 1894), p. 273.

99. Bevier, *History of the First and Second Missouri Confederate Brigades*, pp. 179, 417; Compiled Misouri Service Records; Anderson, *Memoirs*, p. 298.

100. *Official Records*, vol. 24, ser. 1, pt. 1, p. 603; Bearss, *Grant Strikes a Fatal Blow*, p. 392; Bowen to Memminger, 4 June 1863; Bevier, *History of the First and Second Missouri Confederate Brigades*, p. 417.

101. Bowen to Memminger, 4 June 1863; *Official Records*, vol. 24, ser. 1, pt. 1, pp. 607-8, 627, 669; Bowen to Memminger, 2 May 1863.

102. Bearss, *Grant Strikes a Fatal Blow*, p. 392; *Official Records*, vol. 24, ser. 1, pt. 1, pp. 607, 613, 627.

103. Compiled Missouri Service Records.

104. Compiled Missouri Service Records; Bevier, *History of the First and Second Missouri Confederate Brigades*, p. 417.

105. Bowen to Memminger, 4 June 1863; *Official Records*, vol. 24, ser. 1, pt. 1, p. 669.

106. *Official Records*, vol. 24, ser. 1, pt. 1, p. 605; Erickson, ed., "With Grant at Vicksburg," p. 472; *History of the Sixteenth Battery of Ohio Volunteer Light Artillery, U.S.A., from Enlistment, August 20, 1861, to Muster Out, August 2, 1865* (n.p.: Compiled by Committee, 1906), p. 37.

107. Compiled Missouri Service Records; Dysart to Fannie Sharp, 18 Nov. 1863.

108. *History of the Sixteenth Battery*, p. 38.

109. Bearss, *Grant Strikes a Fatal Blow*, p. 393.

110. Compiled Missouri Service Records.

111. Compiled Missouri Service Records; Dyson to Wife, Fall 1862, 5 Dec. 1862, 20 July 1863; Compiled Missouri Service Records; Dyson to Wife, 22 Aug. 1863; List of Students in Dyson's Class, Franklin County, Missouri, 1 March 1861, Dyson Collection, Western Historical Manuscript Collection, University of Missouri, St. Louis.

112. Bevier, *History of the First and Second Missouri Confederate Brigades*, pp. 416–17; Compiled Missouri Service Records.

113. Bevier, *History of the First and Second Missouri Confederate Brigades*, p. 417; Compiled Missouri Service Records.

114. *Official Records*, vol. 24, ser. 1, pt. 1, p. 605; Compiled Missouri Service Records; Bevier, *History of the First and Second Missouri Confederate Brigades*, p. 416.

115. Bevier, *History of the First and Second Missouri Confederate Brigades*, p. 417.

116. Bevier, *History of the First and Second Missouri Confederate Brigades*, p. 417; Bowen to Memminger, 2 May 1863; Hogan to Father, 22 July 1863.

117. Ruyle Memoir, p. 29; Bowen to Memminger, 4 June 1863.

118. Bevier, *History of the First and Second Missouri Confederate Brigades*, pp. 417, 420.

119. Compiled Missouri Service Records.

120. Compiled Missouri Service Records; *History of Monroe and Shelby Counties, Missouri* (St. Louis: National Historical Company, 1884), pp. 1150–51; Adjutant General of Missouri Rcords, Adjutant General Office, Jefferson City, Missouri.

121. Compiled Missouri Service Records; *General History of Macon County, Missouri* (Chicago: Henry Taylor, 1910), pp. 145, 178.

122. Compiled Missouri Service Records; Adjutant General of Missouri Records; 1860 Macon County, Missouri, Census Records; Leathers Family Papers, Dorothy Voncille Liedorff Schmedake, Callao, Missouri; Dysart to Fannie Sharp, 18 Nov. 1863; Leathers Family Papers; Doris Gatterman, Callao, Missouri, to author, 10 Feb. 1989, and Dorothy Voncille Schmedake to author, 9 Jan. 1989.

123. Compiled Missouri Service Records.

124. Bevier, *History of the First and Second Missouri Confederate Brigades*, p. 417; Bearss, *Grant Strikes a Fatal Blow*, p. 393; Compiled Missouri Service Records; Ruyle Memoir, p. 29; Adjutant General of Missouri Records; Mitchell Family Papers, William F. Moore, Redstone, Alabama; "Arthur E. Mitchell," *Confederate Veteran* 20, no. 1 (Jan. 1912): 35.

125. Bevier, *History of the First and Second Missouri Confederate Brigades*, p. 417; Bearss, Battle of Port Gibson Map, sheet 4 of 4; Compiled Missouri Service Records; Joseph O. Jackson, ed., with Forward by Bell I. Wiley, *Some of the Boys . . . The Civil War Letters of Isaac Jackson, 1862–1865* (Carbondale: Southern Illinois University Press, 1960), p. 88.

126. Compiled Missouri Service Records.

127. Jackson, ed., *Some of the Boys*, p. 88; *Official Records*, vol. 24, ser. 1, pt. 1, p. 604; Bearss, *Grant Strikes a Fatal Blow*, p. 394.

128. *Official Records*, vol. 24, ser. 1, pt. 1, p. 604; Compiled Missouri Service Records.

129. Compiled Missouri Service Records.

130. Compiled Missouri Service Records; *Official Records,* vol. 24, ser. 1, pt. 1, p. 612.

131. Compiled Missouri Service Records; Stephen D. Coale to Brother, 18 Feb. 1865, Western Historical Manuscripts Collection, State Historical Society of Missouri, Columbia, Missouri; Bevier, *History of the First and Second Missouri Confederate Brigades,* Appendix, p. 2.

132. *Official Records,* vol. 24, ser. 1, pt. 1, pp. 606, 612; Compiled Missouri Service Records; Smith Memoir, p. 28.

133. *Official Records,* vol. 24, ser. 1, pt. 1, pp. 612, 630.

134. Compiled Missouri Service Records; Bevier, *History of the First and Second Missouri Confederate Brigades,* p. 417.

135. Bearss, *Grant Strikes a Fatal Blow,* p. 393; Bevier, *History of the First and Second Missouri Confederate Brigades,* p. 417; Compiled Missouri Service Records.

136. Compiled Missouri Service Records; Dysart to Fannie Sharp, 18 Nov. 1863; Bevier, *History of the First and Second Missouri Confederate Brigades,* pp. 180, 418.

137. *Official Records,* vol. 24, ser. 1, pt. 1, pp. 191, 194; Bevier, *History of the First and Second Missouri Confederate Brigades,* p. 181; Dabney Herndon Maury, *Recollections of a Virginian* (New York: Charles Scribner's Sons, 1894), p. 189.

138. Compiled Missouri Service Records; Bevier, *History of the First and Second Missouri Confederate Brigades,* pp. 417–18; Bearss, *Grant Strikes a Fatal Blow,* pp. 394–95.

139. Bevier, *History of the First and Second Missouri Confederate Brigades,* pp. 417–18; Compiled Missouri Service Records; Bowen to Memminger, 4 June 1863; Bearss, *Grant Strikes a Fatal Blow,* p. 397.

140. *Official Records,* vol. 24, ser. 1, pt. 1, p. 669; Bowen to Memminger, 4 June 1863 and 2 May 1863; Bevier, *History of the First and Second Missouri Confederate Brigades,* p. 418.

141. Bevier, *History of the First and Second Missouri Confederate Brigades,* p. 418; Hogan to Father, 22 July 1863.

142. Bevier, *History of the First and Second Missouri Confederate Brigades,* pp. 417–19.

143. *Official Records,* vol. 24, ser. 1, pt. 1, p. 666; Bevier, *History of the First and Second Missouri Confederate Brigades,* p. 419.

144. Bevier, *History of the First and Second Missouri Confederate Brigades,* p. 419.

145. *Official Records,* vol. 24, ser. 1, pt. 1, p. 669.

146. Emily Crawford to Mrs. Elizabeth Lewis, 11 June 1863, Lewis Family Papers, Collection of Charles Sullivan, Perkinston, Mississippi.

147. T. B. Cox, "Gen. Pettus Escapes Johnson Island," p. 19; Simon, ed., *The Papers of Ulysses S. Grant,* vol. 8, p. 139; Compiled Missouri Service Records; William C. Davis, *The Battle of New Market* (Garden City, N.J.: Doubleday, 1975), pp. 119–20.

148. Compiled Missouri Service Records; Dysart to Fannie Sharp, 18 Nov. 1863; Emily Crawford to Mrs. Elizabeth Lewis, 11 June 1863, Lewis Family Papers.

149. Dysart to Fannie Sharp, 18 Nov. 1863.

150. Compiled Missouri Service Records.

151. Josie F. Cappleman, "Local Incidents of the War," *Publications of the Mississippi State Historical Society* 4 (1901): 81.

152. *Official Records,* vol. 24, ser. 1, pt. 1, p. 669; Compiled Missouri Service Records; Anderson, *Memoirs,* p. 298.

153. 1860 Franklin County, Missouri, Census Records; George W. Warren Diary, Private Collection of George W. Warren, IV, Montpelier, Virginia; Compiled Missouri Service Records.

154. *Official Records,* vol. 24, ser. 1, pt. 1, pp. 390, 669; Compiled Missouri Service Records; Bevier, *History of the First and Second Missouri Confederate Brigades,* p. 417; Bearss, *Grant Strikes a Fatal Blow,* pp. 406-7.

155. Compiled Missouri Service Records.

## Chapter VI

1. *Official Records,* vol. 24, ser. 1, pt. 1, pp. 683, 669; Elliott Journal, p. 58; (General) John Stevens Bowen to Memminger, 2 May 1863, Bowen Letterbook, Virginia Historical Society, Richmond; Bevier, *History of the First and Second Missouri Confederate Brigades,* p. 419.

2. Compiled Service Records of Confederate Soldiers Who Served in Organizations from the State of Missouri, National Archives, Washington, D.C.; *Official Records,* vol. 24, ser. 1, pt. 1, p. 666; Bowen to Memminger, 2 May 1863; Bevier, *History of the First and Second Missouri Confederate Brigades,* p. 181; Elliott Journal, p. 59.

3. *Official Records,* vol. 24, ser. 1, pt. 1, pp. 666, 669; Ruyle Memoir, p. 29, Anderson, *Memoirs.* p. 299; William C. Wright, *The Confederate Magazine at Fort Wade, Grand Gulf, Mississippi Excavations, 1980-1981* (Jackson: Mississippi Department of Archives and History and the Grand Gulf State Military Monument, 1982), pp. 27-31; W. S. Duff to William T. Sherman, 3 May 1863, Civil War Papers, Missouri Historical Society, St. Louis; Elliott Journal, p. 59.

4. Compiled Missouri Service Records; James Bradley, *The Confederate Mail Carrier* (Mexico: n.p., 1894), p. 162; Edwin C. Bearss, *Grant Strikes a Fatal Blow,* pp. 423-25; Bevier, *History of the First and Second Missouri Confederate Brigades,* pp. 181-83; Anderson, *Memoirs,* p. 301; *Official Records,* vol. 24, ser. 1, pt. 1, pp. 667-69, 816.

5. Compiled Missouri Service Records; Anderson, *Memoirs,* p. 301.

6. Anderson, *Memoirs,* pp. 301-2.

7. Anderson, *Memoirs,* p. 302; Landis Family Papers, Collection of Walter A. Landis, Jr., Faucett, Missouri; *Official Records,* vol. 24, ser. 1, pt. 1, pp. 667, 669, 722-23; Chris L. Rutt, *History of Buchanan and the City of St. Joseph and Representative Citizens* (Chicago: Biographical Publishing Company, 1904), p. 160; Bevier, *History of the First and Second Missouri Confederate Brigades,* p. 182.

8. *Official Records,* vol. 24, ser. 1, pt. 1, p. 669; Anderson, *Memoirs,* pp. 303-5; Elliott Journal, p. 59; *Official Records,* vol. 24, ser. 1, pt. 2, p. 204.

9. Catton, *Grant Moves South,* p. 429; *Official Records,* vol. 24, ser. 1, pt. 3, p. 834; Kenneth Trist Urquhart, ed., *Vicksburg: Southern City Under Siege, William Lovelace Foster's Letter Describing the Defense and Surrender of the*

Confederate Fortress on the Mississippi (New Orleans: Historic New Orleans Collection, 1980), p. 1.

10. Compiled Missouri Service Records; Bevier, *History of the First and Second Missouri Confederate Brigades,* p. 182; Hogan to Father, 22 July 1863, Missouri Historical Society, St. Louis; Elliott Journal, p. 59; *Official Records,* vol. 24, ser. 1, pt. 3, pp. 827, 834; Bearss, *Grant Strikes a Fatal Blow,* p. 453.

11. Bevier, *History of the First and Second Missouri Confederate Brigades,* p. 182; Bearss, *Grant Strikes a Fatal Blow,* p. 454.

12. Compiled Missouri Service Records; Adjutant General of Missouri Records, Adjutant General Office; Jefferson City, Missouri; "Extract of John K. Newman letter," John G. Reilly Collection, Missouri Historical Society, St. Louis; 1860 St. Louis, Missouri, Census Records; Babcock Scrapbook, Missouri Historical Society, St. Louis; Brauckman Scrapbook, Missouri Historical Society, St. Louis; John S. Kelly to William Skaggs, 6 March 1913, Skaggs Collection, box 1, folder 9, Arkansas History Commission, Little Rock, Arkansas; McNamara, "An Historical Sketch of the Sixth Division, Missouri State Guard," p. 2, Missouri Historical Society, St. Louis.

13. Compiled Missouri Service Records; *Official Records,* vol. 39, ser. 1, pt. 42, p. 357.

14. Compiled Missouri Service Records; 1860 Johnson County, Missouri, Census Records.

15. Compiled Missouri Service Records; *History of Henry and St. Clair Counties, Missouri,* pp. 475–76; 1860 Henry County, Missouri, Census Records.

16. *History of Henry and St. Clair Counties, Missouri,* pp. 475–76; Compiled Missouri Service Records; 1860 Henry County, Missouri, Census Records.

17. Uel W. Lamkin, *History of Henry County, Missouri,* (Topeka, Kan.: Historical Publishing Co., 1919), pp. 134–36; Compiled Missouri Service Records; 1860 Henry County, Missouri, Census Records.

18. Compiled Missouri Service Records.

19. Compiled Missouri Service Records; Joseph Boyce Scrapbook, Missouri Historical Society, St. Louis.

20. Compiled Missouri Service Records; 1860 Polk County, Missouri, Census Records.

21. Compiled Missouri Service Records; Anderson, *Memoirs,* p. 306; Cheavens Journal, Western Historical Manuscript Collection, State Historical Society of Missouri, Columbia, Missouri.

22. Compiled Missouri Service Records.

23. Cheavens Journal; Bevier, *History of the First and Second Missouri Confederate Brigades,* pp. 193, 417; Bearss, *Grant Strikes a Fatal Blow,* pp. 406–7; Compiled Missouri Service Records.

24. Anderson, *Memoirs,* p. 306; Compiled Missouri Service Records; Anderson, *Memoirs,* p. 316; 1860 Boone County, Missouri, Census Records; Bevier, *History of the First and Second Missouri Confederate Brigades,* p. 193.

25. Compiled Missouri Service Records.

26. Adjutant General of Missouri Records; *History of Boone County, Missouri* (St. Louis: Western Historical Company, 1882), p. 485; R. I. Holcombe and F. W. Adams, *An Account of the Battle of Wilson's Creek or Oak Hills,* (Springfield: Dow and Adams, 1883), p. 98.

27. Anderson, *Memoirs,* p. 306.

28. Francis A. Lord, *Civil War Collector's Encyclopedia* (New York: Castle Books, 1965), p. 247; *Official Records*, vol. 24, ser. 1, pt. 3, p. 834; Compiled Missouri Service Records.

29. Lord, *Civil War Collector's Encyclopedia*, 247; Francis A. Lord, "Accouterments of the Enfield Musket," *Civil War Times Illustrated* 5, no. 10 (Feb. 1967): 24–27; Jac Weller, "Imported Confederate Shoulder Weapons," *Civil War History* 5, no. 2 (June 1959): 170–71.

30. Bearss, *Grant Strikes a Fatal Blow*, pp. 479–81; Catton, *Grant Moves South*, pp. 432–35.

31. Bearss, *Grant Strikes a Fatal Blow*, pp. 454–59; Catton, *Grant Moves South*, pp. 435–37; Pemberton, *Pemberton*, pp. 146–47; *Official Records*, vol. 24, ser. 1, pt. 3, p. 789; Samuel Carter, III, *The Final Fortress: The Campaign for Vicksburg, 1862–1863* (New York: St. Martin's, 1980), pp. 186–87.

32. Bearss, *Grant Strikes a Fatal Blow*, pp. 477–78, 510–14.

33. Bearss, *Grant Strikes a Fatal Blow*, pp. 554–55; Johnson and Buel, eds., *Battles and Leaders*, 4 vols., vol. 3, pp. 503–7.

34. Bearss, *Grant Strikes a Fatal Blow*, pp. 559–61; *Official Records*, vol. 24, ser. 1, pt. 1, p. 261; *Official Records*, vol. 24, ser. 1, pt. 2, pp. 110, 114.

35. *Official Records*, vol. 24, ser. 1, pt. 1, p. 261.

36. Bearss, *Grant Strikes a Fatal Blow*, pp. 565–67; Ruyle Memoir, p. 30; *Official Records*, vol. 24, ser. 1, pt. 1, pp. 261–62.

37. Pemberton, *Defender of Vicksburg*, p. 150; Ruyle Memoir, p. 30; Hogan to Father, 22 July 1863; Johnson and Buel, eds., *Battles and Leaders*, vol. 3, p. 508; Bearss, *Grant Strikes a Fatal Blow*, pp. 576–77.

38. *Official Records*, vol. 24, ser. 1, pt. 1, p. 262; Ruyle Memoir, p. 30.

39. *Official Records*, vol. 24, ser. 1, pt. 1, p. 262.

40. Johnson and Buel, eds., *Battles and Leaders*, vol. 3, p. 508; Bearss, *Grant Strikes a Fatal Blow*, pp. 576–77.

41. *Official Records*, vol. 24, ser. 1, pt. 1, pp. 125, 262; Ruyle Memoir, p. 30; Bowen Letterbook, Report no. 84, National Archives.

42. Ruyle Memoir, p. 30; Hogan to Father, 22 July 1863; Bearss, *Grant Strikes a Fatal Blow*, pp. 575–77; *Official Records*, vol. 24, ser. 1, pt. 2, p. 110.

43. Ruyle Memoir, p. 30; Bevier, *History of the First and Second Missouri Confederate Brigades*, p. 423; Bowen Letterbook, Report no. 84, National Archives.

44. Hogan to Father, 22 July 1863; Anderson, *Memoirs*, p. 309; Ruyle Memoir, p. 30.

45. Ruyle Memoir, p. 30; Bevier, *History of the First and Second Missouri Confederate Brigades*, p. 424; *Official Records*, vol. 24, ser. 1, pt. 2, pp. 87, 263; Johnson and Buel, eds., *Battles and Leaders*, vol. 3, p. 509.

46. *Official Records*, vol. 24, ser. 1, pt. 2, pp. 93–94, 125–27; *Official Records*, vol. 24, ser. 1, pt. 1, p. 263; Pemberton, *Defender of Vicksburg*, p. 299 Appendices.

47. "Original Letters and Reports Regarding the Siege of Vicksburg," William K. Bixby Collection, Missouri Historical Society, St. Louis; Johnson and Buel, eds., *Battles and Leaders*, vol. 3, pp. 487, 509; Pemberton, *Defender of Vicksburg*, pp. 154–55; Hogan to Father, 22 July 1863; Ruyle Memoir, p. 30.

48. *Official Records*, vol. 24, ser. 1, pt. 1, p. 126, 263; *Official Records*, vol. 24, ser. 1, pt. 2, pp. 93–94; Catton, *Grant Moves South*, p. 440; Johnson and Buel, eds., *Battles and Leaders*, vol. 3, pp. 549–50.

49. *Official Records*, vol. 24, ser. 1, pt. 1, p. 263; Bearss, *Grant Strikes a Fatal Blow*, pp. 583–84; Anderson, *Memoirs*, pp. 309–10; Edwin C. Bearss, *Decision in Mississippi: Mississippi's Important Role in the War Between the States* (Little Rock: Mississippi Commission on the War Between the States, 1962), p. 242; Bowen Letterbook, Report no. 84, National Archives.

50. Bevier, *History of the First and Second Missouri Confederate Brigades*, p. 424; Colonel Amos Riley to Cockrell, 1 July 1863 Report, H. Riley Bock, New Madrid, Missouri; *Official Records*, vol. 24, ser. 1, pt. 2, p. 110; Bearss, *Decision in Mississippi*, p. 645; *St. Louis Missouri Republican*, 5 Dec. 1884.

51. *Official Records*, vol. 24, ser. 1, pt. 2, p. 110; Isaac Vincent Smith Memoir, p. 28, Western Historical Manuscripts Collection, State Historical Society of Missouri, Columbia, Missouri; *St. Louis Missouri Republican*, 5 Dec. 1884; Bevier, *History of the First and Second Missouri Confederate Brigades*, p. 424; Ruyle Memoir, p. 30.

52. Anderson, *Memoirs*, p. 310; Compiled Missouri Service Records; *St. Louis Missouri Republican*, 1 Jan. 1887; "Funeral Oration of Judge John F. Phillips Over Ex-Senator Francis M. Cockrell," Western Historical Manuscripts Collection, State Historical Society of Missouri, St. Louis; *Official Records*, vol. 24, ser. 1, pt. 2, p. 110; *St. Louis Missouri Republican*, 5 Dec. 1884; Babcock Scrapbook; Kearny-Kennerly Scrapbook, 2, Missouri Historical Society, St. Louis.

53. Hubbell Family Papers, Mrs. Leon Rice Taylor, Richmond, Missouri; *Official Records*, vol. 24, ser. 1, pt. 2, p. 110; *St. Louis Missouri Republican*, 1 Jan. 1887; Anderson, *Memoirs*, p. 310.

54. Bearss, *Grant Strikes a Fatal Blow*, pp. 586–92; United States Department of the Interior Geological Survey of Hinds County, Mississippi, Topographical Sheets; *Official Records*, vol. 24, ser. 1, pt. 1, p. 263.

55. Cockrell to Col. B. Ewell, 21 Nov. 1863, Bowen Letterbook, Virginia Historical Society, Richmond.

56. Bearss, *Grant Strikes a Fatal Blow*, pp. 591–92; *Official Records*, vol. 24, ser. 1, pt. 2, p. 43.

57. Anderson, *Memoirs*, p. 310.

58. Anderson, *Memoirs*, p. 311; Bearss, *Grant Strikes a Fatal Blow*, pp. 589–90; Hubbell Family Papers; Compiled Missouri Service Records; *Official Records*, vol. 24, ser. 1, pt. 1, pp. 263–64; Mrs. T. M. Anderson to W. A. Everman, 14 Oct. 1914, Civil War Papers, Missouri Historical Society, St. Louis; Hubbell, "Personal Reminiscences," p. 16, Missouri Historical Society, St. Louis; "Diary of Lieut. Col. Hubbell of 3d Regiment, Missouri Infantry, C.S.A.," *The Land We Love* 6, no. 2, p. 105.

59. Bearss, *Decision in Mississippi*, pp. 250–55.

60. *Official Records*, vol. 24, ser. 1, pt. 2, pp. 94–95; Bearss, *Decision in Mississippi*, pp. 246–50; Bearss, *Grant Strikes a Fatal Blow*, pp. 596–600.

61. *Official Records*, vol. 24, ser. 1, pt. 2, p. 95; *St. Louis Missouri Republican*, 5 Dec. 1884; Bearss, *Decision in Mississippi*, pp. 260–63; *Official Records*, vol. 24, ser. 1, pt. 1, p. 640.

62. Bearss, Battle of Champion Hill Map, sheet 3 of 5; *Official Records*, vol. 24, ser. 1, pt. 2, pp. 105, 120; Bearss, *Grant Strikes a Fatal Blow*, pp. 605–6.

63. *St. Louis Missouri Republican*, 5 Dec. 1884; Smith Memoir, p. 28; Anderson, *Memoirs*, pp. 310–11; Bearss, *Decision in Mississippi*, p. 265.

64. *Official Records*, vol. 24, ser. 1, pt. 1, p. 264; *Official Records*, 24, ser. 1,

pt. 2, p. 110; *Daily Herald*, Vicksburg, Mississippi, 5 Oct. 1902; Bearss, *Decision in Mississippi*, p. 266; Bevier, *History of the First and Second Missouri Confederate Brigades*, pp. 187–88.

65. Bearss, *Decision in Mississippi*, p. 266; *St. Louis Missouri Republican*, 5 Dec. 1884; *Official Records*, vol. 24, ser. 1, pt. 2, p. 110; Bevier, *History of the First and Second Missouri Confederate Brigades*, p. 424; Compiled Missouri Service Records; Bearss, *Grant Strikes a Fatal Blow*, pp. 605–8; Deborah Isaac, "Confederate Days in St. Louis," Extract of a Series of Newspaper articles from the *St. Louis Missouri Republican*, Missouri Historical Society, St. Louis; *Richmond Enquirer*, 12 June 1863.

66. Riley to Cockrell, 1 July 1863; Bevier, *History of the First and Second Missouri Confederate Brigades*, p. 424; *St. Louis Missouri Republican*, 5 Dec. 1884; Hogan to Father, 22 July 1863.

67. *Official Records*, vol. 24, ser. 1, pt. 2, pp. 111, 120; Bevier, *History of the First and Second Missouri Confederate Brigades*, p. 187.

68. *Official Records*, vol. 24, ser. 1, pt. 2, pp. 55, 111; Compiled Missouri Service Records; *Daily Herald*, 5 Oct. 1902.

69. Bevier, *History of the First and Second Missouri Confederate Brigades*, p. 424; Smith Memoir, p. 28; Bearss, Battle of Champion Hill Map, sheet 3 of 5; Ruyle Memoir, p. 30; *Official Records*, vol. 24, ser. 1, pt. 2, p. 110.

70. *Official Records*, vol. 24, ser. 1, pt. 2, pp. 105–6, 110, 120; Bearss, Battle of Champion Hill Map, sheet 3 of 5.

71. *Official Records*, vol. 24, ser. 1, pt. 2, p. 111; Anderson, *Memoirs*, pp. 311–12.

72. *Official Records*, vol. 24, ser. 1, pt. 2, pp. 106, 110–11; Bearss, *Decision in Mississippi*, p. 266; James E. Payne, "Missouri Troops in the Vicksburg Campaign," *Confederate Veteran* 36, no. 9 (Sept. 1928): 341.

73. *Official Records*, vol. 24, ser. 1, pt. 2, pp. 110–11; *Daily Herald*, 5 Oct. 1902; Bevier, *History of the First and Second Missouri Confederate Brigades*, p. 424; Smith Memoir, p. 28; Payne, "Missouri Troops in the Vicksburg Campaign," p. 341; Ruyle Memoir, pp. 30–31.

74. Ruyle Memoir, pp. 30–31.

75. Ruyle Memoir, pp. 30–31; Compiled Missouri Service Records.

76. Ruyle Memoir, pp. 30–31; *Official Records*, vol. 24, ser. 1, pt. 2, pp. 110–11; *History of Randolph and Macon Counties, Missouri* (St. Louis: National Historical Company, 1884), pp. 863–64.

77. *History of Randolph and Macon Counties, Missouri*, pp. 863–64; *Official Records*, vol. 24, ser. 1, pt. 2, pp. 110–11.

78. *Official Records*, vol. 24, ser. 1, pt. 2, pp. 110–11; Smith Memoir, p. 28.

79. *Official Records*, vol. 24, ser. 1, pt. 2, pp. 110–11.

80. *Official Records*, vol. 24, ser. 1, pt. 2, pp. 110–11; *History of Randolph and Macon Counties, Missouri*, pp. 863–64.

81. Smith Memoir, p. 28; *Official Records*, vol. 24, ser. 1, pt. 2, pp. 110–11.

82. Stephen D. Lee, "The Campaign of Vicksburg, Mississippi, in 1863 — from April 15th to and Including the Battle of Champion Hills, or Baker's Creek, May 16th, 1863," *Publications of the Mississippi State Historical Society* 3 (1900), p. 47.

83. Compiled Missouri Service Records; *History of Randolph and Macon Counties, Missouri,* p. 163, 205. "Consolidated Provision Return for First Brigade May 1 to May 10, 1863," Roster sheet in National Archives.

84. Compiled Missouri Service Records; Pemberton, *Defender of Vicksburg,* p. 159.

85. *History of Randolph and Macon Counties, Missouri,* p. 863.

86. History of Randolph and Macon Counties, Missouri, p. 863; *Official Records,* vol. 24, ser. 1, pt. 2, pp. 110-11.

87. Riley to Cockrell, 1 July 1863; *Official Records,* vol. 24, ser. 1, pt. 2, p. 111.

88. Riley to Cockrell, 1 July 1863; Compiled Missouri Service Records; *Official Records,* vol. 24, ser. 1, pt. 2, p. 111.

89. Ruyle Memoir, p. 31; Joseph Boyce, "The Flag of the First Missouri Confederate Infantry," Civil War Collection, Missouri Historical Society, St. Louis; *Official Records,* vol. 24, ser. 1, pt. 2, p. 111; C. H. Riley to A. R. Taylor, 27 June 1886, Joseph Boyce Papers, Missouri Historical Society, St. Louis; Riley to Cockrell, 1 July 1863.

90. *Official Records,* vol. 24, ser. 1, pt. 2, pp. 118-19; Lee, "Campaign of Vicksburg, Mississippi," p. 47; *Official Records,* vol. 10, ser. 1, pt. 1, pp. 616, 621-22; *St. Louis Missouri Republican,* 7 Jan. 1884.

91. Smith Memoir, p. 28; *Official Records,* vol. 24, ser. 1, pt. 2, pp. 118-19; Compiled Missouri Service Records; Cockrell Scrapbook, Missouri Historical Society, St. Louis; *St. Louis Missouri Republican,* 5 Dec. 1884; Kearny-Kennerly Scrapbook, 2.

92. Absalom Roby Dyson to Wife, 8 June 1863, Western Historical Manuscripts Collection; University of Missouri, St. Louis; Compiled Missouri Service Records; Dyson Class Information for Franklin County, Missouri, school, 1 March 1861, Dyson Collection; Bevier, *History of the First and Second Missouri Confederate Brigades,* p. 353; Brauckman Scrapbook.

93. *Official Records,* vol. 24, ser. 1, pt. 2, p. 95; Dunbar Rowland, *History of Mississippi,* vol. 1, p. 879; *Official Records,* vol. 24, ser. 1, pt. 1, p. 669.

94. Compiled Missouri Service Records; Anderson, *Memoirs,* p. 313.

95. Anderson, *Memoirs,* p. 312; *Official Records,* vol. 24, ser. 1, pt. 2, p. 111.

96. Ruyle Memoir, p. 31; Edwin C. Bearss to author, 15 Jan. 1985; Cheavens Journal; Bearss, *Grant Strikes a Fatal Blow,* pp. 609-11.

97. *Official Records,* vol. 24, ser. 1, pt. 2, pp. 49-50, 55; Anderson, *Memoirs,* p. 312; Smith Memoir, pp. 28-29.

98. Smith Memoir, pp. 28-29; *Richmond Enquirer,* 12 June 1863; *Official Records,* vol. 24, ser. 1, pt. 2, p. 43; Bevier, *History of the First and Second Missouri Confederate Brigades,* p. 424; Compiled Missouri Service Records; Cheavens Journal.

99. Bevier, *History of the First and Second Missouri Confederate Brigades,* p. 424; Hogan to Father, 22 July 1863; Ruyle Memoir, p. 31.

100. Bearss, *Grant Strikes a Fatal Blow,* pp. 604, 609-10; *Official Records,* vol. 24, ser. 1, pt. 2, pp. 42, 55; Smith Memoir, p. 29.

101. Smith Memoir, p. 29; *Richmond Enquirer,* 12 June, 1863; *Daily Herald,* 5 Oct. 1902.

102. Bevier, *History of the First and Second Missouri Confederate Brigades,*

p. 188; United States Department of the Interior Geological Survey of Hinds County, Mississippi, Topographical Sheet; Ruyle Memoir, p. 31; Anderson, *Memoirs*, pp. 312–13.

103. Bevier, *History of the First and Second Missouri Confederate Brigades*, p. 425; Ruyle Memoir, p. 31; Anderson, *Memoirs*, pp. 312–13.

104. Hogan to Father, 22 July 1863; *Official Records*, vol. 24, ser. 1, pt. 2, p. 111; Bevier, *History of the First and Second Missouri Confederate Brigades*, pp. 424–25; Compiled Missouri Service Records; Adjutant General of Missouri Records.

105. Ruyle Memoir, p. 31.

106. Compiled Missouri Service Records; *Official Records*, vol. 24, ser. 1, pt. 2, pp. 49–50.

107. Compiled Missouri Service Records; Bevier, *History of the First and Second Missouri Confederate Brigades*, p. 425.

108. *Official Records*, vol. 24, ser. 1, pt. 2, pp. 42, 49–50; *History of the Sixteenth Battery of Ohio Volunteer Light Artillery*, pp. 52, 58.

109. Bevier, *History of the First and Second Missouri Confederate Brigades*, p. 424; Compiled Missouri Service Records; *Official Records*, vol. 24, ser. 1, pt. 2, pp. 51–54.

110. *Official Records*, vol. 24, ser. 1, pt. 2, p. 56.

111. Dyson to Wife, 8 June 1863.

112. Bevier, *History of the First and Second Missouri Confederate Brigades*, pp. 424–25; Ruyle Memoir, p. 31; Compiled Missouri Service Records; *Official Records*, vol. 24, ser. 1, pt. 2, p. 44.

113. Bevier, *History of the First and Second Missouri Confederate Brigades*, pp. 425–26.

114. Compiled Missouri Service Records; 1860 St. Louis, Missouri, Census Records.

115. *Official Records*, vol. 24, ser. 1, pt. 2, p. 44; Compiled Missouri Service Records; Ruyle Memoir, p. 31.

116. Hogan to Father, 22 July 1863; Bevier, *History of the First and Second Missouri Confederate Brigades*, p. 276; Compiled Missouri Service Records; Ruyle Memoir, p. 31; Mitchell Family Papers, William F. Moore, Redstone, Alabama.

117. Bevier, *History of the First and Second Missouri Confederate Brigades*, p. 426; *Official Records*, vol. 24, ser. 1, pt. 2, p. 111; Thomas S. Hawley to Parents, 18 May 1863, Missouri Historical Society, St. Louis; Hogan to Father, 22 July 1863.

118. Bearss, *Grant Stikes a Fatal Blow*, p. 611; *Official Records*, vol. 24, ser. 1, pt. 2, p. 116; Riley to Cockrell, 11 July 1863; Bevier, *History of the First and Second Missouri Confederate Brigades*, p. 189; *St. Louis Missouri Republican*, 5 Dec. 1884.

119. *Official Records*, vol. 24, ser. 1, pt. 2, pp. 49–50.

120. United States Department of the Interior Geological Survey of Hinds County, Mississippi, Topographical Sheet; J. T. Headley, *The Life and Travels of General Grant* (Philadelphia: Hubbard Brothers, 1879), p. 129; *Official Records*, vol. 24, ser. 1, pt. 2, pp. 43–44.

121. *History of the Sixteenth Battery of Ohio Volunteer Light Artillery*, pp. 50–52; *Official Records*, vol. 24, ser. 1, pt. 2, p. 88; A. H. Reynolds, "Vivid

Experiences at Champion Hill, Miss.," *Confederate Veteran* 18, no. 1 (Jan. 1910): pp. 21–22.

122. *History of the Sixteenth Battery of Ohio Volunteer Light Artillery*, pp. 52, 55; Compiled Missouri Service Records; T. M. Eddy, *Patriotism of Illinois* (Chicago: n.p., 1865), p. 463; *Official Records*, vol. 24, ser. 1, pt. 2, pp. 49–50, 111.

123. *Official Records*, vol. 24, ser. 1, pt. 2, p. 111; Riley to Cockrell, 1 July 1863; Bevier, *History of the First and Second Missouri Confederate Brigades*, p. 426; United States Department of the Interior Geological Survey of Hinds County, Mississippi, Topographical Sheet.

124. Bearss, *Grant Strikes a Fatal Blow*, p. 611; Bevier, *History of the First and Second Missouri Confederate Brigades*, p. 426; Hogan to Father, 22 July 1863.

125. Riley to Cockrell, 1 July 1863.

126. *Official Records*, vol. 24, ser. 1, pt. 2, pp. 102, 106, 111; *Daily Herald*, 5 Oct. 1902; *History of the Sixteenth Battery of Ohio Volunteer Light Artillery*, p. 54; Cheavens Journal; Brauckman Scrapbook; *St. Louis Missouri Republican*, 4 July 1885; Champ Clark Scrapbook, vol. 15, Clark Papers, Western Historical Manuscript Collection, State Historical Society of Missouri, Columbia, Missouri.

127. Anderson, *Memoirs*, p. 313; Bearss, *Grant Strikes a Fatal Blow*, pp. 611–12; *St. Louis Missouri Republican*, 5 Dec. 1884.

128. *Official Records*, vol. 24, ser. 1, pt. 1, p. 264; Pemberton, *Defender of Vicksburg*, p. 163, pp. 316–17 Appendices.

129. Bevier, *History of the First and Second Missouri Confederate Brigades*, p. 426; *St. Louis Missouri Republican*, 5 Dec. 1884; William Henry Kavanaugh Memoir, p. 38, Western Historical Manuscripts Collection, State Historical Society of Missouri, Columbia, Missouri; *Daily Herald*, 5 Oct. 1902.

130. Bevier, *History of the First and Second Missouri Confederate Brigades*, p. 426; *Official Records*, vol. 24, ser. 1, pt. 1, pp. 724, 730–31; Anderson, *Memoirs*, p. 313; Kavanaugh Memoir, p. 38; T. B. Sproul, *Confederate Veteran* 2, no. 7 (July 1894), p. 199.

131. Samuel H. M. Byers, *With Fire and Sword* (New York: Neale, 1911), pp. 76–77.

132. Byers, *With Fire and Sword*, 76–77; Kavanaugh Memoir, p. 38; *Official Records*, vol. 24, ser. 1, pt. 1, p. 724; Riley to Cockrell, 1 July 1863; *Official Records*, vol. 24, ser. 1, pt. 2, pp. 118–19.

133. *Official Records*, vol. 24, ser. 1, pt. 2, pp. 42–44; Riley to Cockrell, 1 July 1863; Hawley to Parents, 30 May 1863.

134. *Official Records*, vol. 24, ser. 1, pt. 1, p. 724; Byers, *With Fire and Sword*, p. 79; S. Wentworth Stevenson, "A Southern Campaign," in *The Ladies Benevolent and Industrial Sallymag Society* (Charlottetown, W. H. Bremner, 1868), p. 112.

135. Byers, *With Fire and Sword*, p. 79; *Official Records*, vol. 24, ser. 1, pt. 1, p. 724; *St. Louis Missouri Republican*, 5 Dec. 1884; Riley to Cockrell, 1 July 1863; Payne, "Missouri Troops in the Vicksburg Campaign," *Confederate Veteran* 36 (Sept. 1928): 341; S. G. Trigg, "Fighting Around Vicksburg," *Confederate Veteran* 12, no. 3 (March 1904): 120.

136. J. B. Sanborn, *Memoir of George B. Boomer* (Boston: George C. Rand and Avery, 1864), p. 281; *History of the Sixteenth Battery of Ohio Volunteer Light*

*Artillery*, p. 56; *Official Records*, vol. 24, ser. 1, pt. 2, p. 44; Johnson and Buel, eds., *Battles and Leaders*, vol. 3, pp. 510–11.

137. *Official Records*, vol. 24, ser. 1, pt. 2, pp. 44, 120; Byers, *With Fire and Sword*, p. 80; *St. Louis Missouri Republican*, 5 Dec. 1884; Kavanaugh Memoir, p. 38; Bevier, *History of the First and Second Missouri Confederate Brigades*, p. 426; Anderson, *Memoirs*, p. 313.

138. *Official Records*, vol. 24, ser. 1, pt. 1, pp. 718, 724; Byers, *With Fire and Sword*, p. 84.

139. M. O. Frost, *Regimental History of the Tenth Missouri Volunteer Infantry* (Topeka, Kan.: Frost, 1892), p. 52; Bevier, *History of the First and Second Missouri Confederate Brigades*, p. 426; *Official Records*, vol. 24, ser. 1, pt. 1, pp. 71, 724; *Official Records*, vol. 24, ser. 1, pt. 2, p. 44; Bevier, *History of the First and Second Missouri Confederate Brigades*, pp. 190, 426; Riley to Cockrell, 1 July 1863.

140. Herb Phillips, *Champion Hill!* (n.p.: Champion Hill Battlefield Foundation, n.d.), pp, 4, 11; *Official Records*, vol. 24, ser. 1, pt. 2, p. 111.

141. *Official Records*, vol. 24, ser. 1, pt. 1, p. 264; Bevier, *History of the First and Second Missouri Confederate Brigades*, p. 189; *St. Louis Missouri Republican*, 5 Dec. 1884; *Official Records*, vol. 24, ser. 1, pt. 2, p. 111.

142. *Official Records*, vol. 24, ser. 1, pt. 3, pp. 111–12, 116–17; *Official Records*, vol. 24, ser. 1, pt. 2, pp. 112, 117; Bevier, *History of the First and Second Missouri Confederate Brigades*, p. 426.

143. Bevier, *History of the First and Second Missouri Confederate Brigades*, p. 192; Compiled Missouri Service Records.

144. Bevier, *History of the First and Second Missouri Confederate Brigades*, pp. 192, 426.

145. Hogan to Father, 22 July 1863; *St. Louis Missouri Republican*, 5 Dec. 1884; Anderson, *Memoirs*, p. 314; Edward C. Robbins, "Landis Battery," Civil War Papers, box. no. 1, Missouri Historical Society, St. Louis; Walter A. Landis, Jr., Faucett, Missouri, to author, 4 Nov. 1988.

146. Bevier, *History of the First and Second Missouri Confederate Brigades*, p. 426; *Official Records*, vol. 24, ser. 1, pt. 1, p. 265.

147. Ibid; *Official Records*, vol. 24, ser. 1, pt. 2, p. 112; *Richmond Enquirer*, 12 June 1863; Johnson and Buel, eds., *Battles and Leaders*, vol. 3, p. 48; Smith Memoir, p. 29; John Leavy Manuscript, p. 13, Vicksburg National Military Battlefield Park Archives, Vicksburg, Mississippi; Compiled Missouri Service Records.

148. *Official Records*, vol. 24, ser. 1, pt. 1, p. 265; *Richmond Enquirer*, 12 June 1863; *Official Records*, vol. 24, ser. 1, pt. 2, p. 112.

149. Leavy Manuscript, p. 12; Compiled Missouri Service Records; Appler Diary, p. 17, Missouri Historical Society, St. Louis.

150. Dyson to Wife, 8 June 1863; Johnson and Buel, eds., *Battles and Leaders*, vol. 3, p. 512; *History of the Sixteenth Battery of Ohio Volunteer Light Artillery*, p. 58; Byers, *With Fire and Sword*, pp. 83–84; Compiled Missouri Service Records; Adjutant General of Missouri Records.

## Chapter VII

1. Cheavens Journal, Western Historical Manuscript Collection, State Historical Society of Missouri, Columbia, Missouri; Bevier, *History of the First*

*and Second Missouri Confederate Brigades,* p. 426; Isaac Vincent Smith Memoir, p. 29, Western Historical Manuscripts Collection, State Historical Society of Missouri; Ruyle Memoir, p. 31; Compiled Service Records of Confederate Soldiers Who Served in Organizations from the State of Missouri, National Archives, Washington, D.C.

2. Ruyle Memoir, p. 31; Compiled Missouri Service Records.

3. *Official Records,* vol. 24, ser. 1, pt. 1, pp. 266–67; Bevier, *History of the First and Second Missouri Confederate Brigades,* p. 426; Smith Memoir, p. 29.

4. *Official Records,* vol. 24, ser. 1, pt. 1, 266; Johnson and Buel, eds., *Battles and Leaders of the Civil War,* 4 vols. (New York: Thomas Yoseloff, 1956), vol. 3, p. 487; Smith Memoir, p. 29.

5. *Official Records,* vol. 24, ser. 1, pt. 1, p. 267; *Official Records,* vol. 24, ser. 1, pt. 2, p. 113; John Leavy Manuscript, pp. 14–15, Vicksburg National Military Battlefield Park Archives, Vicksburg, Missouri.

6. Bearss, *Grant Strikes a Fatal Blow,* pp. 656–57, 664; Bevier, *History of the First and Second Missouri Confederate Brigades,* pp. 426–27.

7. Hogan to Father, 22 July 1863, Missouri Historical Society, St. Louis; Smith Memoir, p. 29; Bevier, *History of the First and Second Missouri Confederate Brigades,* p. 426.

8. Hogan to Father, 22 July 1863; Smith Memoir, p. 29; Cheavens Journal; *Official Records,* vol. 24, ser. 1, pt. 2, p. 113; Smith Memoir, p. 29; William Henry Kavanaugh Memoir, p. 39, Western Historical Manuscripts Collection, State Historical Society of Missouri, Columbia, Missouri.

9. Bearss, *Grant Strikes a Fatal Blow,* pp. 664–65; *Official Records,* vol. 24, ser. 1, pt. 1, p. 266; *Official Records,* vol. 24, ser. 1, pt. 2, pp. 113–14; Johnson and Buel, eds., *Battles and Leaders,* vol. 3, pp. 487–88; Smith Memoir, p. 29.

10. *Official Records,* vol. 24, ser. 1, pt. 2, p. 113; Bearss, *Grant Strikes a Fatal Blow,* p. 670; Cheavens Journal.

11. Bearss, *Grant Strikes a Fatal Blow,* p. 670; Bevier, *History of the First and Second Missouri Confederate Brigades,* p. 194; Cheavens Journal; *Official Records,* vol. 24, ser. 1, pt. 2, p. 113.

12. *Official Records,* vol. 24, ser. 1, pt. 2, pp. 136–37.

13. *Official Records,* vol. 24, ser. 1, pt. 2, pp. 136–38; Bearss, *Grant Strikes a Fatal Blow,* pp. 672–73; *Official Records,* vol. 24, ser. 1, pt. 1, p. 267; Hogan to Father, 22 July 1863; Bevier, *History of the First and Second Missouri Confederate Brigades,* p. 426.

14. Bevier, *History of the First and Second Missouri Confederate Brigades,* pp. 426–27.

15. Cheavens Journal; Ruyle Memoir, p. 32; Cheavens Journal; Isaac Hughes Elliott, *History of the Thirty-third Regiment Veteran Volunteer Infantry in the Civil War* (Gibson City, Ill.: Thirty-third Illinois Association Publication, 1902), p. 194; *Official Records,* vol. 24, ser. 1, pt. 1, p. 268; E. W. Strode, "Recollections of an Artilleryman," *Confederate Veteran* 2, no. 12 (Dec. 1894): 379; Compiled Missouri Service Records; Smith Memoir, pp. 29–30.

16. Bevier, *History of the First and Second Missouri Confederate Brigades,* p. 427; Hogan to Father, 22 July 1863; Hogan to Father, 22 July 1863; Joseph D. Jackson, ed., *Some of the Boys ... The Civil War Letters of Isaac Jackson, 1862–1865* (Carbondale: Southern Illinois University Press, 1960), p. 96.

17. *Official Records,* vol. 24, ser. 1, pt. 1, p. 262; Bevier, *History of the First and Second Missouri Confederate Brigades,* pp. 194–95; *Official Records,* vol. 24, ser. 1, pt. 2, p. 113.

18. Richard Sommers, Introduction to *The Official Military Atlas of the Civil War* (New York: Arno, 1978), plate no. 37, map no. 7; Bevier, *History of the First and Second Missouri Confederate Brigades,* pp. 194–95; Jackson, *Some of the Boys,* p. 96; Ephraim McDowell Anderson, *Memoirs: Historical and Personal, Including the Campaigns of the First Missouri Confederate Brigade* (St. Louis, Times Printing Co., 1868), p. 319; Compiled Missouri Service Records.

19. Robert Dunlap Diary, p. 215, John B. Sampson, DeKalb, Missouri; Strode, "Recollections of an Artilleryman," p. 379.

20. Jackson, *Some of the Boys,* p. 96; Anderson, *Memoirs,* p. 319.

21. George Crooke, *The Twenty-first Regiment of Iowa Volunteer Infantry: A Narrative of Its Experience in Active Service* (Milwaukee: King, Fowle, 1891), p. 73; Samuel H. M. Byers, *With Fire and Sword* (New York: Neale, 1911), p. 313; Bevier, *History of the First and Second Missouri Confederate Brigades,* pp. 424–27; Compiled Missouri Service Records; 1860 Franklin County, Missouri, Census Records; Edwin E. Johnson to Sister, 18 August 1863, Dyson Collection.

22. Dunlap Diary, p. 216; Cheavens Journal; Leavy Manuscript, p. 15; *Official Records,* vol. 24, ser. 1, pt. 2, pp. 400–1, 418.

23. Johnson and Buel, eds., *Battles and Leaders,* vol. 3, p. 488; Smith Memoir, p. 29.

24. Anderson, *Memoirs,* p. 320; *Official Records,* ser. 1, pt. 2, p. 113; Smith Memoir, p. 29; *St. Louis Missouri Republican,* 5 Dec. 1884; Byers, *With Fire and Sword,* p. 313.

25. Bearss, *Grant Strikes a Fatal Blow,* p. 677; Crooke, *The Twenty-first Regiment of Iowa Volunteer Infantry,* p. 73; *St. Louis Missouri Republican,* 5 Dec. 1884; *Official Records,* vol. 24, ser. 1, pt. 2, pp. 113–14, 120; Johnson and Buel, eds., *Battles and Leaders,* vol. 3, p. 515; Cheavens Journal; Edward C. Robbins, "Landis Battery," Civil War Papers, box no. 1, Missouri Historical Society, St. Louis; Smith Memoir, p. 30.

26. *Official Records,* vol. 24, ser. 1, pt. 1, p. 617; Johnson and Buel, eds., *Battles and Leaders,* vol. 3, p. 515.

## Chapter VIII

1. Robert Bevier, *History of the First and Second Missouri Confederate Brigades,* pp. 199–200; Hogan to Father, 22 July 1863, Missouri Historical Society, St. Louis; Robert Underwood Johnson and Clarence Clough Buel, eds., *Battles and Leaders of the Civil War,* 4 vols. (New York: Thomas Yoseloff, 1956), vol. 3, p. 515; Charles H. Dana, *Recollections of the Civil War* (New York: Collier Books, 1963), p. 69.

2. Compiled Service Records of Confederate Soldiers Who Served in Organizations from the State of Missouri, National Archives, Washington, D.C.; Hogan to Father, 22 July 1863; *St. Louis Missouri Republican,* 5 Dec. 1884; Anderson, *Memoirs,* p. 319; Bevier, *History of the First and Second Missouri Confederate Brigades,* p. 196; Dyson to Wife, 30 Aug. 1863, Absalom Roby Dyson

Letters, Western Historical Manuscript Collection, University of Missouri, St. Louis.

3. Bevier, *History of the First and Second Missouri Confederate Brigades*, p. 199; Cheavens Journal, Western Historical Manuscripts Collection, State Historical Society of Missouri, Columbia, Missouri; *Milestones, to Live and Die in Dixie* (N.p.: Westinghouse Integrated Logistics Support, n.d.), p. 2.

4. John Leavy Manuscript, p. 21, Vicksburg National Military Battlefield Park Archives, Vicksburg, Mississippi; *The Mobile, Alabama, Register and Advertiser*, 19 July 1863; Edwin C. Bearss, *The Campaign for Vicksburg: Unvexed to the Sea* (Dayton: Morningside House, 1986), vol. 3, p. 675.

5. Theodore D. Fisher Diary, p. 2, Missouri Historical Society, St. Louis; Anderson, *Memoirs*, p. 327; *The War of the Rebellion: A Compilation of the Official Records of the Union and Confederate Armies*, 128 vols. (Washington, D.C., 1880–1901), vol. 24, ser. 1, pt. 2, pp. 397, 414; *St. Louis Missouri Republican*, 5 Dec. 1884; Anderson, *Memoirs*, p. 327; Frances Marion Cockrell Scrapbook, 4, Missouri Historical Society, St. Louis; Bearss, *Unvexed to the Sea*, pp. 750, 753; Hogan to Father, 22 July 1863.

6. Bearss, *Unvexed to the Sea*, pp. 753–54; Virginia Calohan Harrell, *Vicksburg and the River* (Vicksburg, Miss.: Virginia Calohan Harrell, 1986), pp. 9–10, 92; *Official Records*, vol. 24, ser. 1, pt. 2, p. 414; Bearss, *Unvexed to the Sea*, p. 754.

7. Bevier, *History of the First and Second Missouri Confederate Brigades*, p. 429; Isaac Vincent Smith Memoir, p. 30, Western Historical Manuscripts Collection, State Historical Society of Missouri, Columbia, Missouri; *Vicksburg, Official National Park Handbook* (Washington, D.C.: United States Department of the Interior, 1986), pp. 45–46; Fisher Diary, p. 1; Johnson and Buel, eds., *Battles and Leaders*, vol. 3, p. 537; *Richmond Enquirer*, 5 June 1863; Kenneth Trist Urquhart, *Vicksburg: Southern City Under Siege, William Lovelace Foster's Letter Describing the Defense and Surrender of the Confederate Fortress on the Mississippi* (New Orleans: Historic New Orleans Collection, 1980), p. 7.

8. *Official Records*, vol. 24, ser. 1, pt. 2, pp. 414, 419–20; Bearss, *Unvexed to the Sea*, p. 741; Leavy Manuscript, p. 21.

9. Johnson and Buel, eds., *Battles and Leaders*, vol. 3, p. 517.

10. Bearss, *Unvexed to the Sea*, p. 761; *Official Records*, vol. 24, ser. 1, pt. 2, pp. 267–68; Robbins to Sister, 24 Jan. 1863, Robbins Papers, Mercantile Library, St. Louis.

11. Riley to Cockrell, 26 July 1863, H. Riley Bock, New Madrid, Missouri; *Official Records*, vol. 24, ser. 1, pt. 2, p. 414; Bevier, *History of the First and Second Missouri Confederate Brigades*, p. 202; Riley to Cockrell, 26 July 1863; Johnson and Buel, eds., *Battles and Leaders*, vol. 3, p. 489.

12. *Official Records*, vol. 24, ser. 1, pt. 2, pp. 267–68, 414; Data on battlefield marker of troop positions, Vicksburg National Military Park, Vicksburg, Mississippi; Bearss, *Unvexed to the Sea*, p. 761.

13. Johnson and Buel, eds., *Battles and Leaders*, vol. 3, p. 489; Robbins to Sister, 24 Jan. 1863; *Official Records*, vol. 24, ser. 1, pt. 2, pp. 263–64.

14. Riley to Cockrell, 26 July 1863; *Official Records*, vol. 24, ser. 1, pt. 2, pp. 263–65.

15. Hogan to Father, 22 July 1863; Bevier, *History of the First and Second Missouri Confederate Brigades*, p. 202.

16. Compiled Missouri Service Records; Hogan to Father, 22 July 1863.

17. *Official Records*, vol. 24, ser. 1, pt. 2, pp. 264, 414.

18. Compiled Missouri Service Records.

19. Bearss, *Unvexed to the Sea*, p. 773; Earl S. Miers, *The Web of Victory: Grant at Vicksburg* (Baton Rouge: Louisiana State University Press, 1955), pp. 204–5.

20. Hogan to Father, 22 July 1863; Bevier, *History of the First and Second Missouri Confederate Brigades*, p. 202.

21. *Official Records*, vol. 24, ser. 1, pt. 2, p. 415; Bevier, *History of the First and Second Missouri Confederate Brigades*, p. 202; Compiled Missouri Service Records; *Richmond Enquirer*, 5 June 1863.

22. Dana, *Recollections of the Civil War*, p. 97; Compiled Missouri Service Records; Mitchell Family Papers, William F. Moore, Redstone, Alabama; Arington Wayne Simpson Diary, Western Historical Manuscripts Collection, State Historical Society of Missouri, Columbia, Missouri; William A. Ruyle Memoir, p. 32, Dee Ruyle, Bolivar, Missouri.

23. Bevier, *History of the First and Second Missouri Confederate Brigades*, pp. 197, 429.

24. Harrell, *Vicksburg and the River*, pp. 17, 21, 27, 29, 35, 43, 49; Babcock Scrapbook, Missouri Historical Society, St. Louis; Jonathan Beasley, "Blacks — Slave and Free — Vicksburg, 1850–1860," *Journal of Mississippi History* 38, no. 1 (Feb. 1976): 3.

25. *Official Records*, vol. 24, ser. 1, pt. 3, p. 904; Compiled Missouri Service Records; *Official Records*, vol. 24, ser. 1, pt. 2, p. 415; Riley to Cockrell, 26 July 1863.

26. Miers, *Web of Victory*, p. 206; Johnson and Buel, eds., *Battles and Leaders*, vol. 3, p. 518; Bearss, *Unvexed to the Sea*, p. 792.

27. Dana, *Recollections of the Civil War*, p. 97; Johnson and Buel, eds., *Battles and Leaders*, vol. 3, p. 518; Catton, *Grant Moves South*, p. 452; J. H. Jones, "The Rank and File at Vicksburg," *Publications of the Mississippi State Historical Society* 7 (1903): 20; Bearss, *Unvexed to the Sea*, p. 813; *Official Records*, vol. 24, ser. 1, pt. 2, p. 415; Riley to Cockrell, 26 July 1863.

28. Riley to Cockrell, 26 July 1863; *Official Records*, vol. 24, ser. 1, pt. 2, p. 415; Data on battlefield marker of troop positions, Vicksburg National Military Park; Bearss, *Unvexed to the Sea*, pp. 816, n. 8, 818; Compiled Missouri Service Records; Riley to Cockrell, 22 July 1863; "Roster Field and Line Officers, First Missouri Confederate Infantry," box 2, Civil War Papers, Missouri Historical Society, St. Louis.

29. Crooke, *The Twenty-first Regiment of Iowa Volunteer Infantry*, p. 77; Bevier, *History of the First and Second Missouri Confederate Brigades*, p. 204.

30. Robert J. Rombauer Order Book 1863, Journal and Diaries, Missouri Historical Society, St. Louis; Joseph B. Mitchell, *The Badge of Gallantry: Recollections of Civil War Congressional Medal of Honor Winners* (New York: Macmillian, 1968), pp. 111–22; *St. Louis Missouri Republican*, 5 Dec. 1884; Francis V. Greene, *The Mississippi, Campaigns of the Civil War* (New York: Charles Scribner's Sons, 1885), p. 179.

31. Mitchell, *Badge of Gallantry*, pp. 114–15, 118; Necrologies Scrapbook, 7, p. 2, Missouri Historical Society, St. Louis; *St. Louis Missouri Republican*, 5 Dec. 1884; *Richmond Enquirer*, 5 June 1863.

32. Bearss, *Unvexed to the Sea*, p. 815; Greene, *The Mississippi*, p. 179.

33. Mitchell, *Badge of Gallantry*, pp. 115–16; Bearss, *Unvexed to the Sea*, p. 816; Necrologies Scrapbook, 7, p. 2; Rombauer Order Book 1863; Harvey M. Trimble, *History of the Ninety-third Regiment Illinois Volunteer Infantry, from Organization to Muster Out* (Chicago: Blakely, 1898), p. 36.

34. Bevier, *History of the First and Second Missouri Confederate Brigades*, p. 204; Jones, "Rank and File at Vicksburg," p. 21; *St. Louis Missouri Republican*, 5 Dec. 1884; Mitchell, *Badge of Gallantry*, pp. 90, 113; Compiled Missouri Service Records.

35. Bevier, *History of the First and Second Missouri Confederate Brigades*, p. 42; *Official Records*, vol. 24, ser. 1, pt. 2, p. 415; Compiled Missouri Service Records.

36. Bearss, *Unvexed to the Sea*, p. 816.

37. Mitchell, *Badge of Gallantry*, pp. 116–17; Smith Memoir, p. 30; *Official Records*, vol. 24, ser. 1, pt. 2, p. 415; W. J. Ervin, "Genius and Heroism of Lieut. K. H. Faulkner," *Confederate Veteran* 14, no. 11 (Nov. 1906): 497.

38. Robbins to Sister, 24 Jan. 1863; Bearss, *Unvexed to the Sea*, p. 839.

39. Smith Memoir, p. 30; Bevier, *History of the First and Second Missouri Confederate Brigades*, p. 204; Compiled Missouri Service Records; Mitchell Family Papers.

40. Miers, *Web of Victory*, p. 214; W. J. Smith to Mrs. Bowen, 23 March 1893, Bowen Papers, Missouri Historical Society, St. Louis; Rombauer Order Book 1863; Hogan to Father, 22 July 1863.

41. Seth James Wells, *The Diary of Seth Wells* (Detroit: W. H. Rowe, 1915), p. 79; Johnson and Buel, eds., *Battles and Leaders*, vol. 3, pp. 546–50.

42. Johnson and Buel, eds., *Battles and Leaders*, vol. 3, p. 518; Bearss, *Unvexed to the Sea*, p. 1079; Bevier, *History of the First and Second Missouri Confederate Brigades*, pp. 205, 429; *St. Louis Missouri Republican*, 5 Dec. 1884; David D. Porter, *The Naval History of the Civil War* (New York: Sherman, 1886), pp. 321–25; *St. Louis Missouri Republican*, 5 Dec. 1885; Cheavens Journal.

43. Compiled Missouri Service Records; Bevier, *History of the First and Second Missouri Confederate Brigades*, pp. 429, 432; *Official Records*, vol. 24, ser. 1, pt. 2, p. 415; Edwin C. Bearss, ed., "Charles E. Affeld Describes the Mechanicsburg Expedition," *Journal of the Illinois State Historical Society* 56, no. 2, (1972): 237.

44. Compiled Missouri Service Records; Anderson, *Memoirs*, p. 338.

45. Bevier, *History of the First and Second Missouri Confederate Brigades*, p. 429; Compiled Missouri Service Records; 1860 Johnson County, Missouri, Census Records.

46. Compiled Missouri Service Records; William Hyde and Howard L. Conrad, *Encyclopedia of the History of St. Louis*, 4 vols. (St. Louis: Southern Historical Company, 1899), vol. 2, pp. 1136–37.

47. Crooke, *Twenty-first Regiment*, p. 78; Bevier, *History of the First and Second Missouri Confederate Brigades*, pp. 199, 429; Compiled Missouri Service Records; Leavy Manuscript, pp. 23–24; *Mobile Register and Advertiser*, 19 July 1863; *St. Louis Missouri Republican*, 5 Dec. 1884; *Union and Confederate Annals: The Blue and Gray in Friendship Meet, and Heroic Deeds Recited*, 1, no. 1 (June 1884): 39; Osburn H. Oldroyd, *A Soldier's Story of the Siege of Vicksburg* (Springfield: H. W. Rokker, 1885), p. 158; Theodore D. Fisher Diary, p. 4, Missouri

Historical Society, St. Louis; Joseph Boyce, "Rev. John Bannon Chaplain Price's Missouri Confederate Division": Paper Read March 8, 1914, at Confederate Veteran Meeting, Camp 731, St. Louis, Missouri, United Confederate Veterans, Missouri Historical Society, St. Louis.

48. Anderson, *Memoirs*, p. 333; *St. Louis Missouri Republican*, 5 Dec. 1884; Fisher Diary, p. 2; Urquhart, *Vicksburg*, p. 21.

49. Urquhart, *Vicksburg*, p. 21; C. A. Powell, "Brother Fought Against Brother," *Confederate Veteran* 10, no. 10 (Oct. 1902): 463; Emma Balfour, *Vicksburg, a City Under Siege: Diary of Emma Balfour May 16, 1863–June 2, 1863* (n.p.: Phillip C. Weinberger, 1983), p. 128.

50. "Facts Concerning Albert Carlisle Mitchell," including Absalom Grimes Sketch, p. 5, Absalom Grimes Papers, Missouri Historical Society, St. Louis; Compiled Missouri Service Records; Milo M. Quaife, *Absalom Grimes: Confederate Mail Runner* (New Haven: Yale University Press, 1926), pp. 214–16; Bell Irvin Wiley, *The Life of Johnny Reb: The Common Soldier of the Confederacy* (Baton Rouge: Louisiana State University, 1978), p. 200.

51. Adjutant General of Missouri Records, Adjutant General Office, Jefferson City, Missouri.

52. L. Moody Simms, Jr., "A Louisiana Engineer at the Siege of Vicksburg: Letters of Henry Ginder, *Louisiana History* 8 (1967): 374; *Official Records*, vol. 24, ser. 1, pt. 2, pp. 363, 411–12.

53. *Official Records*, vol. 24, ser. 1, pt. 2, p. 412; Urquhart, *Vicksburg*, pp. 47, 54; William H. Tunnard, *A Southern Record: The History of the Third Regiment Louisiana Infantry* (Dayton: Morningside, 1970), p. 260.

54. *Official Records*, vol. 24, ser. 1, pt. 2, p. 412; Urquhart, *Vicksburg*, p. 47; Fisher Diary, p. 3.

55. Leavy Manuscript, p. 22; Urquhart, *Vicksburg*, pp. 33, 38.

56. Compiled Missouri Service Records; Lemmon Family Papers.

57. *Official Records*, vol. 24, ser. 1, pt. 1, p. 274; Hogan to Father, 22 July 1863; *Official Records*, vol. 24, ser. 1, pt. 2, p. 175.

58. Compiled Missouri Service Records; Warren Diary; Milton D. Rafferty, *Historical Atlas of Missouri* (Norman: University of Oklahoma, 1981), plate no. 38; Russel L. Gerlach, "Population Origins in Rural Missouri," *Missouri Historical Review* 71, no. 1 (Oct. 1976): 10–11, 14–19; Compiled Missouri Service Records; *St. Louis Missouri Republican*, 5 Dec. 1884.

59. Compiled Missouri Service Records; Leavy Manuscript, pp. 21–22.

60. Bevier, *History of the First and Second Missouri Confederate Brigades*, p. 435; Dysart to Sharp, 18 Nov. 1863, Compiled Missouri Service Records.

61. Compiled Missouri Service Records; George Elliott Journal, p. 70, Tennessee State Library and Archives, Nashville; Obediah Taylor Photograph, Eleanor S. Brockenbrough Library, Confederate Museum, Richmond, Virginia; General Directory for the City of Vicksburg, Mississippi (Vicksburg: H. C. Clarke, 1860), p. 22.

62. John B. Bannon Diary, Yates Snowden Collection, South Carolina Library, University of South Carolina, Columbia, South Carolina; *St. Louis Missouri Republican*, 5 Dec. 1884; James J. Pillar, *The Catholic Church in Mississippi, 1837–1865* (New Orleans: Hauser, 1964), p. 233; The Reverend Laurence J. Kenny and Joseph P. Morrissey, "Father John Bannon, S.J.," *United States Catholic Historical Society Publications* 26 (1936): 94; Hogan to Father, 22 July 1863.

63. Compiled Missouri Service Records; Harrell, *Vicksburg and the River*, p. 45.

64. Elliott Journal, p. 70; Fisher Diary, p. 4; Bevier, *History of the First and Second Missouri Confederate Brigades*, pp. 330–31.

65. Nannie M. Tilley, ed., *Federals on the Frontier: The Diary of Benjamin F. McIntyre, 1862–1864* (Austin: University of Texas Press, 1963), p. 167.

66. Fisher Diary, p. 3; Hogan to Father, 22 July 1863.

67. Fisher Diary, p. 6; Compiled Missouri Service Records; Dyson to Wife, 30 Aug. 1863; Leavy Manuscript, p. 34.

68. *Official Records*, vol. 24, ser. 1, pt. 1, p. 278; *St. Louis Missouri Republican*, 5 Dec. 1884; Bevier, *History of the First and Second Missouri Confederate Brigades*, p. 431; Cheavens Journal, p. 41; Anderson, *Memoirs*, pp. 377, 339; Fisher Diary, p. 7; Frank Moore, ed., *The Rebellion Record* (New York: n.p., 1862–1868), vol. 7, p. 172.

69. *Daily Citizen*, Vicksburg, Mississippi, 2 July 1863; Hyde and Conrad, *Encyclopedia of the History of St. Louis*, vol. 4, p. 2444; Bevier, *History of the First and Second Missouri Confederate Brigades*, pp. 431, 435–36; Ruyle Memoir, p. 32.

70. Compiled Missouri Service Records.

71. Bevier, *History of the First and Second Missouri Confederate Brigades*, pp. 432–33.

72. Compiled Missouri Service Records; Adjutant General of Missouri Records; 1860 Macon County, Missouri, Census Records; *General History of Macon County, Missouri* (Chicago: Henry Taylor, 1910), pp. 15–16.

73. Bevier, *History of the First and Second Missouri Confederate Brigades*, p. 431; Dysart to Sharp, Nov. 18, 1863.

74. Dysart to Sharp, Nov. 18, 1863; Compiled Missouri Service Records.

75. Compiled Missouri Service Records; McCown Family Papers, Collection of Garland McCown of Garland, Texas, and Frank D. McCown of Fort Worth, Texas.

76. Homer L. Calkins, ed., "From Elkhorn to Vicksburg: James H. Fauntelroy's Diary for the Year 1862," *Civil War History* 2 (Jan. 1956): 31; Wayne C. Temple, ed., *Campaigning with Grant* (New York: Century, 1897), pp. 363–64; Compiled Missouri Service Records.

77. Fisher Diary, p. 5; *Official Records*, vol. 24, ser. 1, pt. 2, pp. 332–33; Bevier, *History of the First and Second Missouri Confederate Brigades*, p. 212; Bearss, *Unvexed to the Sea*, p. 741; Moore, ed., *Rebellion Record*, vol. 7, p. 172; Johnson and Buel, eds., *Battles and Leaders*, vol. 3, pp. 491, 526–27; Dana, *Recollections of the Civil War*, p. 97; Tunnard, *A Southern Record*, pp. 234–35, 258, 266, 547; Compiled Missouri Service Records; *The History of Johnson County Missouri*, pp. 672–73.

78. Johnson and Buel, eds., *Battles and Leaders*, vol. 3, p. 491; *Official Records*, vol. 24, ser. 1, pt. 2, pp. 332–33; Tunnard, *A Southern Record*, pp. 259–60, 266; Fisher Diary, p. 5.

79. Fisher Diary, p. 6; Joseph Dill Alison Diary, Southern Historical Collection, University of North Carolina, Chapel Hill, North Carolina; Tunnard, *A Southern Record*, pp. 264, 396; *Official Records*, vol. 24, ser. 1, pt. 2, p. 202.

80. Alonzo Brown, *History of the Fourth Regiment of Minnesota Infantry Volunteers During the Great Rebellion* (St. Paul: Pioneer Press, 1892), p. 227; *Richmond Enquirer*, 1 July 1863.

81. Miers, *Web of Victory*, pp. 280–81; Elliott Journal, p. 65; *Official Records*, vol. 24, ser. 1, pt. 2, pp. 202, 376; *Mobile Register and Advertiser*, 19 July, 1863; Richard Wheeler, *The Siege of Vicksburg* (New York: Thomas Y. Crowell, 1978), p. 221; Johnson and Buel, eds., *Battles and Leaders*, vol. 3, p. 527; Elliott Journal, p. 65.

82. T. M. Eddy, *Patriotism of Illinois* (Chicago: n.p., 1865), p. 471; *Official Records*, vol. 24, ser. 1, pt. 2, pp. 207, 415; Johnson and Buels, eds., *Battles and Leaders*, vol. 3, pp. 491, 527; Bearss, *Unvexed to the Sea*, p. 920; Elliott Journal, p. 65; James Payne, "Missouri Troops in the Vicksburg Campaign," *Confederate Veteran* 36 (Sept. 1928): 378.

83. Tunnard, *A Southern Record*, pp. 258–59; Elliott Journal, p. 65; *Official Records*, vol. 24, ser. 1, pt. 2, pp. 372, 376–77, 415–16; *Richmond Enquirer*, 14 Aug. 1863; *Mobile Register and Advertiser*, 19 July 1863; Compiled Missouri Service Records; Bevier, *History of the First and Second Missouri Confederate Brigades*, p. 430; *Mobile Register and Advertiser*, 19 July 1863; Necrologies Scrapbook, p. 106, no. 11c, Missouri Historical Society, St. Louis; Moore, ed., *Rebellion Record*, vol. 7, p. 203; *Mobile Register and Advertiser*, 19 July 1863; Bearss, *Unvexed to the Sea*, p. 821.

84. William E. Connelley, *Doniphan's Expedition and the Conquest of New Mexico and California* (Topeka, Kan.: n.p., 1907), p. 538; Compiled Missouri Service Records; Necrologies Scrapbook, p. 106, no. 11c; Hogan to Father, 22 July 1863; Ruyle Memoir, pp. 32–33; Bevier, *History of the First and Second Missouri Confederate Brigades*, pp. 199, 430.

85. Hogan to Father, 22 July 1863; Moore, ed., *Rebellion Record*, vol. 7, p. 167; William S. Morris, *History of the Thirty-first Regiment Illinois Volunteers, Organized by John A. Logan* (Evansville: Keller, 1902), pp. 73–74; Miers, *Web of Victory*, pp. 281–82.

86. Payne, "Missouri Troops in the Vicksburg Campaign," pp. 377–78; *Mobile Register and Advertiser*, 19 July 1863; Moore, ed., *Rebellion Record*, vol. 7, p. 203; Compiled Missouri Service Records.

87. Orville James Victor, *The History Civil, Political and Military of the Southern Rebellion*, 4 vols. (New York: J. D. Torrey, 1861–1865), vol. 4, p. 75; Compiled Missouri Service Records; Ruyle Memoir, p. 33; Simpson Diary; Tunnard, *A Southern Record*, p. 259; "A Hero in the Strife," *Confederate Veteran* 2, no. 9 (Sept. 1894): 282; Bevier, *History of the First and Second Missouri Confederate Brigades*, p. 211; Morris, *History of the Thirty-first Regiment*, p. 74.

88. Tunnard, *A Southern Record*, p. 259; Compiled Missouri Service Records; Mitchell Papers; Ruyle Memoir,. p. 33.

89. Bevier, *History of the First and Second Missouri Confederate Brigades*, p. 84; Johnson and Buel, eds., *Battles and Leaders*, vol. 3, p. 527; Dana, *Recollections of the Civil War*, pp. 97–98; William Henry Kavanaugh Memoir, p. 42, Western Historical Manuscripts Collection, State Historical Society of Missouri, Columbia, Missouri; Moore, ed., *Rebellion Record*, vol. 7, p. 203; Compiled Missouri Service Records; Ruyle Memoir, p. 33; Simpson Diary.

90. *Official Records*, vol. 24, ser. 1, pt. 2, p. 294.

91. Compiled Missouri Service Records; Ruyle Memoir, p. 33; *Official Records*, vol. 24, ser. 1, pt. 2, p. 294; Miers, *Web of Victory*, p. 283.

92. Victor, *History of the Southern Rebellion*, vol. 4, p. 75; "A Hero of the Strife," p. 282; Stephen D. Lee, "The Siege of Vicksburg," *Publications of the*

Mississippi State Historical Society 3 (1900): 66; Hogan to Father, 22 July 1863; Compiled Missouri Service Records; *Official Records*, vol. 24, ser. 1, pt. 2, p. 372.

93. Elliott Journal, p. 65; Moore, ed., *Rebellion Record*, vol. 7, p. 173.

94. Elliott Journal, p. 65; *Official Records*, vol. 24, ser. 1, pt. 2, p. 202.

95. Compiled Missouri Service Records; Dyson Class Information for Franklin County, Missouri, school, 1 March 1861; Adjutant General of Missouri Records; Compiled Missouri Service Records; Dyson to Wife, 22 Aug. 1863; *Official Records*, vol. 24, ser. 1, pt. 2, pp. 202, 333; Elliott Journal, p. 65.

96. *Official Records*, vol. 24, ser. 1, pt. 2, p. 416; Compiled Missouri Service Records.

97. Tunnard, *A Southern Record*, p. 260; *Official Records*, vol. 24, ser. 1, pt. 2, p. 294, 372; Moore, ed., *Rebellion Record*, vol. 7, p. 173; *Official Records*, vol. 24, ser. 1, pt. 2, p. 416.

98. Elliott Journal, p. 65; Compiled Missouri Service Records; 1860 Polk County, Missouri, Census Records.

99. Historic Homes of Missouri Scrapbook, 9, Missouri Historical Society, St. Louis; Compiled Missouri Service Records.

100. Bevier, *History of the First and Second Missouri Confederate Brigades*, p. 429; Hogan to Father, 22 July 1863.

101. Hyde and Conrad, *Encyclopedia*, vol. 4, p. 2444; Bearss, *Unvexed to the Sea*, p. 1127.

102. Bearss, *Unvexed to the Sea*, p. 1282; Smith Memoir, pp. 31–32; Hyde and Conrad, *Encyclopedia*, vol. 4, p. 2444; Johnson and Buel, eds., *Battles and Leaders*, vol. 3, p. 492; "Words of a Veteran About Vicksburg," *Confederate Veteran* 2, no. 10 (Oct. 1894): 312; Hogan to Father, 22 July 1863.

103. Compiled Missouri Service Records; Anderson, *Memoirs*, p. 358; Bevier, *History of the First and Second Missouri Confederate Brigades*, p. 431.

104. Leavy Manuscript, p. 38; *Richmond Enquirer*, 14 Aug. 1863; Lida Lord Reed, "A Woman's Experiences During the Siege of Vicksburg," *The Century Magazine* 61 (April 1901): 926; *Richmond Enquirer*, 14 Aug. 1863.

105. Hogan to Father, 22 July 1863; *St. Louis Missouri Republican*, 5 Dec. 1884; James J. Pillar, *The Catholic Church in Mississippi, 1837–1865* (New Orleans: Hauser, 1964), pp. 106, 132–33, 191; *Richmond Enquirer*, 14 Aug. 1863.

106. Compiled Missouri Service Records; Leavy Manuscript, p. 37; Bearss, *Unvexed to the Sea*, pp. 903–4; John Colby, "Bullets, Hardtack and Mud," *Journal of the West* 4, no. 2 (April 1965): Elliott Journal, p. 66; *Richmond Enquirer*, 14 Aug. 1863; Leavy Manuscript, p. 37.

107. Fisher Diary, p. 7; Moore, ed., *Rebellion Record*, vol. 7, p. 173; *St. Louis Missouri Republican*, 5 Dec. 1884; Johnson and Buel, eds., *Battles and Leaders*, vol. 3, p. 491; *Official Records*, vol. 24, ser. 1, pt. 2, pp. 202–3; Hogan to Father, 22 July 1863.

108. Fisher Diary, p. 7; Moore, ed., *Rebellion Record*, vol. 7, p. 173; Tunnard, *A Southern Record*, pp. 263–66.

109. Moore, ed., *Rebellion Record*, vol. 7, p. 173; Johnson and Buel, eds., *Battles and Leaders*, vol. 3, p. 491; Simms, "A Louisiana Engineer," p. 375; Oscar Kraines, "Incorruptible Cockrell: Presidential Troubleshooter and Senate Watch Dog, the Life and Times of Francis Marion Cockrell," p.11, Missouri Historical Society, St. Louis; Dana, *Recollections of the Civil War*, p. 97; Compiled Missouri Service Records.

110. Johnson and Buel, eds., *Battles and Leaders*, vol. 3, p. 550; Leavy Manuscript, p. 42; Compiled Missouri Service Records; 1860 Henry County, Missouri, Census Records; Stephen D. Coale to Brother, 28 Jan. 1864, 2 Feb. 1864, 20 Feb. 1864, 28 Feb. 1864, 18 Feb. 1865, 13 March 1865, Western Historical Manuscripts Collection, State Historical Society of Missouri, Columbia, Missouri.

111. Anderson, *Memoirs*, p. 347; Johnson and Buel, eds., *Battles and Leaders*, vol. 3, p. 491; *Official Records*, vol. 24, ser. 1, pt. 2, pp. 202–3; Tunnard, *A Southern Record*, p. 264.

112. Fisher Diary, p. 7; Smith Memoir, p. 32; *Official Records*, vol. 24, ser. 1, pt. 2, p. 416; M. A. DeWolfe, ed., *Home Letters of General Sherman* (New York: Charles Scribner's Sons, 1909), p. 267.

113. *Official Records*, vol. 24, ser. 1, pt. 2, p. 416; Payne, "Missouri Troops in the Vicksburg Campaign," p. 378.

114. Fisher Diary, p. 7; *St. Louis Missouri Republican*, 5 Dec. 1884; *Official Records*, vol. 24, ser. 1, pt. 2, p. 173; Elliott Journal, p. 66; Bevier, *History of the First and Second Missouri Confederate Brigades*, p. 430.

115. Fisher Diary, p. 7; Smith Memoir, p. 32; Hogan to Father, 22 July 1863; Payne, "Missouri Troops in the Vicksburg Campaign," p. 378; *Official Records*, vol. 24, ser. 1, pt. 2, pp. 173, 416; Elliott Journal, p. 66; "The Bravest Soldier," newspaper clipping, Kearny-Kennerly Scrapbook, 2, Missouri Historical Society, St. Louis; Anderson, *Memoirs*, p. 347; *Richmond Enquirer*, 14 Aug. 1863.

116. Fisher Diary, p. 7; *St. Louis Missouri Republican*, 5 Dec. 1884; Johnson and Buel, eds., *Battles and Leaders*, vol. 3, p. 491.

117. Anderson, *Memoirs*, p. 352; *Official Records*, vol. 24, ser. 1, pt. 2, p. 416; Leavy Manuscript, p. 40.

118. *Centralia, Missouri, Fireside Guard*, 16 March 1917; Fisher Diary, pp. 7–8; Cockrell Scrapbook, 5; Tunnard, *A Southern Record*, p. 266; Kavanaugh Memoir, p. 42; *Official Records*, vol. 24, ser. 1, pt. 2, p. 416; *St. Louis Missouri Republican*, 5 Dec. 1884.

119. Johnson and Buel, eds., *Battles and Leaders*, vol. 3, p. 528; Fisher Diary, p. 7; *St. Louis Missouri Republican*, 5 Dec. 1884; Compiled Missouri Service Records; Adjutant General of Missouri Records.

120. Kavanaugh Memoir, p. 43; Tunnard, *A Southern Record*, p. 266; Cockrell Scrapbook, 4; *St. Louis Missouri Republican*, 5 Dec. 1884; Phillips Funeral Oration for Cockrell, 6 June 1917, Western Historical Manuscripts Collection, State Historical Society of Missouri, Columbia, Missouri.

121. *St. Louis Missouri Republican*, 5 Dec. 1884; Johnson and Buel, eds., *Battles and Leaders*, vol. 3, pp. 491, 522; Compiled Missouri Service Records; Fisher Diary, p. 7; *St. Louis Missouri Republican*, 5 Dec. 1884; *Official Records*, vol. 24, ser. 1, pt. 2, pp. 186, 416; Fisher Diary, p. 7.

122. Johnson and Buel, eds., *Battles and Leaders*, vol. 3, p. 491; Bevier, *History of the First and Second Missouri Confederate Brigades*, p. 430.

123. Payne, "Missouri Troops in the Vicksburg Campaign," p. 378; Anderson, *Memoirs*, p. 353; *Official Records*, vol. 24, ser. 1, pt. 2, p. 416.

124. Fisher Diary, p. 8; *Official Records*, vol. 24, ser. 1, pt. 2, p. 416; *St. Louis Missouri Republican*, 5 Dec. 1884.

125. *Official Records*, vol. 24, ser. 1, pt. 1, pp. 281–82; Compiled Missouri Service Records; *St. Louis Missouri Republican*, 5 Dec. 1884.

126. Bevier, *History of the First and Second Missouri Confederate Brigades*,

p. 431; "Words of a Veteran About Vicksburg," p. 312; Mary Ann Loughborough, *My Cave Life in Vicksburg* (New York: D. Appleton, 1864), p. 113; Moore, ed., *Rebellion Record*, vol. 7, p. 172; *Official Records*, vol. 24, ser. 1, pt. 2, p. 417.

127. Bevier, *History of the First and Second Missouri Confederate Brigades*, p. 217; Anderson, *Memoirs*, p. 356; William L. Webb, *Battles and Biographies of Missourians* (Kansas City: Hudson-Kimerly, 1903), p. 129; *St. Louis Missouri Republican*, 5 Dec. 1884.

128. Leavy Manuscript, p. 43; Fisher Diary, p. 8; Bevier, *History of the First and Second Missouri Confederate Brigades*, pp. 217, 433-34.

129. Bearss, *Unvexed to the Sea*, pp. 1284-85; Camp Jackson Papers, Missouri Historical Society, St. Louis; *St. Louis Missouri Republican*, 5 Dec. 1884; Compiled Missouri Service Records.

130. Bevier, *History of the First and Second Missouri Confederate Brigades*, pp. 433-34; *Official Records*, vol. 24, ser. 1, pt. 2, p. 175.

131. Johnson and Buel, eds., *Battles and Leaders*, vol. 3, p. 530; *St. Louis Missouri Republican*, 5 Dec 1884; *Official Records*, vol. 24, ser. 1, pt. 1, p. 283; Bevier, *History of the First and Second Missouri Confederate Brigades*, pp. 433-34.

132. Bevier, *History of the First and Second Missouri Confederate Brigades*, 433-34; Harrell, *Vicksburg and the River*, p. 43.

133. Bevier, *History of the First and Second Missouri Confederate Brigades*, p. 434; Urquhart, *Vicksburg*, pp. 55-56, 59; Hogan to Father, 22 July 1863; Tunnard, *A Southern Record*, p. 271; Necrologies Scrapbook, no. 11c, p. 215; Adjutant General of Missouri Records.

134. Bannon Diary; Vickers, *Under Both Flags*, p. 107; Hogan to Father, 22 July 1863; Seth James Wells, "The Siege of Vicksburg," in *The Diary of Seth J. Wells* (Detroit: W. H. Rowe, 1915), p. 88.

135. Anderson, *Memoirs*, p. 357; *St. Louis Missouri Republican*, 5 Dec. 1884; Bearss, *Unvexed to the Sea*, p. 1304.

136. Compiled Missouri Service Records; Leavy Manuscript, p. 44; Vickers, *Under Both Flags*, p. 105; *St. Louis Missouri Republican*, 7 Aug. 1886.

137. Fisher Diary, p. 8; Hogan to Father, 22 July 1863; *St. Louis Missouri Republican*, 5 Dec. 1884; Anderson, *Memoirs*, p. 360; Johnson and Buel, eds., *Battles and Leaders*, vol. 3, p. 534; Hogan to Father, 22 July 1863; *St. Louis Missouri Republican*, 5 Dec. 1884; Leavy Manuscript, pp. 47-48; List of exchanged Camp Jackson prisoners, Camp Jackson Papers.

138. Bevier, *History of the First and Second Missouri Confederate Brigades*, p. 434; Compiled Missouri Service Records; Cheavens Journal.

139. Bevier, *History of the First and Second Missouri Confederate Brigades*, p. 442; *Official Records*, vol. 24, ser. 1, pt. 2, p. 417; Compiled Missouri Service Records.

140. *Official Records*, vol. 24, ser. 1, pt. 2, p. 417; U.D.C., *Reminiscences of the Women of Missouri During the Sixties*, p. 57; Johnson and Buel, eds., *Battles and Leaders*, vol. 3, p. 550; John Stevens Bowen carte de viste, Missouri Historical Society Photographic Department; *St. Louis Missouri Republican*, 5 Dec. 1884.

141. Compiled Missouri Service Record; Bob Priddy, *Across Our Wide Missouri*, 2 vols. (Independence: Providence Press, 1982-84), vol. 1, p. 292; Cockrell to General Samuel Cooper, 12 Sept. 1863, Bowen Letterbook, Virginia Historical Society, Richmond.

142. Compiled Missouri Service Records; Hogan to Father, 22 July 1963; Anderson, *Memoirs*, p. 363; Hogan to Father, 22 July 1863; Johnson and Buel, eds., *Battles and Leaders*, vol. 3, p. 532; Bevier, *History of the First and Second Missouri Confederate Brigades*, p. 413.

143. Bevier, *History of the First and Second Missouri Confederate Brigades*, p. 443.

144. Compiled Missouri Service Records.

# BIBLIOGRAPHY

## Manuscripts

Acock, Robert E. Papers, 1854–1866. Western Historical Manuscript Collection, State Historical Society of Missouri, Columbia, Missouri.

Alison, Joseph Dill. Diary. Southern Historical Collection, University of North Carolina, Chapel Hill, North Carolina.

Appler Diary. Missouri Historical Society. St. Louis, Missouri.

Babcock Scrapbook. Missouri Historical Society. St. Louis, Missouri.

Badger Collection. Missouri Historical Society, St. Louis, Missouri.

Bannon, John B. Diary. Yates Snowden Collection, South Carolina Library, University of South Carolina, Columbia, South Carolina.

Bearss, Edwin C. Battle of Port Gibson-Troop Movement Map. United States Department of the Interior National Park Service, Division of Design and Construction Prepared by Eastern Office. Arlington, Virginia.

Bedford Family Papers. Western Historical Manuscript Collection, State Historical Society of Missouri, Columbia, Missouri.

Billion Scrapbook. Missouri Historical Society, St. Louis, Missouri.

Bixby, William K. Collection. Missouri Historical Society, St. Louis, Missouri.

Bowen, (General) John Stevens. Collection. Missouri Historical Society, St. Louis, Missouri.

————. Genealogy. Georgia Historical Society, Savannah, Georgia.

————. Letterbook. Virginia Historical Society, Richmond, Virginia.

————. Carte de viste. Missouri Historical Society Photographic Department.

Boyce, Joseph. Papers, Scrapbook, and Manuscript. Missouri Historical Society, St. Louis, Missouri.

Brauckman Scrapbook. Missouri Historical Society, St. Louis, Missouri.

Breckenridge, William C. Papers. Western Historical Manuscript Collection, State Historical Society of Missouri, Columbia, Missouri.

Camp Jackson Papers. Missouri Historical Society, St. Louis, Missouri.

Carondelet Historical Society Archives, St. Louis, Missouri.

Catalogue of the Officers and Students of McGee College, 1854–1855. Missouri Historical Society, St. Louis, Missouri.

Census Records. 1860, Dunklin County, Missouri.

----. 1860, Henry County, Missouri.

----. 1860, Johnson County, Missouri.

----. 1850, Polk County, Missouri.

----. 1860, Polk County, Missouri.

----. 1860, St. Louis, Missouri.

Cheavens, Henry. Journal. Western Historical Manuscript Collection, State Historical Society of Missouri, Columbia, Missouri.

Civil War Collection. Missouri Historical Society, St. Louis, Missouri.

Civil War Papers 1900–1962, Missouri Historical Society, St. Louis, Missouri.

Clark, Champ. Clark Papers. Western Historical Manuscript Collection, State Historical Society of Missouri, Columbia, Missouri.

Cockrell, Francis Marion. Scrapbook. Missouri Historical Society, St. Louis, Missouri.

Compiled Service Records of Confederate Soldiers Who Served in Organizations from the State of Missouri. National Archives, Washington, D.C.

"Consolidated Provision Return for First Brigade, May 1–May 10, 1863." Roster Sheet. National Archives, Washington, D.C.

Danner, Albert C. Historical Memorandum. Dorothy Danner Tribets, Mobile, Alabama.

Dunlap, Robert. Diary. John B. Sampson, DeKalb, Missouri.

Dyson, Absalom Roby. Letters. Western Historical Manuscript Collection, University of Missouri, St. Louis, Missouri.

Elliott, George. Journal. Tennessee State Library and Archives, Nashville, Tennessee.

Fisher, Theodore D. Diary. Missouri Historical Society, St. Louis, Missouri.

Fordyce Collection. Missouri Historical Society, St. Louis, Missouri.

Greenwood, George. Service Record. Adjutant General of Missouri Records, Adjutant General Office, Jefferson City, Missouri.

Grimes, Absalom. Papers. Missouri Historical Society, St. Louis, Missouri.

Harris, Thomas A. "Speech of the Hon. Thomas A. Harris Delivered at the Camp of the First Missouri Brigade, C.S.A., April 30th, 1864, near Tuscaloosa, Alabama." Western Reserve Historical Society, Cleveland, Ohio.

Historic Homes of Missouri. Scrapbook. Missouri Historical Society, St. Louis, Missouri.

Hubbell Family Papers. Missouri Historical Society, St. Louis, Missouri.

Kavanaugh, William Henry. Memoir. Western Historical Manuscripts Collection, State Historical Society of Missouri, Columbia, Missouri.

Kearny-Kennerly Scrapbook. Missouri Historical Society. St. Louis, Missouri.

Kennedy's St. Louis City Directory of 1859 and 1860.

Knapp, John. Collection. Camp Jackson Papers, Missouri Historical Society, St. Louis, Missouri.

Kraines, Oscar. "Incorruptible Cockrell: Presidential Troubleshooter and Senate Watch Dog, the Life and Times of Frances Marion Cockrell." Manuscript. Missouri Historical Society, St. Louis, Missouri.

Landis Family Papers. Collection of Walter A. Landis, Jr. Faucett, Missouri.

Leathers Family Papers. Dorothy Voncille Liedorff Schmedake. Callao, Missouri.

Leavy, John. Manuscript. Vicksburg National Military Battlefield Park Archives, Vicksburg, Mississippi.

Lewis Family Papers. Collection of Charles Sullivan, Perkinston, Mississippi.

Little, Henry. Diary, U.S. Army Military Historical Institute, Carlisle, Pennsylvania.

McCown Family Papers. Collection of Garland McCown of Garland, Texas, and Frank D. McCown, Fort Worth, Texas.

McEwen Papers. Missouri Historical Society, St. Louis, Missouri.

McNamara, John. "An Historical Sketch of the Sixth Division, Missouri State Guard." Missouri Historical Society, St. Louis, Missouri.

Miller, Edwin L. Papers. Western Historical Manuscript Collection, State Historical Society of Missouri, Columbia, Missouri.

Mitchell Family Papers. William F. Moore, Redstone, Alabama.

Necrologies Scrapbook. Missouri Historical Society, St. Louis, Missouri.

Pankey Family Papers. Mrs. Mary Pankey, Cardwell, Missouri.

Payne, James E. Account. Vicksburg National Military Park.

Raynor, (Colonel) William H. Diary. Vicksburg National Military Park, National Park Service Archives, Vicksburg, Mississippi.

Reilly, John G. Collection. Missouri Historical Society, St. Louis, Missouri.

Reynolds, Thomas C. "General Sterling Price and the Confederacy." Missouri Historical Society, St. Louis, Missouri.

Robbins Papers. Mercentile Library Archives, St. Louis, Missouri.

Rombauer, Robert J. Order Book 1863. Journal and Diaries. Missouri Historical Society, St. Louis, Missouri.

Ruyle, William A. Memoir. Dee Ruyle, Bolivar, Missouri.

St. John's Evangelist Church Archives, St. Louis, Missouri.

Simpson, Avington Wayne. Diary. Western Historical Manuscript Collections, State Historical Society of Missouri, Columbia, Missouri.

Skaggs, William. Collection of Confederate Veteran Letters. Arkansas History Commission, Little Rock, Arkansas.

Snyder, John F. Papers. Missouri Historical Society, St. Louis, Missouri.

Snyder, William. Letters. New Madrid Historical Museum, New Madrid, Missouri.

Soulard, Antonine P. Papers. Missouri Historical Society, St. Louis, Missouri.

Taylor, Obediah. Photograph. Eleanor S. Brockenbrough Library. Confederate Museum, Richmond, Virginia.

U.S. Department of the Interior. Geological Survey and Topographical Map for Claiborne County, Mississippi.

————. Geological Survey and Topographical Map for Hinds County, Mississippi.

Warren, George W. Diary. Private Collection of George W. Warren, IV. Montpelier, Virginia.

Warren Letters. Private Collection of Ellen R. Deremer, Alexandria, Virginia.

Wheatley Family Papers. Carlos W. Bowman Collection, San Carlos, California.

## Books

Alden, Henry M., and Alfred H. Guernsey, eds., *Harper's Pictorial History of the Civil War*. New York: Fairfax Press, n.d.

Anderson, Ephraim McDowell. *Memoirs: Historical and Personal, Including the Campaigns of the First Missouri Confederate Brigade*. St. Louis: Times Printing Co., 1868.

Andrews, J. Cutler. *The South Reports the Civil War*. Princeton, N.J.: Princeton University Press, 1970.

Aptheker, Herbert. *American Negro Slave Revolts*. New York: International, 1974.

Balfour, Emma. *Vicksburg, A City Under Siege: Diary of Emma Balfour May 16, 1863–June 2, 1863*. N.p.: Phillip C. Weinberger, 1983.

Ballard, Michael B. *Pemberton: A Biography*. Jackson: University Press of Mississippi, 1991.

Balthis, Laura V., ed. *Early Recollections of George W. Dameron: Biographical Sketches of Log Cabin Pioneers*. Huntsville: Herald Print Company, 1898.

*The Battle of Shiloh and the Organizations Engaged*. Washington, D.C.: Government Publication, 1902.

Bearss, Edwin C. *The Campaign for Vicksburg: Unvexed to the Sea*. Dayton: Morningside House, Vol. 3, 1986.

----. *Decision in Mississippi: Mississippi's Important Role in the War Between the States*. Little Rock: Mississippi Commission on the War Between the States, 1962.

----. *Grant Strikes a Fatal Blow*, Vol. 2.

Bettersworth, John K. *Confederate Mississippi: The People and Policies of a Cotton State in Wartime*. Baton Rouge: Louisiana State University Press, 1943.

Bevier, Robert. *History of the First and Second Missouri Confederate Brigades, 1861–1865 and from Wakarusa to Appomattox, A Military Anagraph*. St. Louis: Bryan, Brand, 1879.

Black, Robert C., III. *The Railroads of the Confederacy*. Chapel Hill: University of North Carolina Press, 1952.

Boatner, Mark M., III. *The Civil War Dictionary*. New York: David McKay, 1959.

Bodine, T. V. *The Chronology of a County Editor: The Writings of T. V. Bodine*. Edited by Paul Alexander. N.p., n.d.

Bradley, James. *The Confederate Mail Carrier*. Mexico: n.p., 1894.

Brown, Alonzo. *History of the Fourth Regiment of Minnesota Infantry Volunteers During the Great Rebellion*. St. Paul: Pioneer Press, 1892.

Brown, D. Alexander. *Grierson's Raid: A Cavalry Adventure of the Civil War*. Urbana: University of Illinois Press, 1962.

Byers, Samuel H. M. *With Fire and Sword*. New York: Neale, 1911.

*Campbell's Gazetteer of Missouri*. St. Louis: R. A. Campbell, 1874.

Carter, Samuel, III. *The Final Fortress: The Campaign for Vicksburg 1862–1863*. New York: St. Martin's, 1980.

Castel, Albert. *General Sterling Price and the Civil War in the West*. Baton Rouge: Louisiana State University Press, 1968.

Catton, Bruce. *Grant Moves South*. Boston: Little, Brown, 1960.

Chance, Joseph E. *The Second Texas Infantry: From Shiloh to Vicksburg*. Austin: Eakin, 1984.

Cockrell, Ewing. *History of Johnson County, Missouri*. Kansas City: Historical Company, 1881.

Cockrell, Monroe F., ed. *The Lost Account of the Battle of Corinth and the Court Martial of Gen. Van Dorn*. Jackson: McCowart Mercer, 1955.

Comte de Paris, Louis Philippe Albert D'Orléans. *The Civil War in America*. 4 vols. Philadelphia: Joseph H. Coates, 1876.

Connell, Thomas L., and Barbara L. Bellows. *God and General Longstreet: The Lost Cause and the Southern Mind*. Baton Rouge: Louisiana State University Press, 1982.

Connelley, William E. *Doniphan's Expedition and the Conquest of New Mexico and California.* Topeka, Kan.: n.p., 1907.

Connelly, Thomas Lawrence. *Civil War Tennessee: Battles and Leaders.* Knoxville: University of Tennessee Press, 1979.

Cooper, William J., Jr. *Liberty and Slavery: Southern Politics to 1860.* New York: Knopf, 1983.

Crooke, George. *The Twenty-first Regiment of Iowa Volunteer Infantry: A Narrative of Its Experience in Active Service.* Milwaukee: King, Fowle, 1891.

Dana, Charles A. *Recollections of the Civil War.* New York: Collier Books, 1963.

Davis, William C. *The Battle of New Market.* Garden City, N.J.: Doubleday, 1975.

Dethloff, Henry C., ed. *Thomas Jefferson and American Democracy.* Lexington, Mass.: D. C. Heath, 1971.

DeWolfe, M. A., ed. *Home Letters of General Sherman.* New York: Charles Scribner's Sons, 1909.

Douglas, Henry. *History of Southeast Missouri.* Chicago: Goodspeed, 1888.

Dowdey, Clifford. *Experiment in Rebellion.* Garden City, N.J.: Doubleday, 1946.

Duffield, H. M. Introduction to *Deeds of Valor, From Records in the Archives of the United States Government: How American Heros Won the Medal of Honor.* Detroit: Perrien Keydel, 1906.

Duke, Basil. *Reminiscences of Basil Duke.* New York: n.p., 1969.

Dunaway, Maxine. *1862 Rebel List of Polk County, Missouri, Including Slave Owners from 1861 Tax Assessment Book.* Springfield: Maxine Dunaway, 1984.

————. *1840 Polk County Census.* Springfield: Maxine Dunaway, 1978.

Durree, Daniel Steele. *An Illustrated History of Missouri.* Cincinnati: R. Clarke, 1876.

Duychinck, Evert Augustus. *National History of the War for the Union.* 3 vols. New York: Johnson, Fry, 1861–1865.

Eaton, Clement. *Jefferson Davis.* New York: Free Press, 1977.

————. *A History of the Southern Confederacy.* New York: Free Press, 1954.

Eddy, T. M. *Patriotism of Illinois.* Chicago: n.p., 1865.

Edwards, Edward. *History of the Volunteer Fire Department of St. Louis.* St. Louis: Veteran Volunteer Fireman's Historical Society, 1906.

Elliott, Isaac Hughes. *History of the Thirty-third Regiment Veteran Volunteer Infantry in the Civil War.* Gibson City, Ill.: Thirty-third Illinois Association Publication, 1902.

Ewing, R. C. *Historical Memoirs: Containing a Brief History of the Cumberland Presbyterian Church in Missouri and Biographical Sketches of a Number of Ministers Who Contributed to the Organization and the Establishment of That Church in the Country West of the Mississippi.* Nashville: Cumberland Presbyterian Board of Publication, 1874.

Faherty, William Barnaby. *Better the Dream, Saint Louis: University and Community, 1818–1968.* St. Louis: St. Louis University Press, 1968.

————. *The Catholic Ancestry of Saint Louis.* St. Louis: Bureau of Information, Archdiocese of Saint Louis, 1965.

————. *Dream by the River: Two Centuries of Saint Louis Catholicism, 1766–1967.* St. Louis: Piraeus, 1973.

Faust, Drew Gilpin. *The Creation of Confederate Nationalism: Idealogy and Identity in the Civil War South.* Baton Rouge: Louisiana State University Press, 1988.

Fay, Edwin Hedge. *This Infernal War.* Austin: University of Texas Press, 1958.

Forister, Robert H. *History of Stoddard County, Missouri*. N.p.: Stoddard County Historical Society, n.d.

*From Kerry Patch to Little Paderhorn: A Visit in the Irish-German Communities of Nineteenth Century St. Louis*. St. Louis: Landmarks Association of St. Louis, 1966.

Frost, M. O. *Regimental History of the Tenth Missouri Volunteer Infantry*. Topeka, Kan.: Frost, 1892.

Fuller, J. F. C. *The Generalship of Ulysses S. Grant*. New York: Da Capo, 1991.

*General Directory for the City of Vicksburg, Mississippi*. Vicksburg: H. C. Clarke, 1860.

*General History of Macon County, Missouri*. Chicago: Henry Taylor, 1910.

Gentry, Claude. *The Battle of Corinth*. Baldwyn: Magnolia, 1976.

Gerlach, Russell L. *Settlement Patterns in Missouri: A Study of Population Origins*. Columbia: University of Missouri Press, 1986.

*The Golden Years: 50th Anniversary: Johnson County Historical Society, 1920–1970*. Clinton: Printery, 1970.

Grant, Ulysses S. *Personal Memoirs of U. S. Grant*. New York: Century, 1903.

Greene, Francis V. *The Mississippi, Campaigns of the Civil War*. New York: Charles Scribner's Sons, 1885.

Harrell, Virginia Calohan. *Vicksburg and the River*. Vicksburg: Virginia Calohan Harrell, 1986.

Hartje, Robert G. *Van Dorn*. Nashville: Vanderbilt University Press, 1967.

Headley, J. T. *The Life and Travels of General Grant*. Philadelphia: Hubbard Brothers, 1879.

*Historical Review of Franklin County, Missouri, Sesqui-Centennial 1818–1968*. Union, Mo: Moore Enterprises, 1968.

*History of Boone County, Missouri*. St. Louis: Western Historical Company, 1882.

*History of Franklin, Jefferson, Washington, Crawford, Gasconade Counties, Missouri*. Chicago: Goodspeed, 1888.

*History of Henry and St. Clair Counties, Missouri*. St. Joseph: Goodspeed, 1883.

*History of Hickory, Polk, Cedar, Dade and Barton Counties, Missouri*. Chicago: Goodspeed, 1889.

*History of Lewis, Clark, Knox and Scotland Counties, Missouri*. Chicago: Goodspeed, 1887.

*History of Monroe and Shelby Counties, Missouri*. St. Louis: National Historical Company, 1884.

*History of Newton, Lawrence, Barry and McDonald Counties, Missouri*. Chicago: Goodspeed, 1888.

*History of Randolph and Macon Counties, Missouri*. St. Louis: National Historical Company, 1884.

*History of the Sixteenth Battery of Ohio Volunteer Light Artillery, U.S.A., from Enlistment, August 20, 1861, to Muster Out, August 2, 1865*. N.p.: Compiled by Committee, 1906.

*History of Vernon County, Missouri*. Chicago: Goodspeed, 1911.

Holcombe, R. I., and F. W. Adams. *An Account of the Battle of Wilson's Creek or Oak Hills*. Springfield: Dow and Adams, 1883.

Horgan, Reverend John Joseph. *On the Mission in Missouri 1857–1868*. Kansas City: John A. Heilmann, 1892.

Horn, Stanley. *The Army of Tennessee.* Norman: University of Oklahoma Press, 1952.

Horner, Miles. *History and Genealogy of Buffalo Township, Cardwell, Missouri 1843–1972.* Kennett, Mo.: Guy Derby, 1973.

Hubert, Charles F. *History of the Fiftieth Illinois Infantry.* Kansas City: Western Veteran Publishing Company, 1894.

Hurt, R. Douglas. *Agriculture and Slavery in Missouri's Little Dixie.* Columbia: University of Missouri Press, 1992.

Hyde, William, and Howard L. Conrad. *Encyclopedia of the History of St. Louis.* 4 vols. St. Louis: Southern Historical Company, 1899.

Jackson, Joseph O., ed. *Some of the Boys . . . The Civil War Letters of Isaac Jackson, 1862–1865.* Carbondale: Southern Illinois University Press, 1960.

Johnson, Robert Underwood, and Clarence Clough Buel, eds. *Battles and Leaders of the Civil War.* 4 vols. New York: Thomas Yoseloff, 1956.

Jones, Archer. *Confederate Strategy from Shiloh to Vicksburg.* Baton Rouge: Louisiana State University Press, 1961.

Kennedy, Frances H., ed. *The Civil War Battlefield Guide.* Boston: Houghton Mifflin, 1990.

Kiel, Herman Gottlieb. *The Centennial Biographical Directionary of Franklin County, Missouri.* Washington, D.C.: H. G. Riel, 1925.

Kitchens, Ben Earl. *Rosecrans Meets Price: The Battle of Iuka, Mississippi.* Florence: Thornwood, 1985.

Knox, Thomas W. *Campfire and Cotton-Field: Southern Adventure in Time of War.* Philadelphia: Jones Brothers, 1865.

Lamers, William M. *The Edge of Glory: A Biography of Gen. William S. Rosecrans, U.S.A.* New York: Harcourt, Brace and World, 1961.

Lamkin, Uel W. *History of Henry County, Missouri.* Topeka, Kan.: Historical Publishing Company, 1919.

Lehmann, Karl. *Thomas Jefferson: American Humanist.* New York: MacMillan, 1947.

Livermore, William Roscoe, and John Codman Ropes, *The Story of the Civil War: A Concise Account of a War in the United States of America Between 1861 and 1865.* 4 vols. New York: G. P. Putnam's Sons, 1904–1913.

Logan, Sheridan A. *Old Saint Jo: Gateway to the West 1799–1932.* N.p.: John Sublett Foundation, 1979.

Lord, Francis A. *Civil War Collector's Encyclopedia.* New York: Castle Books, 1965.

Loughborough, Mary Ann. *My Cave Life in Vicksburg.* New York: D. Appleton, 1864.

McCormick, David I., comp., and Mrs. Mindwell Crompton Wilson, ed. *Indiana Battle Flags: And a Record of Indiana Organizations in the Mexican, Civil and Spanish American Wars.* Indianapolis: n.p., 1929.

McDonald, Lyla Merrill. *Iuka's History Embodying Dudley's Battle of Iuka.* Corinth: Rankin Printery, 1923.

McElroy, John. *The Struggle for Missouri.* Washington, D.C.: National Tribune, 1909.

MacManus, Seumas. *The Story of the Irish Race.* New York: Devin-Adair, 1944.

McWhiney, Grady, and Robert Wiebe, eds. *Historical Vistas: Readings in United States History.* Boston: Allyn and Bacon, 1963.

Madaus, Howard Michael, and Robert D. Needham. *The Battle Flags of the Confederate Army of Tennessee.* Milwaukee: Milwaukee Public Museum, 1976.

Marshall, Howard Wight. *Folk Architecture in Little Dixie: A Regional Culture in Missouri.* Columbia: University of Missouri Press, 1981.

Maury, Dabney Herndon. *Recollections of a Virginian.* New York: Charles Scribner's Sons, 1894.

Mears, Phyllis E. *Macon County, Missouri, Obituaries 1889–1903.* Decorah, Mo.: Anundsen, 1987.

Meyer, Duane. *The Heritage of Missouri — A History.* St. Louis: State Publishing Company, 1973.

Miers, Earl S. *The Web of Victory: Grant at Vicksburg.* Baton Rouge: Louisiana State University Press, 1955.

*Milestones, to Live and Die in Dixie.* N.p.: Westinghouse Integrated Logistics Support, n.d.

Miller, Reverend George. *Missouri's Memorable Decade 1860–1870: An Historical Sketch — Personal — Political — Religious.* Columbia: E. W. Stephens, 1898.

Missouri House of Representatives Journal, Twenty-first Assembly, First Session.

Mitchell, Joseph B. *The Badge of Gallantry: Recollections of Civil War Congressional Medal of Honor Winners.* New York: Macmillian, 1968.

Monaghan, Jay. *Civil War on the Western Border, 1854–1865.* New York: Bonanza Books, n.d.

————. *Swamp Fox of the Confederacy: The Life and Military Services of M. Jeff Thompson.* Tuscaloosa: Confederate Publishing Company, 1956.

Moore, Frank, ed. *The Rebellion Record.* 11 vols. New York: n.p., 1862–1868.

Morris, William S. *History of the Thirty-first Regiment Illinois Volunteers, Organized by John A. Logan.* Evansville, Ill.: Keller, 1902.

Needham, Robert D. *The Battle Flags of the Confederate Army of Tennessee.* Milwaukee: Milwaukee Public Library, 1976.

Nevins, Allan. *Ordeal of the Union, The War for the Union: War Becomes Revolution 1862–1863.* 8 vols. New York: Charles Scribner's Sons, 1960.

Niehaus, Earl F. *The Irish in New Orleans 1800–1860.* Baton Rouge: Louisiana State University Press, 1965.

Norton, Albert Herman. *Rebel Religion: The Story of Confederate Chaplains.* St. Louis, Bethany, 1961.

*Official Proceedings of the Sixth Annual Reunion of Missouri Division, United Confederate Veterans.* St. Joseph: Combe, 1902.

*Official Roster of the Soldiers of the State of Ohio in the War of the Rebellion 1861–1866.* Akron: Werner, 1887.

O'Hanlon, John. *Life and Scenery in Missouri: Reminiscences of a Missionary Priest.* Dublin: James Duffy, 1890.

Oldroyd, Osburn H. *A Soldier's Story of the Siege of Vicksburg.* Springfield: H. W. Rokker, 1885.

*Organization and Status of Missouri Troops in Service During the Civil War.* Washington, D.C.: U.S. Government Printing Office, 1902.

Parrish, William E. *The Civil War: A Second American Revolution?* New York: Holt, Rinehart and Winston, 1970.

————. *A History of Missouri, 1860–1875.* 3 vols. Columbia: University of Missouri, 1973.

Pemberton, John C. *Pemberton, Defender of Vicksburg.* Chapel Hill: University of North Carolina Press, 1942.

Peterson, Merrill D. *The Jefferson Image in the American Mind.* New York: Oxford University Press, 1960.

Phillips, Herb. *Champion Hill!* n.p.: Champion Hill Battlefield Foundation, n.d.

Pierson, George Wilson. "The Frontier and American Institutions, A Criticism of the Turner Theory." In *The Turner Thesis, Concerning the Role of the Frontier in American History,* edited by George Rogers Taylor. Boston: D. C. Heath, 1956.

Pillar, James J. *The Catholic Church in Mississippi, 1837–1865.* New Orleans: Hauser, 1964.

Porter, David D. *The Naval History of the Civil War.* New York: Sherman, 1886.

*Portrait and Biographical Record of Johnson and Pettis Counties, Missouri.* Chicago: Chapman, 1895.

*Portrait and Biographical Record of Ralls, Marion and Pike and Randolph Counties, Missouri.* Chicago: Chapman, 1895.

Pratt, Fletcher. *Civil War on Western Waters.* New York: Henry Holt, 1956.

Priddy, Bob. *Across Our Wide Missouri.* 2 vols. Independence: Providence Press, 1982–84.

Primm, James Neal and Steven Rowan. Introduction to *Germans for a Free Missouri: Translations from the St. Louis Radical Press 1857–1862.* Columbia: University of Missouri Press, 1983.

––––. *Lion of the Valley: St. Louis, Missouri.* Boulder, Colo.: Pruett, 1981.

Quaife, Milo M. *Absalom Grimes: Confederate Mail Runner.* New Haven: Yale University Press, 1926.

Rafferty, Milton D. *Historical Atlas of Missouri.* Norman: University of Oklahoma, 1981.

Romero, Sidney J. *Religion in the Rebel Ranks.* Lanham: University Press of America, 1983.

Rose, Victor M. *Ross' Texas Brigade.* Louisville: Courier Journal, 1881.

Rowland, Dunbar. *History of Mississippi.* 2 vols. Hattiesburg: University and College Press of Mississippi, 1972.

––––, ed. *Jefferson Davis, Constitutionalist: His Letters, Papers and Speeches.* 6 vols. Jackson: Mississippi Department of Archives and History, 1923.

Rozwenc, Edwin C., ed. *The Causes of the American Civil War.* Boston: D. C. Heath, 1961.

Rutt, Chris L. *History of Buchanan and the City of St. Joseph and Representative Citizens.* Chicago: Biographical Publishing Company, 1904.

Sanborn, J. B. *Memoir of George B. Boomer.* Boston: George C. Rand and Avery, 1864.

Schooley, Herschel. *Centennial History of Audrain County, Missouri.* Mexico: McIntyre, 1937.

Schroeder, Adolph E. "To Missouri Where the Sun of Freedom Shines: Dream and Reality on the Western Frontier." In *The German-American Experience in Missouri,* edited by Marshall and Goodrich.

Shoemaker, Floyd C. *Missouri and Missourians: Land of Contrasts and People of Achievements.* Chicago: Lewis, 1943.

Shrum, Edison. *The History of Scott County, Missouri; Up to the Year 1880.* Sikeston: Standard Printing Company, Scott County Historical Society.

Simon, John T. *The Papers of Ulysses S. Grant, April 1–July 6, 1863.* Carbondale: Southern Illinois University Press, 1979.

Smyth-Davis, Mary F. *History of Dunklin County, Missouri, 1845–1895*. St. Louis: Nixon-Jones, 1896.

Snead, Thomas. *The Fight for Missouri*. (New York: Charles Scribner's Sons, 1886).

Snider, Felix, and Earl Collins. *Cape Girardeau: Biography of a City*. Cape Girardeau: Ramfire, 1956.

Sommers, Richard. Introduction to *The Official Military Atlas of the Civil War*. New York: Arno, 1978.

Stanley, Lois, George F. Wilson, and Mary Helen Wilson. *Death Records from Missouri Newspapers: The Civil War Years, January 1861–December 1865*. Decorah, Mo.: Anundsen, 1983.

Stevens, Walter B. *Centennial History of Missouri (The Central State): One Hundred Years in the Union 1820–1921*. 5 vols. Chicago: S. J. Clarke, 1921.

Stevenson, S. Wentworth. "A Southern Campaign." In *The Ladies Benevolent and Industrial Sallymag Society*. Charlottetown, W. H. Bremner, 1868.

Temple, Wayne C., ed. *Campaigning with Grant*. New York: Century, 1897.

Thomas, Emory M. *The Confederacy as a Revolutionary Experience*. N.J.: Prentice-Hall, 1971.

Tilley, Nannie M., ed. *Federals on the Frontier: The Diary of Benjamin F. McIntyre, 1862–1864*. Austin: University of Texas Press, 1963.

Towey, Martin G. "Kerry Patch Revisited: Irish Americans in St. Louis in the Turn of the Century Era." In *Irish-American Communities in the Turn of the Century Era 1880–1920*, edited by Timothy J. Meagher. New York: Greenwood, 1986.

Trexler, Harrison Anthony. *Slavery in Missouri, 1804–1865*. Baltimore: Johns Hopkins Press, 1914.

Trimble, Harvey M. *History of the Ninety-third Regiment Illinois Volunteer Infantry, from Organization to Muster Out*. Chicago: Blakely, 1898.

Tucker, Glenn. *Zeb Zance: Champion of Personal Freedom*. Indianapolis: Bobbs-Merrill, 1965.

Tunnard, William H. *A Southern Record: The History of the Third Regiment Louisiana Infantry*. Dayton: Morningside, 1970.

Turner, George Edgar. *Victory Rode the Rails: The Strategic Place of the Railroads in the Civil War*. New York: Bobbs-Merrill, 1953.

United Daughters of the Confederacy, Missouri Chapter. *Reminiscences of the Women of Missouri During the Sixties*. Jefferson City, Mo.: Hugh Stephens Printing Company, n.d.

Urquhart, Kenneth Trist, ed. *Vicksburg: Southern City Under Siege, William Lovelace Foster's Letter Describing the Defense and Surrender of the Confederate Fortress on the Mississippi*. New Orleans: Historic New Orleans Collection, 1980.

U. S. Department of the Interior. *Vicksburg, Official National Park Handbook*. Washington, D.C., 1986.

Vickers, George M. *Under Both Flags*. (Philadelphia: Peoples Publishing Company, 1896).

Victor, Orville James. *The History Civil, Political and Military of the Southern Rebellion*. 4 vols. New York: J. D. Torrey, 1861–1865.

Wakelyn, Jon L. *Biographical Dictionary of the Confederacy*. Westport: Greenwood, 1977.

Waller, Alexander H. *History of Randolph County, Missouri*. Topeka: Historical Publishing Company, 1920.

*The War of the Rebellion: A Compilation of the Official Records of the Union and Confederate Armies.* 128 vols. Washington, D.C., 1880–1901.

Warner, Ezra, Jr. *Generals in Gray: Lives of the Confederate Commanders.* Baton Rouge: Louisiana State University Press, 1959.

Webb, William L. *Battles and Biographies of Missourians.* Kansas City: Hudson-Kimerly, 1903.

Wells, Seth James. *The Diary of Seth J. Wells.* Detroit: W. H. Rowe, 1915.

Wheeler, Richard. *The Siege of Vicksburg.* New York: Thomas Y. Crowell, 1978.

Wiley, Bell Irvin. *The Life of Billy Yank: The Common Soldier of the Union.* Baton Rouge: Louisiana State University Press, 1978.

————. *The Life of Johnny Reb: The Common Soldier of the Confederacy.* Baton Rouge: Louisiana State University, 1978.

Williams, Kenneth P. *Lincoln Finds a General: A Military Study of the Civil War.* 5 vols. New York: Macmillan, 1949–1959.

Williams, Walter. *History of Northeast Missouri.* 3 vols. Chicago: Lewis, 1913.

Williamson, Joel. *New People: Miscegenation and Mulattoes in the United States.* New York: New York University Press, 1984.

Wilson, James Harrison. *The Life of Ulysses S. Grant, General of the Armies of the United States.* Springfield: Gurdon Bill, 1968.

Wiltse, Charles M. *The Jeffersonian Tradition in American Democracy.* New York: Hill and Wang, 1960.

Woodruff, (Mrs.) Howard W. *Polk County Marriage Records, 1836–1859.* Kansas City: Mrs. Howard W. Woodruff, 1970.

Woodward, C. Vann. "The Southern Ethic in a Puritan World." In *Myth and Southern History: The Old South,* edited by Patrick Gerster and Nicholas Cords. Chicago: Rand McNally, 1974.

————. *American Counterpoint: Slavery and Racism in the North-South Dialogue.* Boston: Little, Brown, 1971.

Wright, William C. *The Confederate Magazine at Fort Wade, Grand Gulf, Mississippi Excavations, 1980–1981.* Jackson: Mississippi Department of Archives and History and the Grand Gulf State Military Monument, 1982.

Wyman, Mark. *Immigrants in the Valley: Irish, Germans and Americans in the Upper Mississippi Country 1830–1860.* Chicago: Nelson-Hall, 1984.

## Articles

Anders, Leslie. "Men from Home: Missouri Volunteers in the Pacification of Mobile Alabama, 1865–1866." *Missouri Historical Review* 69 (April 1975).

Bannon, John B. "Experiences of a Confederate Army Chaplain." *Letters and Notices of the English Jesuit Province* (Oct. 1867).

Bearss, Edwin C. "Grand Gulf's Role in the Civil War." *Civil War History* 5 (1959).

————, ed. "Charles E. Affeld Describes the Mechanicsburg Expedition." *Journal of the Illinois State Historical Society* 56, no. 2 (1972).

Beasley, Jonathan. "Blacks — Slave and Free — Vicksburg, 1850–1860." *Journal of Mississippi History* 38 (Feb. 1976).

*Bulletin of Johnson County Historical Society* (April 1976).

Calkins, Homer L., ed. "From Elkhorn to Vicksburg: James H. Fauntelroy's Diary for the Year 1862." *Civil War History* 2 (Jan. 1956).

Cappleman, Josie F. "Local Incidents of the War." *Publications of the Mississippi State Historical Society* 4 (1901).

Chambers, William Pit. "My Journal: The Story of a Soldier's Life Told by Himself." *Publications of the Mississippi State Historical Society* 5 (1925).

Colby, John. "Bullets, Hardtack and Mud." *Journal of the West* 4, no. 2 (April 1965).

"Colonel David Young Pankey." *Confederate Veteran* 18 (April 1910).

"Colonel Eugene Erwin." *Confederate Veteran* 4 (Aug. 1896).

Cox, T. B. "Gen. Pettus Escapes Johnson's Island." *Confederate Veteran* 13 (Jan. 1905).

"Diary of Lieutenant Colonel Hubbell of 3d Regiment Missouri Infantry, C.S.A.," *The Land We Love* 6, no. 2, p. 99.

"Dr. Benjamin Givens Dysart." *Confederate Veteran* 12 (April 1904).

Erickson, Edgar L., ed. "With Grant at Vicksburg: From the Civil War Diary of Captain Charles E. Wilcox." *Journal of the Illinois State Historical Society* 30 (Jan. 1938).

Ervin, W. J. "Genius and Heroism of Lieut. K. H. Faulkner." *Confederate Veteran* 14 (Nov. 1906).

Frederick, J. V., ed. "An Illinois Soldier in North Mississippi: Diary of John Wilson, February 15–December 30, 1862." *The Journal of Mississippi History* 1 (July 1939).

Gerlach, Russel L. "Population Origins in Rural Missouri." *Missouri Historical Review* 71 (Oct. 1976).

Godsey, Roy. "Southeast Missouri: An Agricultural Empire." *Monthly Bulletin of the Missouri State Board of Agriculture* 21 (Oct. 1923).

Goodrich, James W. "Robert Eaton Acock: The Gentleman from Polk." *Missouri Historical Review* 73 (April 1979).

Gordon, James. "The Battle and Retreat from Corinth." *Mississippi State Historical Society Publications* 4 (1901).

Gunn, Jack W. "The Battle of Iuka." *The Journal of Mississippi History* 24 (July 1962).

Hernon, Joseph M., Jr. "The Irish Nationalists and Southern Secession." *Civil War History* 12 (March 1966).

"A Hero in the Strife." *Confederate Veteran* 2 (Sept. 1894).

Jones, J. H. "The Rank and File at Vicksburg." *Publications of the Mississippi State Historical Society* 7 (1903).

King, W. H. "Early Experiences in Missouri." *Confederate Veteran* 17 (Oct. 1909).

Kirkpatrick, Arthur R. "Missouri's Delegation in the Confederate Congress." *Civil War History* 5 (June 1959).

Lampe, A. B. "St. Louis Fire Department 1820–1850." *Missouri Historical Review* 62 (April 1968).

Lee, Stephen D. "The Campaign of Vicksburg, Mississippi, in 1863—from April 15th to and Including the Battle of Champion Hills, or Baker's Creek, May 16th, 1863." *Publications of the Mississippi State Historical Society* 3 (1900).

Lord, Francis A. "Accouterments of the Enfield Musket." *Civil War Times Illustrated* 5 (Feb. 1967).

Maury, Dabney H. "Recollections of Campaign Against Grant in North Mississippi in 1862–1863." *Southern Historical Society Papers* 13 (Jan.–Dec. 1885).

Miller, Robert E. "One of the Ruling Class, Thomas Caute Reynolds: Second Confederate Governor of Missouri." *Missouri Historical Review* 80 (July 1986).

Mitchell, The Reverend Benjamin Looney. "A Confederate Participant Describes the Battle of Wilson Creek." *Ozark Mountaineer* 7 (Feb. 1959).

Moore, John Hebron. "Railroads of Antebellum Mississippi." *Journal of Mississippi History* 41 (Feb. 1979).

Mullen, Jay Carlton. "Pope's New Madrid and Island Number Ten Campaigns." *Missouri Historical Review* 59 (April 1965).

Parrish, William E. "The Palmyra 'Massacre': A Tragedy of Guerilla Warfare." *Journal of Confederate History* 1, no. 2 (Winter 1988).

Payne, James E. "Early Days of War in Missouri." *Confederate Veteran* 37 (Feb. 1931).

––––. "From Missouri." *Confederate Veteran* 38 (Sept. 1930).

––––. "Missouri Troops in the Vicksburg Campaign." *Confederate Veteran* 36 (Sept. 1928).

––––. "The Sixth Missouri at Corinth." *Confederate Veteran* 36 (Dec. 1928).

––––. "Skylarking Along the Line." *Confederate Veteran* 38 (March 1930).

"Polk County Rangers." *The Résumé: Newsletter of the Historical Society of Polk County, Missouri* (Jan. 1991).

Powell, C. A. "Brother Fought Against Brother." *Confederate Veteran* 10 (Oct. 1902).

Reed, Lida Lord. "A Woman's Experiences During the Siege of Vicksburg." *The Century Magazine* 61 (April 1901).

Renny, (Reverend) Laurence J., and Joseph P. Morrissey. "Father John Bannon, S.J." *United States Catholic Historical Society Publications* 26 (1936).

Reynolds, A. H. "Vivid Experiences at Champion Hill, Miss." *Confederate Veteran* 18 (Jan. 1910).

Schneider, John C. "Riot and Reaction in St. Louis, 1854–1856." *Missouri Historical Review* 68 (Jan. 1974).

Shalhope, Robert E. "Eugene Genovese, the Missouri Elite and Civil War Historiography." *Bulletin of the Missouri Historical Society* 26 (July 1970).

Simms, L. Moody, Jr. "A Louisiana Engineer at the Siege of Vicksburg: Letters of Henry Ginder." *Louisiana History* 8 (1967).

Sproul, T. B. *Confederate Veteran* 2 (July 1894).

Stanton, Donald J., Goodwin F. Berquist, Jr., and Paul C. Bowers. "Missouri's Forgotten General: M. Jeff Thompson and the Civil War." *Missouri Historical Review* 70 (April 1976).

Strode, E. W. "Recollections of an Artilleryman." *Confederate Veteran* 2 (Dec. 1894).

Swindler, William F. "The Southern Press in Missouri 1861–1864." *Missouri Historical Review* 35 (April 1941).

Thompson, William C. "From Shiloh to Port Gibson." *Civil War Times Illustrated* 3 (Oct. 1964).

Towey, Martin G., and Margaret Lopiccolo Sullivan. "The Knights of Father Mathew: Parallel Ethnic Reform." *Missouri Historical Review* 75 (Jan. 1981).

Trigg, S. G. "Fighting Around Vicksburg." *Confederate Veteran* 12, no. 3 (March 1904).

Tucker, Phillip Thomas. "Reconnaissance in Tensas Parish, April 1863: Missouri Confederates in Louisiana." *Louisiana History* 31 (Spring 1990).

*Union and Confederate Annals: The Blue and Gray in Friendship Meet, and Heroic Deeds Recited* 1 (Jan. and June, 1884).

Weller, Jac. "Imported Confederate Shoulder Weapons." *Civil War History* 5. no. 2 (June 1959).
"Words of a Veteran About Vicksburg." *Confederate Veteran* 2 (Oct. 1894).

## *Thesis*

Nichols, Bruce. "The Civil War in Johnson County, Missouri." Master of Arts Thesis, Central Missouri State University, 1974.

# INDEX

325